DATE DUE		

NO NEED FOR TENCHI!
Volume 9: The Quest for More Money
VIZ Media Edition

STORY AND ART BY HITOSHI OKUDA

English Adaptation/Fred Burke
Translation/Shuko Shikata
Transcription for Reformat Edition/Alison King
Touch-up Art & Lettering/Curtis Yee
Design/Courtney Utt
Editor/Shaenon K. Garrity

Managing Editor/Annette Roman
Editorial Director/Elizabeth Kawasaki
Editor in Chief/Alvin Lu
Sr. Director of Acquisitions/Rika Inouye
Sr. VP of Marketing/Liza Coppola
Executive VP of Sales & Marketing/John Easum
Publisher/Hyoe Narita

Published by VIZ Media, LLC
P.O. Box 77010
San Francisco, CA 94107

10 9 8 7 6 5 4 3 2 1
First printing, November 2006

www.viz.com
store.viz.com

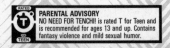

VIZ MANGA

No Need for Tenchi! ™

Volume 9:
The Quest for More Money

STORY AND ART BY

HITOSHI OKUDA

CONTENTS

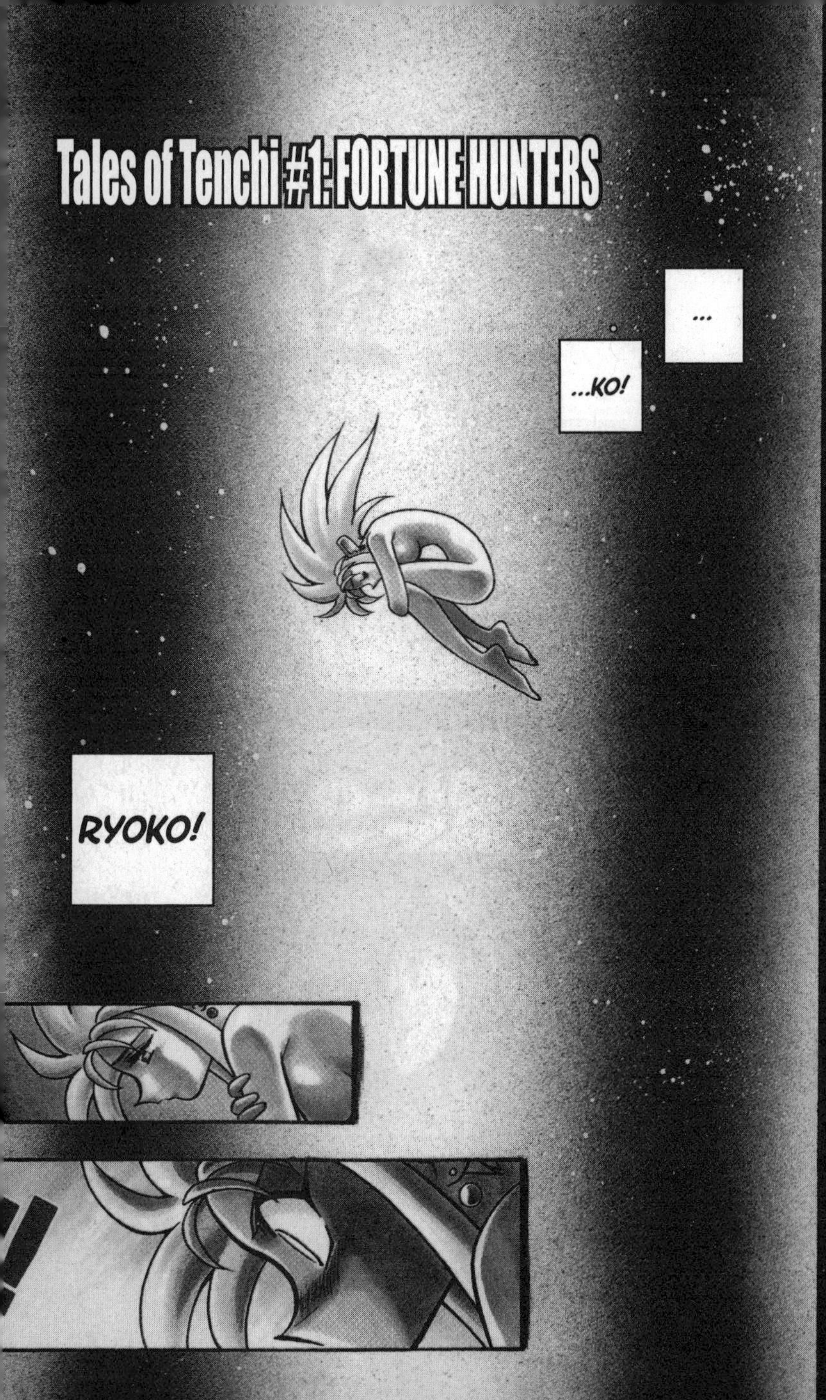

Tales of Tenchi #1: FORTUNE HUNTERS

...

...KO!

RYOKO!

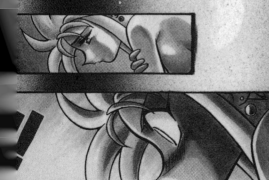

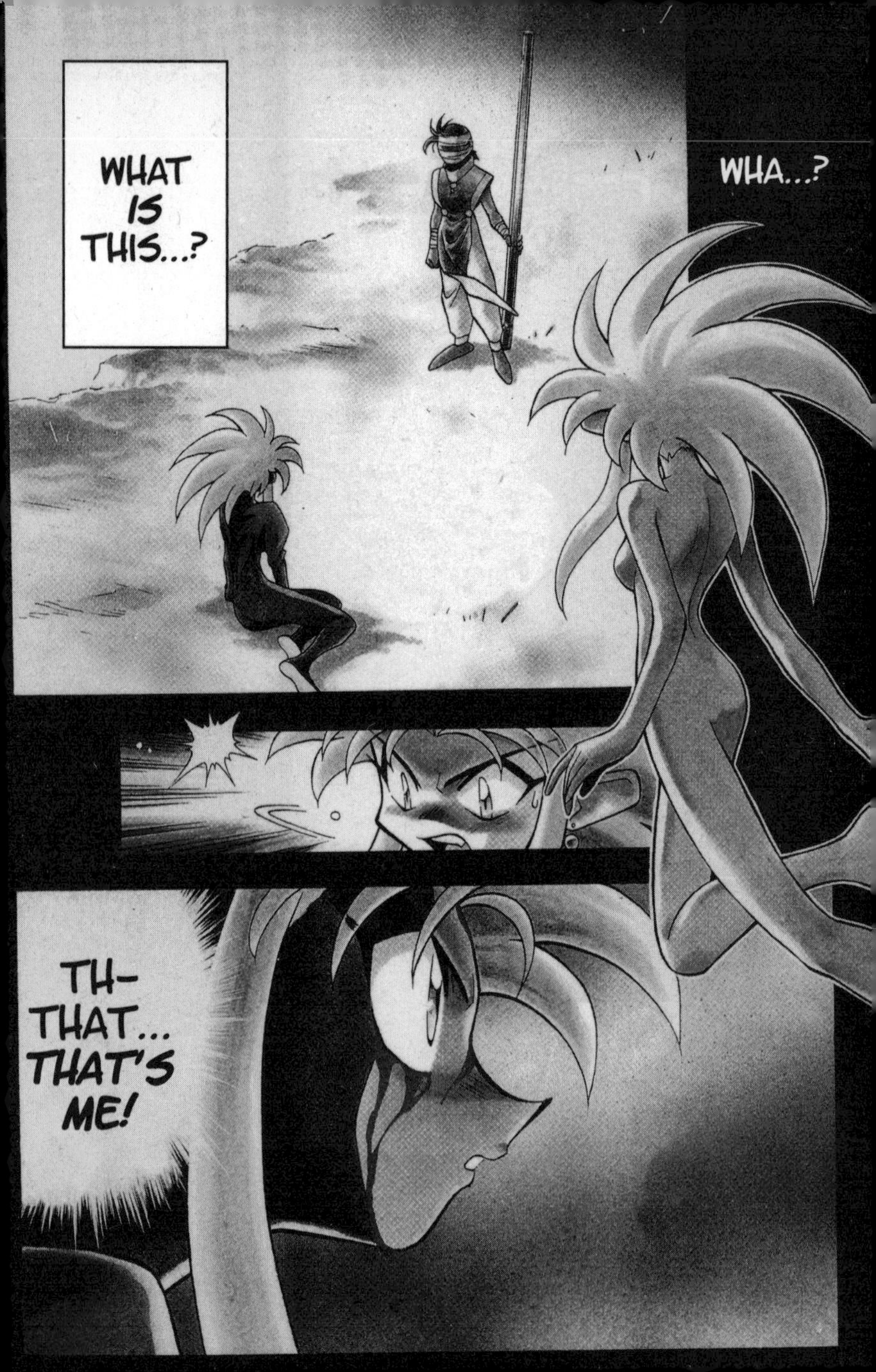
WHA...?
WHAT IS THIS...?
TH- THAT... THAT'S ME!

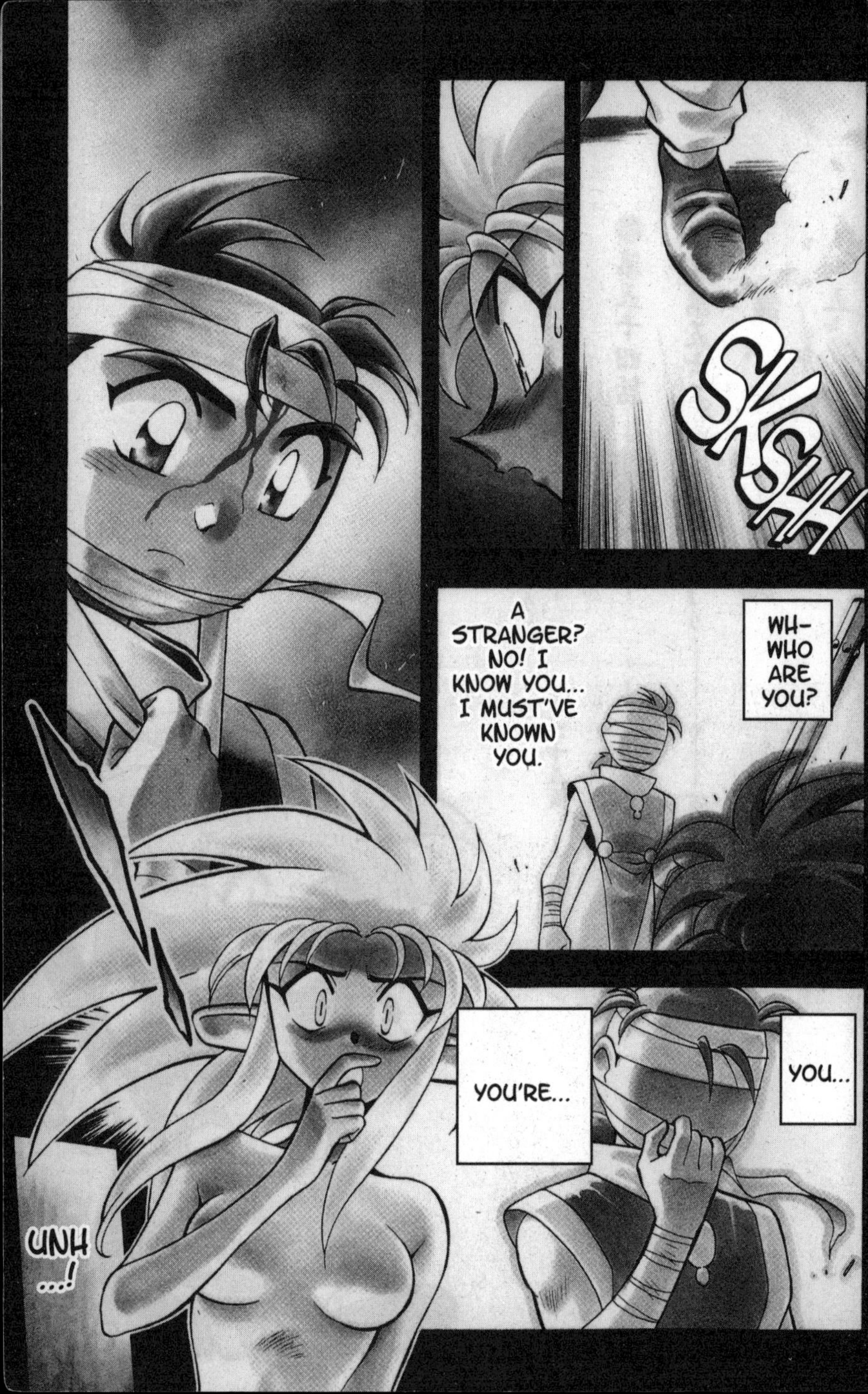
SKSHH
WH- WHO ARE YOU?
A STRANGER? NO! I KNOW YOU... I MUST'VE KNOWN YOU.
YOU...
YOU'RE...
UNH ...!

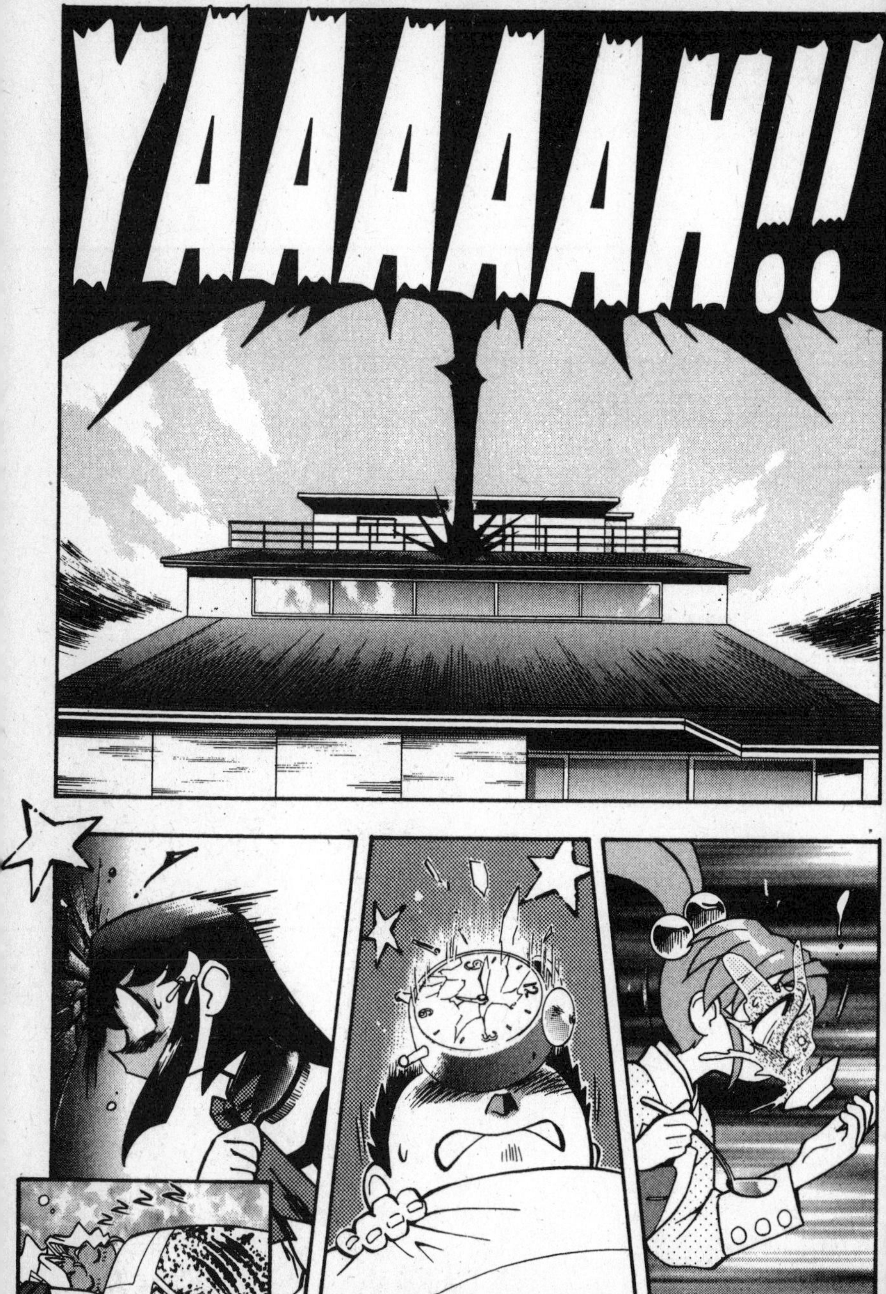

YAAAAH!!

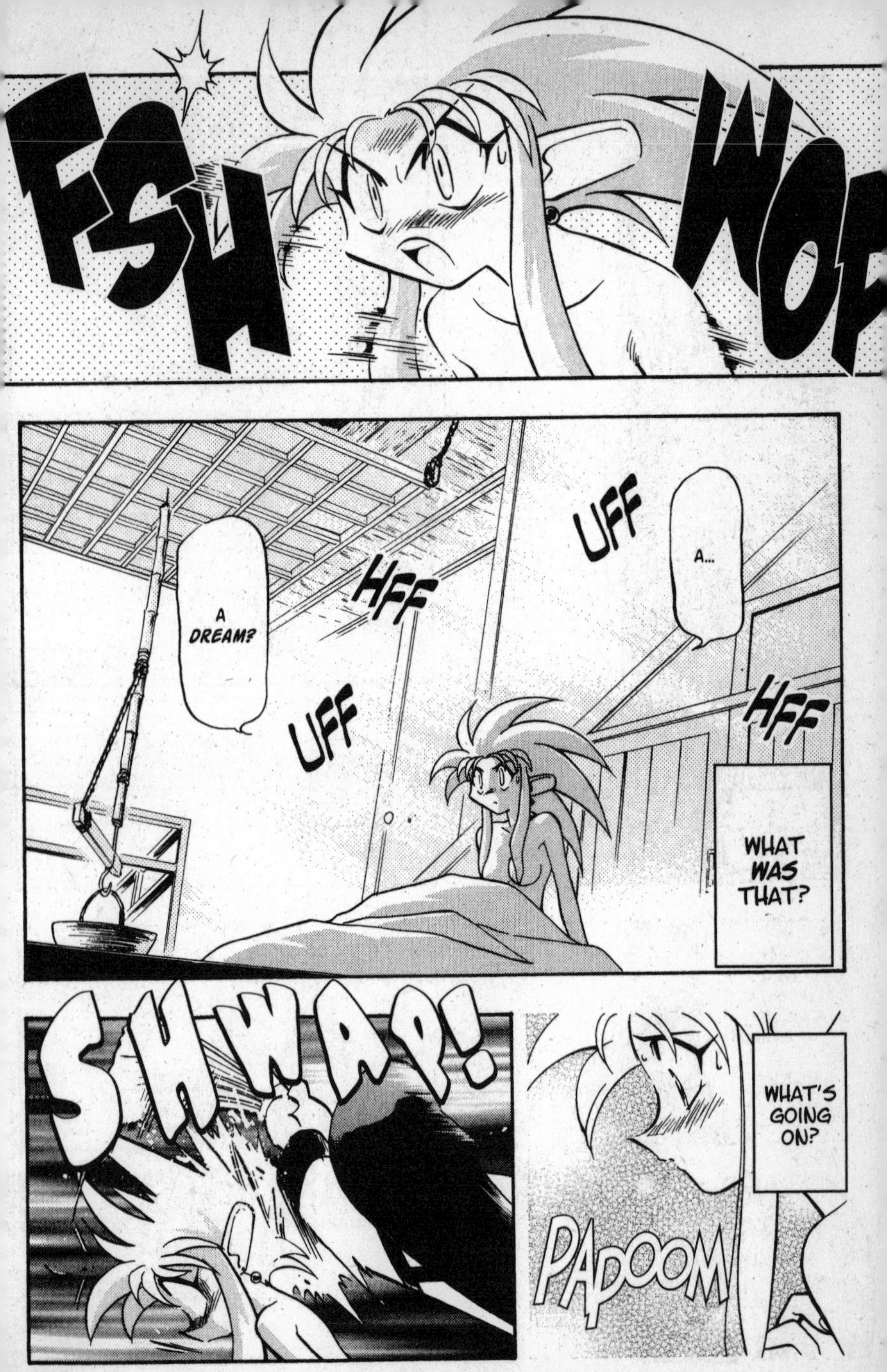
WOF
FSH
A...
UFF
HFF
WHAT WAS THAT?
HFF
A DREAM?
UFF
WHAT'S GOING ON?
PADOOM
SHWAP!

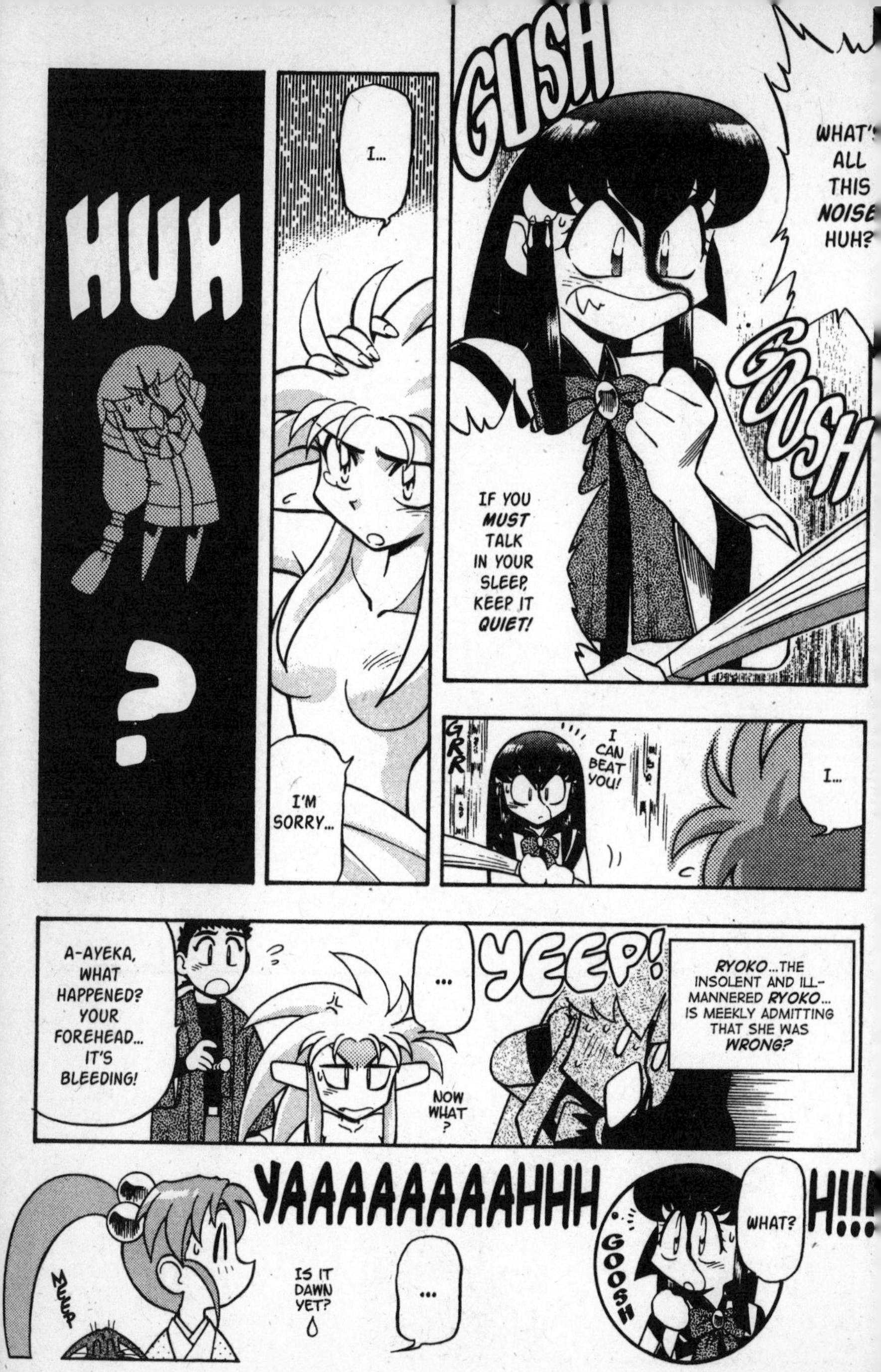
GUSH
WHAT'S ALL THIS NOISE HUH?
GOOSH
IF YOU MUST TALK IN YOUR SLEEP, KEEP IT QUIET!
I...
I CAN BEAT YOU!
GRR
I...
I'M SORRY...
HUH
?
RYOKO...THE INSOLENT AND ILL-MANNERED RYOKO... IS MEEKLY ADMITTING THAT SHE WAS WRONG?
YEEP!
...
NOW WHAT?
A-AYEKA, WHAT HAPPENED? YOUR FOREHEAD... IT'S BLEEDING!
WHAT?
GOOSH
YAAAAAAAAAHHHH!!!
...
IS IT DAWN YET?

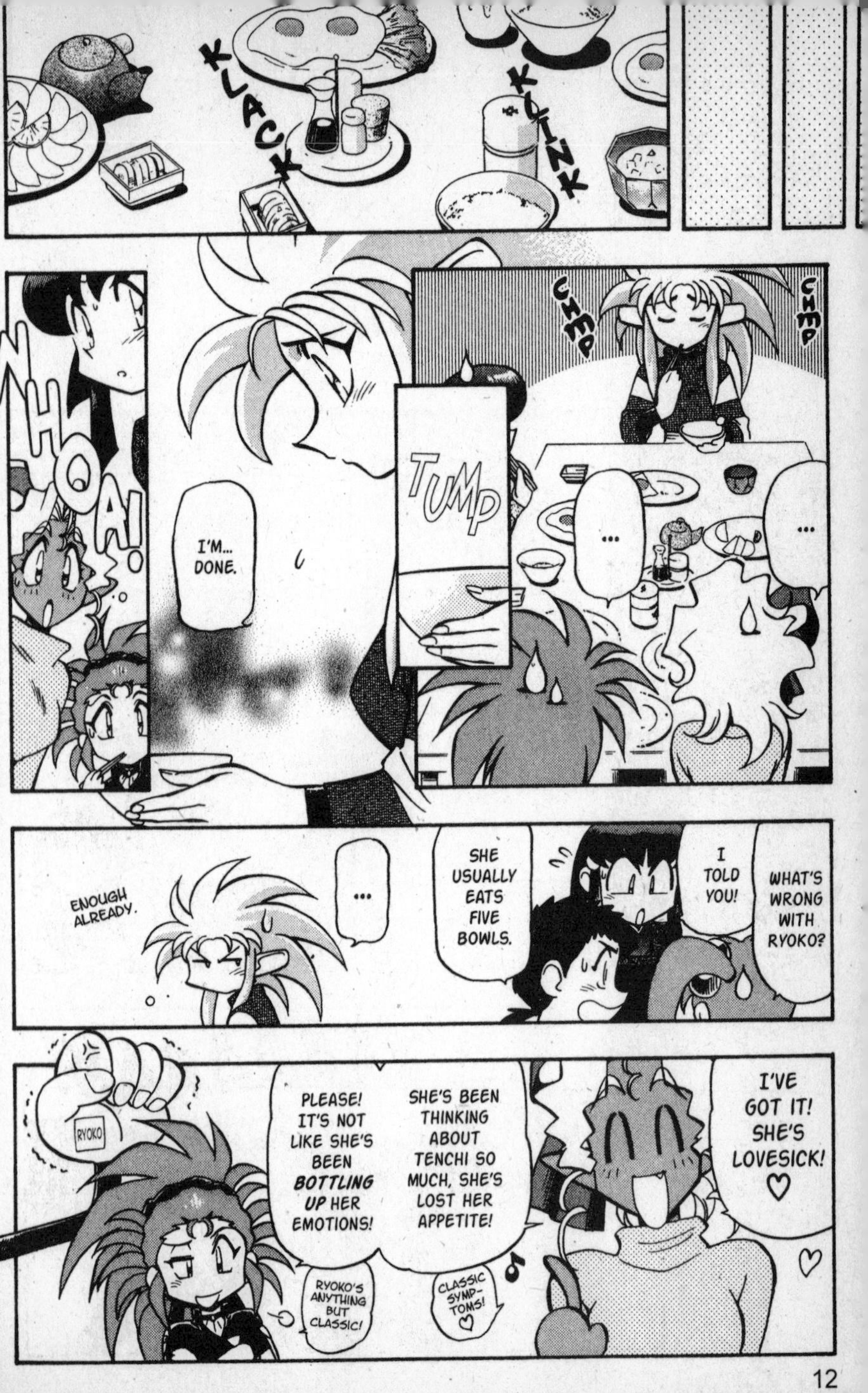
KLINK
KLACK
CHMP
CHMP
...
...
TUMP
I'M... DONE.
WHOA!
WHAT'S WRONG WITH RYOKO?
I TOLD YOU!
SHE USUALLY EATS FIVE BOWLS.
...
ENOUGH ALREADY.
I'VE GOT IT! SHE'S LOVESICK! ♡
CLASSIC SYMPTOMS! ♡
SHE'S BEEN THINKING ABOUT TENCHI SO MUCH, SHE'S LOST HER APPETITE!
PLEASE! IT'S NOT LIKE SHE'S BEEN ***BOTTLING UP*** HER EMOTIONS!
RYOKO'S ANYTHING BUT CLASSIC!
RYOKO

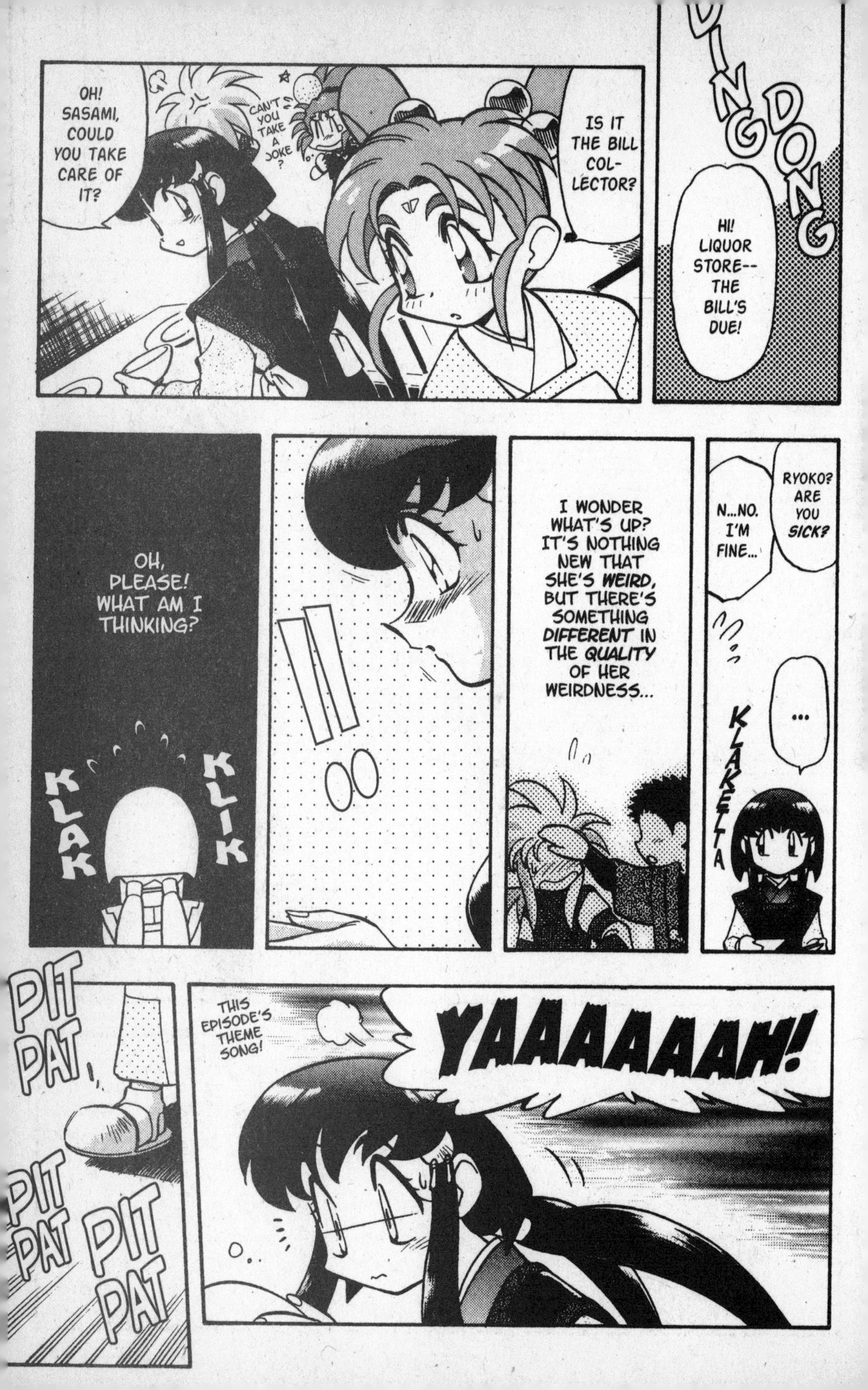
DING DONG
HI! LIQUOR STORE-- THE BILL'S DUE!
IS IT THE BILL COLLECTOR?
CAN'T YOU TAKE A JOKE?
OH! SASAMI, COULD YOU TAKE CARE OF IT?
RYOKO? ARE YOU *SICK?*
N...NO. I'M FINE...
...
KLAKETA
I WONDER WHAT'S UP? IT'S NOTHING NEW THAT SHE'S *WEIRD,* BUT THERE'S SOMETHING *DIFFERENT* IN THE *QUALITY* OF HER WEIRDNESS...
OH, PLEASE! WHAT AM I THINKING?
KLIK
KLAK
THIS EPISODE'S THEME SONG!
YAAAAAAAH!
PIT PAT
PIT PAT
PIT PAT

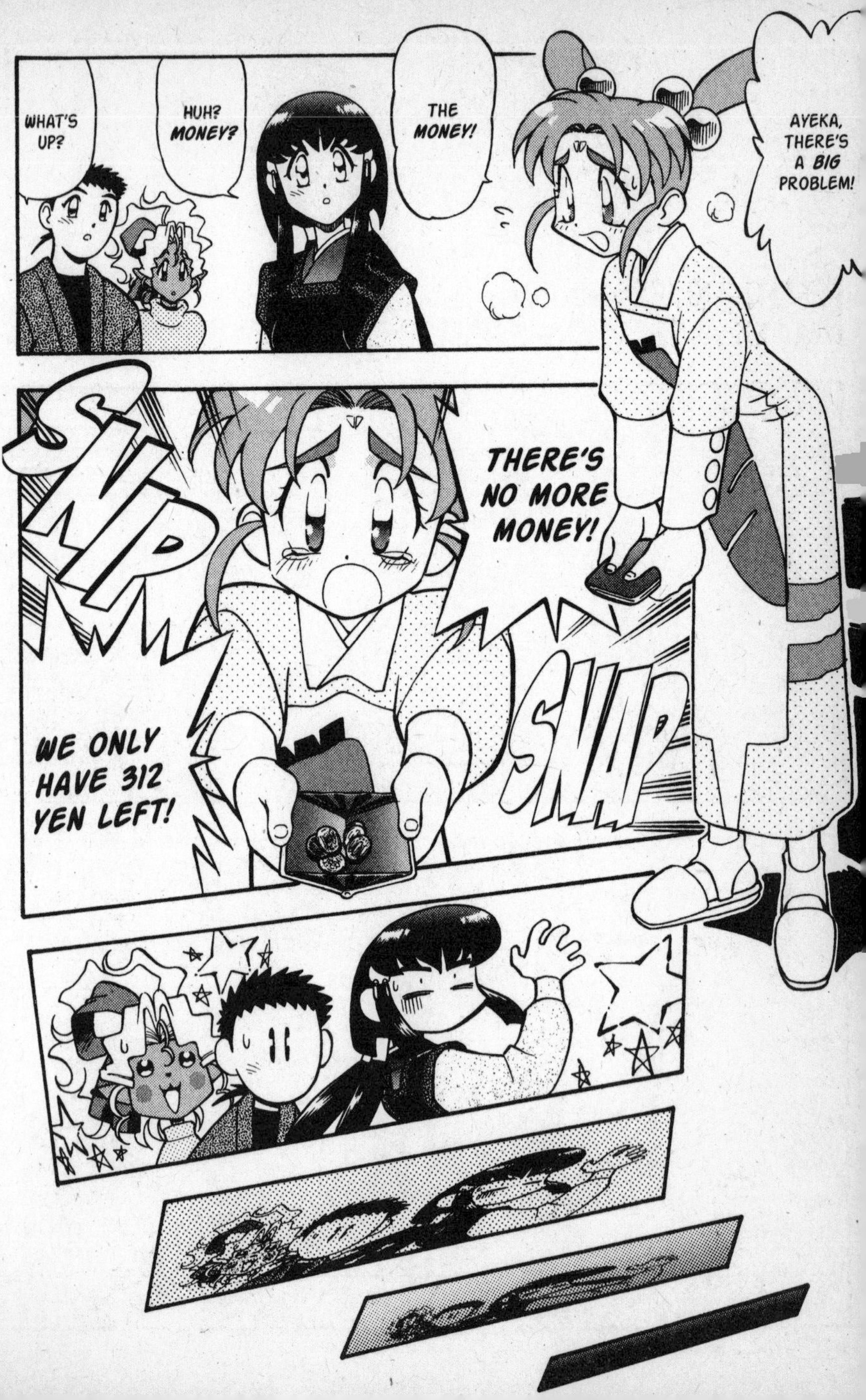
AYEKA, THERE'S A BIG PROBLEM!
THE MONEY!
HUH? MONEY?
WHAT'S UP?
THERE'S NO MORE MONEY!
SNIP
SNAP
WE ONLY HAVE 312 YEN LEFT!

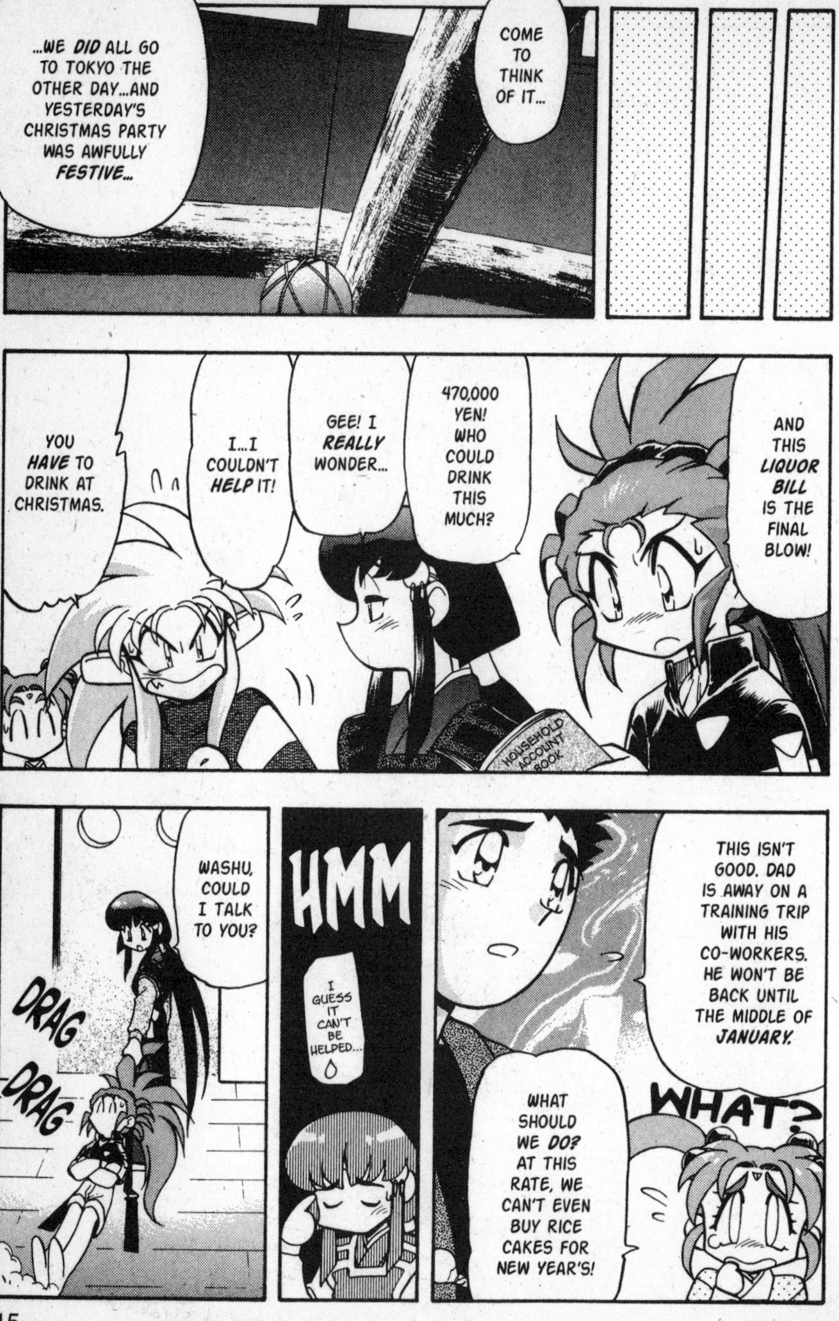
COME TO THINK OF IT...
...WE DID ALL GO TO TOKYO THE OTHER DAY...AND YESTERDAY'S CHRISTMAS PARTY WAS AWFULLY FESTIVE...
AND THIS LIQUOR BILL IS THE FINAL BLOW!
470,000 YEN! WHO COULD DRINK THIS MUCH?
GEE! I REALLY WONDER...
I...I COULDN'T HELP IT!
YOU HAVE TO DRINK AT CHRISTMAS.
HOUSEHOLD ACCOUNT BOOK
THIS ISN'T GOOD. DAD IS AWAY ON A TRAINING TRIP WITH HIS CO-WORKERS. HE WON'T BE BACK UNTIL THE MIDDLE OF JANUARY.
WHAT?
WHAT SHOULD WE DO? AT THIS RATE, WE CAN'T EVEN BUY RICE CAKES FOR NEW YEAR'S!
HMM
I GUESS IT CAN'T BE HELPED...
WASHU, COULD I TALK TO YOU?
DRAG
DRAG

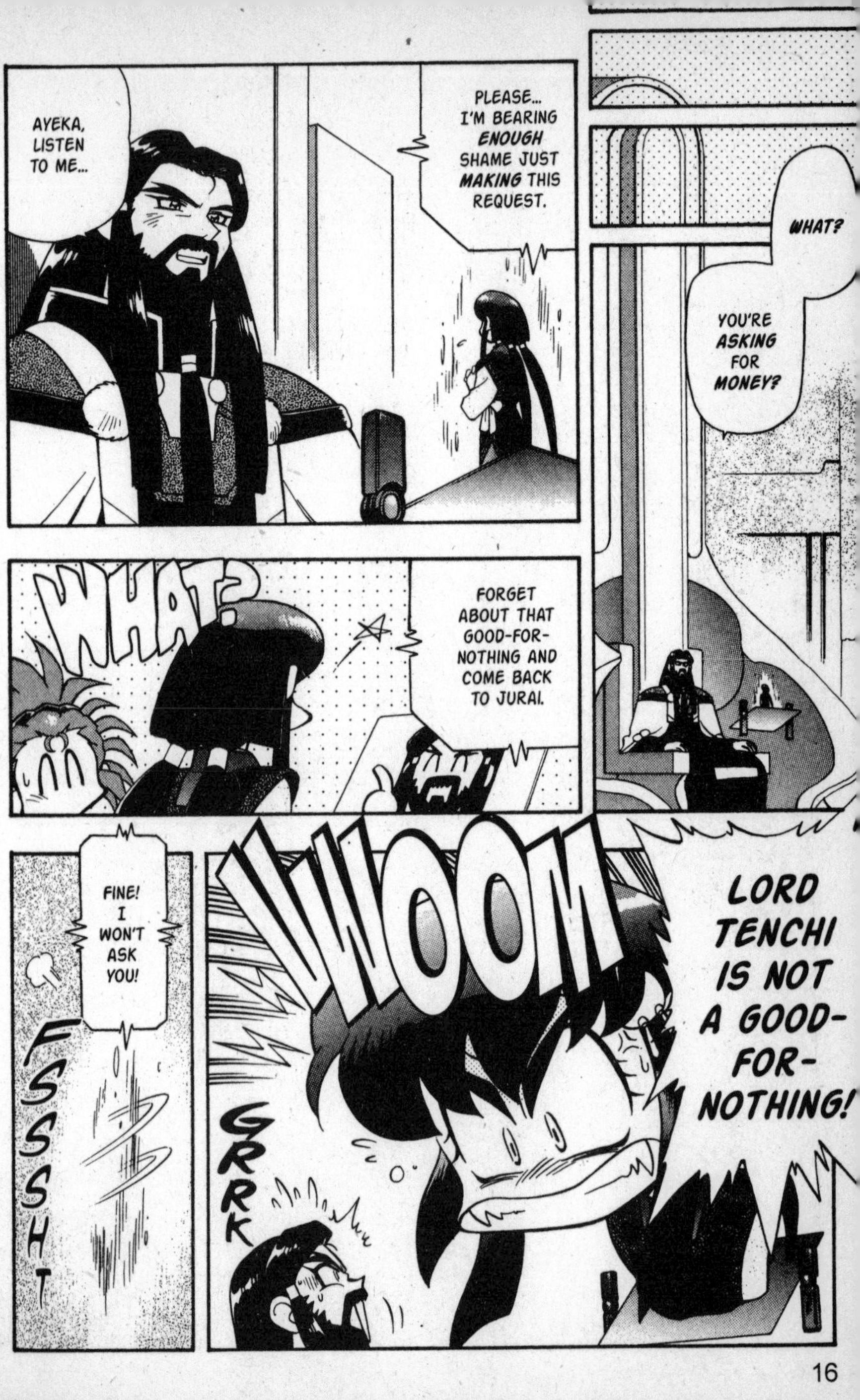
WHAT?
YOU'RE ASKING FOR MONEY?
PLEASE... I'M BEARING ENOUGH SHAME JUST MAKING THIS REQUEST.
AYEKA, LISTEN TO ME...
FORGET ABOUT THAT GOOD-FOR-NOTHING AND COME BACK TO JURAI.
WHAT?
LORD TENCHI IS NOT A GOOD-FOR-NOTHING!
WOOM
GRRK
FINE! I WON'T ASK YOU!
FSSSHT

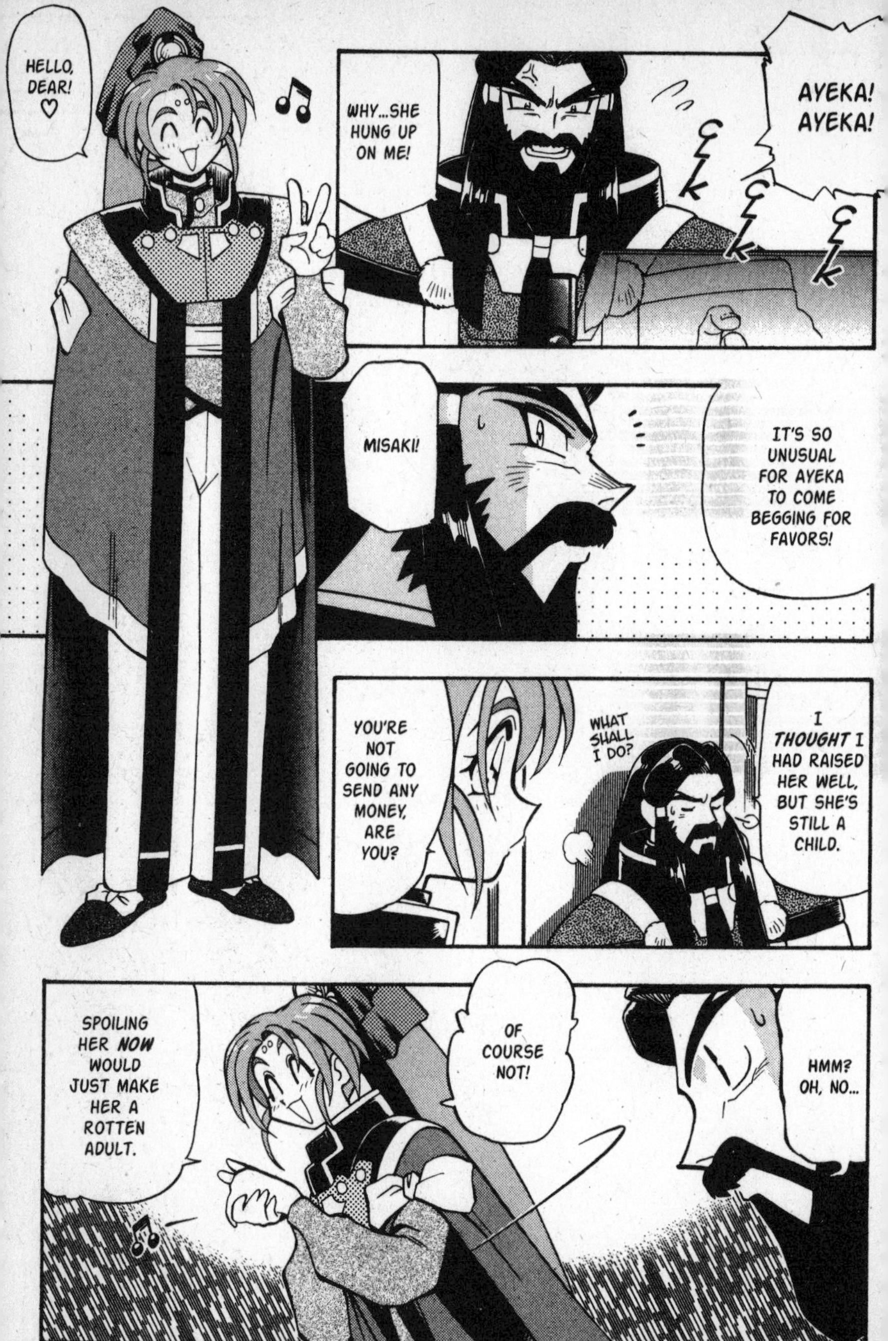
AYEKA! AYEKA!
CLK
CLK
CLK
WHY...SHE HUNG UP ON ME!
IT'S SO UNUSUAL FOR AYEKA TO COME BEGGING FOR FAVORS!
MISAKI!
I *THOUGHT* I HAD RAISED HER WELL, BUT SHE'S STILL A CHILD.
WHAT SHALL I DO?
YOU'RE NOT GOING TO SEND ANY MONEY, ARE YOU?
HELLO, DEAR! ♡
HMM? OH, NO...
OF COURSE NOT!
SPOILING HER *NOW* WOULD JUST MAKE HER A ROTTEN ADULT.

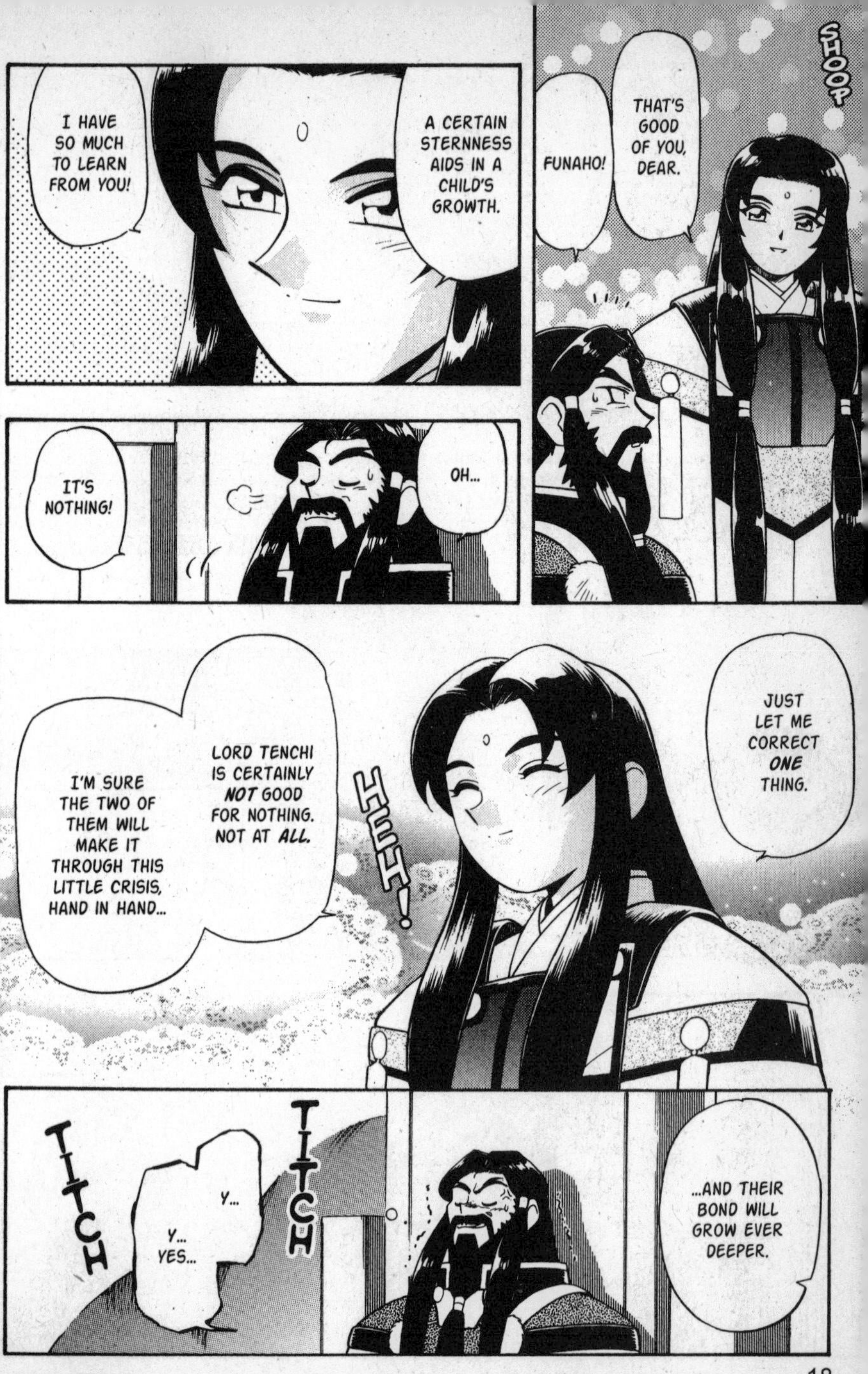
SHOOP
THAT'S GOOD OF YOU, DEAR.
FUNAHO!
A CERTAIN STERNNESS AIDS IN A CHILD'S GROWTH.
I HAVE SO MUCH TO LEARN FROM YOU!
OH...
IT'S NOTHING!
JUST LET ME CORRECT ONE THING.
HEH!
LORD TENCHI IS CERTAINLY NOT GOOD FOR NOTHING. NOT AT ALL.
I'M SURE THE TWO OF THEM WILL MAKE IT THROUGH THIS LITTLE CRISIS, HAND IN HAND...
...AND THEIR BOND WILL GROW EVER DEEPER.
TITCH
Y... Y... YES...
TITCH

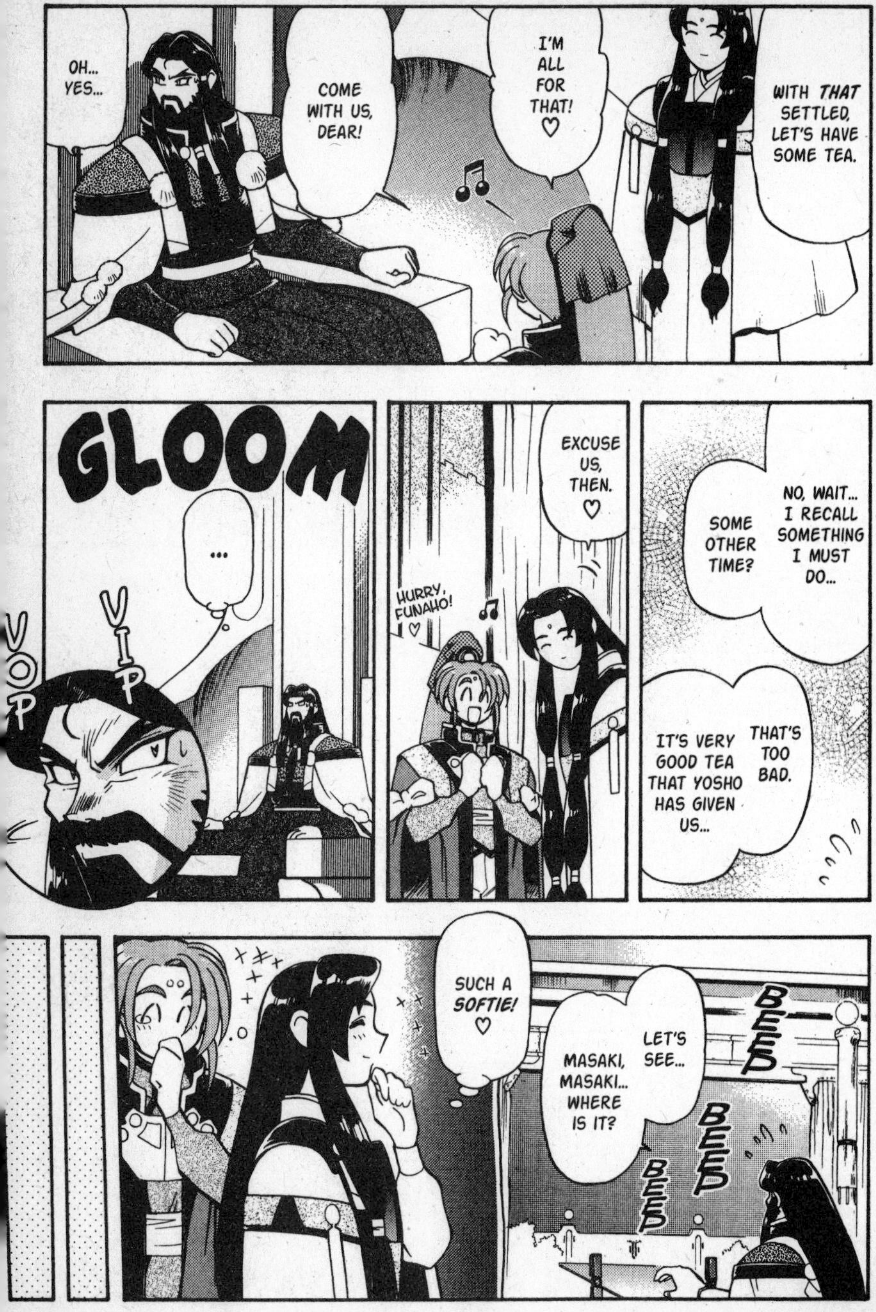
WITH THAT SETTLED, LET'S HAVE SOME TEA.
I'M ALL FOR THAT! ♡
COME WITH US, DEAR!
OH... YES...
NO, WAIT... I RECALL SOMETHING I MUST DO...
SOME OTHER TIME?
THAT'S TOO BAD.
IT'S VERY GOOD TEA THAT YOSHO HAS GIVEN US...
EXCUSE US, THEN. ♡
HURRY, FUNAHO! ♡
GLOOM
...
VIP
VOP
BEEP
BEEP
BEEP
LET'S SEE...
MASAKI, MASAKI... WHERE IS IT?
SUCH A SOFTIE! ♡

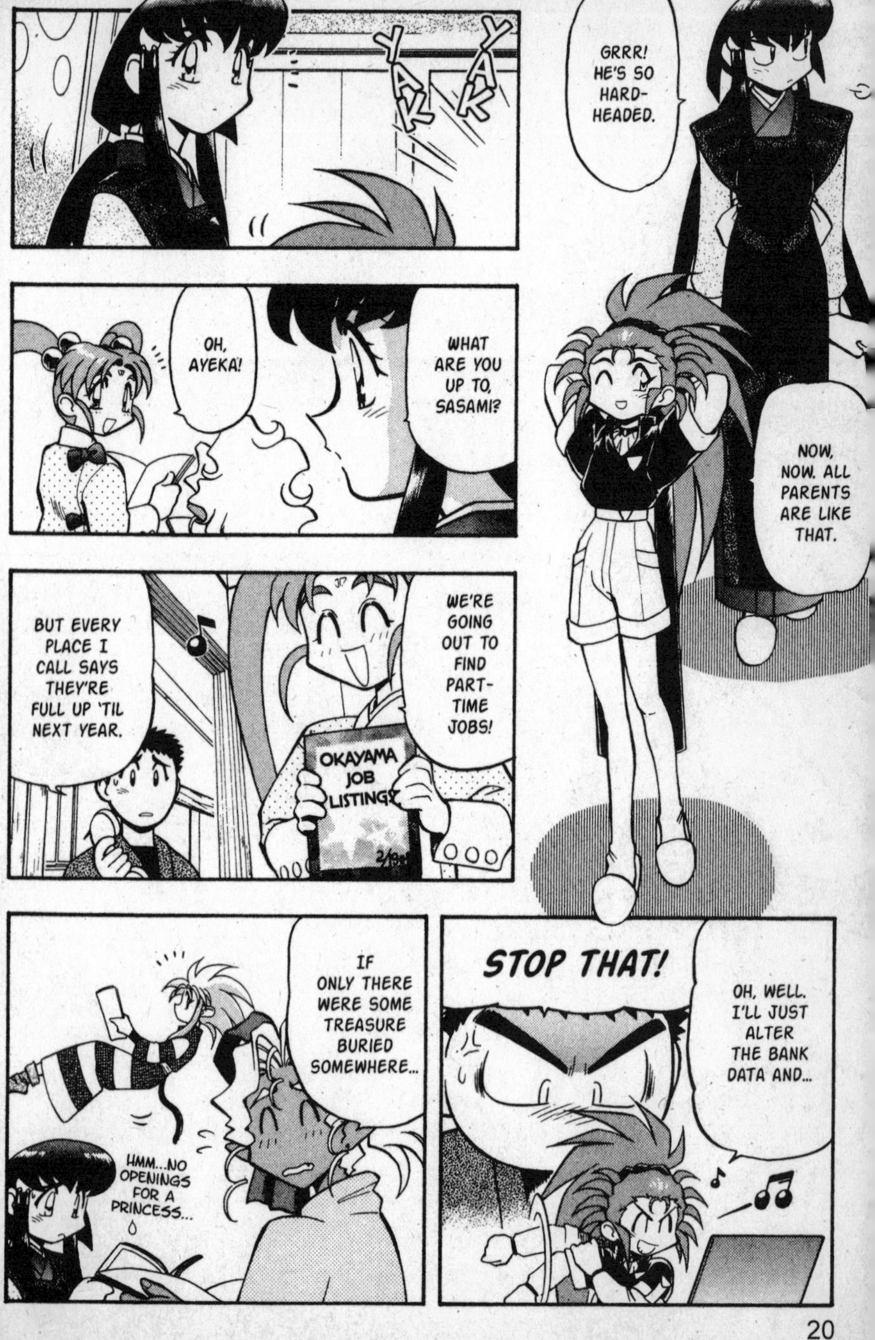
GRRR! HE'S SO HARD-HEADED.
NOW, NOW. ALL PARENTS ARE LIKE THAT.
YAK YAK
WHAT ARE YOU UP TO, SASAMI?
OH, AYEKA!
WE'RE GOING OUT TO FIND PART-TIME JOBS!
OKAYAMA JOB LISTINGS
BUT EVERY PLACE I CALL SAYS THEY'RE FULL UP 'TIL NEXT YEAR.
OH, WELL. I'LL JUST ALTER THE BANK DATA AND...
STOP THAT!
IF ONLY THERE WERE SOME TREASURE BURIED SOMEWHERE...
HMM...NO OPENINGS FOR A PRINCESS...

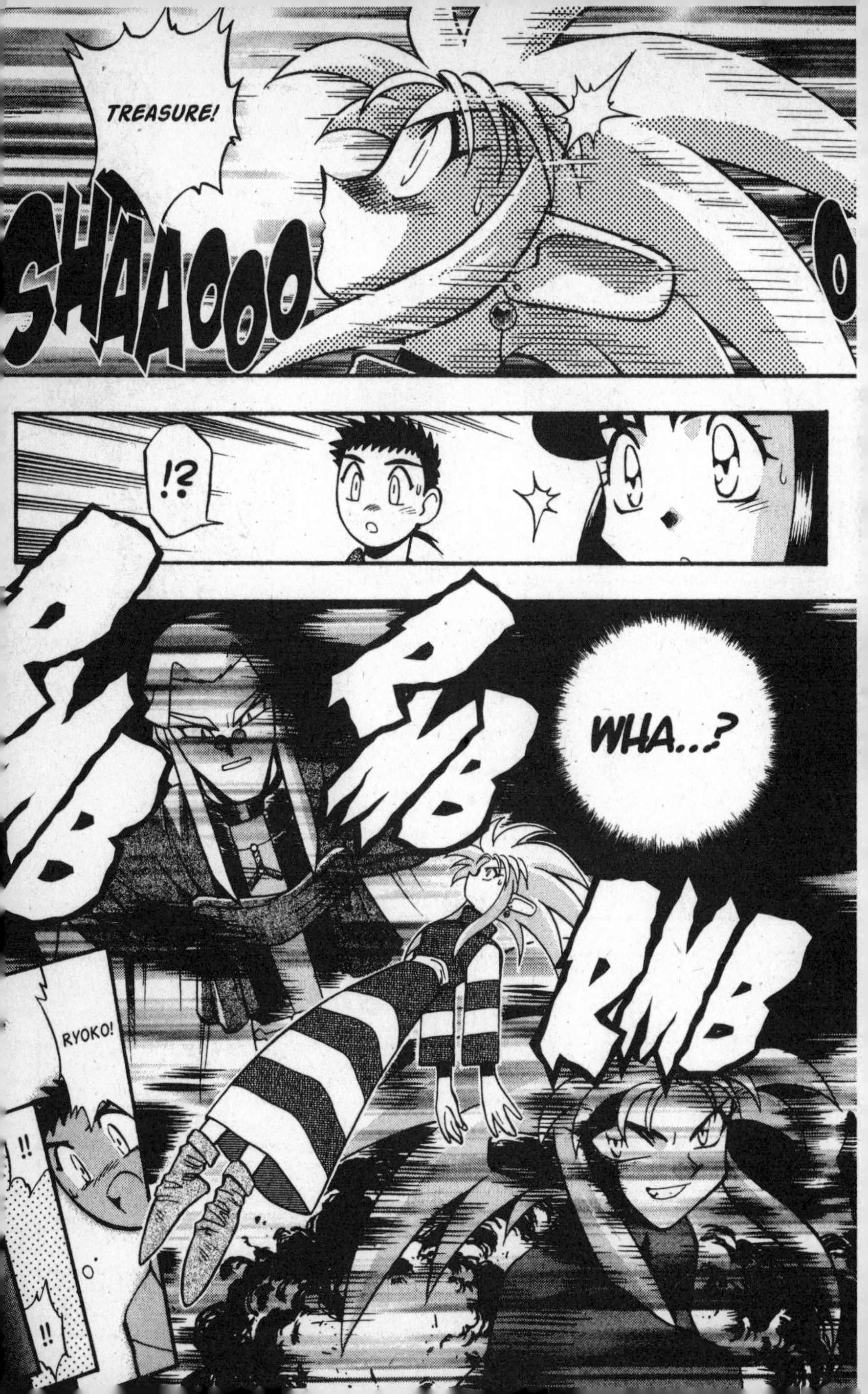
TREASURE!
SHAAOOO
!?
BMB
BMB
WHA...?
BMB
RYOKO!
!!
!!

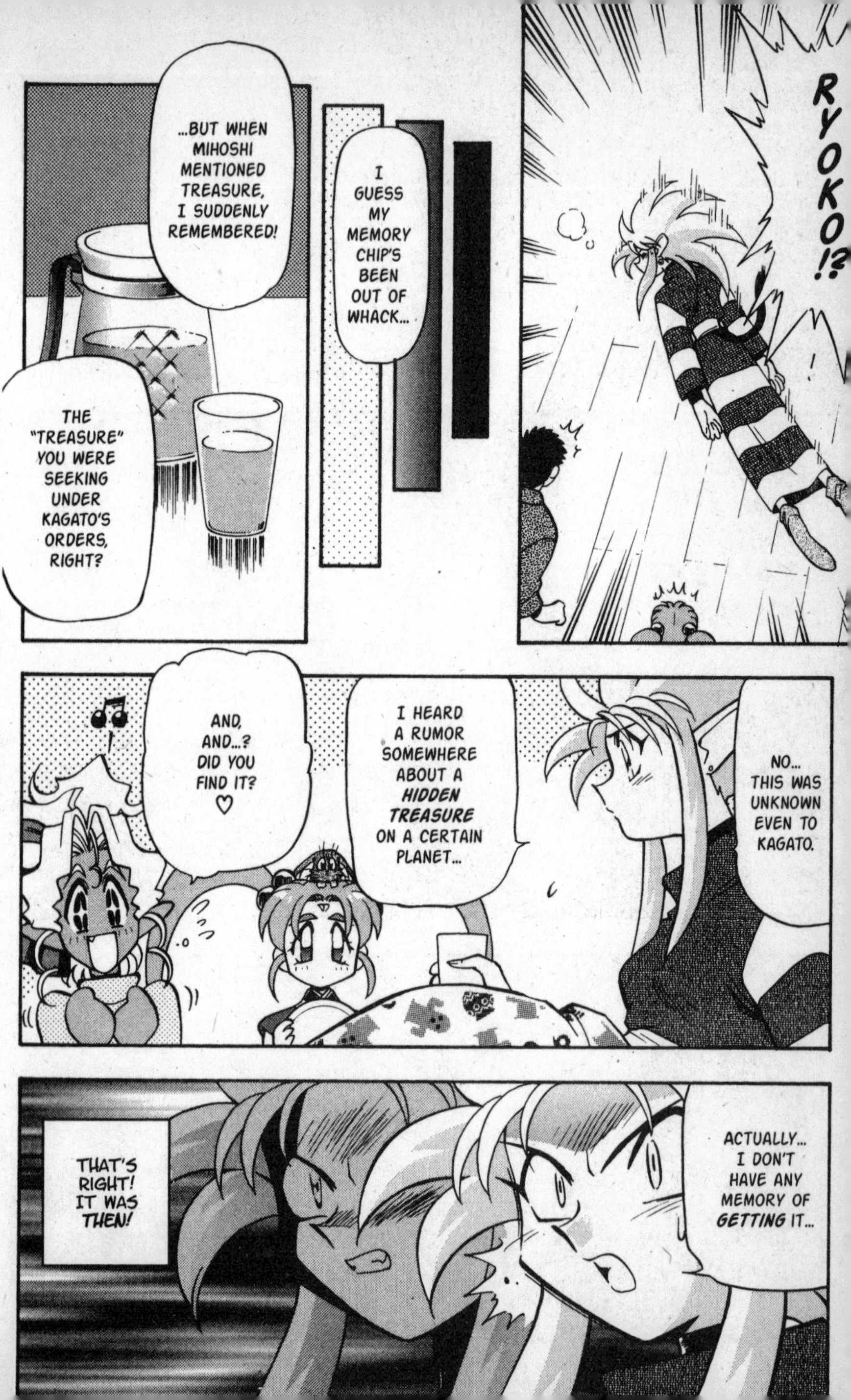
RYOKO!?
I GUESS MY MEMORY CHIP'S BEEN OUT OF WHACK...
...BUT WHEN MIHOSHI MENTIONED TREASURE, I SUDDENLY REMEMBERED!
THE "TREASURE" YOU WERE SEEKING UNDER KAGATO'S ORDERS, RIGHT?
NO... THIS WAS UNKNOWN EVEN TO KAGATO.
I HEARD A RUMOR SOMEWHERE ABOUT A *HIDDEN TREASURE* ON A CERTAIN PLANET...
AND, AND...? DID YOU FIND IT? ♡
ACTUALLY... I DON'T HAVE ANY MEMORY OF *GETTING* IT...
THAT'S RIGHT! IT WAS *THEN*!

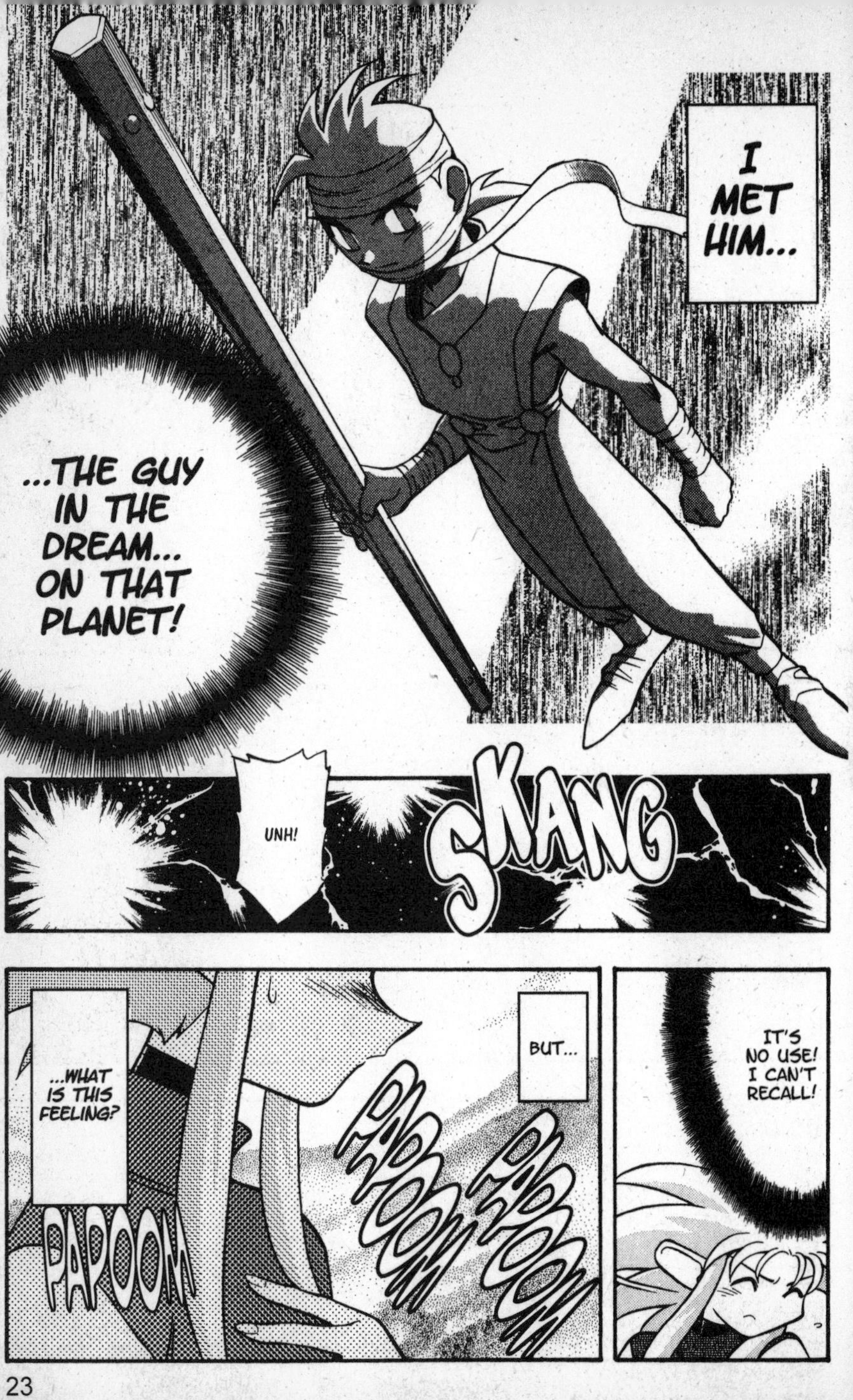
I MET HIM...
...THE GUY IN THE DREAM... ON THAT PLANET!
SKANG
UNH!
IT'S NO USE! I CAN'T RECALL!
BUT...
PAPOOM
PAPOOM
...WHAT IS THIS FEELING?
PAPOOM

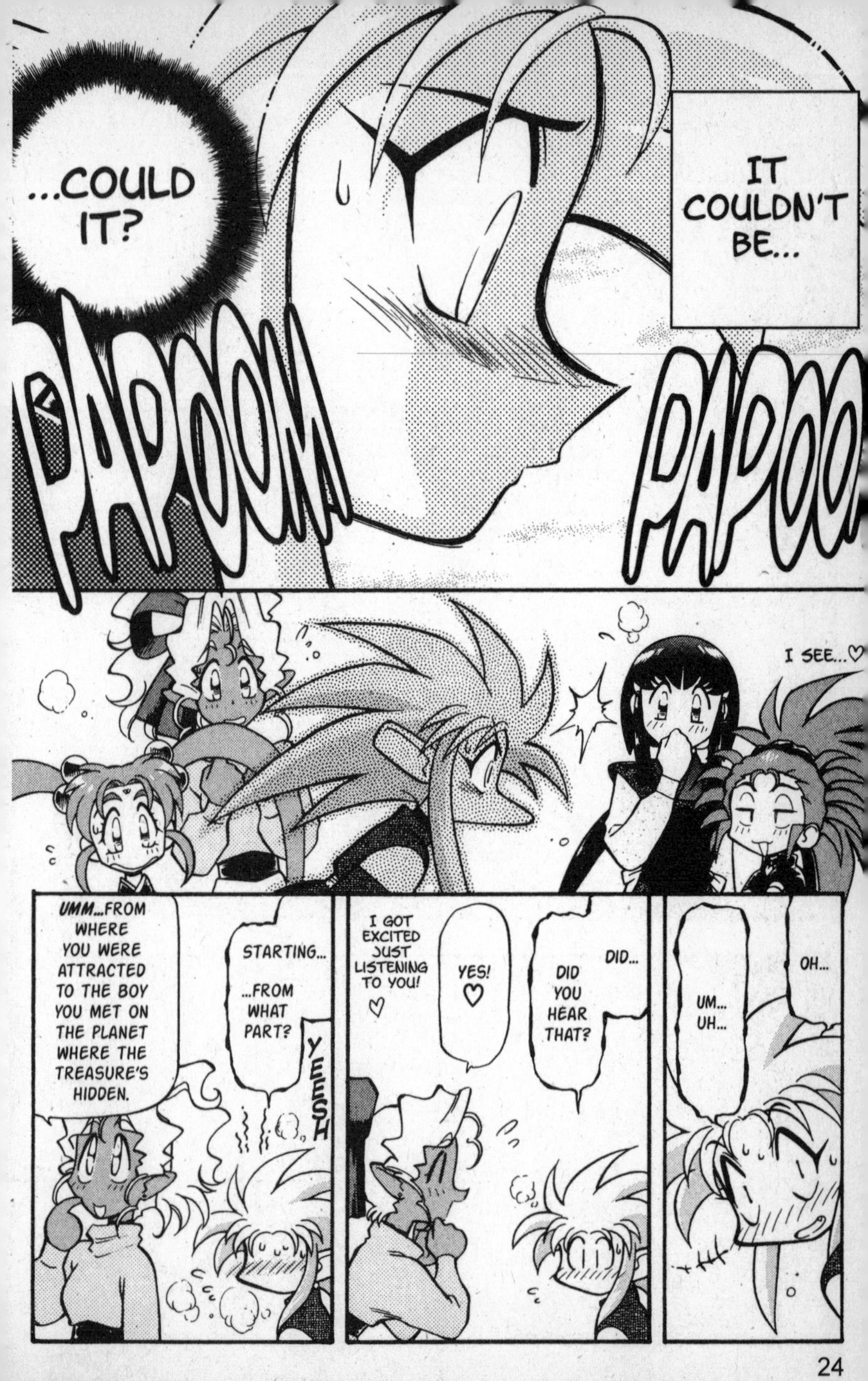

IT COULDN'T BE...
...COULD IT?
PAPOO
PAPOOM
I SEE...♡
OH...
UM... UH...
DID...
DID YOU HEAR THAT?
YES! ♡
I GOT EXCITED JUST LISTENING TO YOU! ♡
STARTING...
...FROM WHAT PART?
YEESH
UMM...FROM WHERE YOU WERE ATTRACTED TO THE BOY YOU MET ON THE PLANET WHERE THE TREASURE'S HIDDEN.

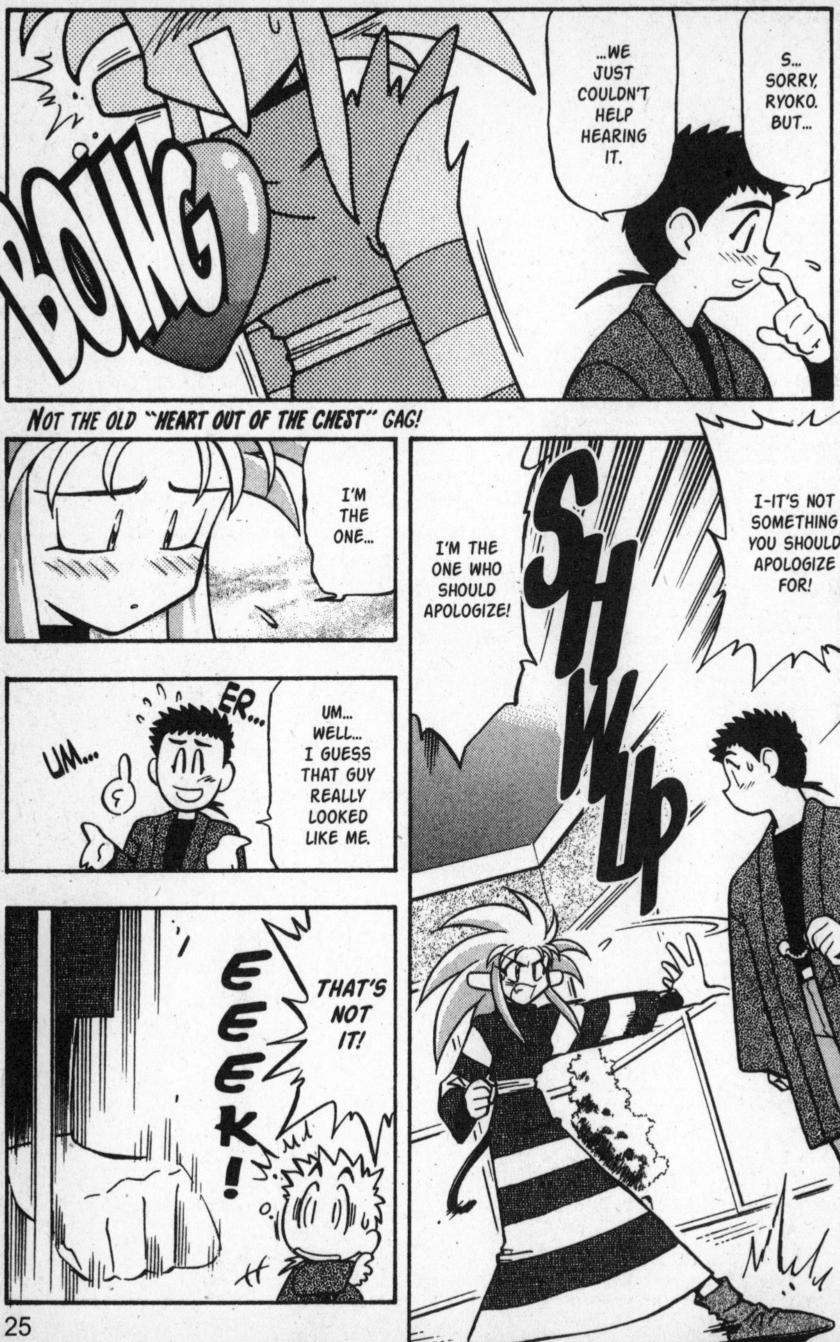
S... SORRY, RYOKO. BUT...
...WE JUST COULDN'T HELP HEARING IT.
BOING
NOT THE OLD "HEART OUT OF THE CHEST" GAG!
I-IT'S NOT SOMETHING YOU SHOULD APOLOGIZE FOR!
SHWUP
I'M THE ONE WHO SHOULD APOLOGIZE!
I'M THE ONE...
ER...
UM... WELL... I GUESS THAT GUY REALLY LOOKED LIKE ME.
UM...
THAT'S NOT IT!
EEEEK!

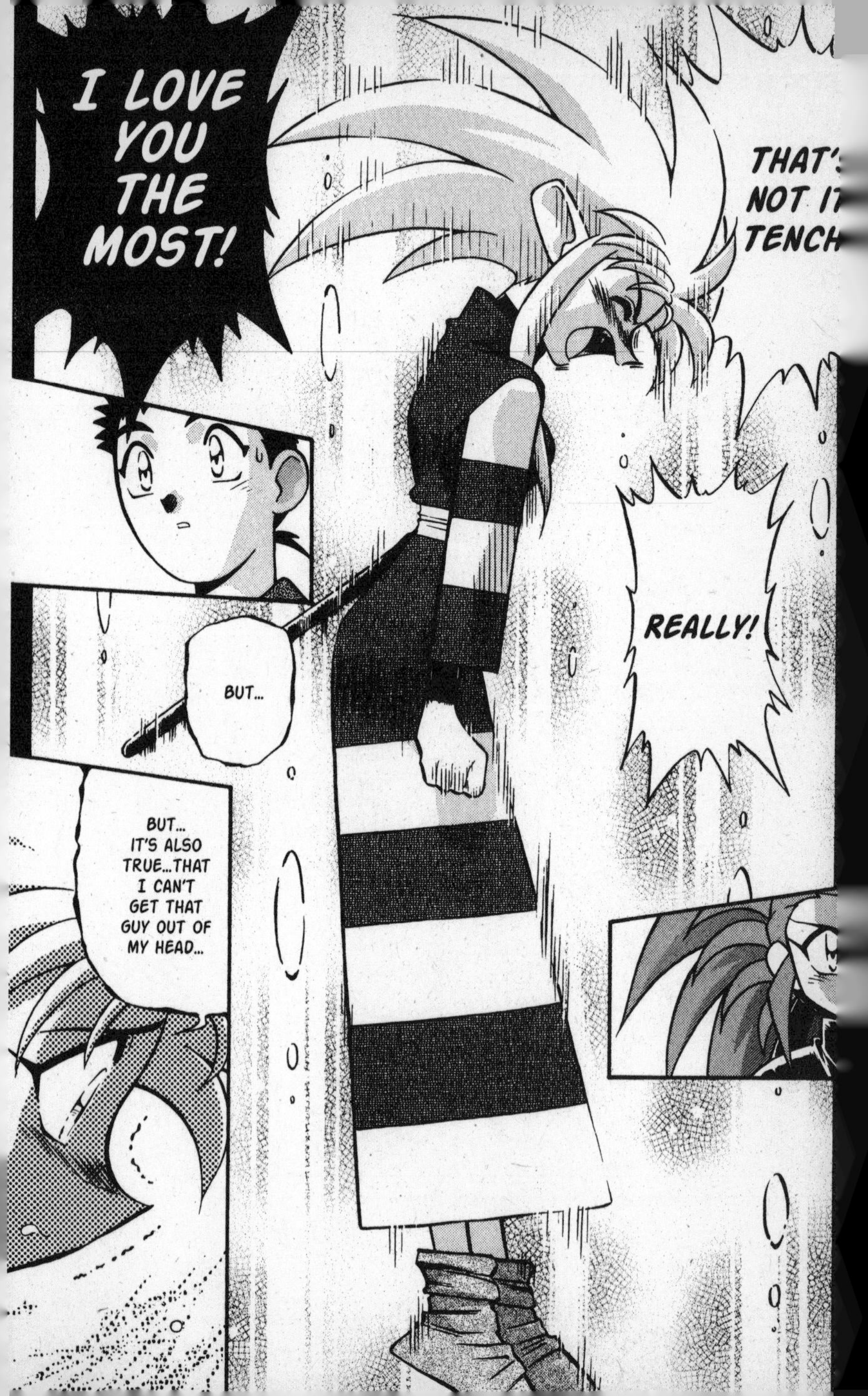
THAT'S NOT IT TENCH
REALLY!
I LOVE YOU THE MOST!
BUT...
BUT... IT'S ALSO TRUE...THAT I CAN'T GET THAT GUY OUT OF MY HEAD...

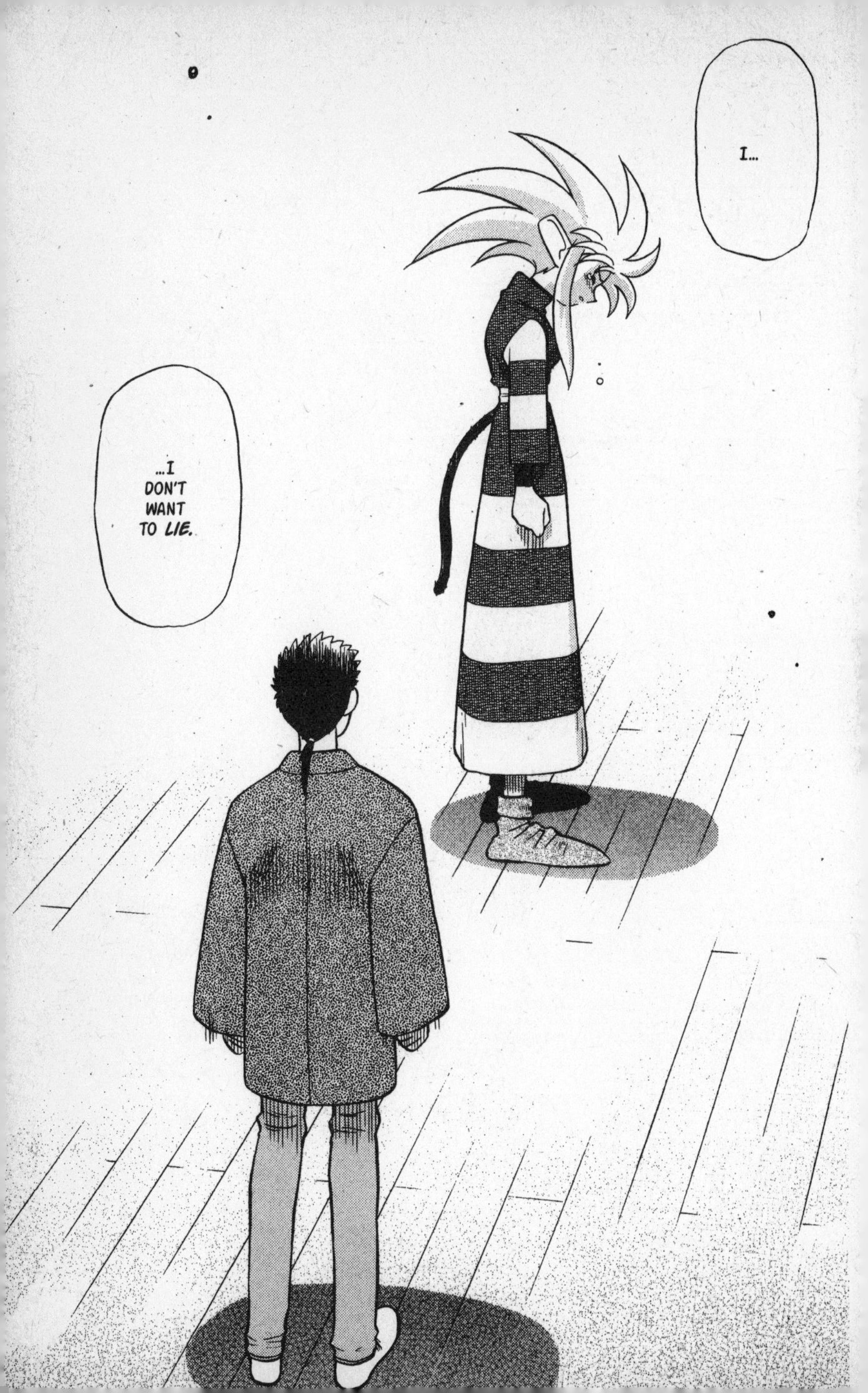
I...
...I DON'T WANT TO *LIE.*

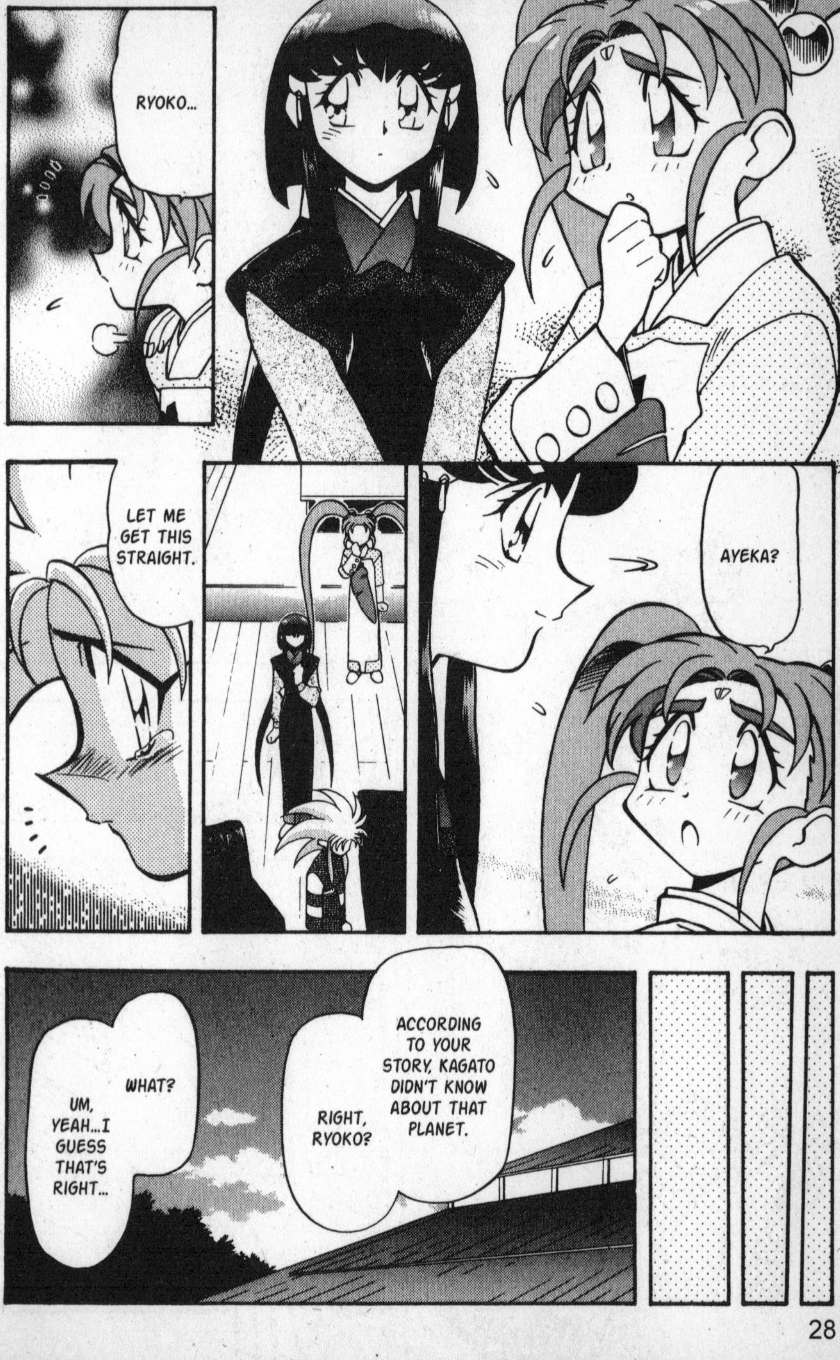
RYOKO...
AYEKA?
LET ME GET THIS STRAIGHT.
ACCORDING TO YOUR STORY, KAGATO DIDN'T KNOW ABOUT THAT PLANET.
RIGHT, RYOKO?
WHAT?
UM, YEAH...I GUESS THAT'S RIGHT...

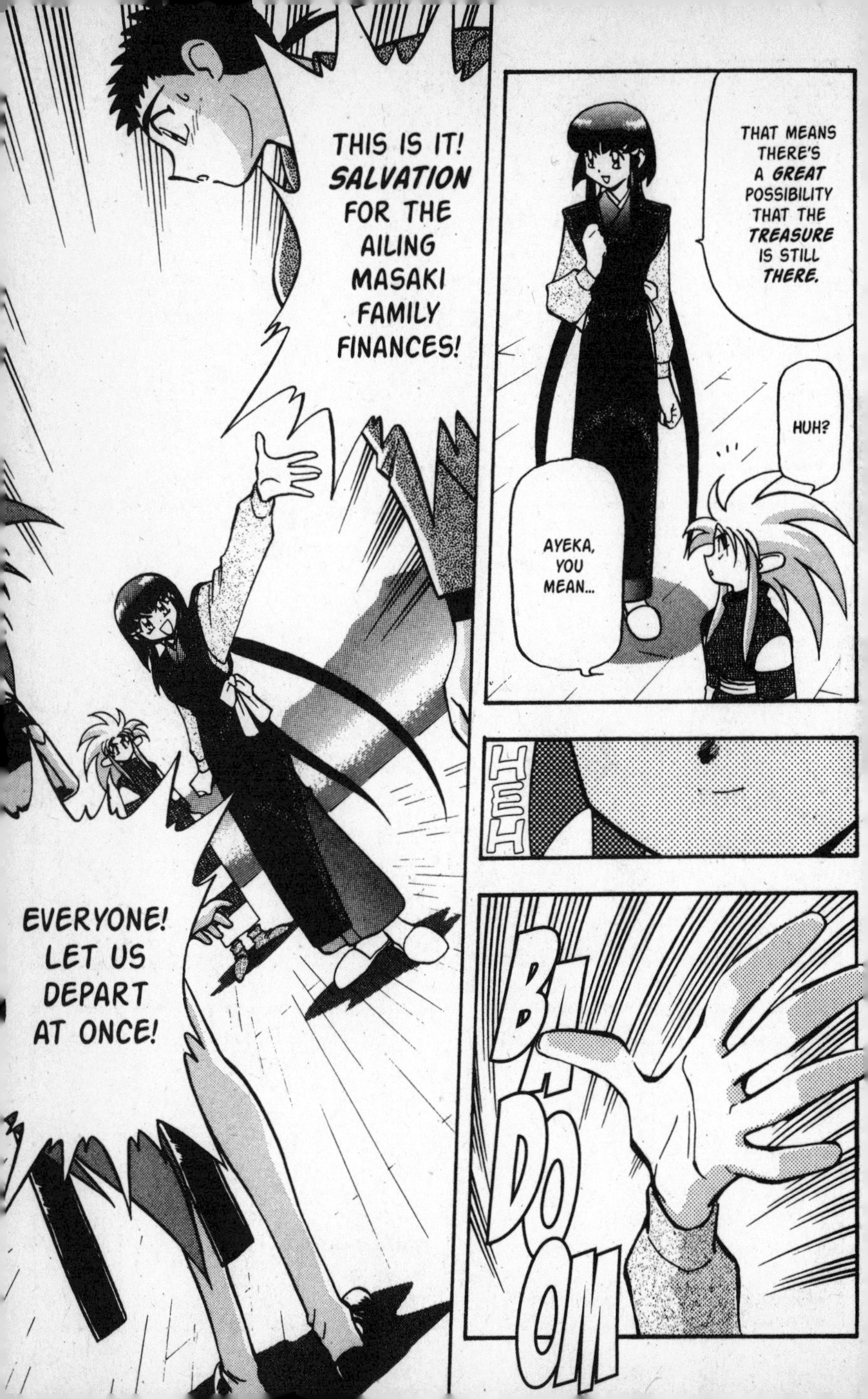
THAT MEANS THERE'S A *GREAT* POSSIBILITY THAT THE *TREASURE* IS STILL *THERE.*
HUH?
AYEKA, YOU MEAN...
HEH
BADOOM
THIS IS IT! *SALVATION* FOR THE AILING MASAKI FAMILY FINANCES!
EVERYONE! LET US DEPART AT ONCE!

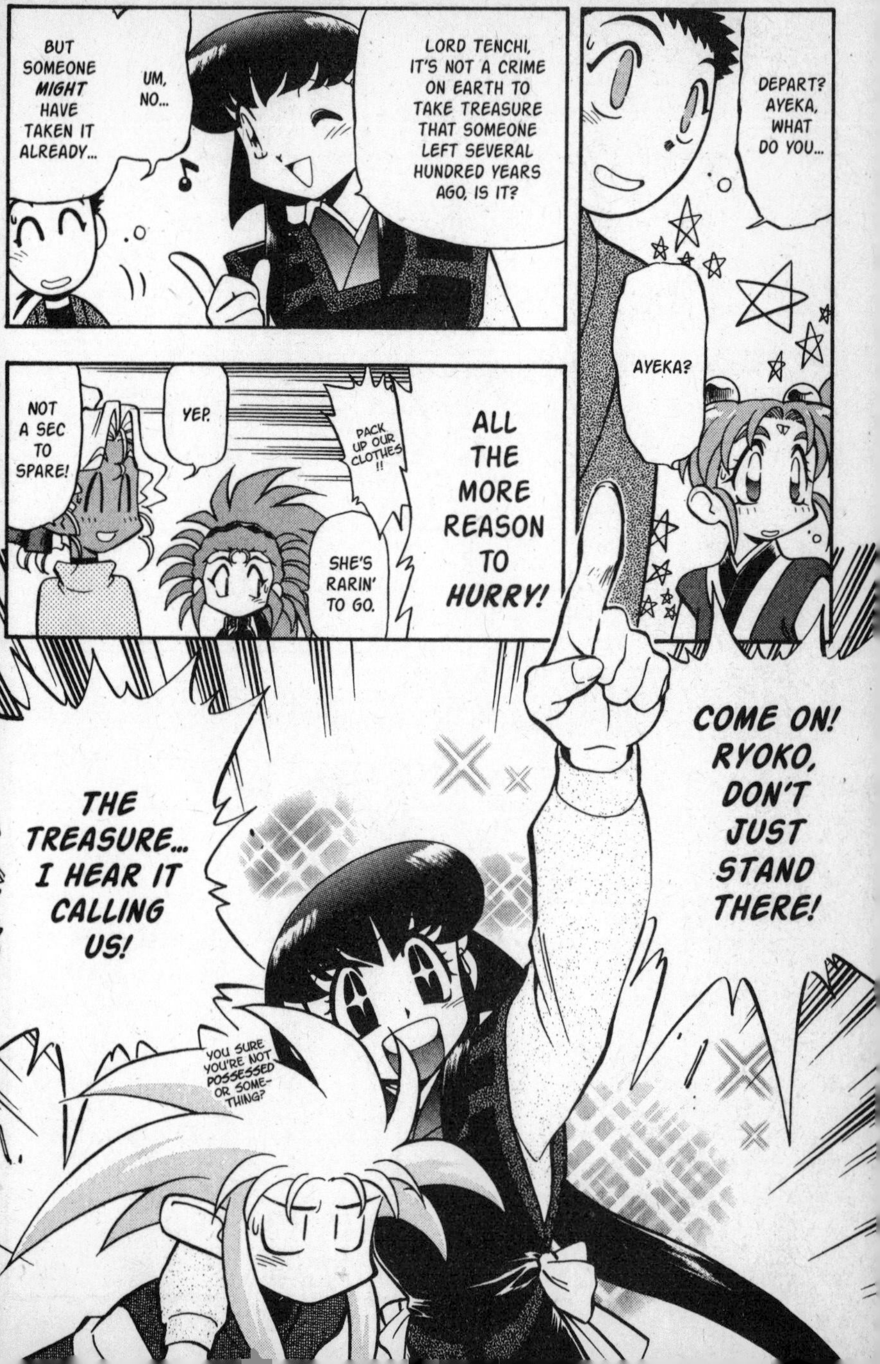
DEPART? AYEKA, WHAT DO YOU...
AYEKA?
LORD TENCHI, IT'S NOT A CRIME ON EARTH TO TAKE TREASURE THAT SOMEONE LEFT SEVERAL HUNDRED YEARS AGO, IS IT?
UM, NO...
BUT SOMEONE *MIGHT* HAVE TAKEN IT ALREADY...
ALL THE MORE REASON TO *HURRY!*
PACK UP OUR CLOTHES!!
SHE'S RARIN' TO GO.
YEP.
NOT A SEC TO SPARE!
COME ON! RYOKO, DON'T JUST STAND THERE!
THE TREASURE... I HEAR IT CALLING US!
YOU SURE YOU'RE NOT POSSESSED OR SOME-THING?

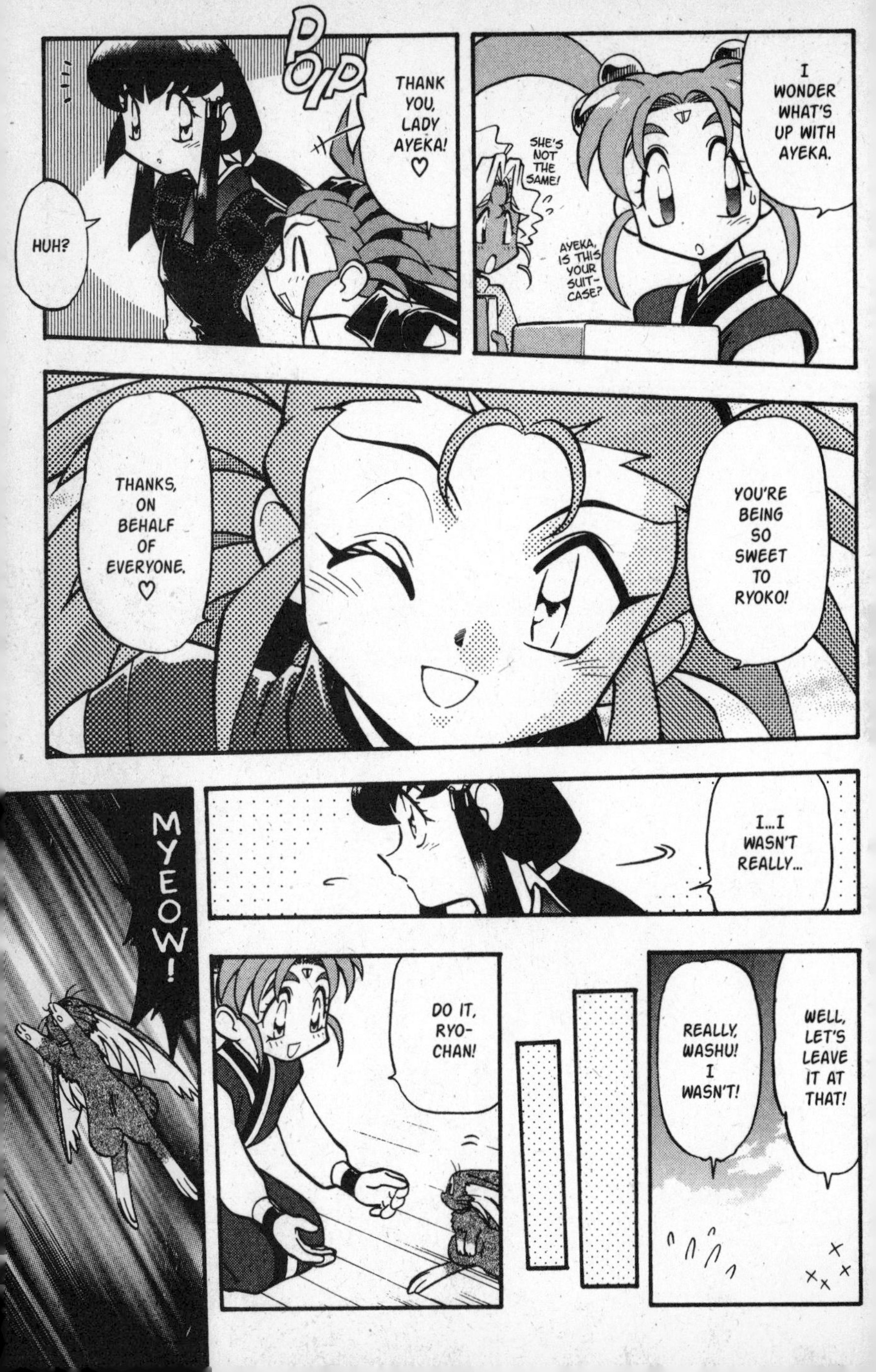
I WONDER WHAT'S UP WITH AYEKA.
SHE'S NOT THE SAME!
AYEKA, IS THIS YOUR SUIT-CASE?
POP
THANK YOU, LADY AYEKA! ♡
HUH?
YOU'RE BEING SO SWEET TO RYOKO!
THANKS, ON BEHALF OF EVERYONE. ♡
I...I WASN'T REALLY...
WELL, LET'S LEAVE IT AT THAT!
REALLY, WASHU! I WASN'T!
DO IT, RYO-CHAN!
MYEOW!

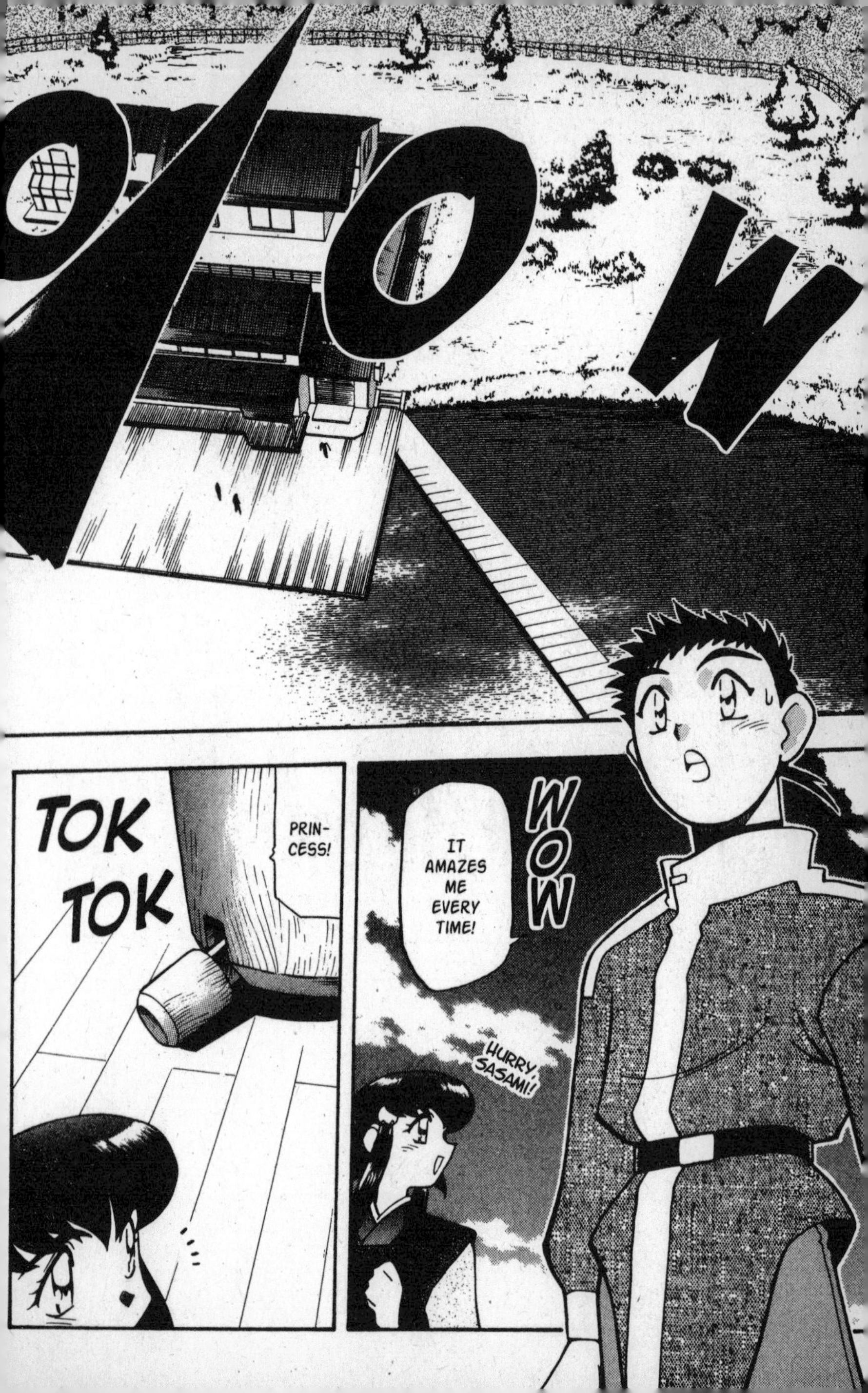
WOW
WOW
IT AMAZES ME EVERY TIME!
HURRY, SASAMI!
PRIN-CESS!
TOK TOK
...

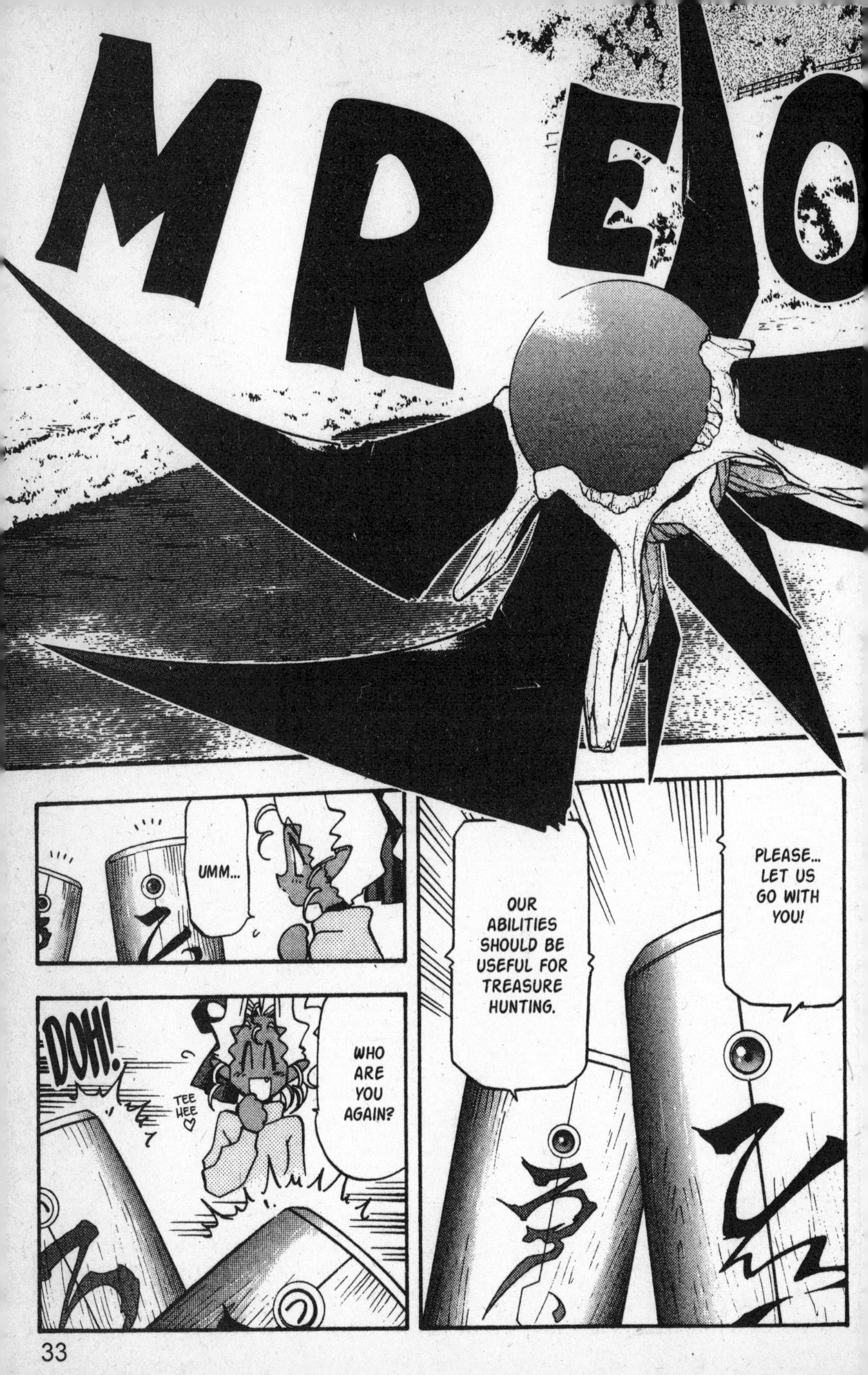
MREO
PLEASE... LET US GO WITH YOU!
OUR ABILITIES SHOULD BE USEFUL FOR TREASURE HUNTING.
UMM...
WHO ARE YOU AGAIN?
DOH!
TEE HEE ♡

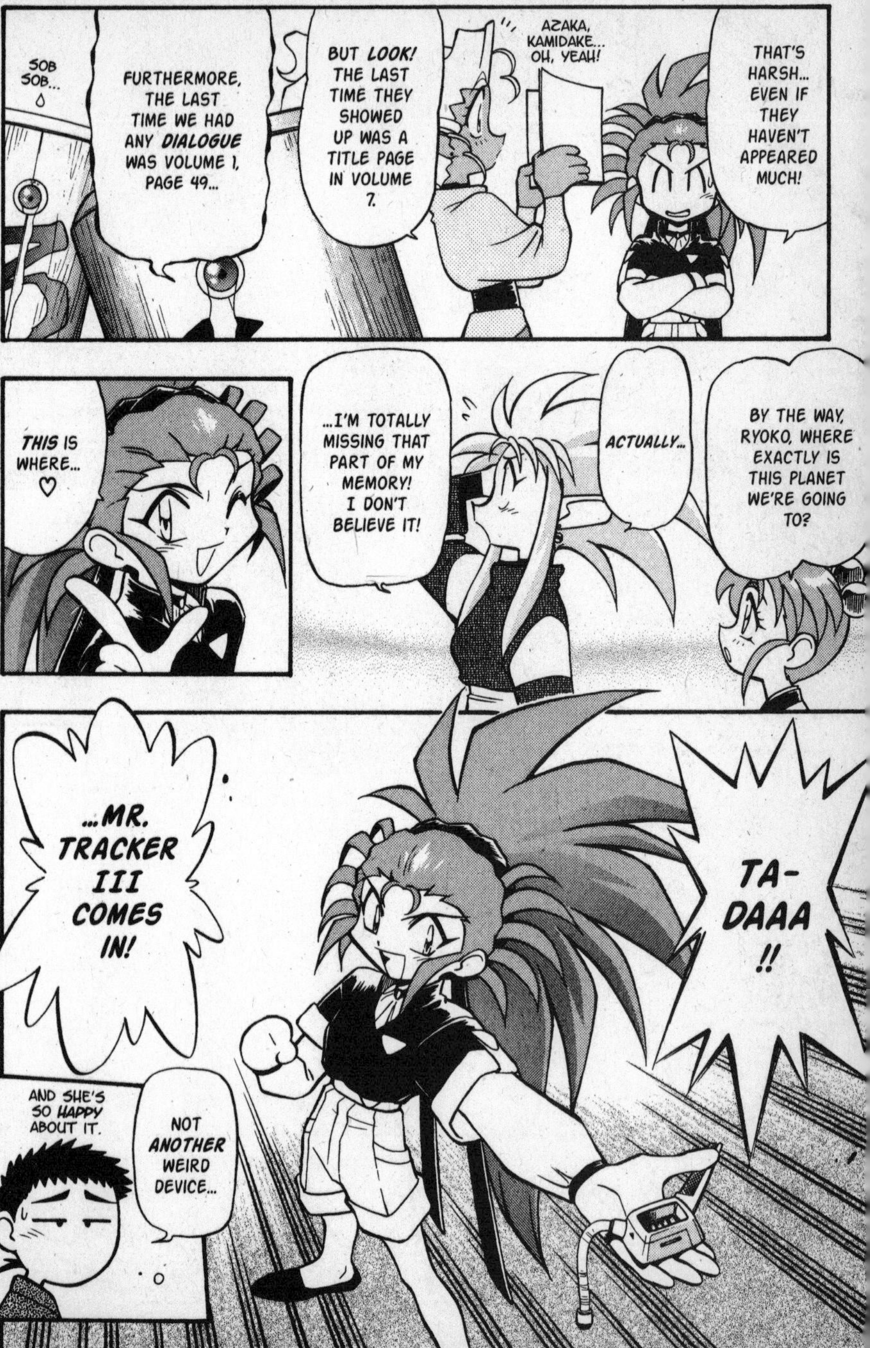
THAT'S HARSH... EVEN IF THEY HAVEN'T APPEARED MUCH!
AZAKA, KAMIDAKE... OH, YEAH!
BUT *LOOK!* THE LAST TIME THEY SHOWED UP WAS A TITLE PAGE IN VOLUME 7.
FURTHERMORE, THE LAST TIME WE HAD ANY *DIALOGUE* WAS VOLUME 1, PAGE 49...
SOB SOB...
BY THE WAY, RYOKO, WHERE EXACTLY IS THIS PLANET WE'RE GOING TO?
ACTUALLY...
...I'M TOTALLY MISSING THAT PART OF MY MEMORY! I DON'T BELIEVE IT!
THIS IS WHERE... ♡
TA-DAAA!!
...MR. TRACKER III COMES IN!
NOT *ANOTHER* WEIRD DEVICE...
AND SHE'S SO *HAPPY* ABOUT IT.

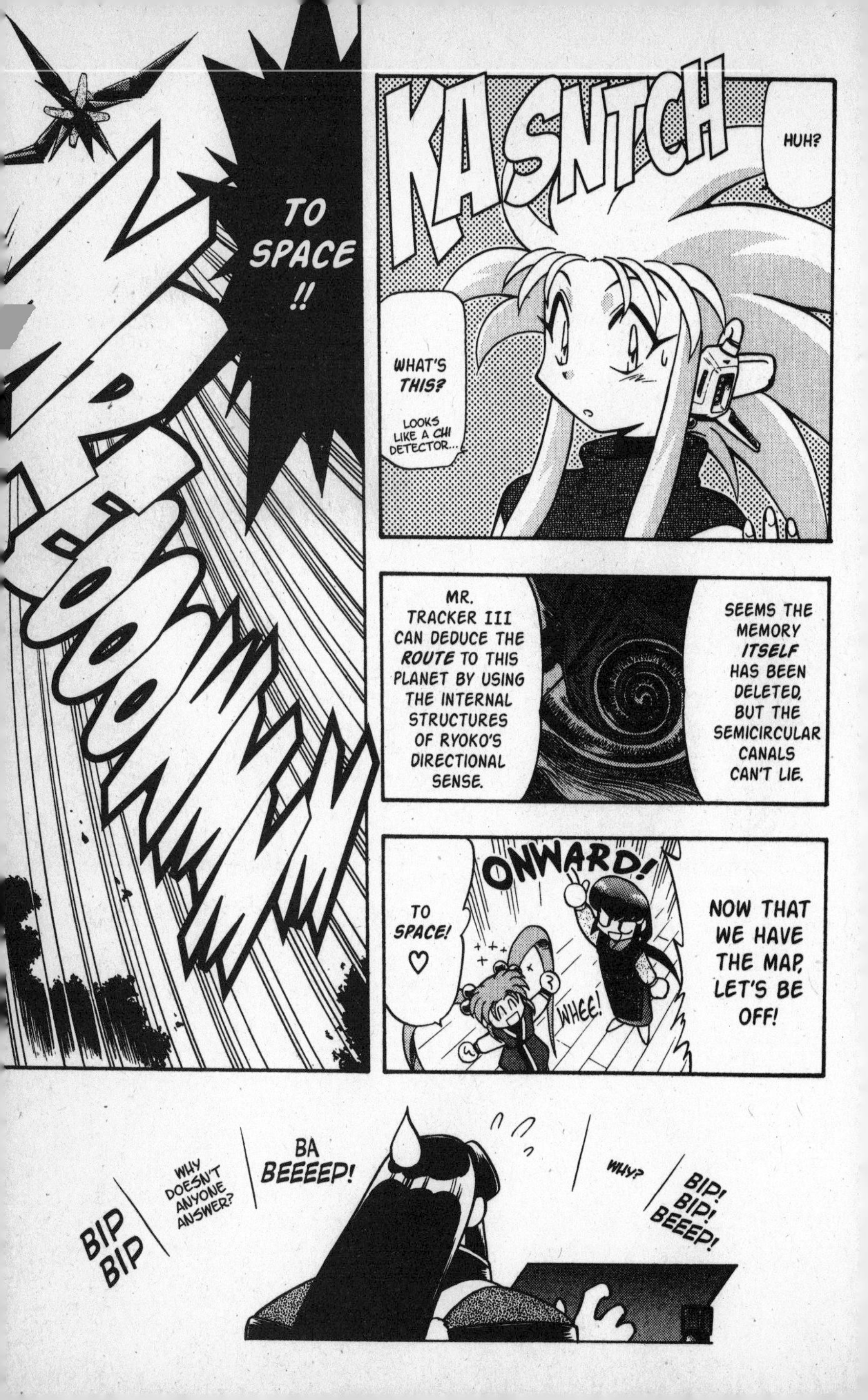
HUH?
KASNTCH
WHAT'S THIS?
LOOKS LIKE A CHI DETECTOR...
SEEMS THE MEMORY ITSELF HAS BEEN DELETED, BUT THE SEMICIRCULAR CANALS CAN'T LIE.
MR. TRACKER III CAN DEDUCE THE ROUTE TO THIS PLANET BY USING THE INTERNAL STRUCTURES OF RYOKO'S DIRECTIONAL SENSE.
NOW THAT WE HAVE THE MAP, LET'S BE OFF!
ONWARD!
WHEE!
TO SPACE! ♡
TO SPACE !!
BIP! BIP! BEEEP!
WHY?
BA BEEEEP!
WHY DOESN'T ANYONE ANSWER?
BIP BIP

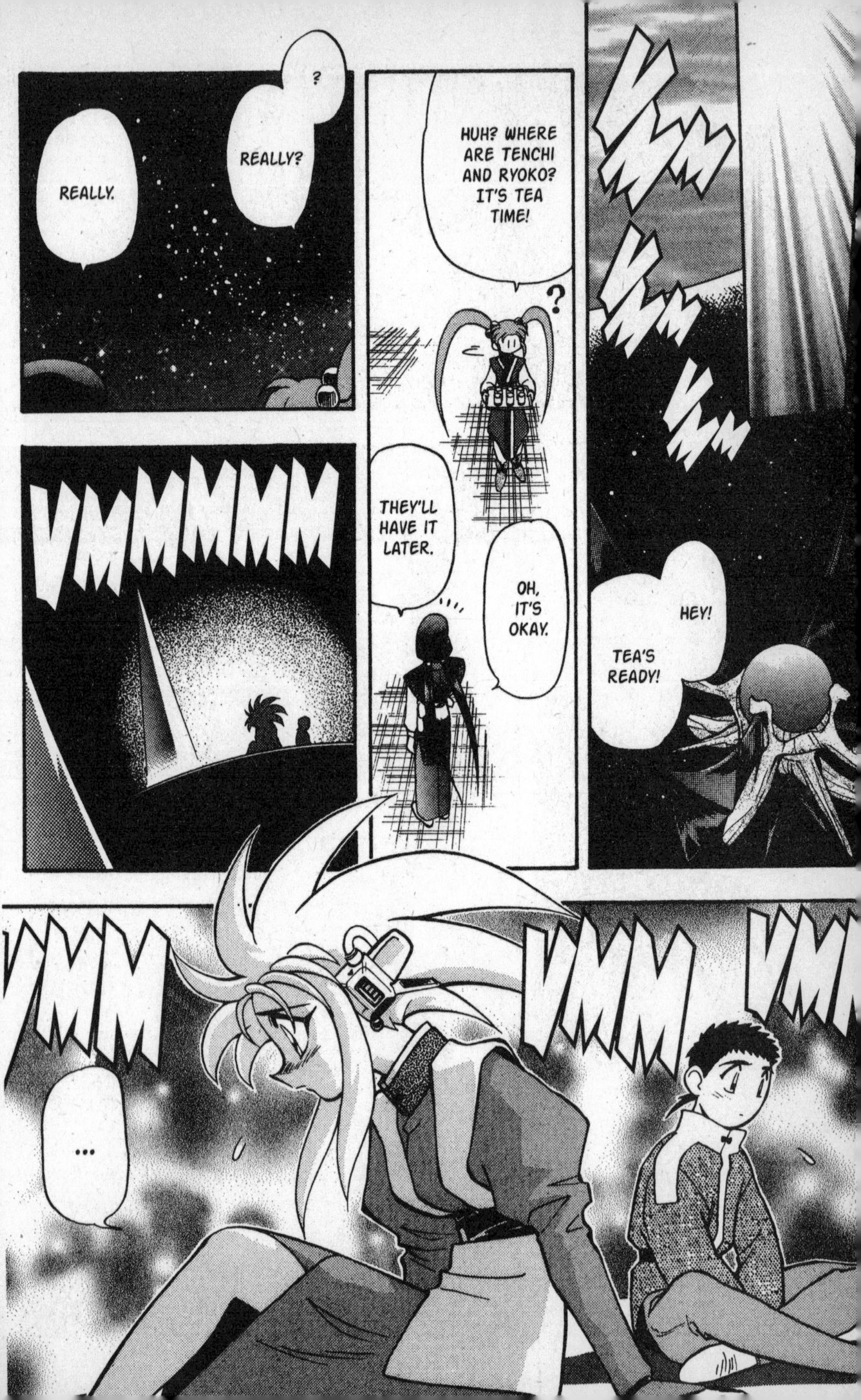
VMM
VMM
VMM
HEY!
TEA'S READY!
HUH? WHERE ARE TENCHI AND RYOKO? IT'S TEA TIME!
?
OH, IT'S OKAY.
THEY'LL HAVE IT LATER.
?
REALLY?
REALLY.
VMMMMM
VMM
VMM
VMM
...

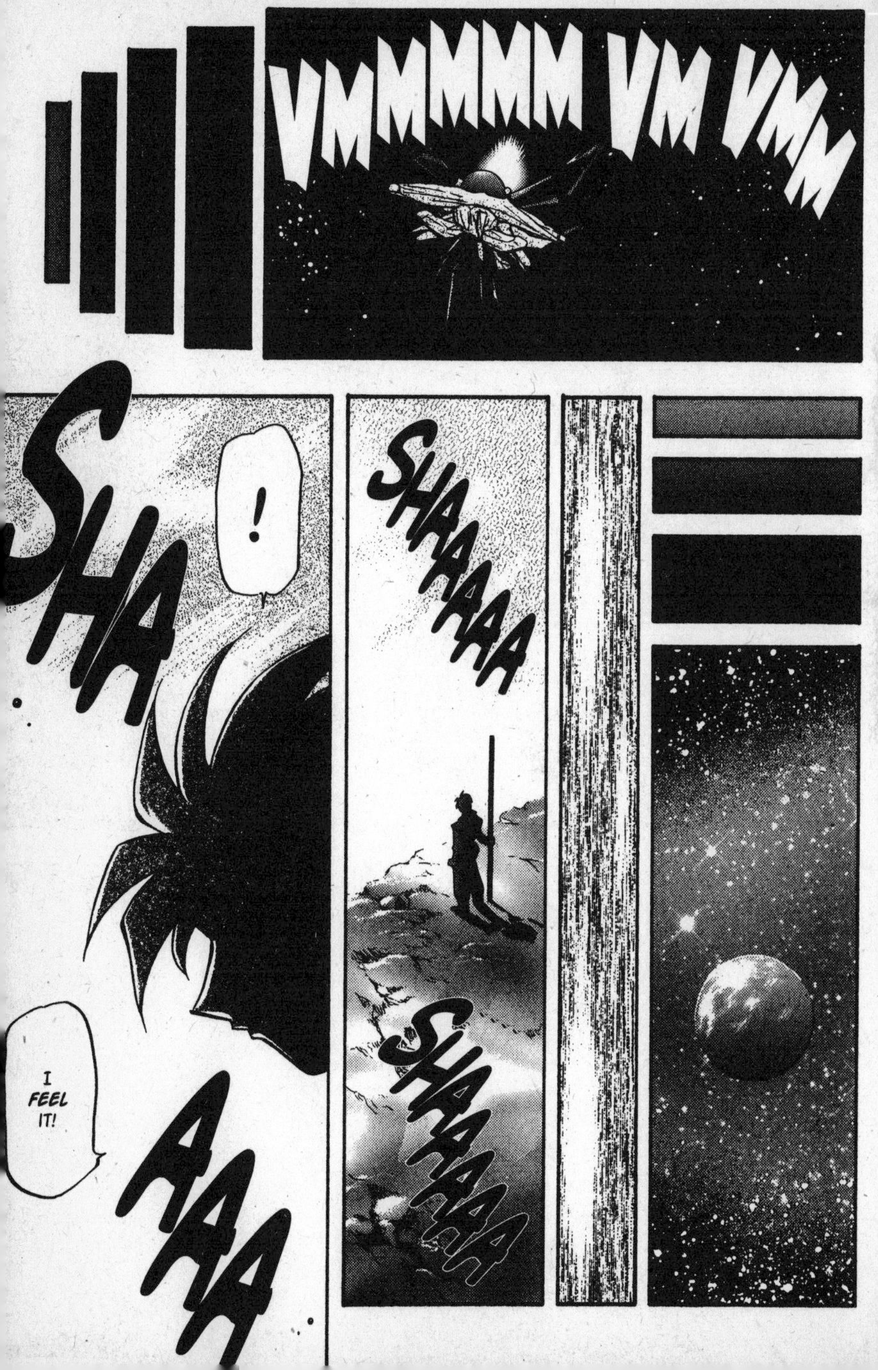
VMMMMM VM VMM
SHAAAAA
SHAAAAA
!
SHA
I FEEL IT!
AAAA

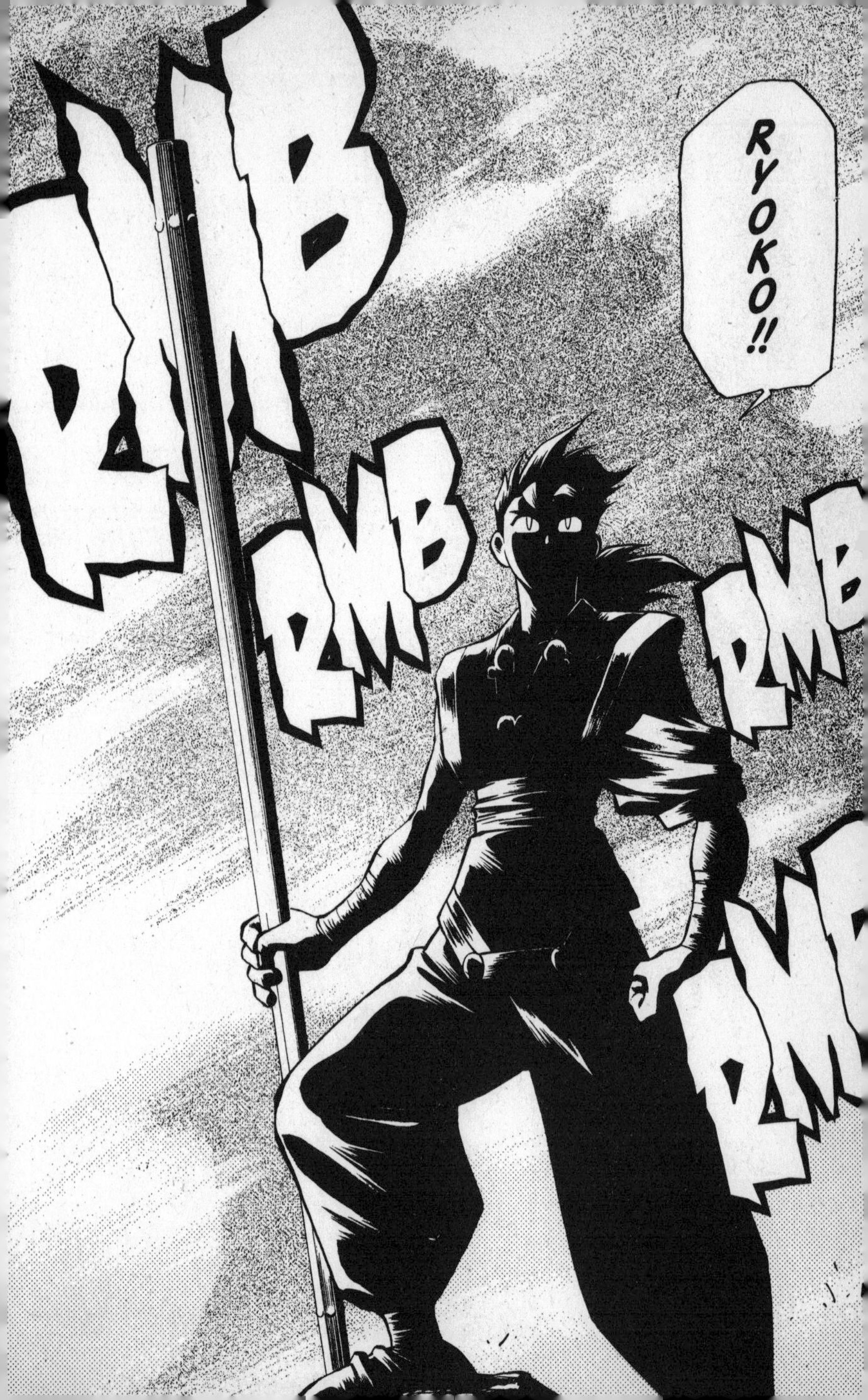
RYOKO!!
RMB
RMB
RMB
RMB

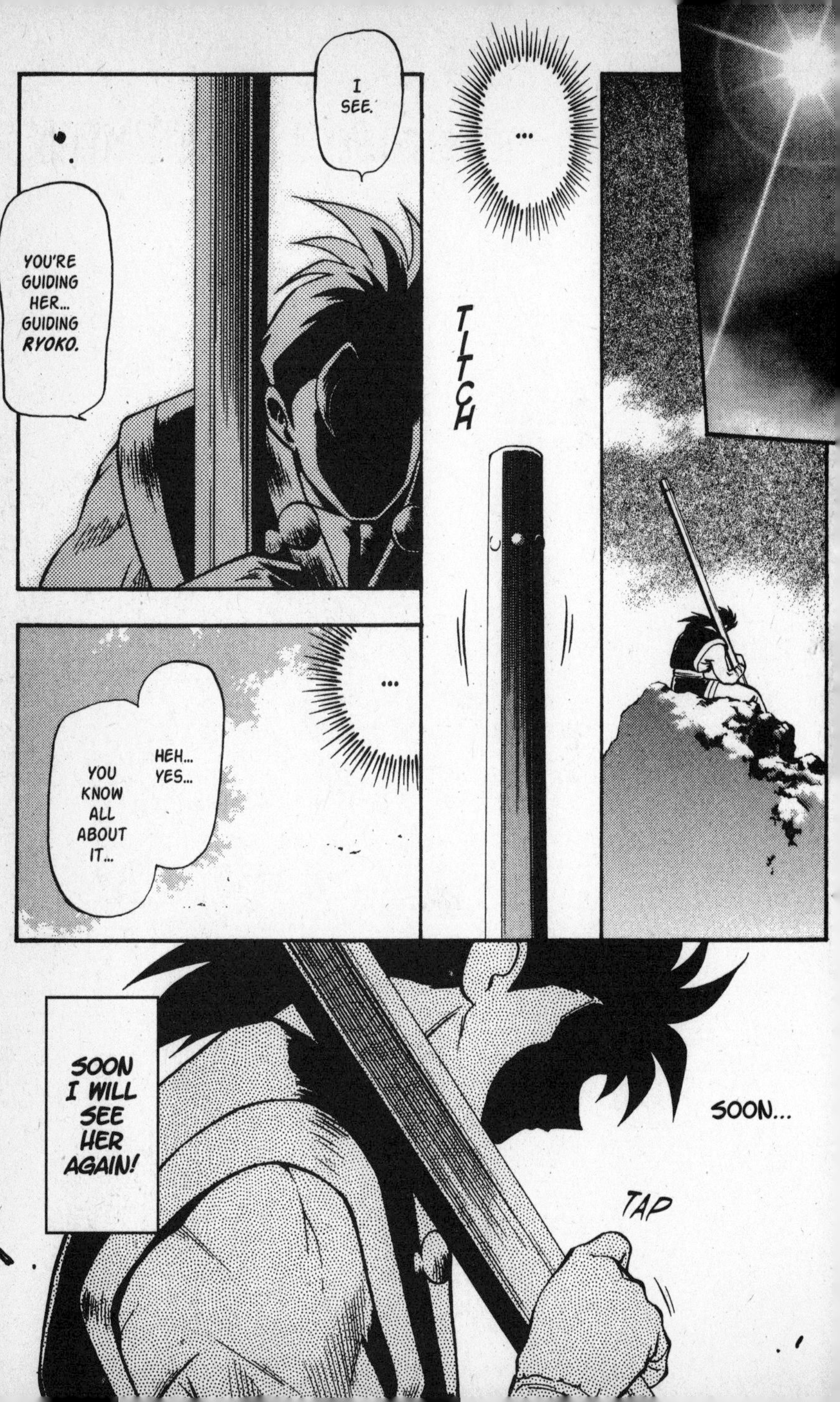
...
TITCH
I SEE.
YOU'RE GUIDING HER... GUIDING RYOKO.
...
HEH... YES...
YOU KNOW ALL ABOUT IT...
SOON...
TAP
SOON I WILL SEE HER AGAIN!

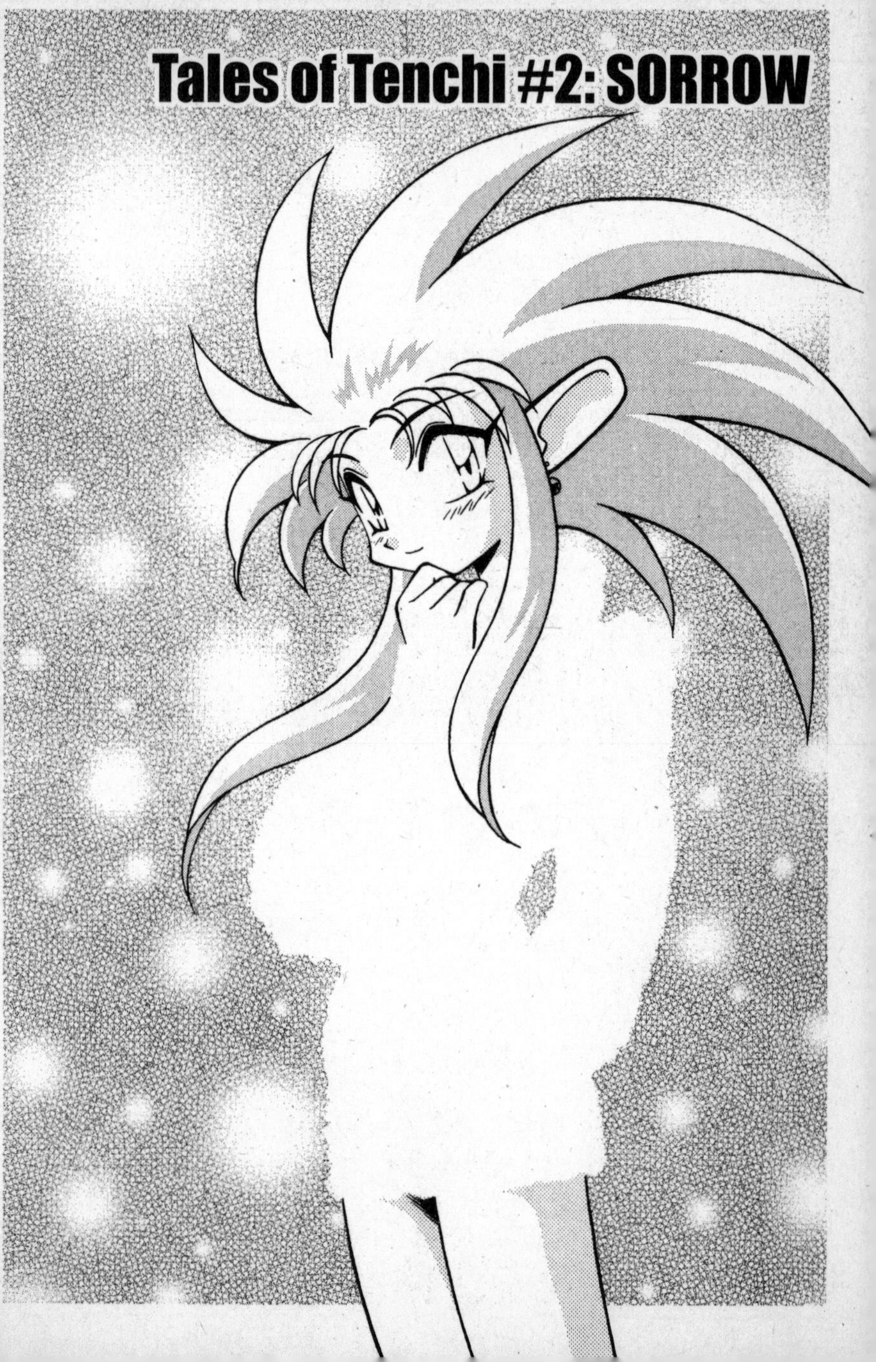
Tales of Tenchi #2: SORROW

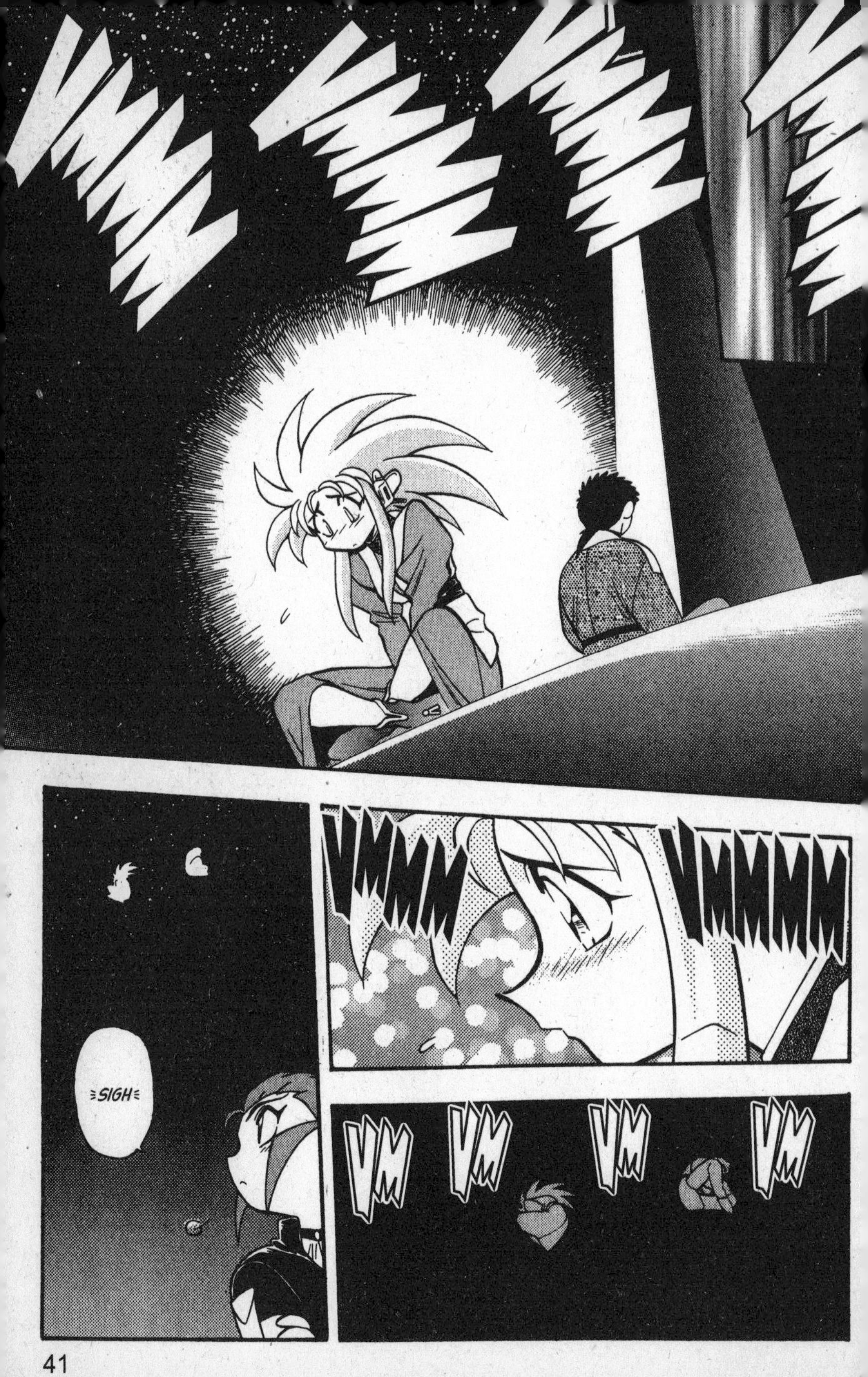
VMMMMM
VMMM
VM
VM
VM
VM
SIGH

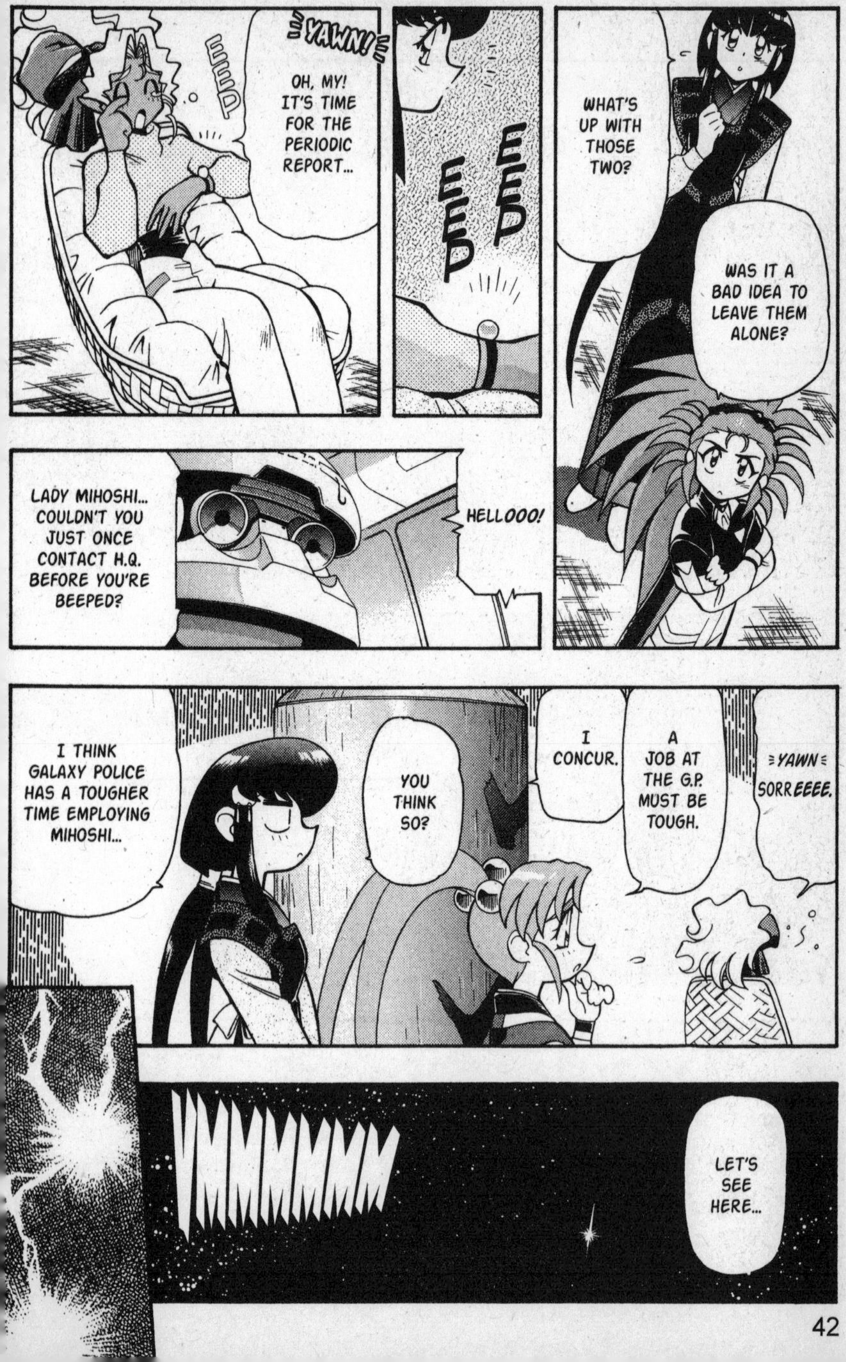
WHAT'S UP WITH THOSE TWO?
WAS IT A BAD IDEA TO LEAVE THEM ALONE?
EEEP
EEEP
YAWN!
OH, MY! IT'S TIME FOR THE PERIODIC REPORT...
EEEP
HELLOOO!
LADY MIHOSHI... COULDN'T YOU JUST ONCE CONTACT H.Q. BEFORE YOU'RE BEEPED?
YAWN
SORREEEE.
A JOB AT THE G.P. MUST BE TOUGH.
I CONCUR.
YOU THINK SO?
I THINK GALAXY POLICE HAS A TOUGHER TIME EMPLOYING MIHOSHI...
LET'S SEE HERE...
VMMMMMM

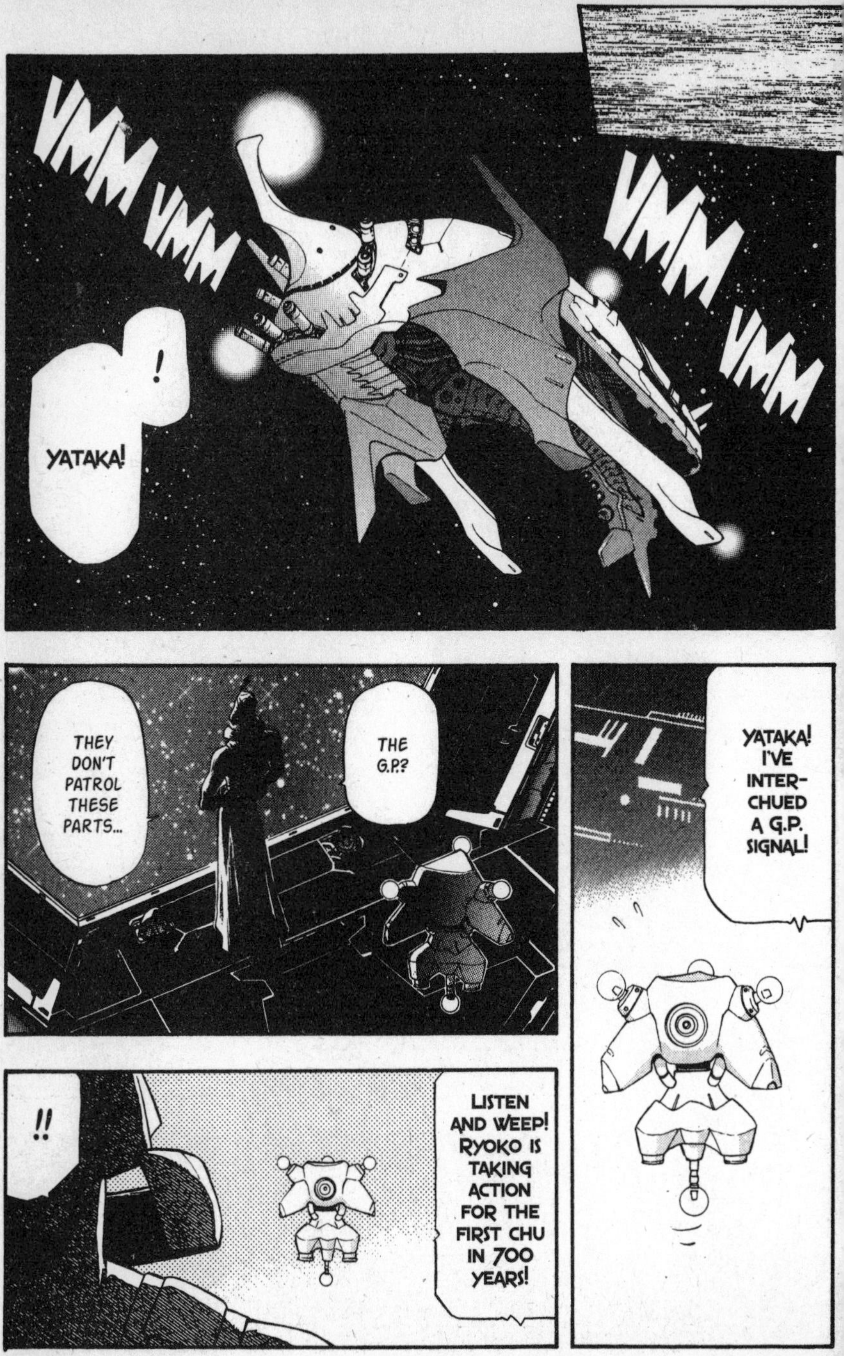
VMM VMM
VMM VMM
!
YATAKA!
YATAKA! I'VE INTER-CHUED A G.P. SIGNAL!
THE G.P.?
THEY DON'T PATROL THESE PARTS...
LISTEN AND WEEP! RYOKO IS TAKING ACTION FOR THE FIRST CHU IN 700 YEARS!
!!

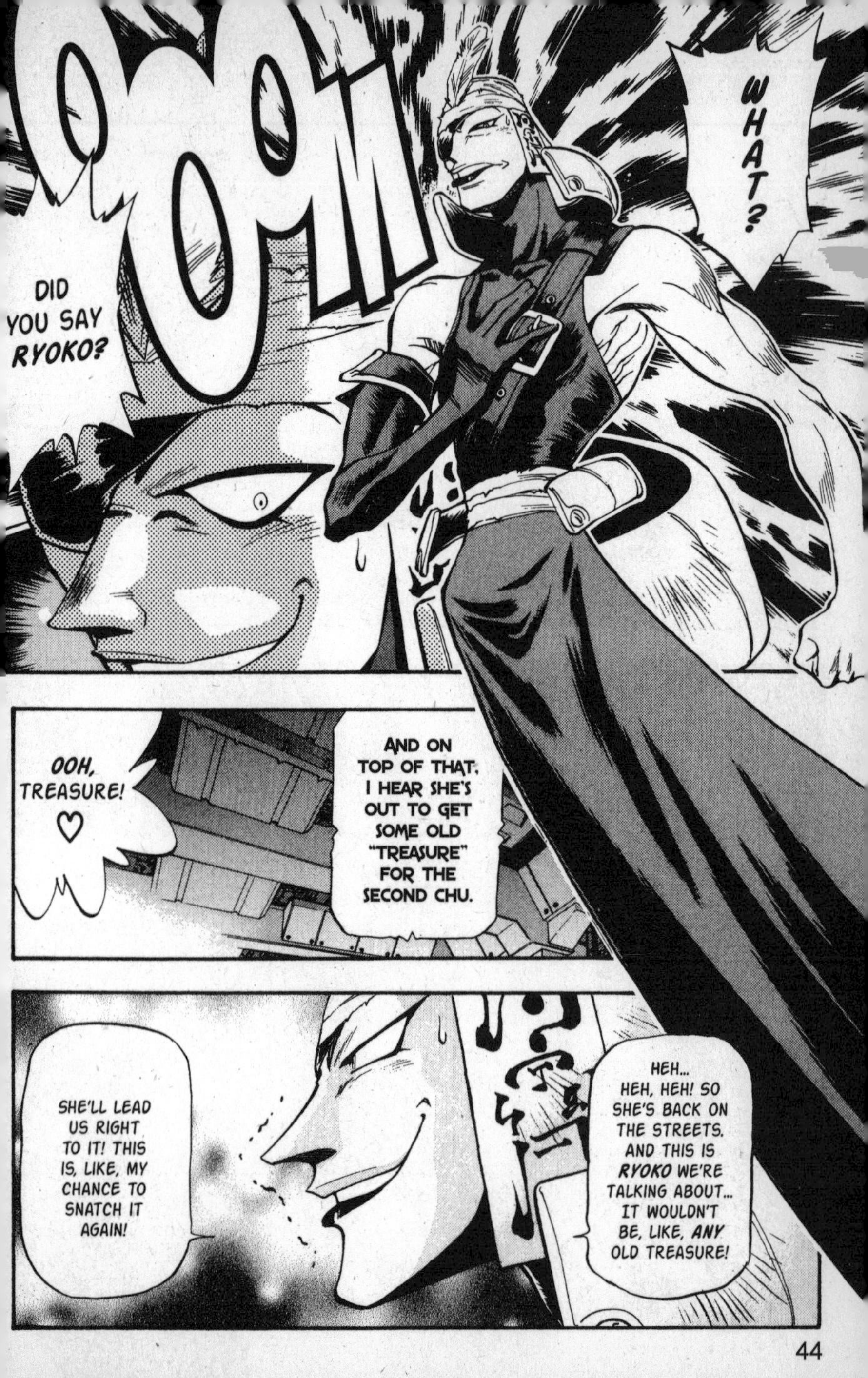
WHAT?
OOM!
DID YOU SAY *RYOKO?*
AND ON TOP OF THAT, I HEAR SHE'S OUT TO GET SOME OLD "TREASURE" FOR THE SECOND CHU.
OOH, TREASURE! ♡
HEH... HEH, HEH! SO SHE'S BACK ON THE STREETS. AND THIS IS *RYOKO* WE'RE TALKING ABOUT... IT WOULDN'T BE, LIKE, *ANY* OLD TREASURE!
SHE'LL LEAD US RIGHT TO IT! THIS IS, LIKE, MY CHANCE TO SNATCH IT AGAIN!

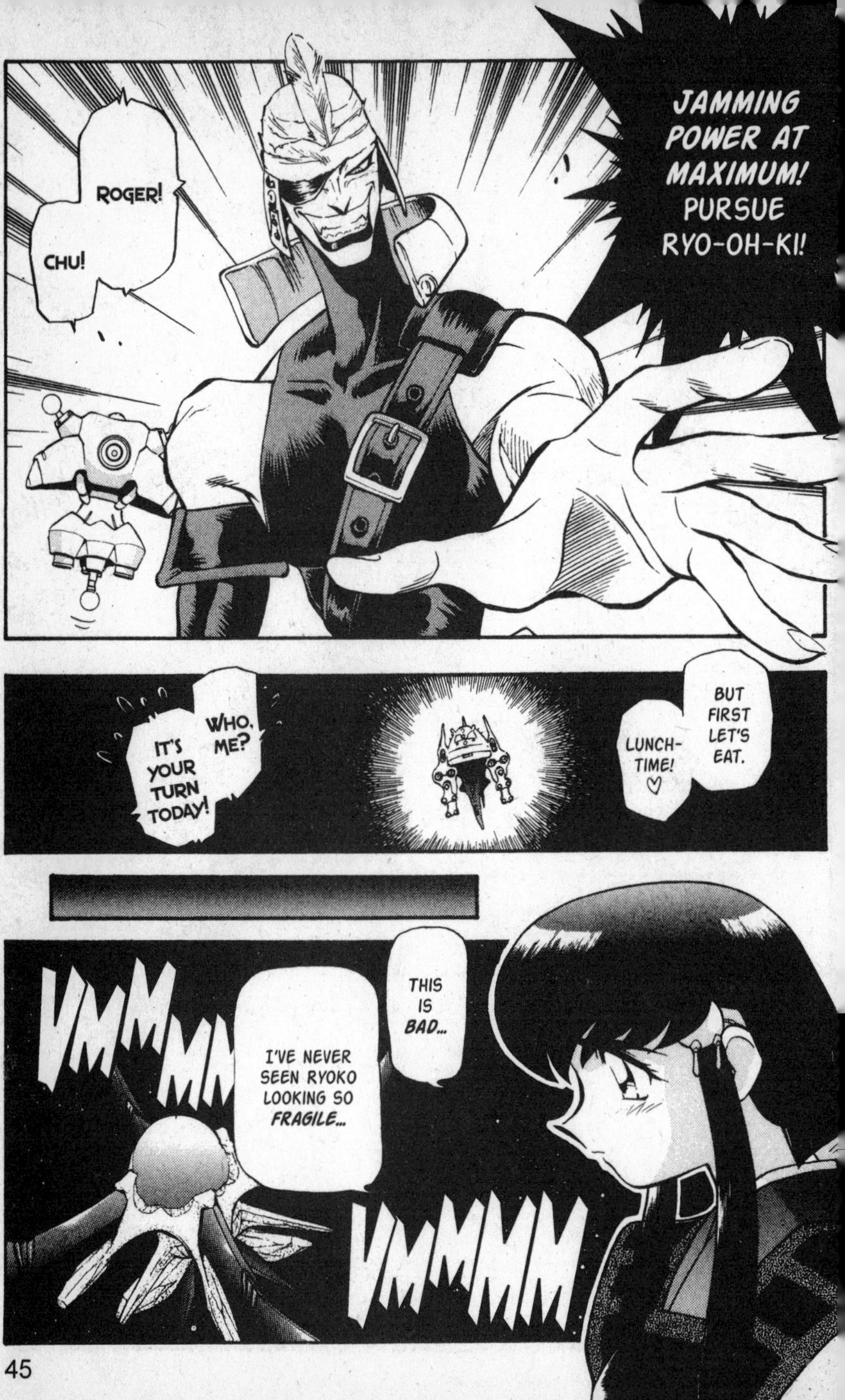
JAMMING POWER AT MAXIMUM! PURSUE RYO-OH-KI!
ROGER!
CHU!
BUT FIRST LET'S EAT.
LUNCH-TIME! ♡
IT'S YOUR TURN TODAY!
WHO, ME?
THIS IS BAD...
I'VE NEVER SEEN RYOKO LOOKING SO FRAGILE...
VMMMM
VMMMM

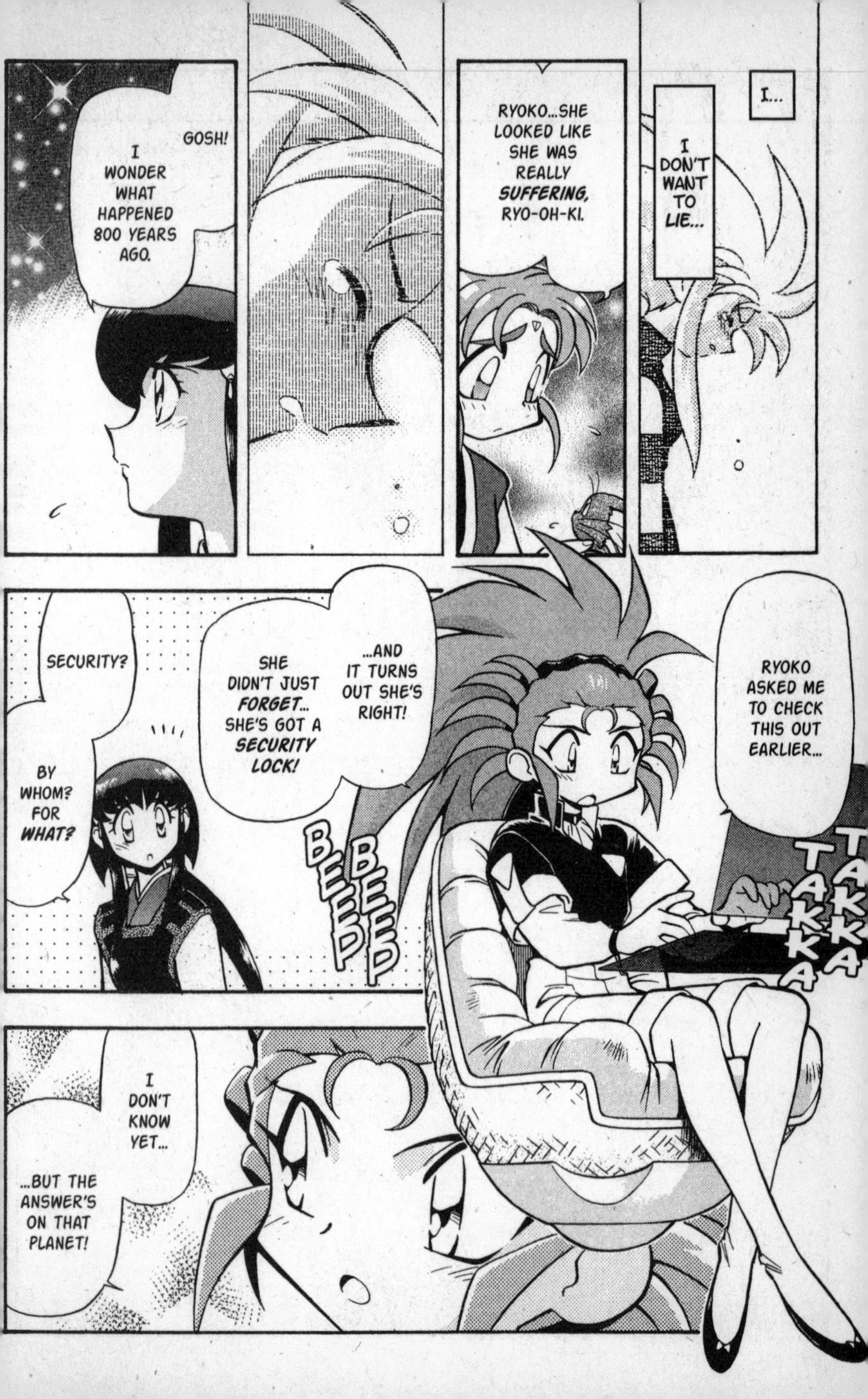
I...
I DON'T WANT TO LIE...
RYOKO...SHE LOOKED LIKE SHE WAS REALLY SUFFERING, RYO-OH-KI.
GOSH!
I WONDER WHAT HAPPENED 800 YEARS AGO.
RYOKO ASKED ME TO CHECK THIS OUT EARLIER...
TAKKA TAKKA
TAKKA
...AND IT TURNS OUT SHE'S RIGHT!
SHE DIDN'T JUST FORGET... SHE'S GOT A SECURITY LOCK!
BEEP BEEP
SECURITY?
BY WHOM? FOR WHAT?
I DON'T KNOW YET...
...BUT THE ANSWER'S ON THAT PLANET!

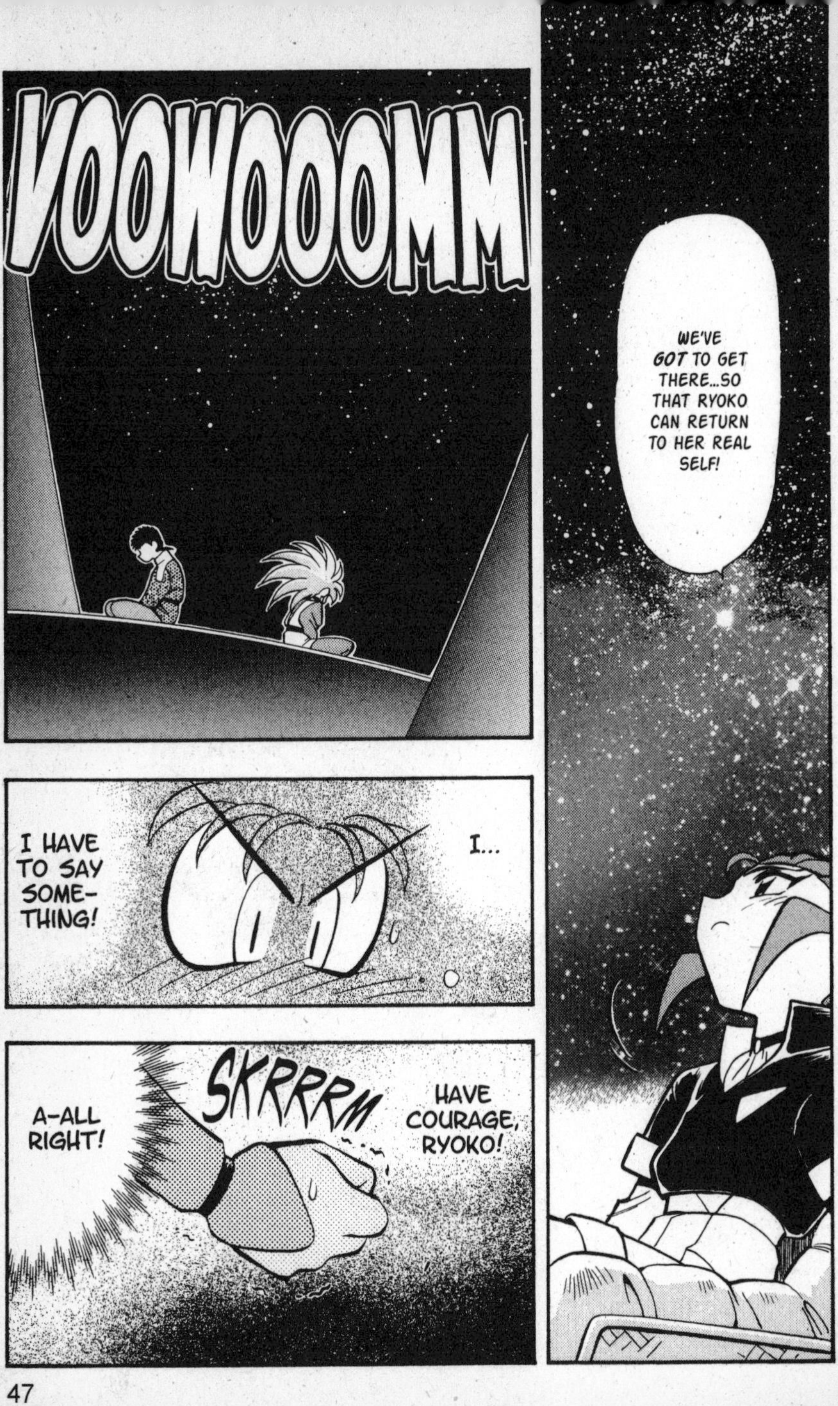
WE'VE GOT TO GET THERE...SO THAT RYOKO CAN RETURN TO HER REAL SELF!
VOOWOOOMM
I...
I HAVE TO SAY SOME-THING!
HAVE COURAGE, RYOKO!
SKRRRM
A-ALL RIGHT!

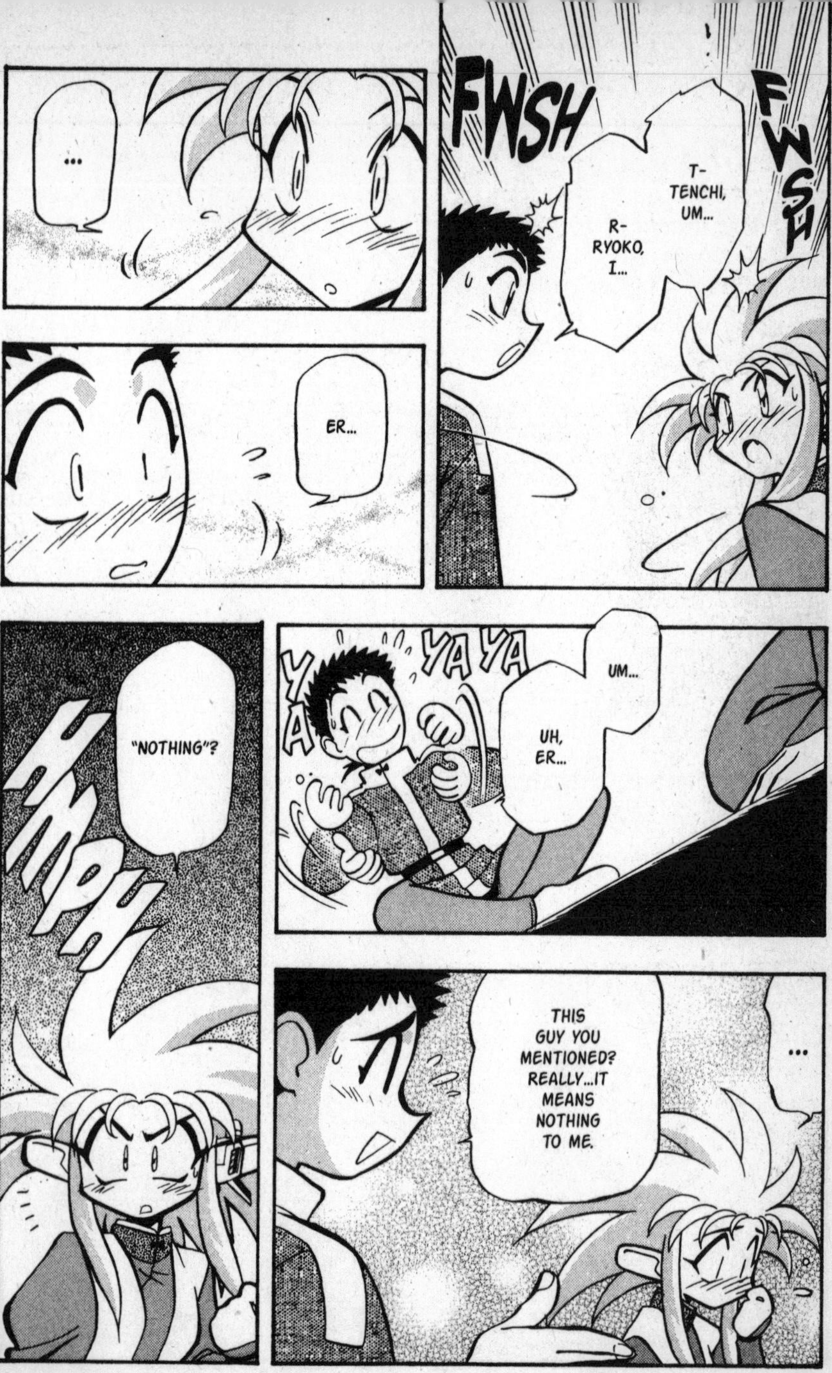
FWSH
T-
TENCHI,
UM...
FWSH
R-
RYOKO,
I...
...
ER...
UM...
YA YA
UH,
ER...
YA
YA
...
THIS GUY YOU MENTIONED? REALLY...IT MEANS NOTHING TO ME.
HMPH
"NOTHING"?

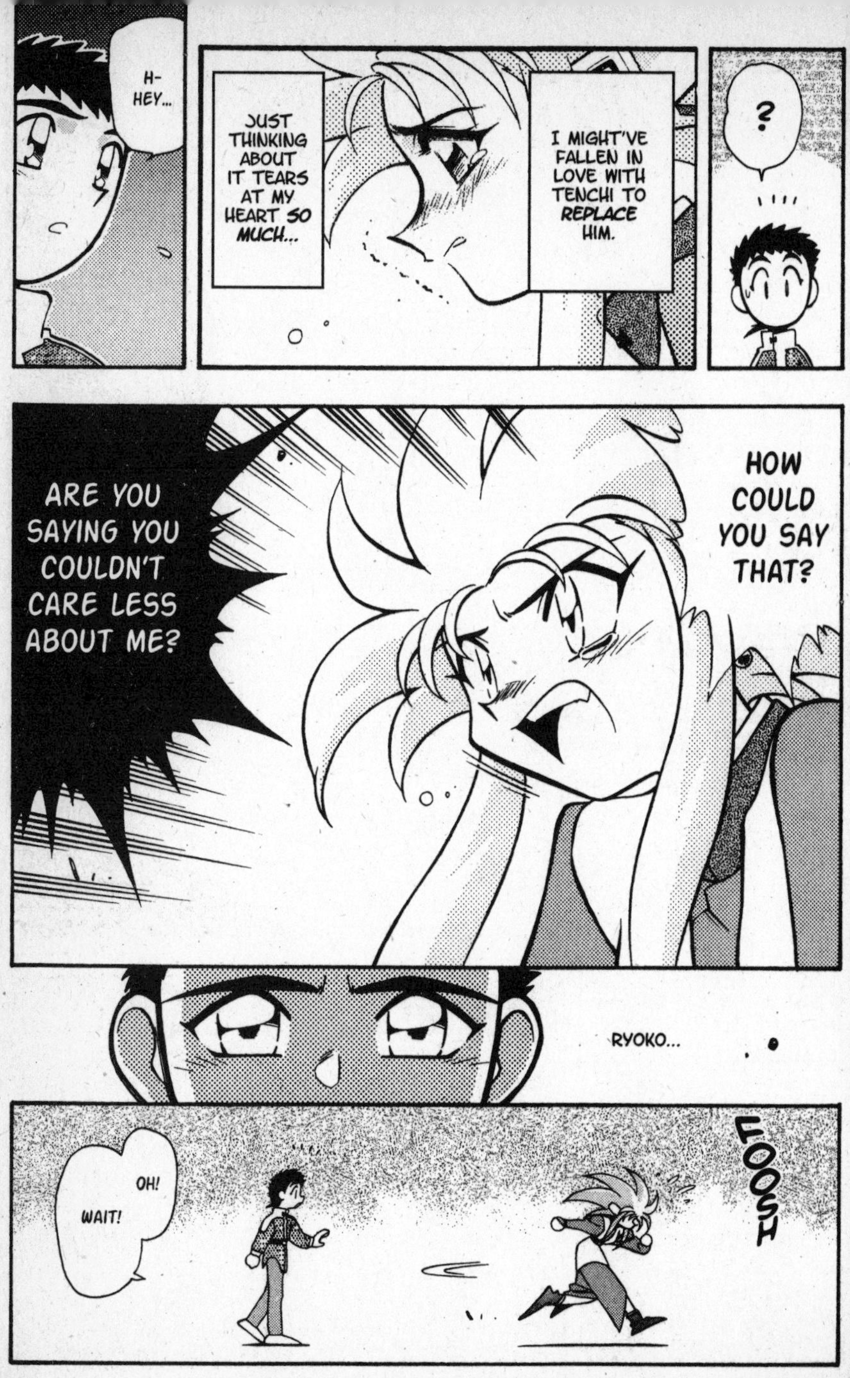
?
I MIGHT'VE FALLEN IN LOVE WITH TENCHI TO REPLACE HIM.
JUST THINKING ABOUT IT TEARS AT MY HEART SO MUCH...
H- HEY...
HOW COULD YOU SAY THAT?
ARE YOU SAYING YOU COULDN'T CARE LESS ABOUT ME?
RYOKO...
FOOSH
OH!
WAIT!

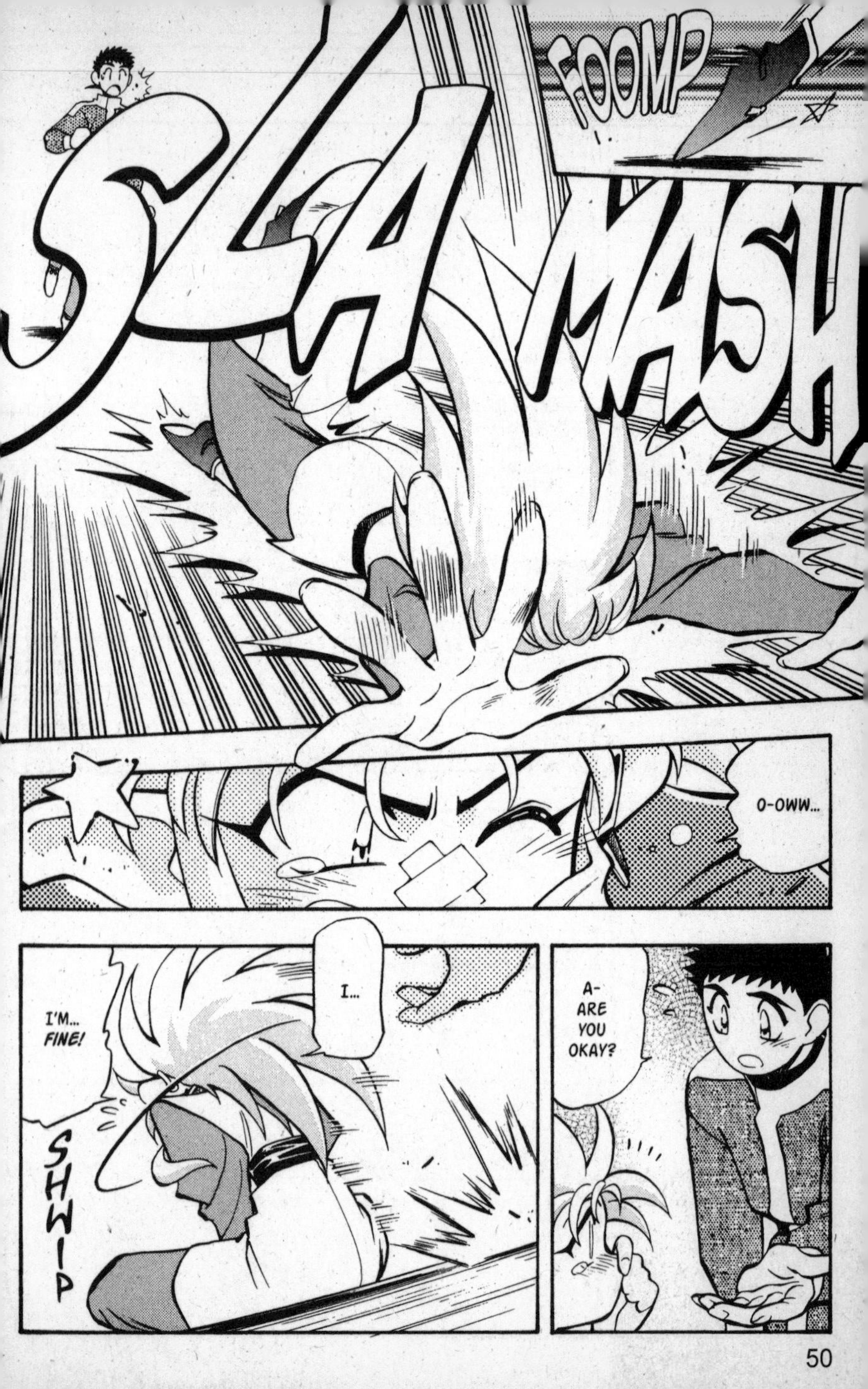
FOOMP
SLAMASH
O-OWW...
A-ARE YOU OKAY?
I...
I'M... *FINE!*
SHWIP

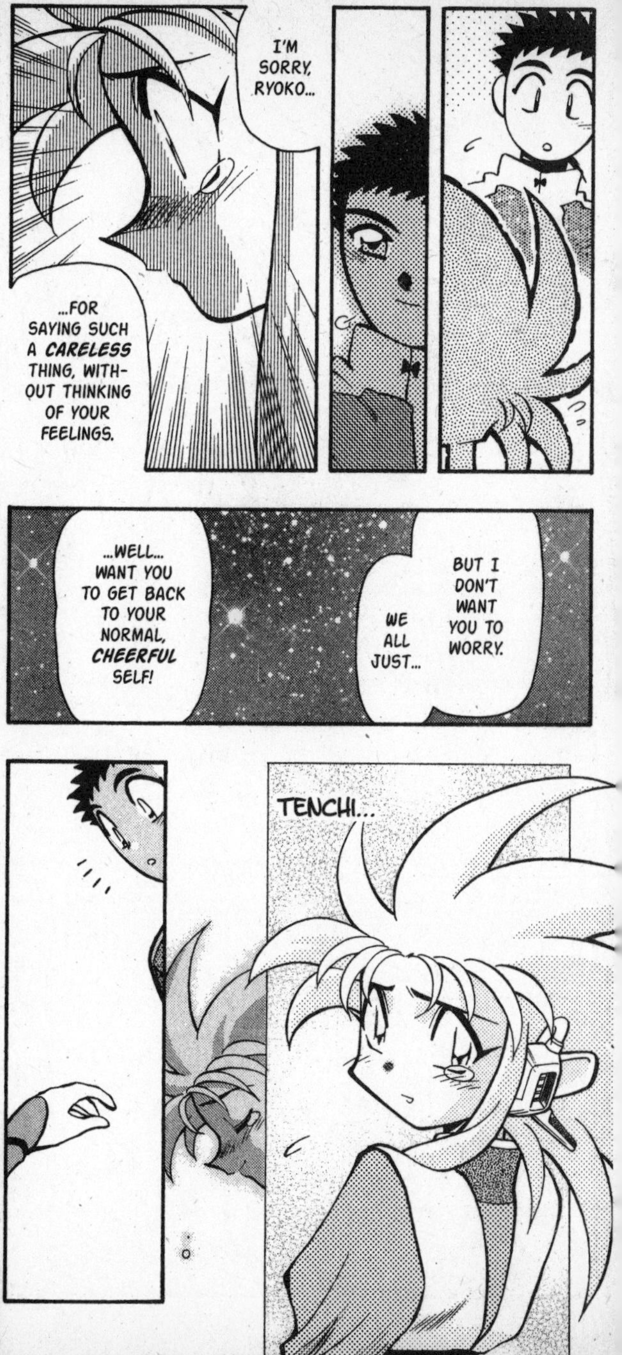
I'M SORRY, RYOKO...
...FOR SAYING SUCH A CARELESS THING, WITH-OUT THINKING OF YOUR FEELINGS.
BUT I DON'T WANT YOU TO WORRY.
WE ALL JUST...
...WELL... WANT YOU TO GET BACK TO YOUR NORMAL, CHEERFUL SELF!
TENCHI...
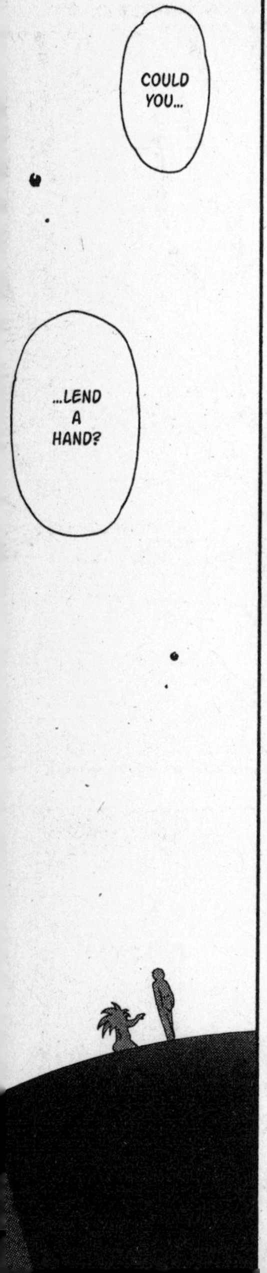
COULD YOU...
...LEND A HAND?

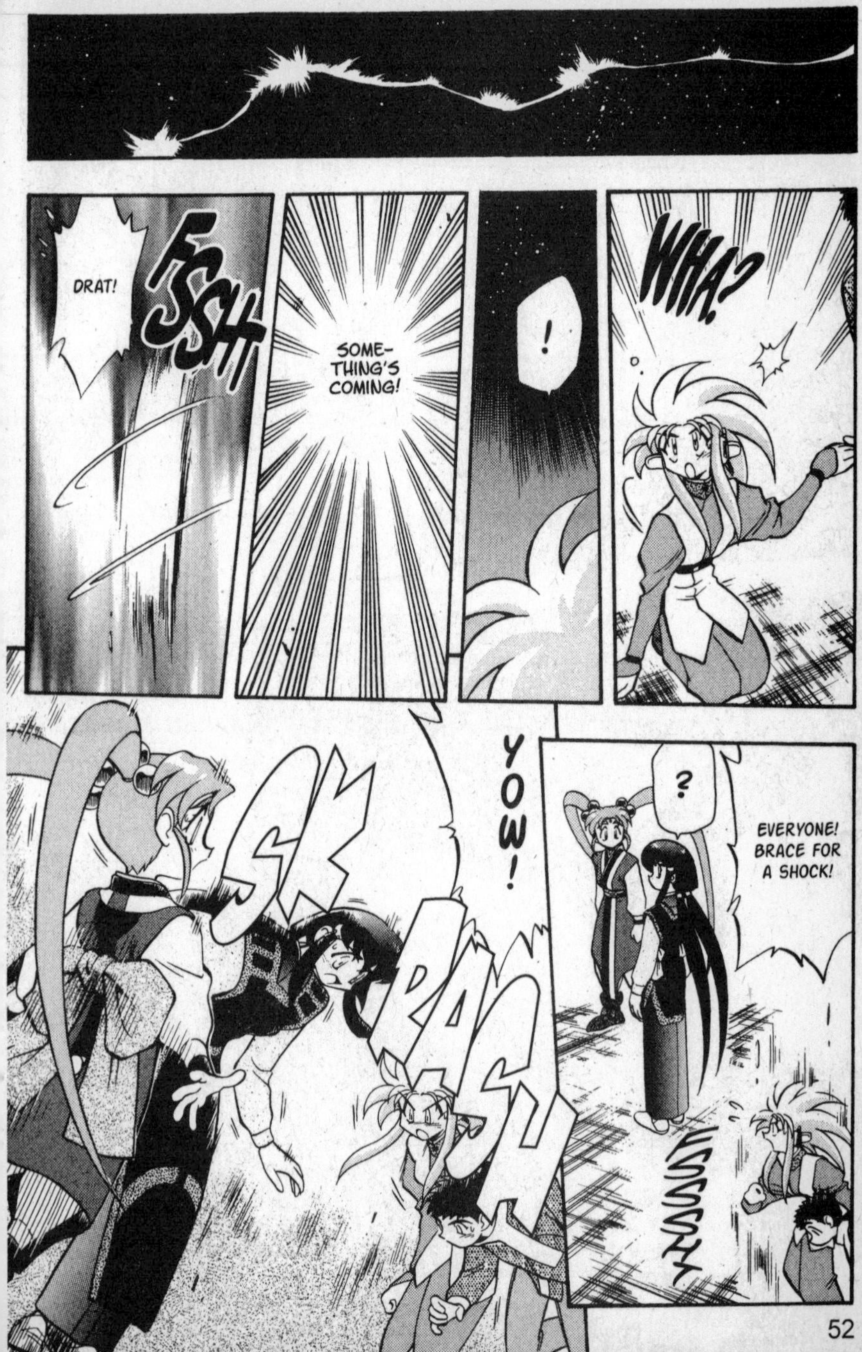
WHA?
!
SOME-THING'S COMING!
DRAT!
FSSHH
?
EVERYONE! BRACE FOR A SHOCK!
YOW!

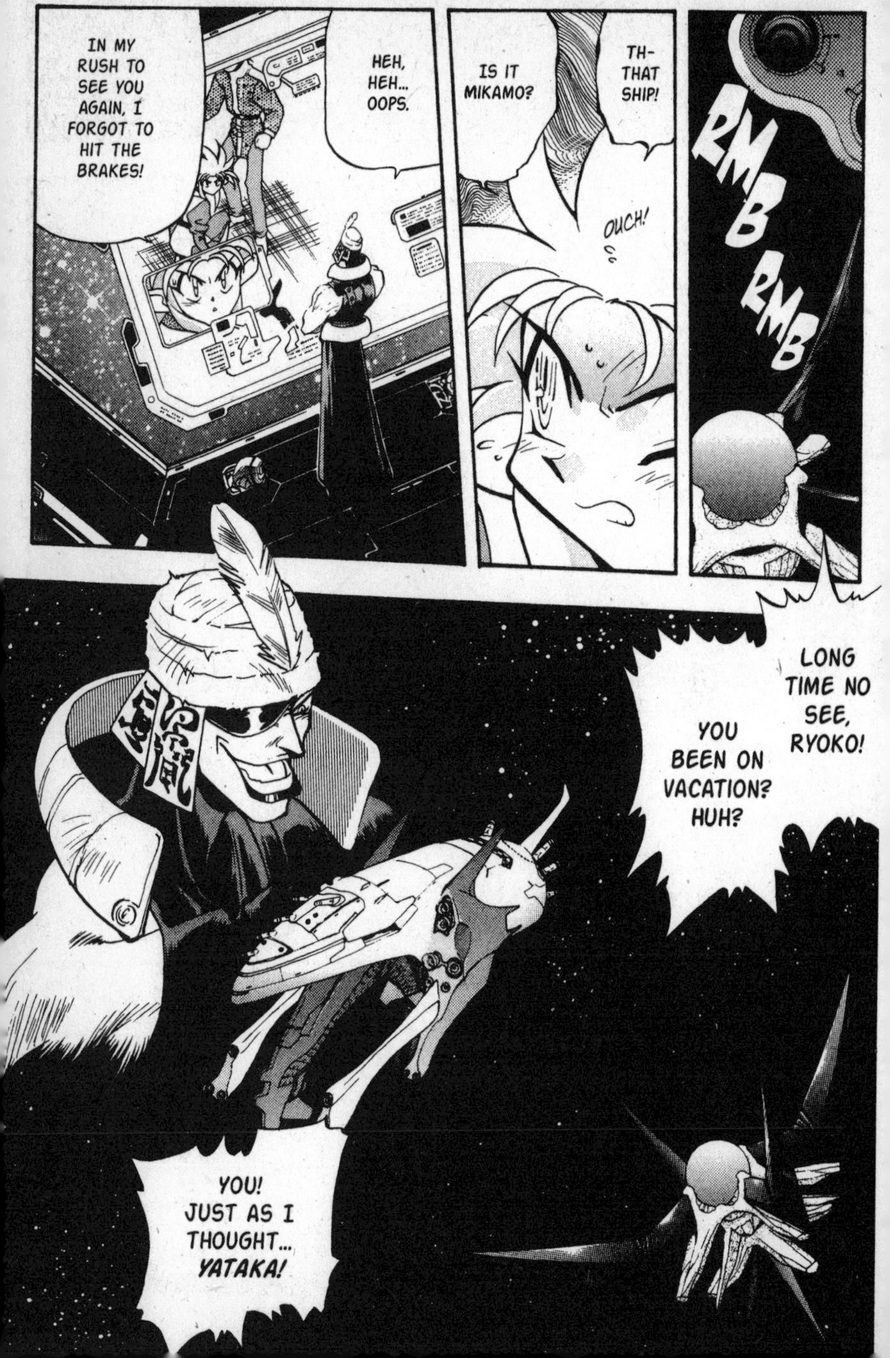
RMB
RMB
RMB
TH-THAT SHIP!
IS IT MIKAMO?
OUCH!
HEH, HEH... OOPS.
IN MY RUSH TO SEE YOU AGAIN, I FORGOT TO HIT THE BRAKES!
LONG TIME NO SEE, RYOKO!
YOU BEEN ON VACATION? HUH?
YOU! JUST AS I THOUGHT... *YATAKA!*

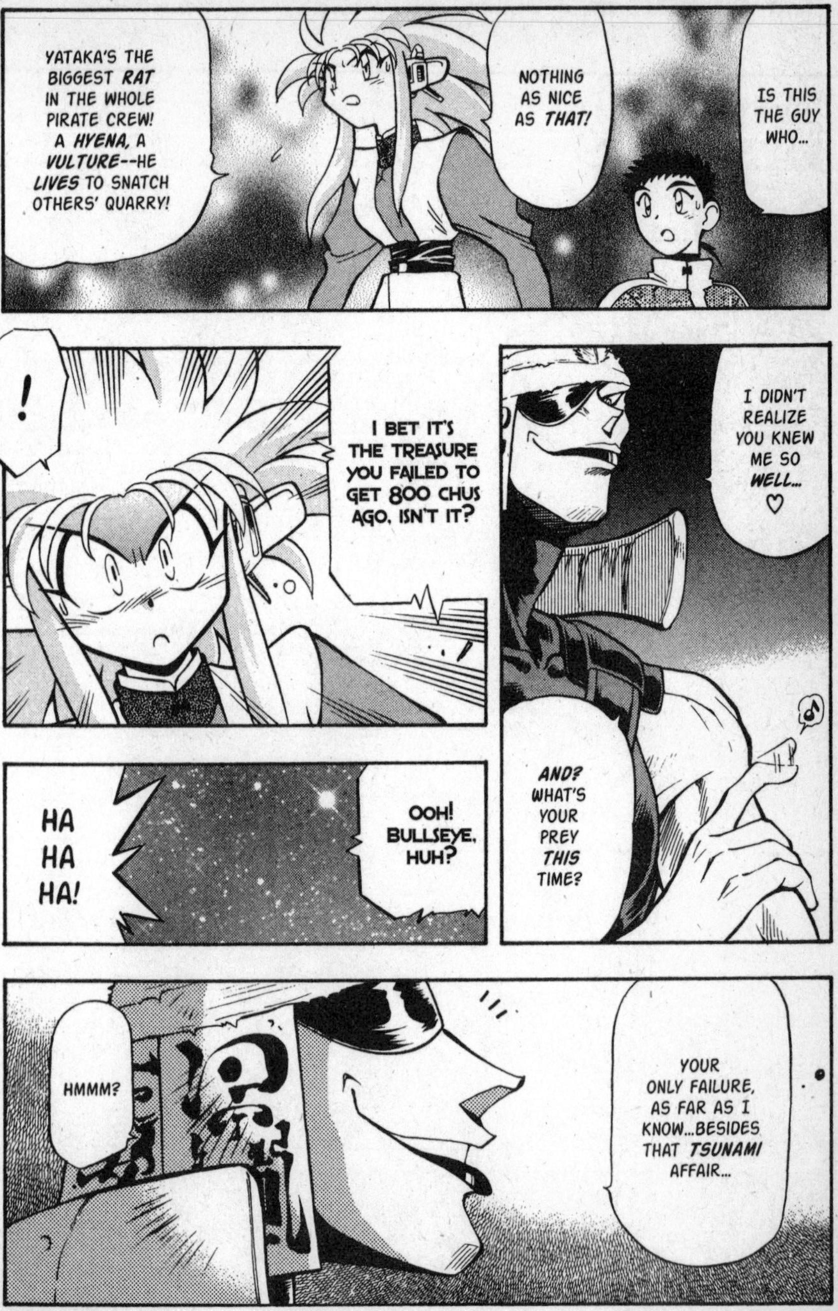
IS THIS THE GUY WHO...
NOTHING AS NICE AS *THAT!*
YATAKA'S THE BIGGEST *RAT* IN THE WHOLE PIRATE CREW! A *HYENA,* A *VULTURE*--HE *LIVES* TO SNATCH OTHERS' QUARRY!
I DIDN'T REALIZE YOU KNEW ME SO *WELL...* ♡
AND? WHAT'S YOUR PREY *THIS* TIME?
I BET IT'S THE TREASURE YOU FAILED TO GET 800 CHUS AGO, ISN'T IT?
!
OOH! BULLSEYE, HUH?
HA HA HA!
YOUR ONLY FAILURE, AS FAR AS I KNOW...BESIDES THAT *TSUNAMI* AFFAIR...
HMMM?

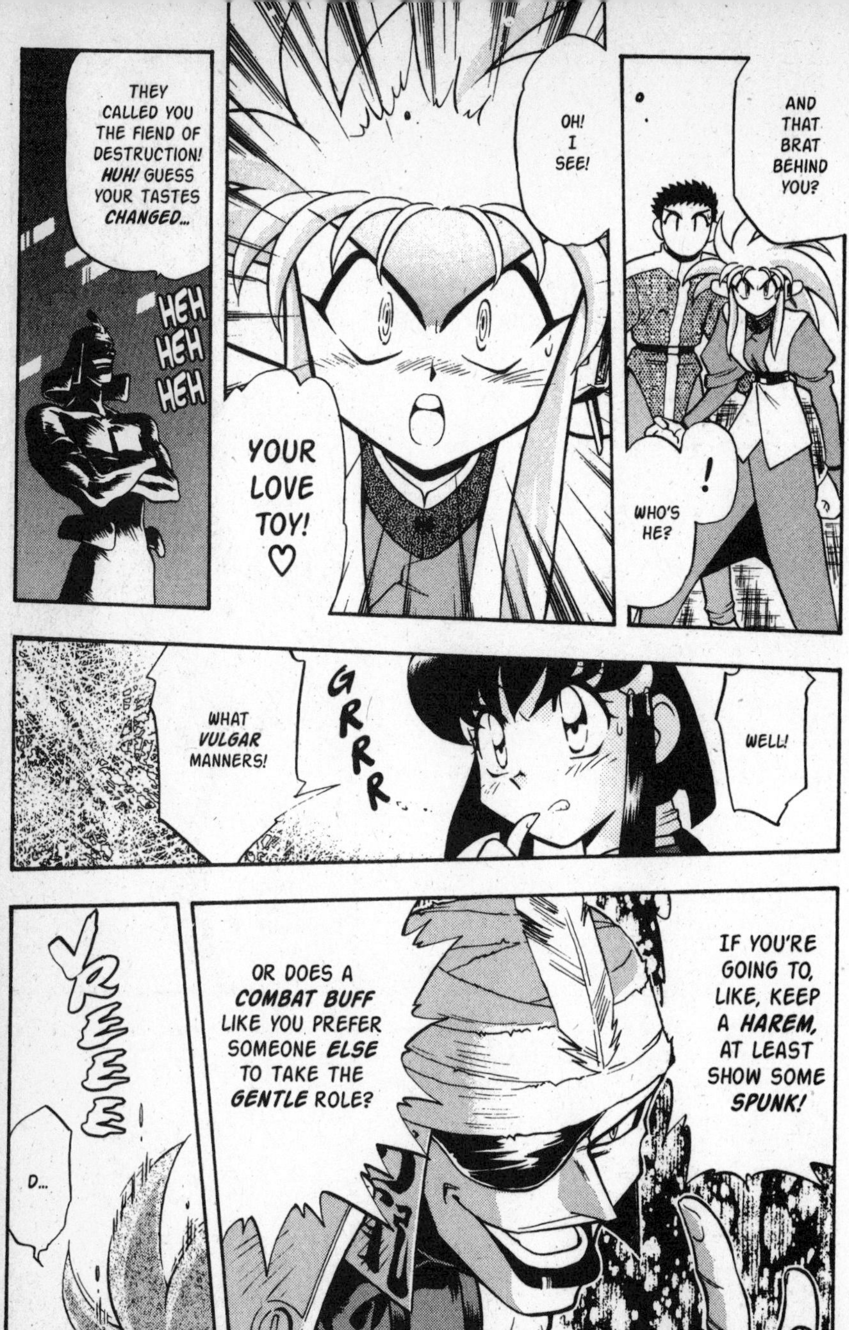
AND THAT BRAT BEHIND YOU?
!
WHO'S HE?
OH! I SEE!
YOUR LOVE TOY! ♡
THEY CALLED YOU THE FIEND OF DESTRUCTION! HUH! GUESS YOUR TASTES CHANGED...
HEH HEH HEH
WELL!
GRRRR...
WHAT VULGAR MANNERS!
IF YOU'RE GOING TO, LIKE, KEEP A HAREM, AT LEAST SHOW SOME SPUNK!
OR DOES A COMBAT BUFF LIKE YOU PREFER SOMEONE ELSE TO TAKE THE GENTLE ROLE?
VREEEE!
D...

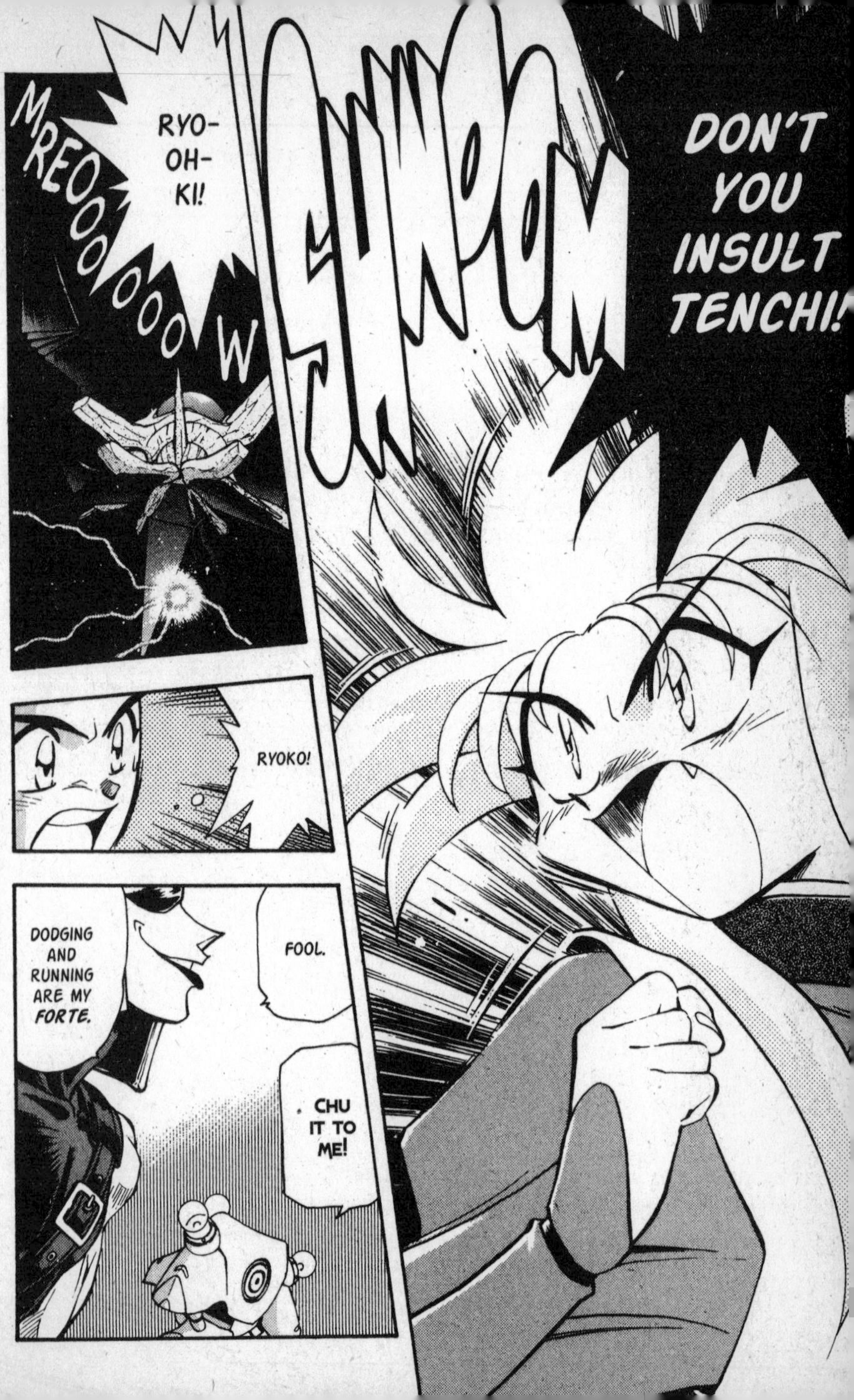
DON'T YOU INSULT TENCHI!
SHWOOM
MREOOOOOOOW
RYO-OH-KI!
RYOKO!
FOOL.
DODGING AND RUNNING ARE MY *FORTE*.
CHU IT TO ME!

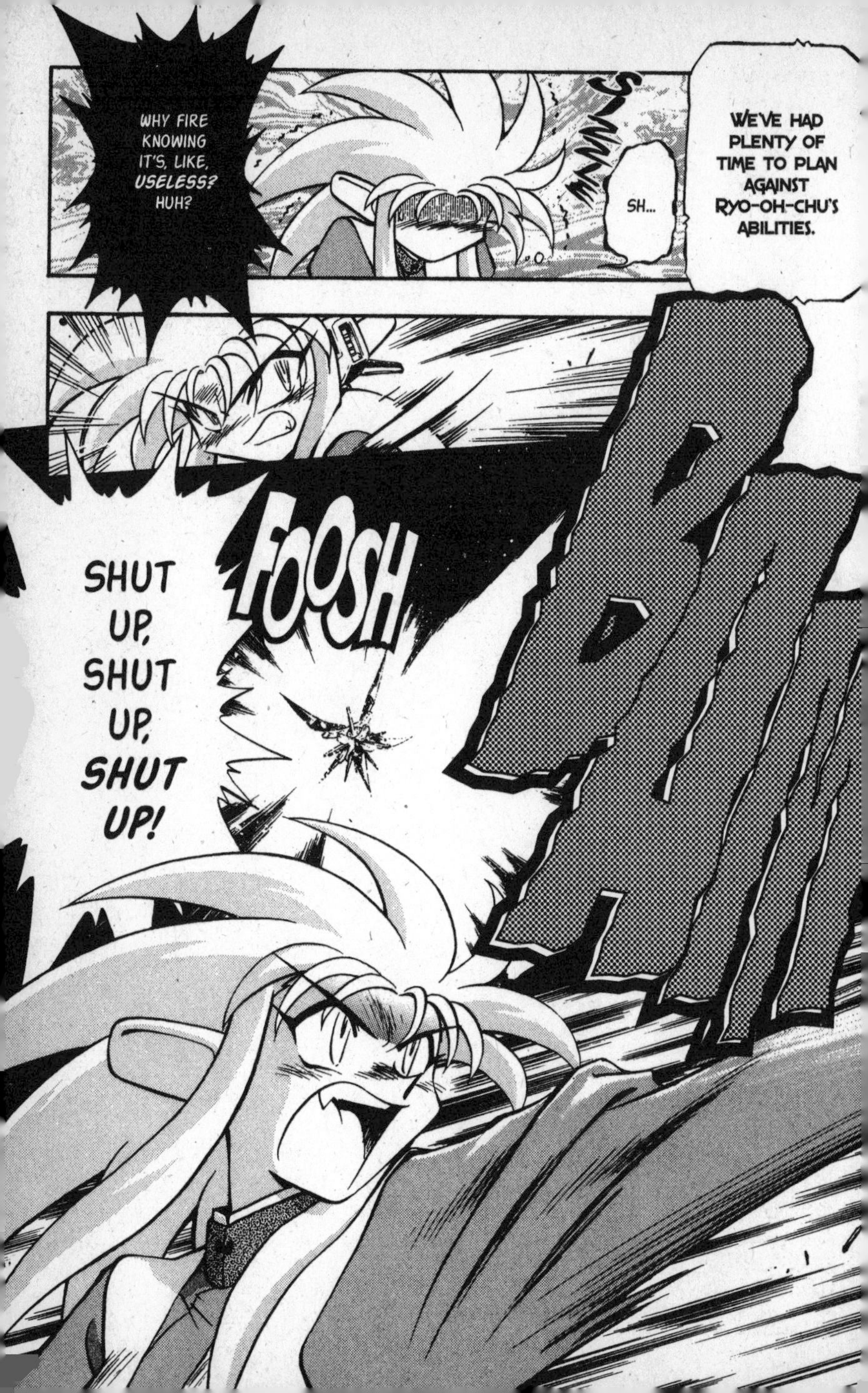
WE'VE HAD PLENTY OF TIME TO PLAN AGAINST RYO-OH-CHU'S ABILITIES.
SH...
WHY FIRE KNOWING IT'S, LIKE, USELESS? HUH?
FOOSH
SHUT UP, SHUT UP, SHUT UP!

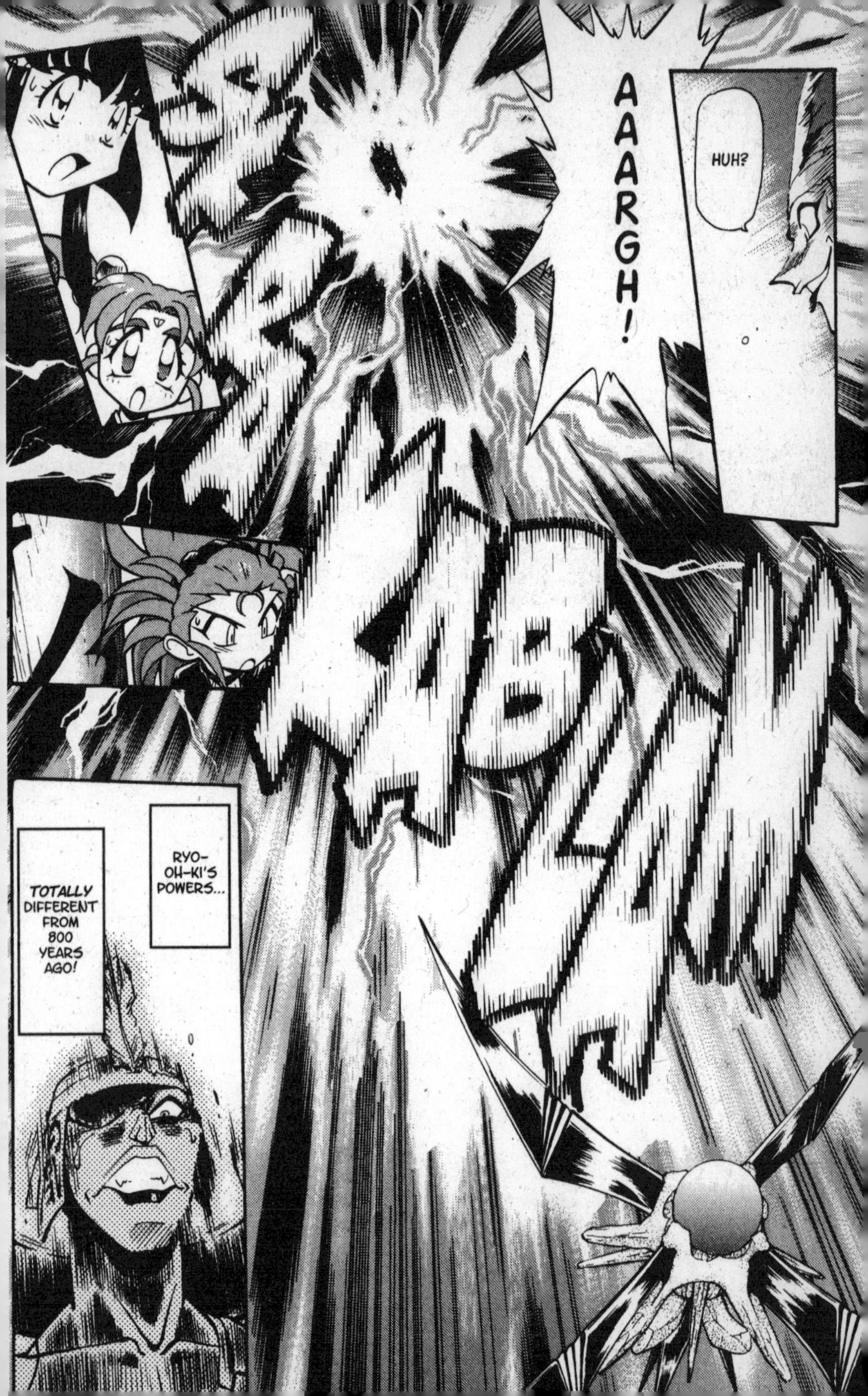
HUH?
AAAARGH!
RYO-OH-KI'S POWERS...
TOTALLY DIFFERENT FROM 800 YEARS AGO!

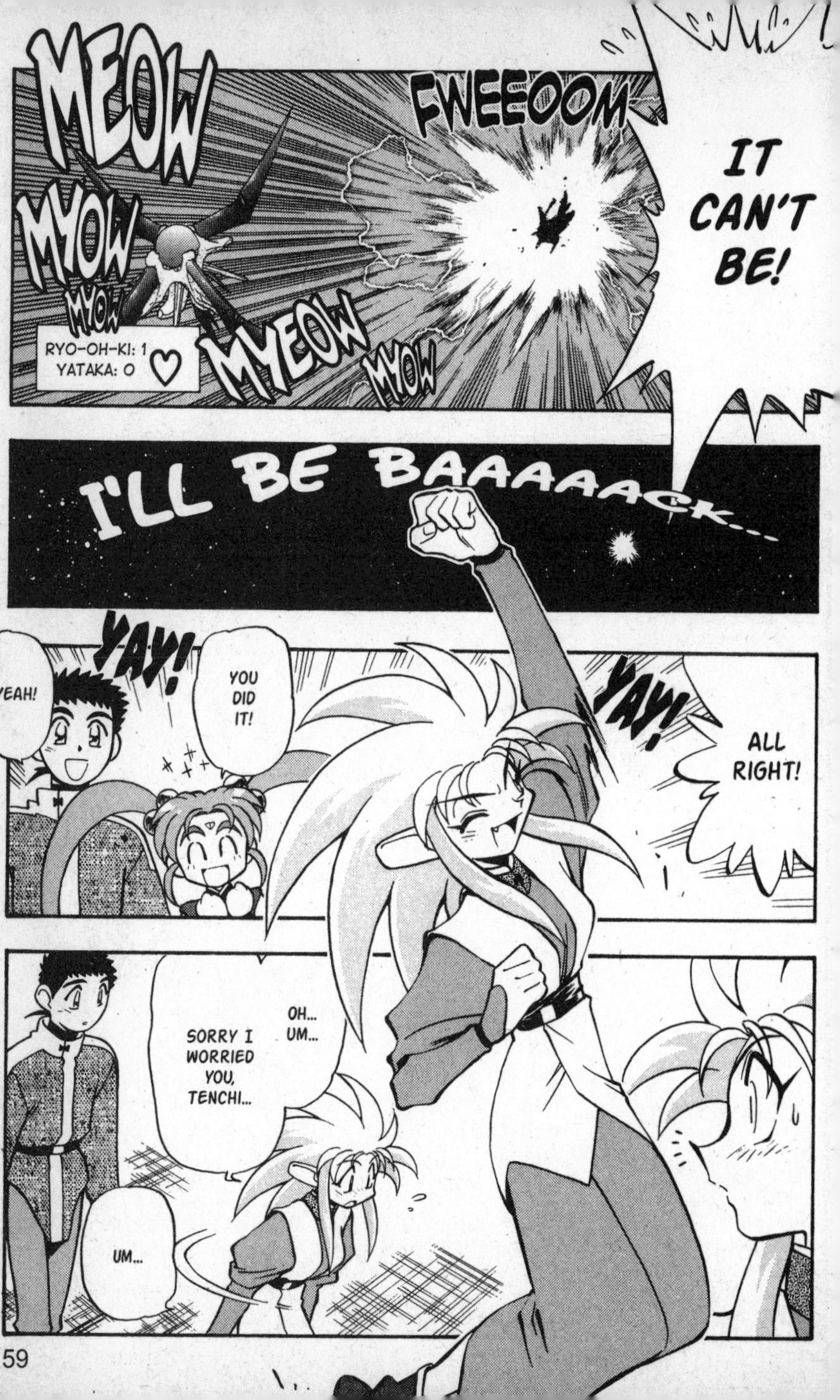
IT CAN'T BE!
FWEEOOM
MEOW
MYOW
MYOW
RYO-OH-KI: 1
YATAKA: 0
MYEOW
MYOW
I'LL BE BAAAAACK...
ALL RIGHT!
YAY!
YOU DID IT!
YAY!
YEAH!
OH... UM...
SORRY I WORRIED YOU, TENCHI...
UM...

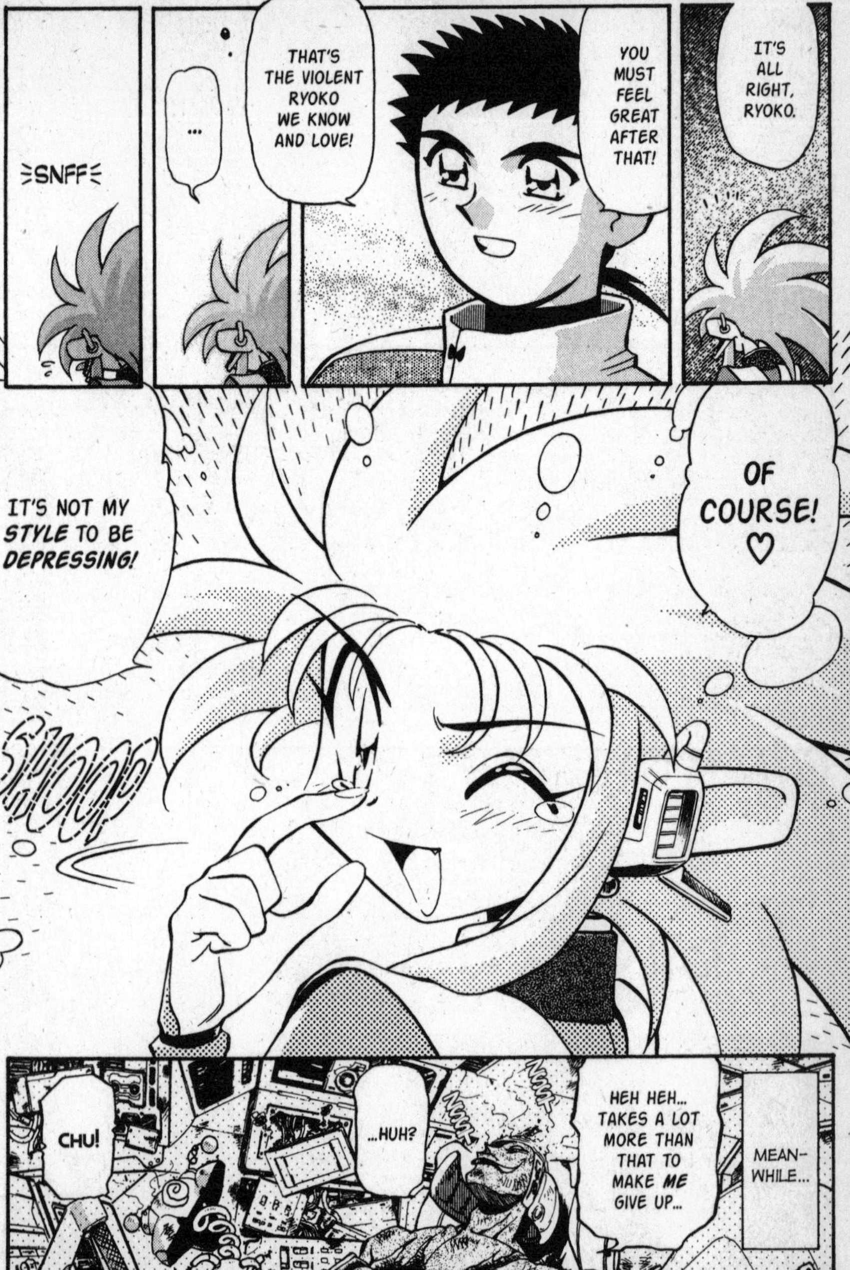
IT'S ALL RIGHT, RYOKO.
YOU MUST FEEL GREAT AFTER THAT!
THAT'S THE VIOLENT RYOKO WE KNOW AND LOVE!
...
SNFF
OF COURSE! ♡
IT'S NOT MY *STYLE* TO BE *DEPRESSING!*
MEAN-WHILE...
HEH HEH... TAKES A LOT MORE THAN THAT TO MAKE *ME* GIVE UP...
...HUH?
CHU!

UH-OH! STILL ALIVE...

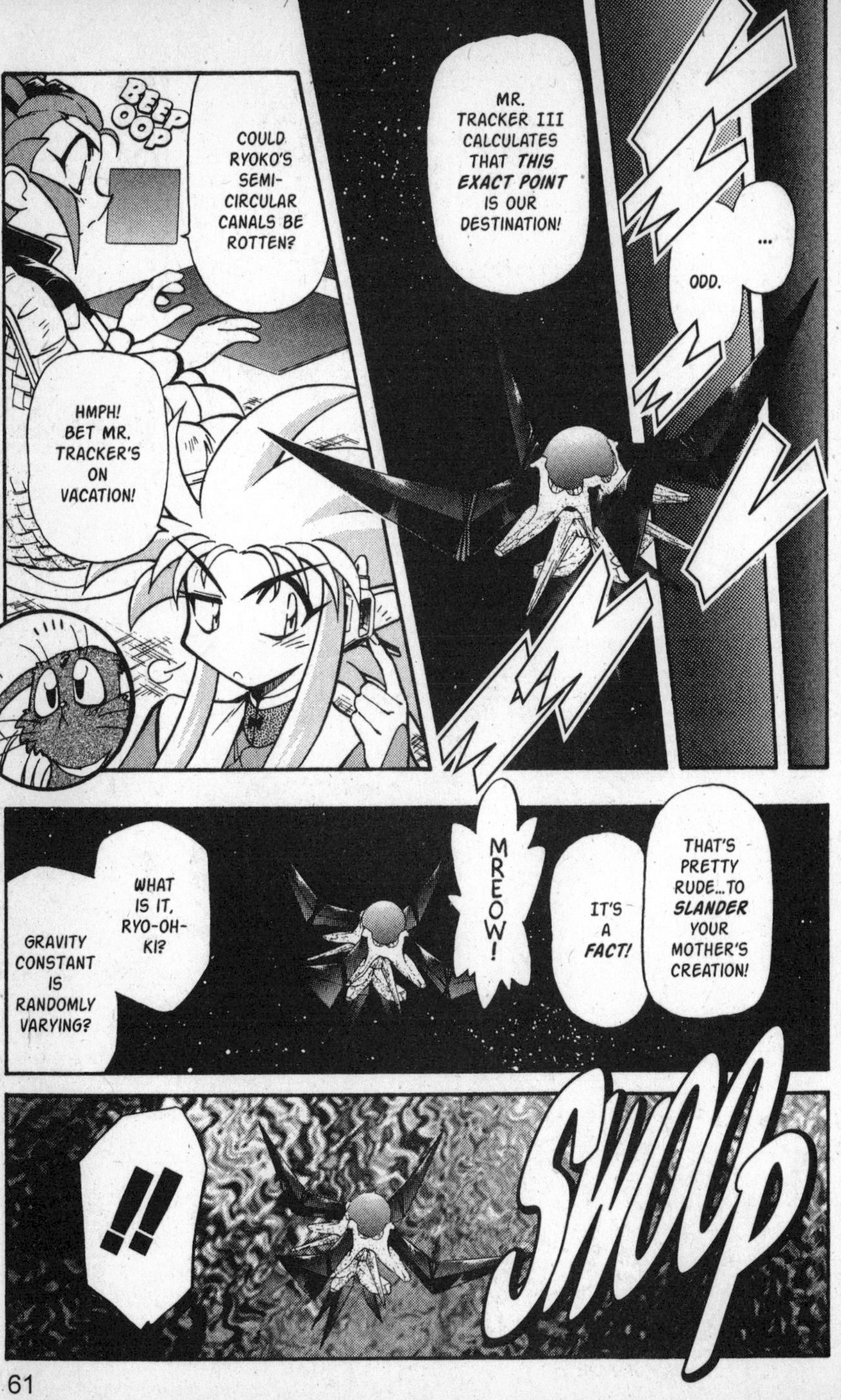
...
ODD.
MR. TRACKER III CALCULATES THAT THIS EXACT POINT IS OUR DESTINATION!
COULD RYOKO'S SEMI-CIRCULAR CANALS BE ROTTEN?
BEEP OOP
HMPH! BET MR. TRACKER'S ON VACATION!
THAT'S PRETTY RUDE...TO SLANDER YOUR MOTHER'S CREATION!
IT'S A FACT!
MREOW!
WHAT IS IT, RYO-OH-KI?
GRAVITY CONSTANT IS RANDOMLY VARYING?
SHOOP
!!

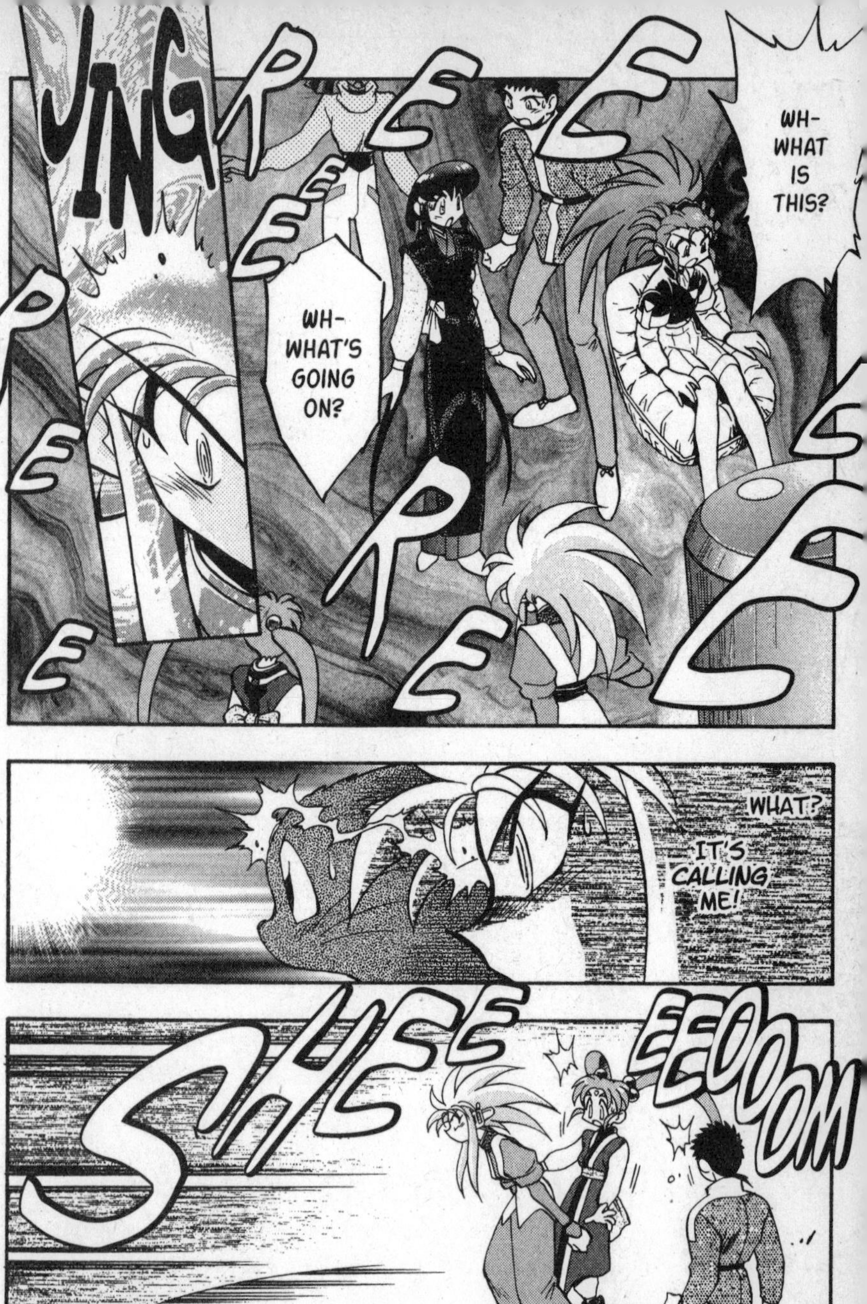
WH- WHAT IS THIS?
JING
PREEEE
WH- WHAT'S GOING ON?
REEE
REE
REEE
WHAT?
IT'S CALLING ME!
SHEEEEOOOOM
..!

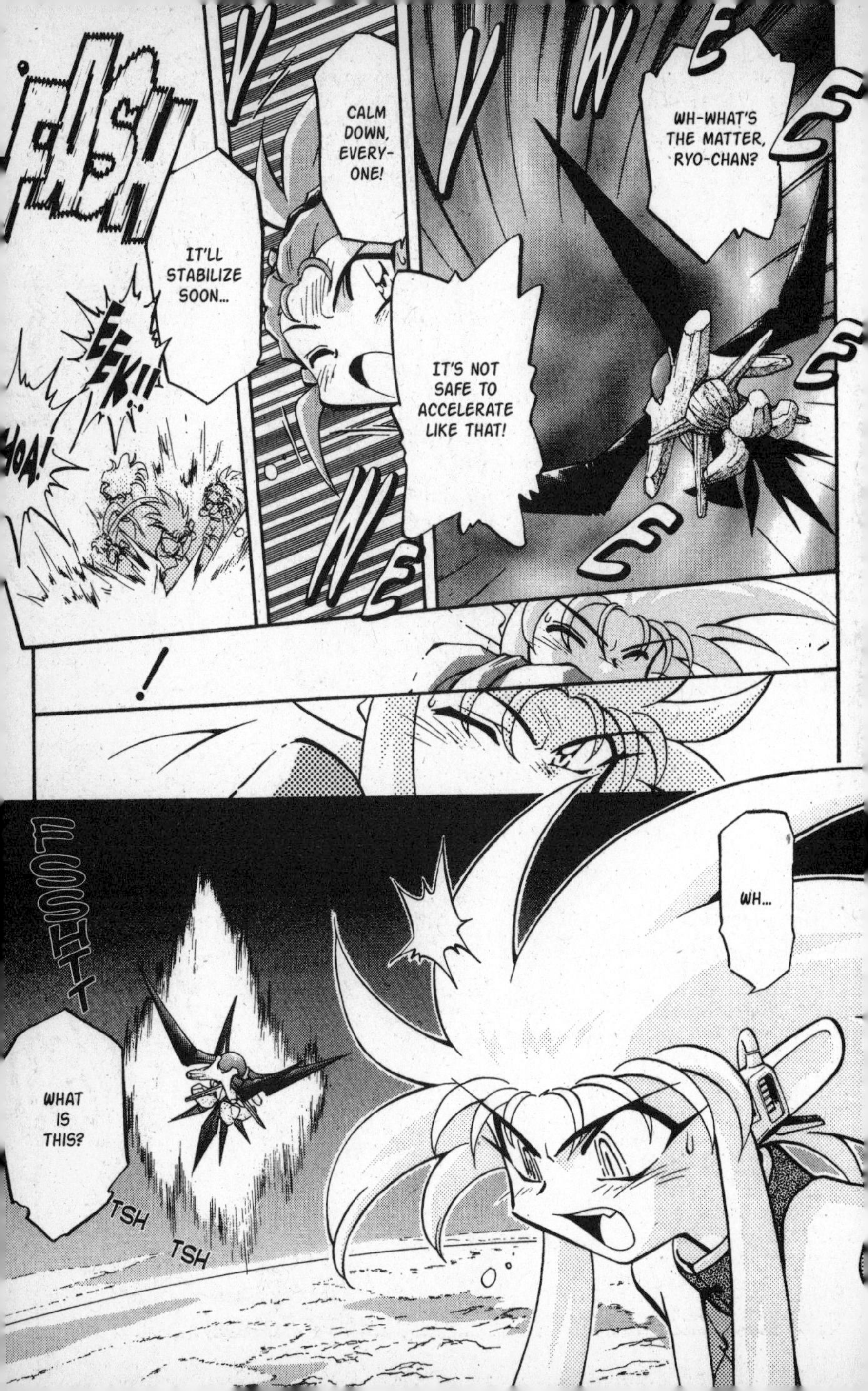
WH-WHAT'S THE MATTER, RYO-CHAN?
IT'S NOT SAFE TO ACCELERATE LIKE THAT!
CALM DOWN, EVERY-ONE!
IT'LL STABILIZE SOON...
EEEK!!
HOA!
!
WH...
FSSHTT
WHAT IS THIS?
TSH
TSH

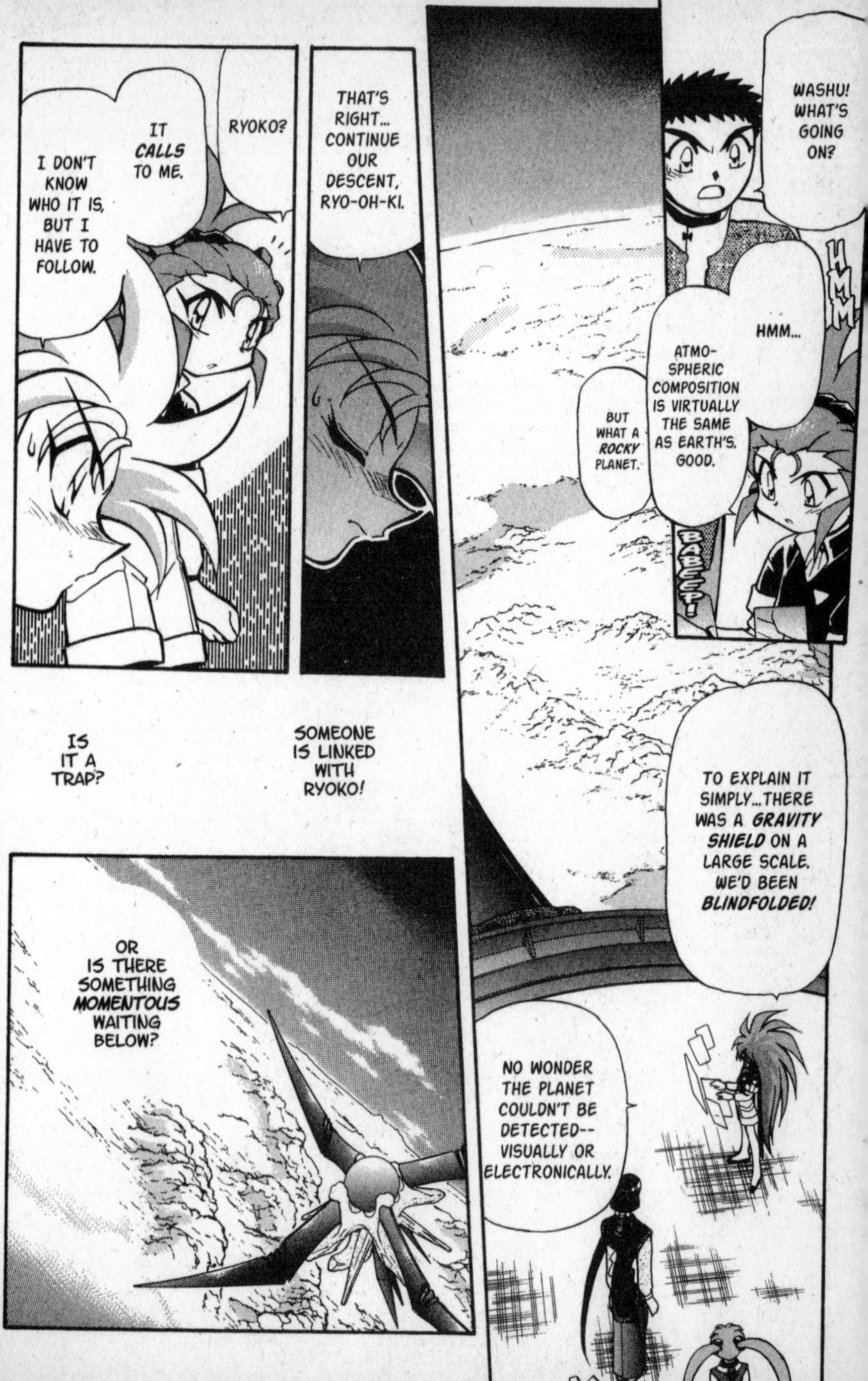

WASHU! WHAT'S GOING ON?
HMM
HMM...
ATMOSPHERIC COMPOSITION IS VIRTUALLY THE SAME AS EARTH'S. GOOD.
BUT WHAT A *ROCKY* PLANET.
BABEEP!
TO EXPLAIN IT SIMPLY...THERE WAS A ***GRAVITY SHIELD*** ON A LARGE SCALE. WE'D BEEN ***BLINDFOLDED!***
NO WONDER THE PLANET COULDN'T BE DETECTED-- VISUALLY OR ELECTRONICALLY.
THAT'S RIGHT... CONTINUE OUR DESCENT, RYO-OH-KI.
RYOKO?
IT *CALLS* TO ME.
I DON'T KNOW WHO IT IS, BUT I HAVE TO FOLLOW.
SOMEONE IS LINKED WITH RYOKO!
IS IT A TRAP?
OR IS THERE SOMETHING ***MOMENTOUS*** WAITING BELOW?

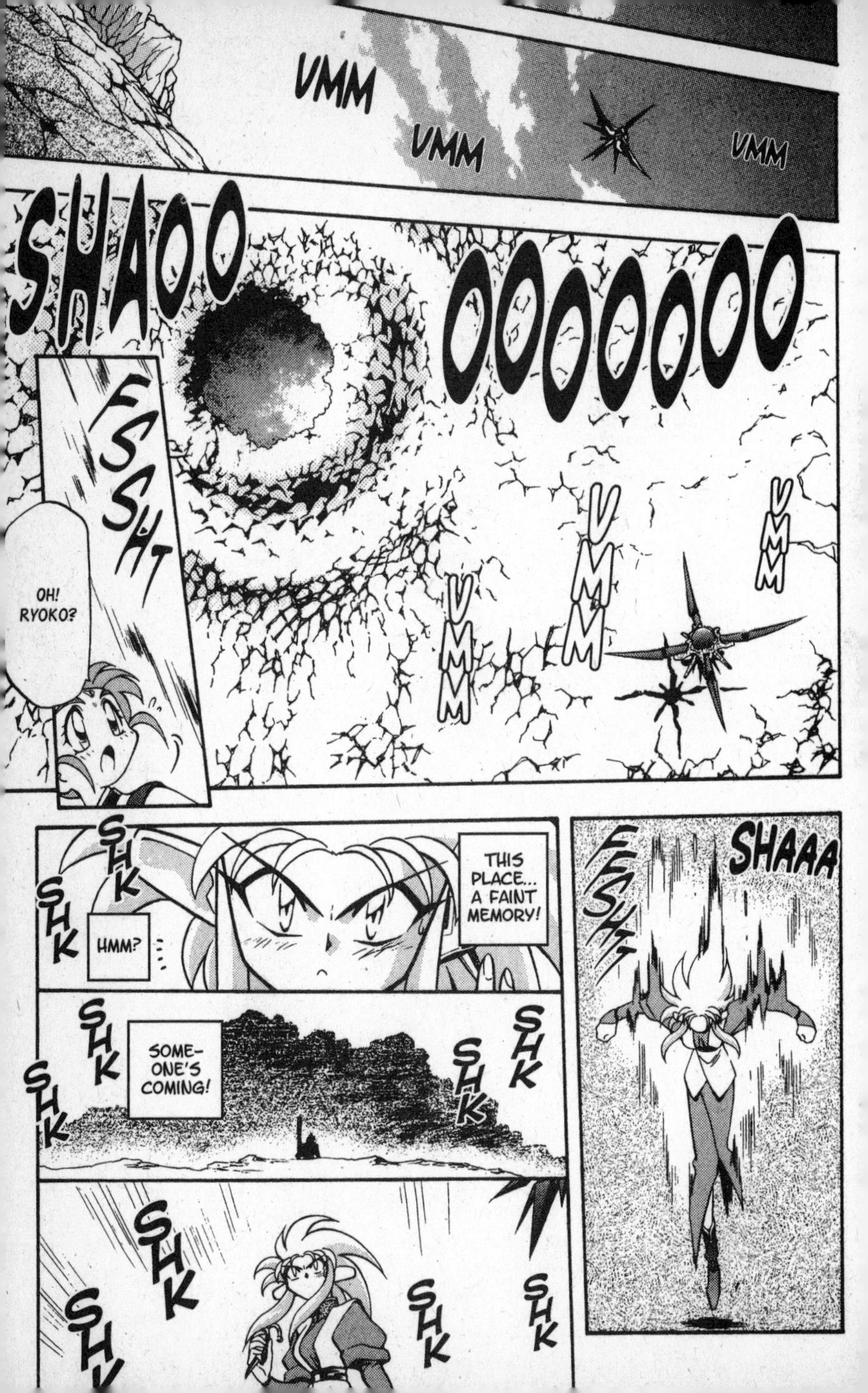
UMM
UMM
UMM
SHAOOOOOOOOO
VMMM
VMMM
VMMM
FSSSHT
OH! RYOKO?
SHAAA
FFSHT
SHK SHK SHK
THIS PLACE... A FAINT MEMORY!
HMM?
SHK SHK SHK SHK SHK
SOME-ONE'S COMING!
SHK SHK SHK SHK

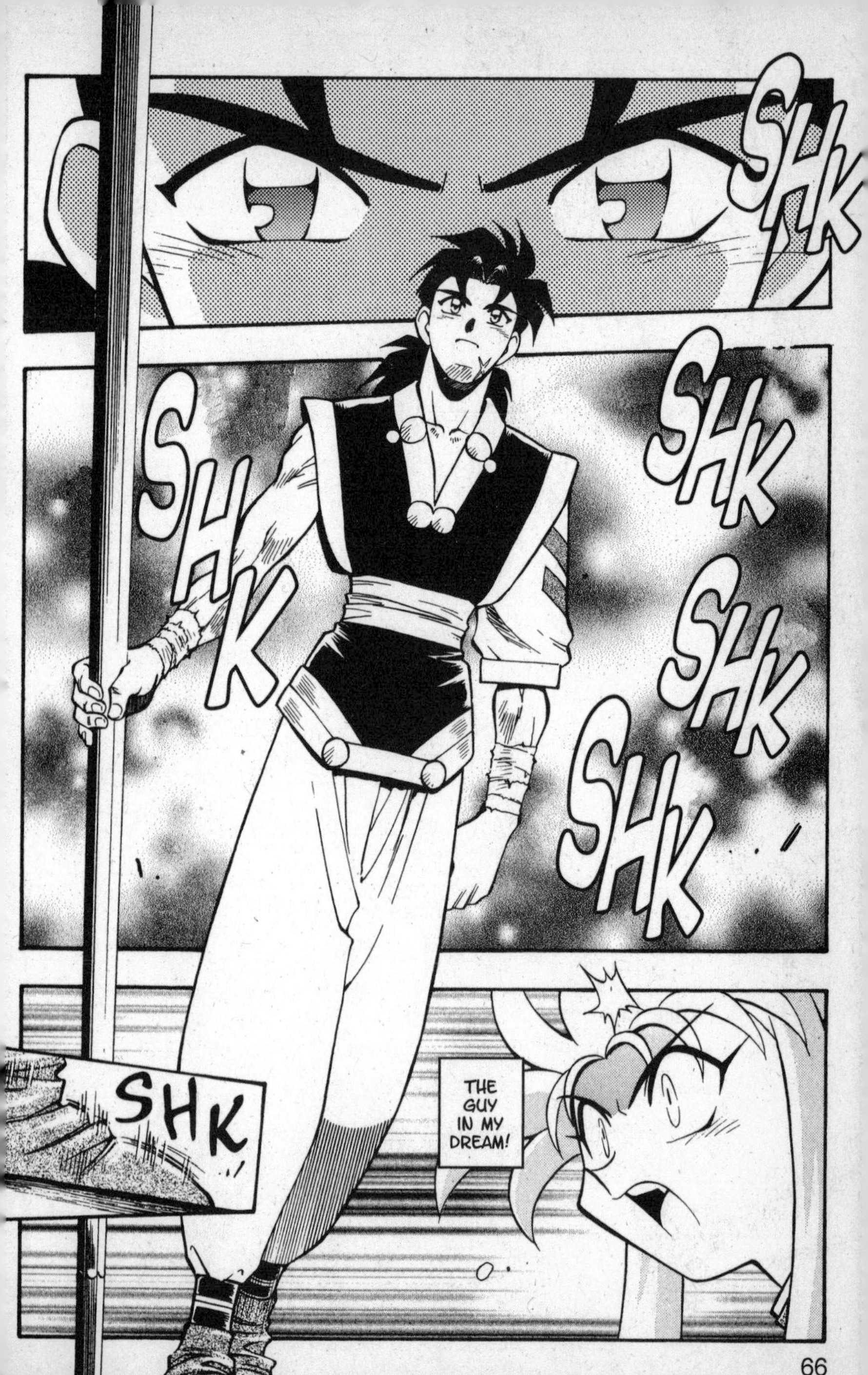
SHK
SHK
SHK
SHK
SHK
THE GUY IN MY DREAM!
SHK

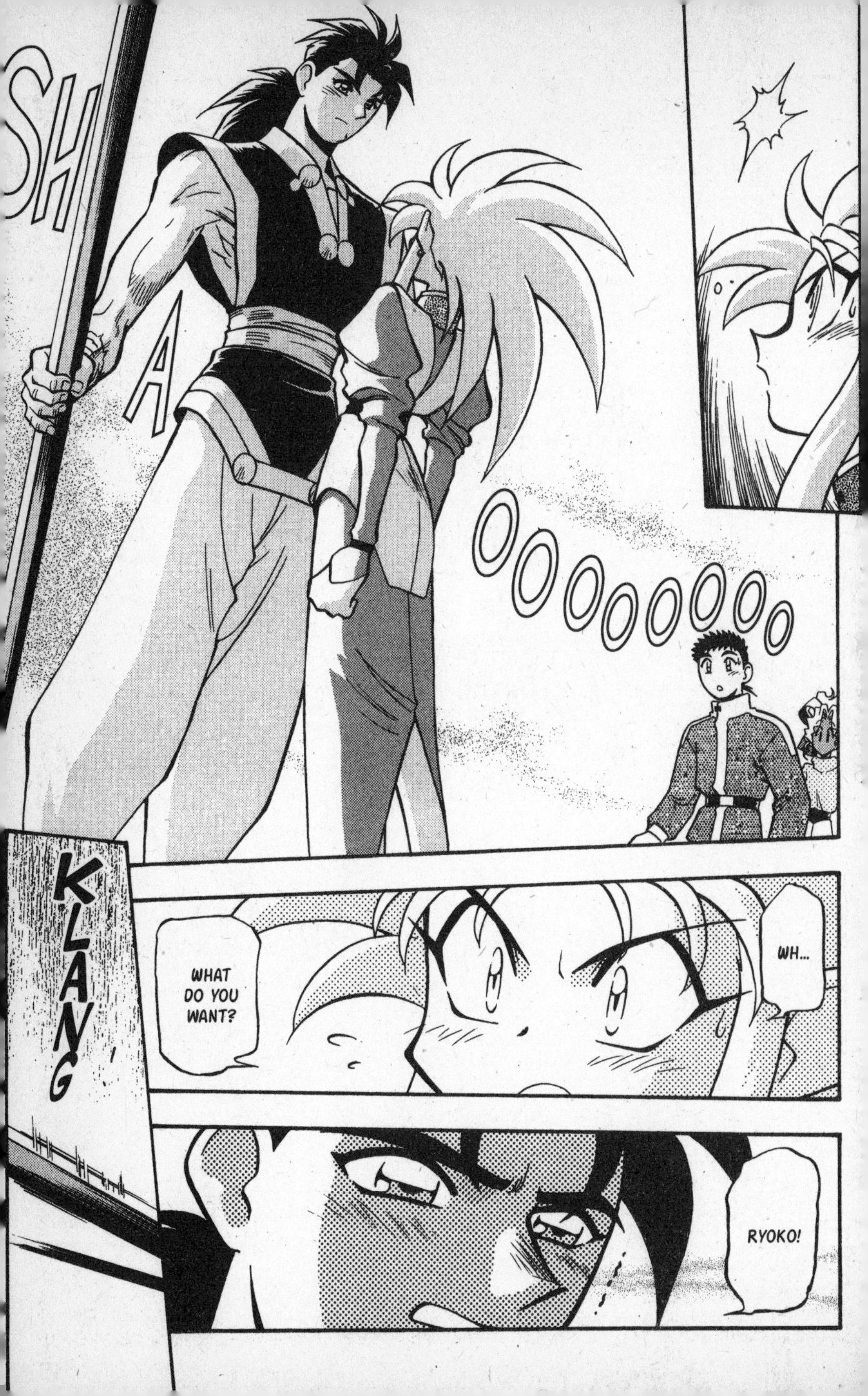
SHA
OOOOOOOO
WH...
WHAT DO YOU WANT?
RYOKO!
KLANG

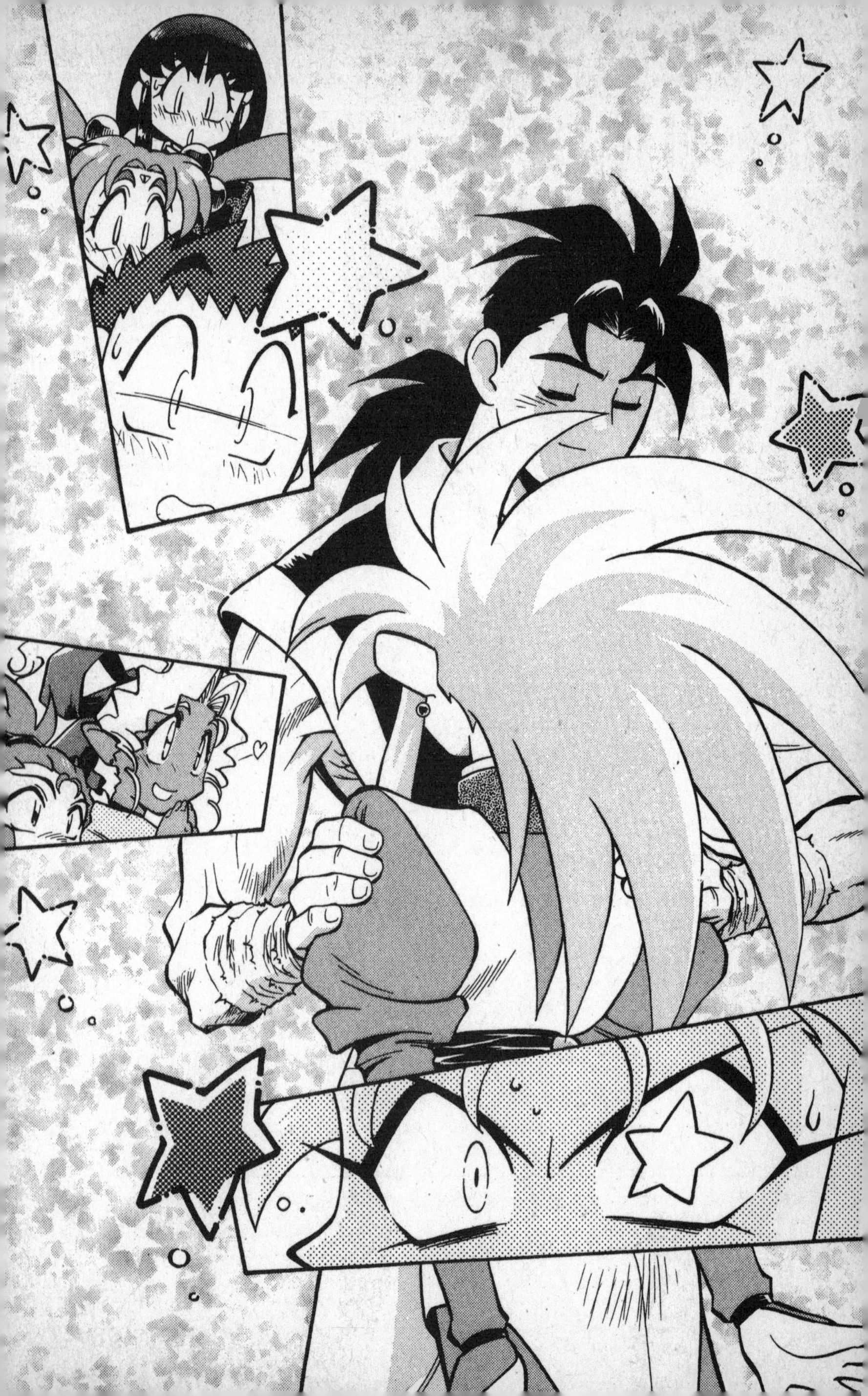

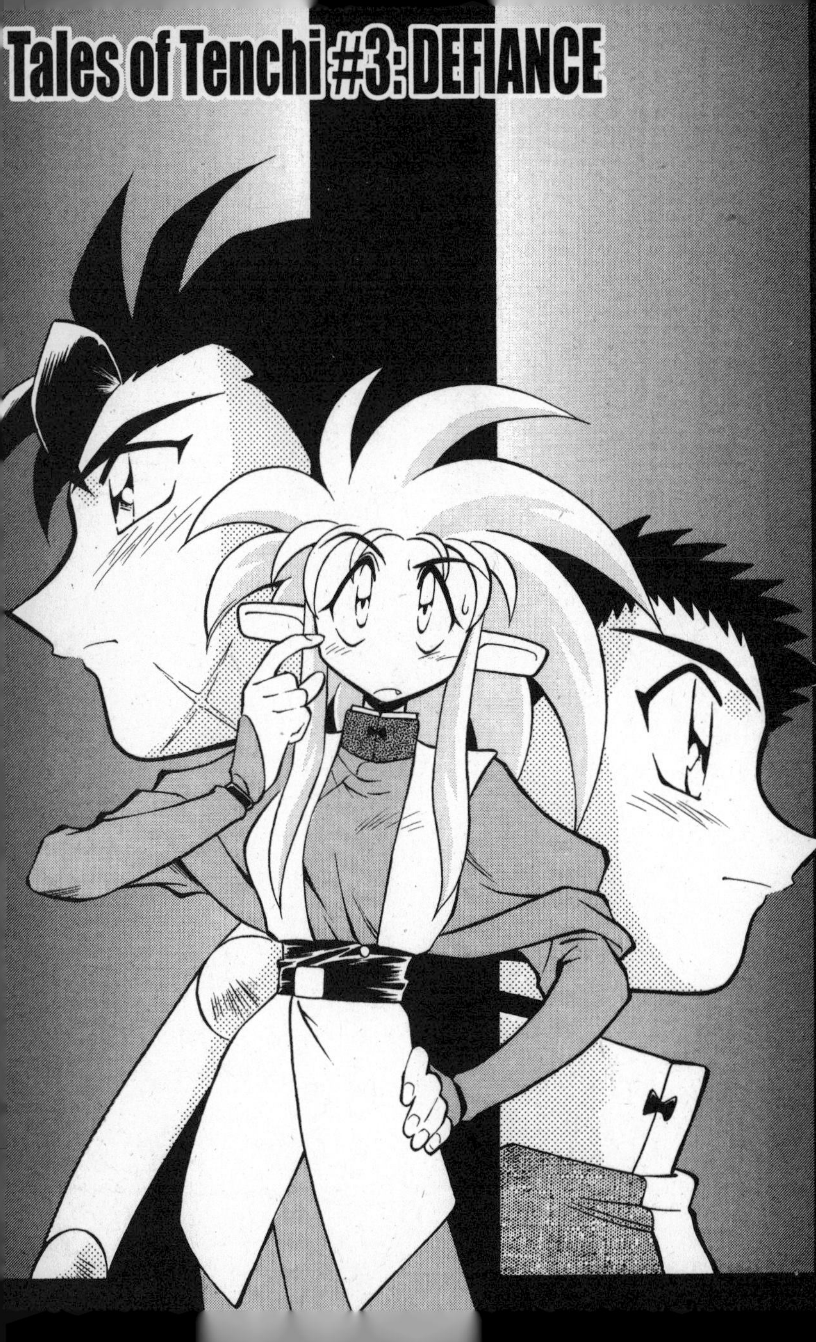
Tales of Tenchi #3: DEFIANCE

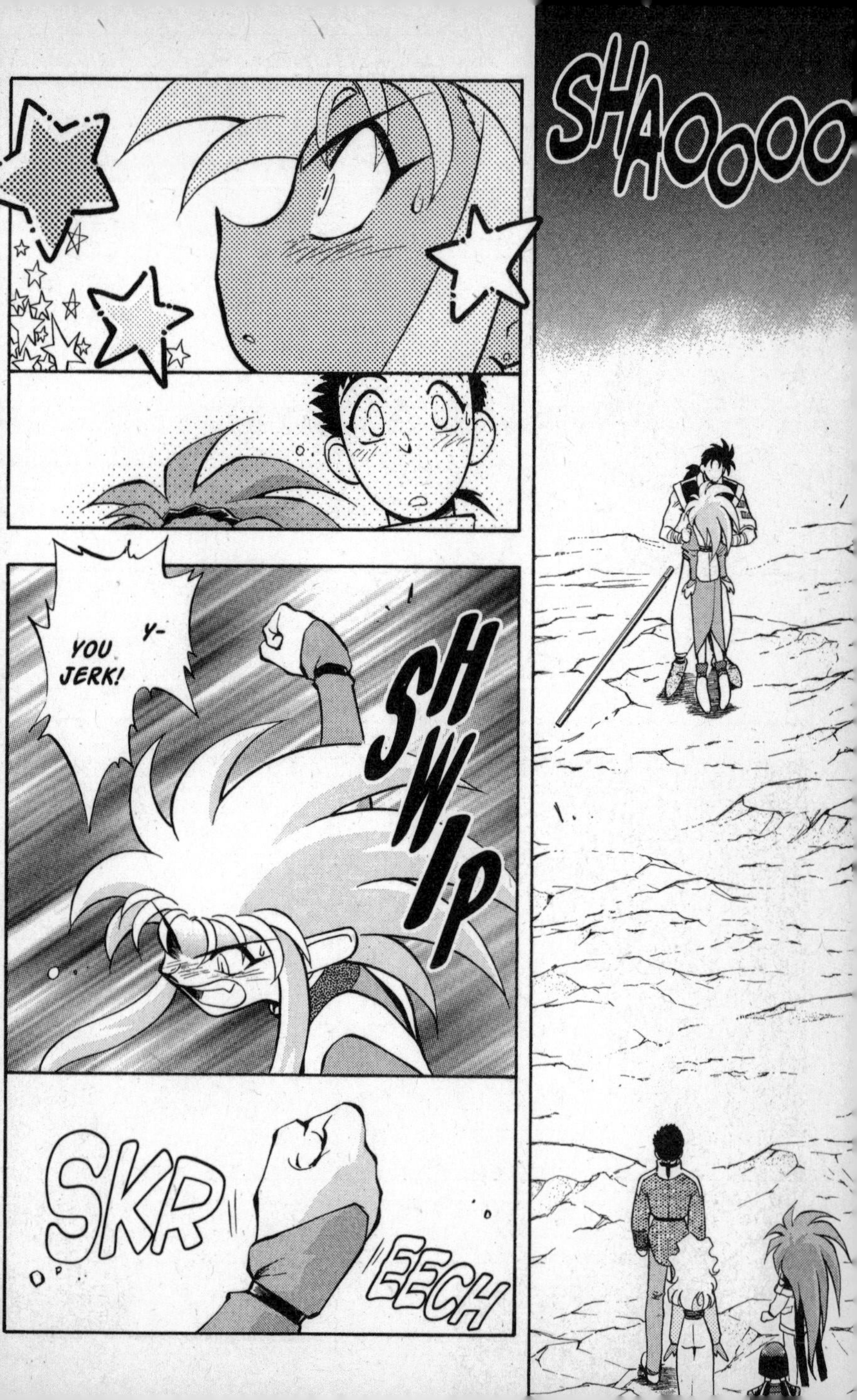
SHAOOOO
Y- YOU JERK!
SHWIP
SKR
EECH

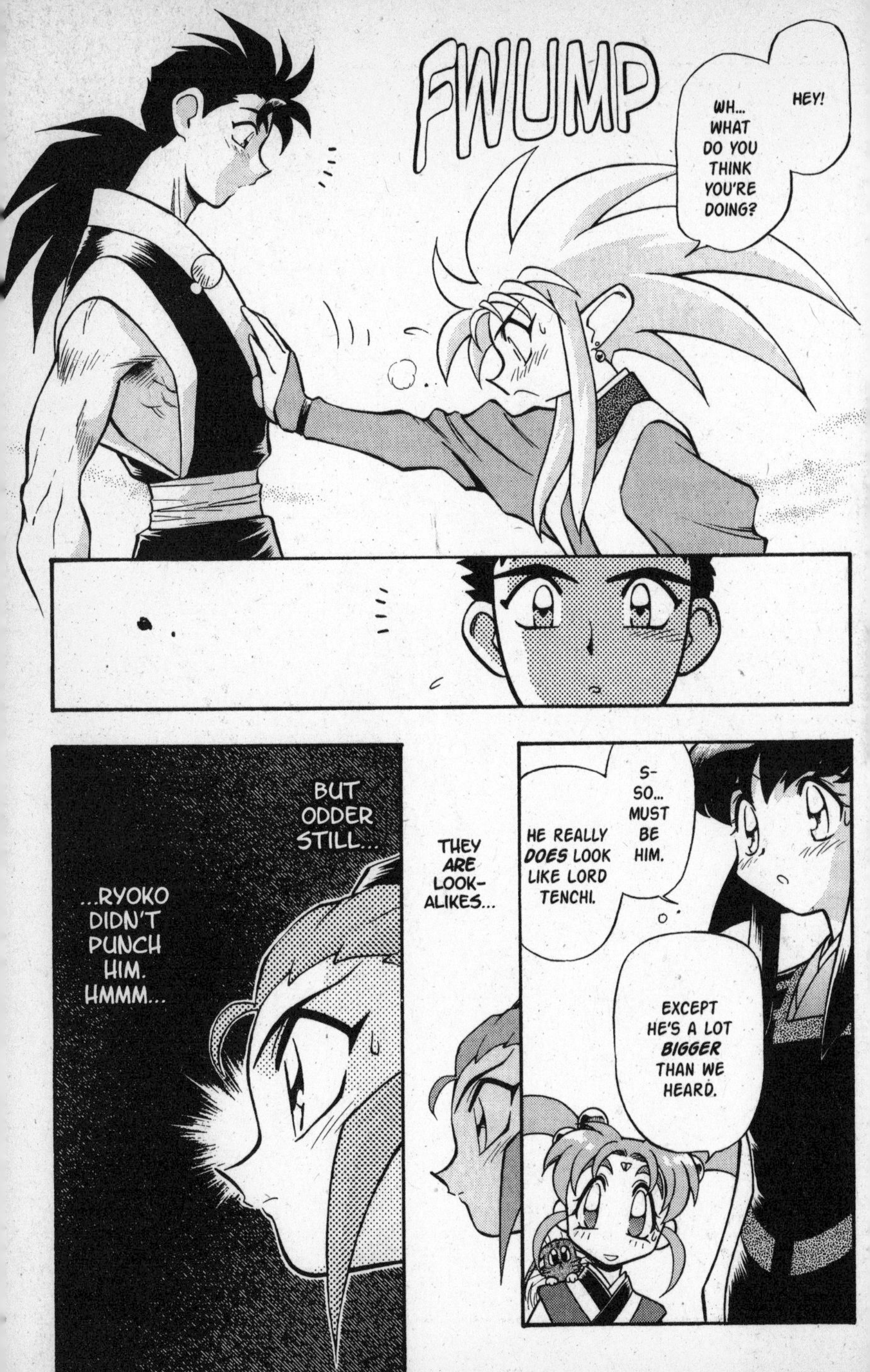
FWUMP
HEY!
WH... WHAT DO YOU THINK YOU'RE DOING?
S-SO... MUST BE HIM.
HE REALLY DOES LOOK LIKE LORD TENCHI.
THEY ARE LOOK-ALIKES...
EXCEPT HE'S A LOT BIGGER THAN WE HEARD.
BUT ODDER STILL...
...RYOKO DIDN'T PUNCH HIM. HMMM...

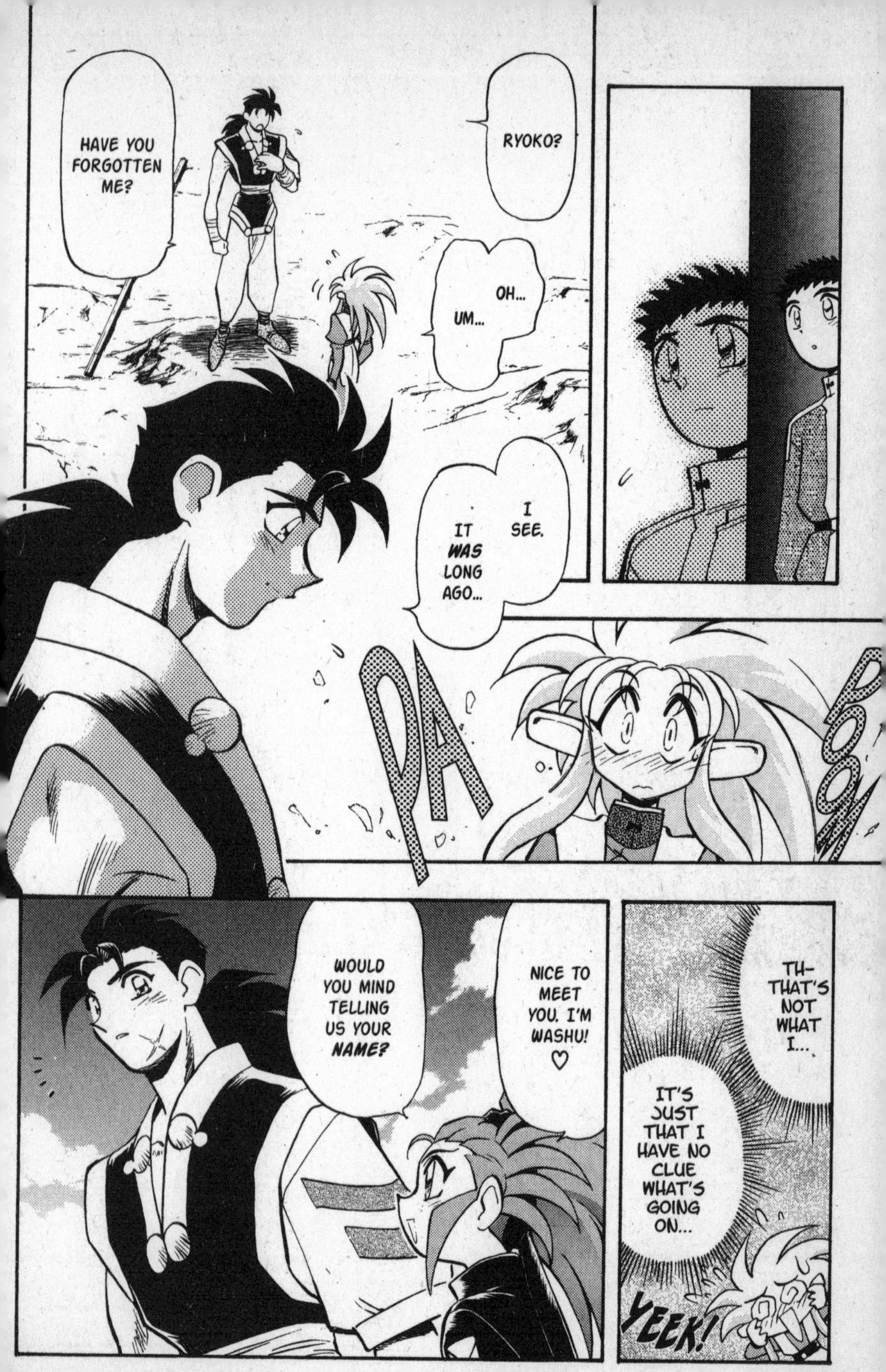
RYOKO?
HAVE YOU FORGOTTEN ME?
OH... UM...
I SEE. IT *WAS* LONG AGO...
BOOM
PA
TH-THAT'S NOT WHAT I...
IT'S JUST THAT I HAVE NO CLUE WHAT'S GOING ON...
YEEK!
NICE TO MEET YOU. I'M WASHU! ♡
WOULD YOU MIND TELLING US YOUR *NAME?*

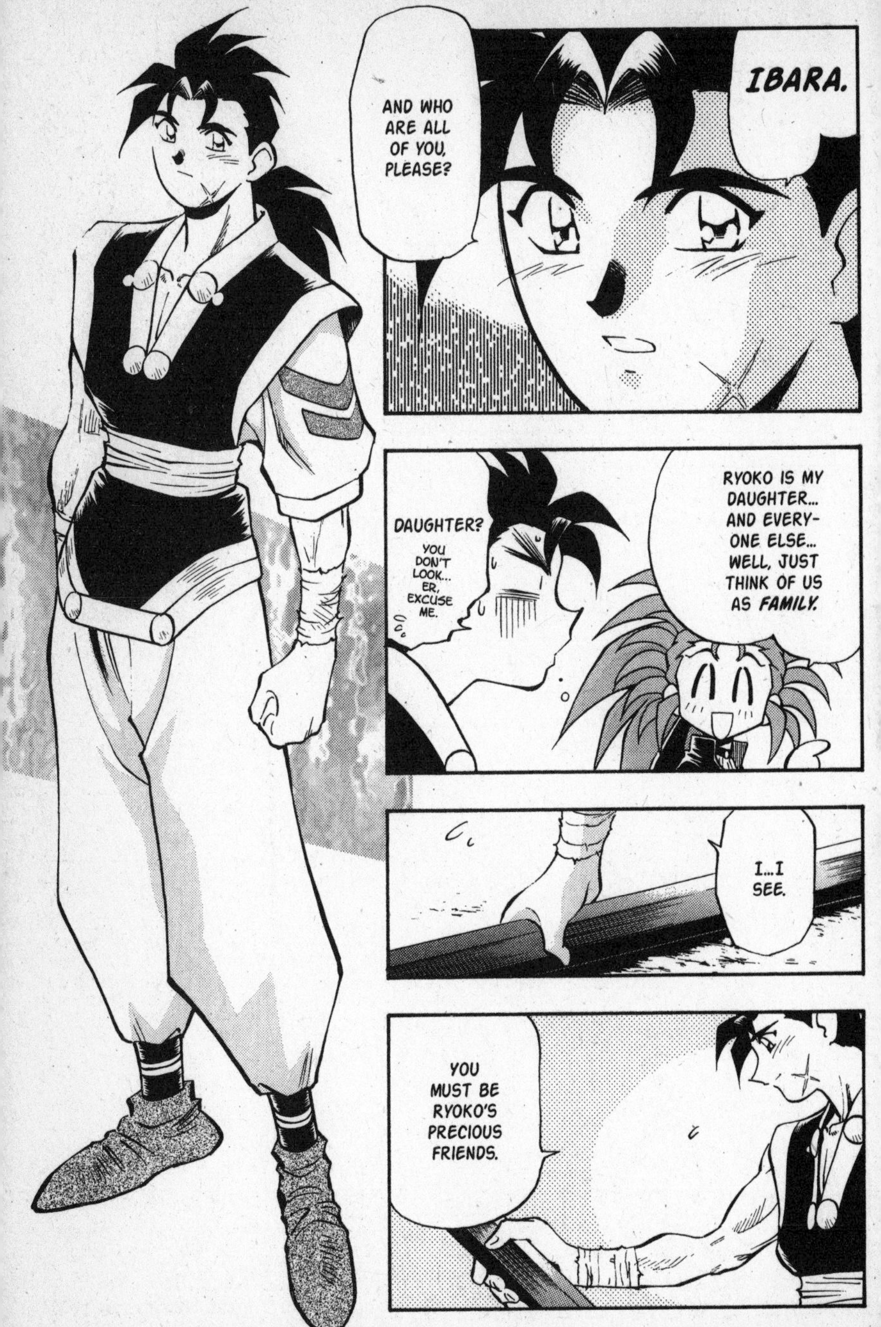
IBARA.
AND WHO ARE ALL OF YOU, PLEASE?
RYOKO IS MY DAUGHTER... AND EVERY-ONE ELSE... WELL, JUST THINK OF US AS *FAMILY.*
DAUGHTER?
YOU DON'T LOOK... ER, EXCUSE ME.
I...I SEE.
YOU MUST BE RYOKO'S PRECIOUS FRIENDS.

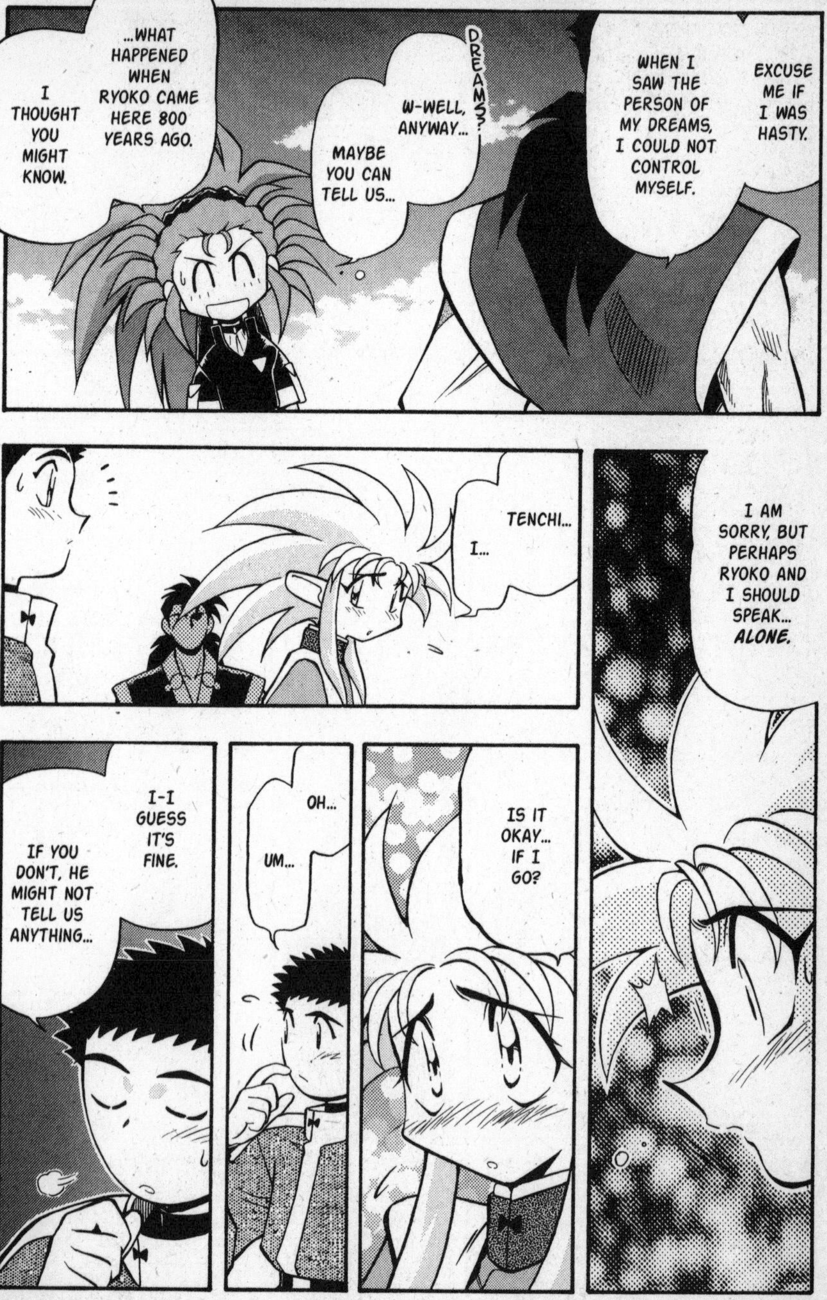
EXCUSE ME IF I WAS HASTY.
WHEN I SAW THE PERSON OF MY DREAMS, I COULD NOT CONTROL MYSELF.
DREAMS?
W-WELL, ANYWAY...
MAYBE YOU CAN TELL US...
...WHAT HAPPENED WHEN RYOKO CAME HERE 800 YEARS AGO.
I THOUGHT YOU MIGHT KNOW.
I AM SORRY, BUT PERHAPS RYOKO AND I SHOULD SPEAK... ***ALONE.***
TENCHI...
I...
IS IT OKAY... IF I GO?
OH...
UM...
I-I GUESS IT'S FINE.
IF YOU DON'T, HE MIGHT NOT TELL US ANYTHING...

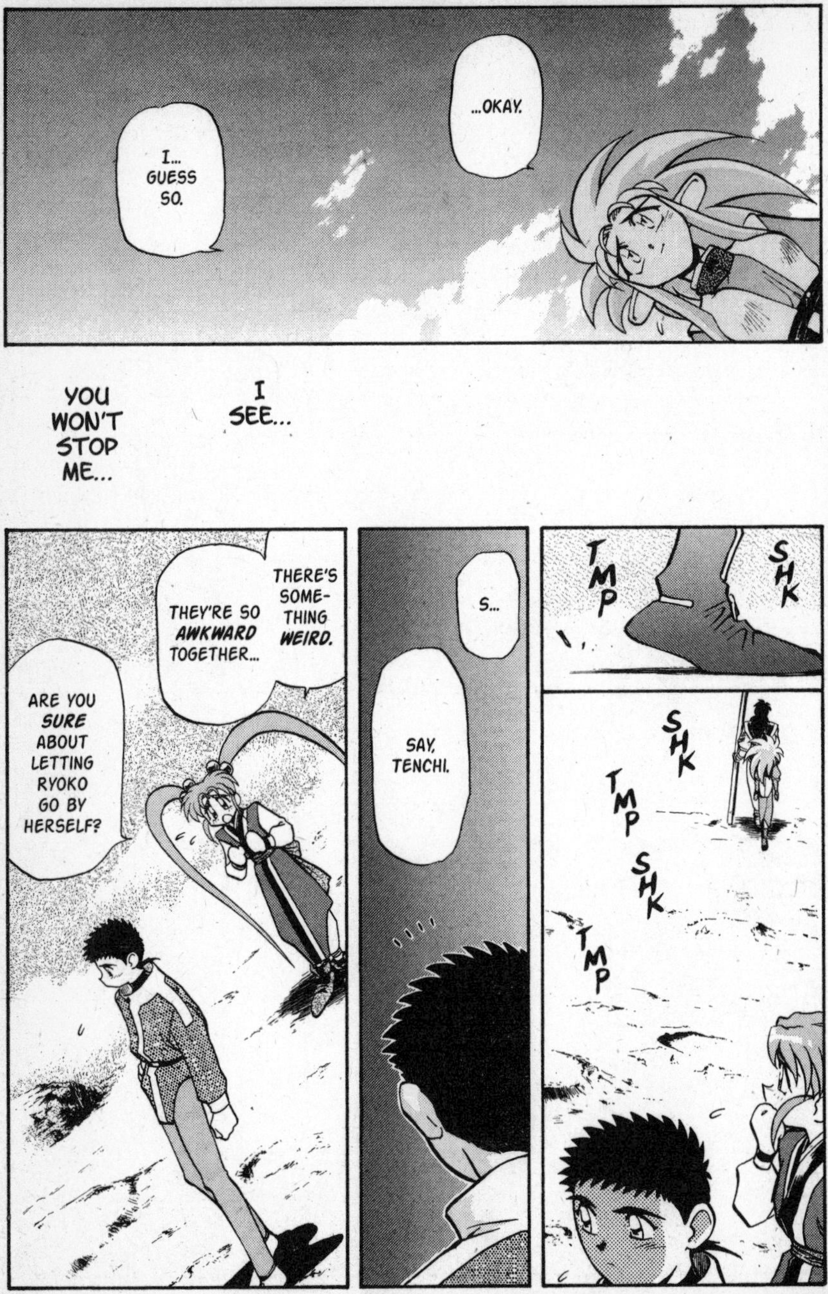
...OKAY.
I... GUESS SO.
I SEE...
YOU WON'T STOP ME...
SHK
TMP
SHK
TMP
SHK
TMP
S...
SAY, TENCHI.
THERE'S SOME-THING WEIRD.
THEY'RE SO AWKWARD TOGETHER...
ARE YOU SURE ABOUT LETTING RYOKO GO BY HERSELF?

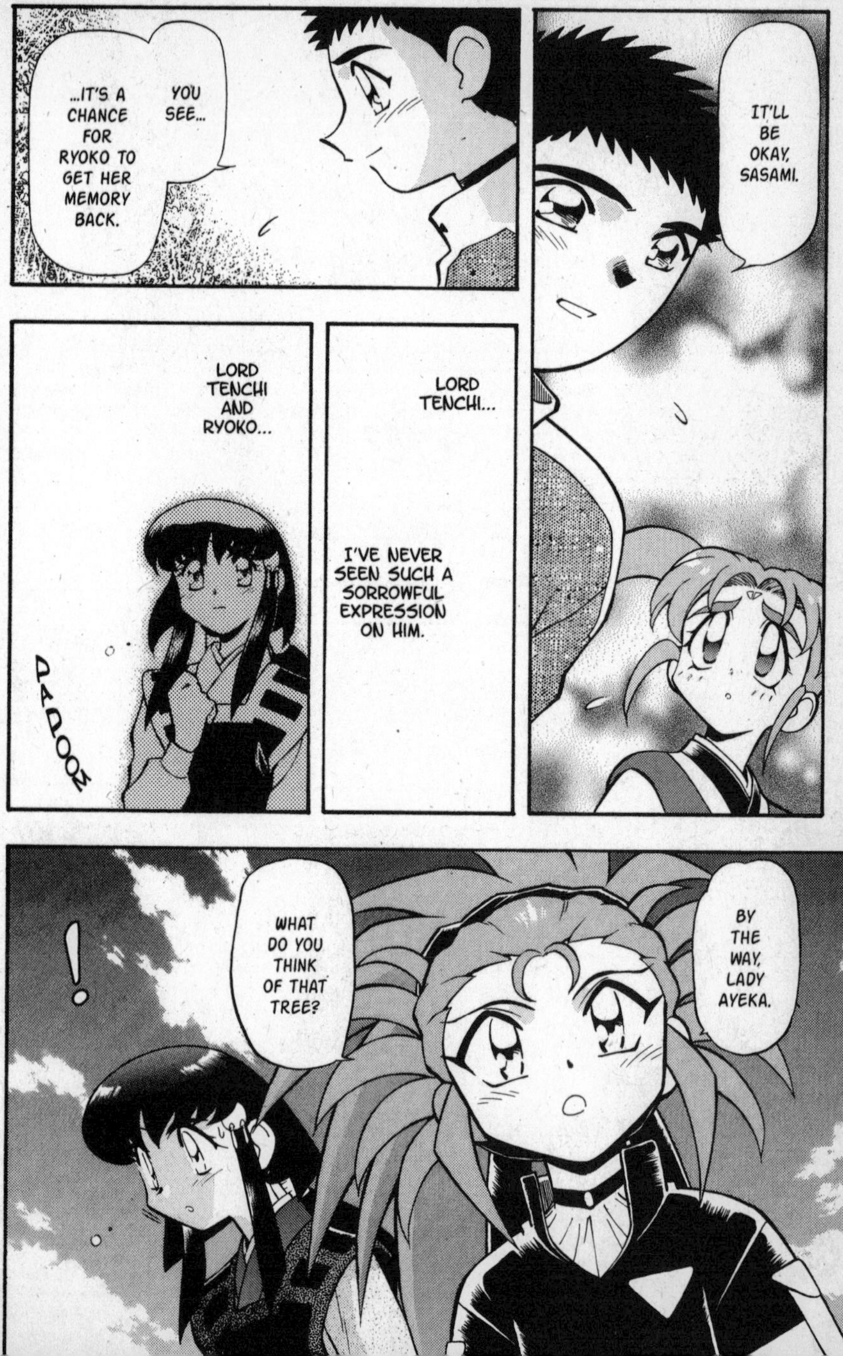
IT'LL BE OKAY, SASAMI.
YOU SEE...
...IT'S A CHANCE FOR RYOKO TO GET HER MEMORY BACK.
LORD TENCHI...
I'VE NEVER SEEN SUCH A SORROWFUL EXPRESSION ON HIM.
LORD TENCHI AND RYOKO...
DADOOM
BY THE WAY, LADY AYEKA.
WHAT DO YOU THINK OF THAT TREE?
!

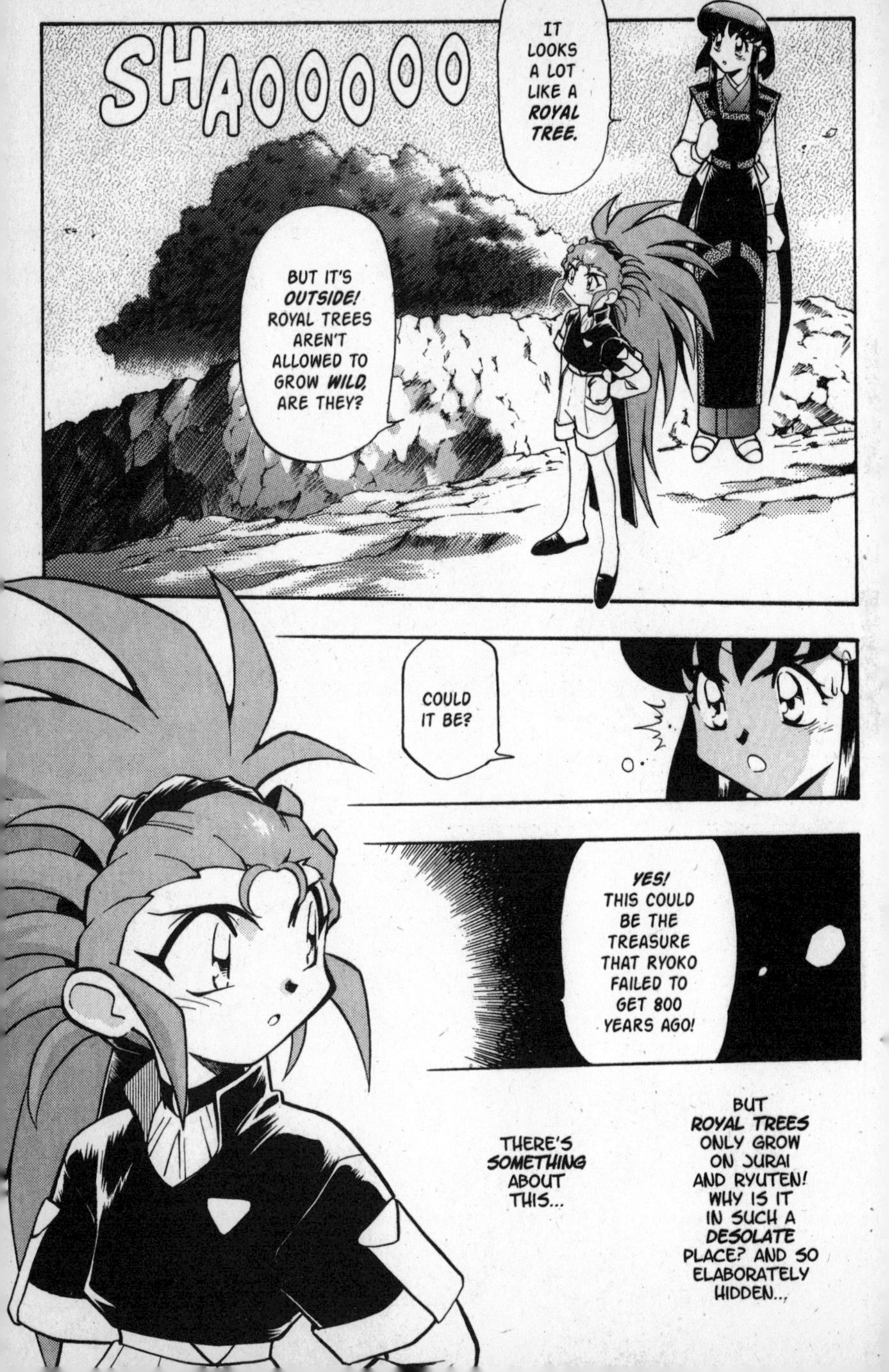
IT LOOKS A LOT LIKE A ROYAL TREE.
SHAOOOOO
BUT IT'S OUTSIDE! ROYAL TREES AREN'T ALLOWED TO GROW WILD, ARE THEY?
COULD IT BE?
YES! THIS COULD BE THE TREASURE THAT RYOKO FAILED TO GET 800 YEARS AGO!
BUT ROYAL TREES ONLY GROW ON JURAI AND RYUTEN! WHY IS IT IN SUCH A DESOLATE PLACE? AND SO ELABORATELY HIDDEN...
THERE'S SOMETHING ABOUT THIS...

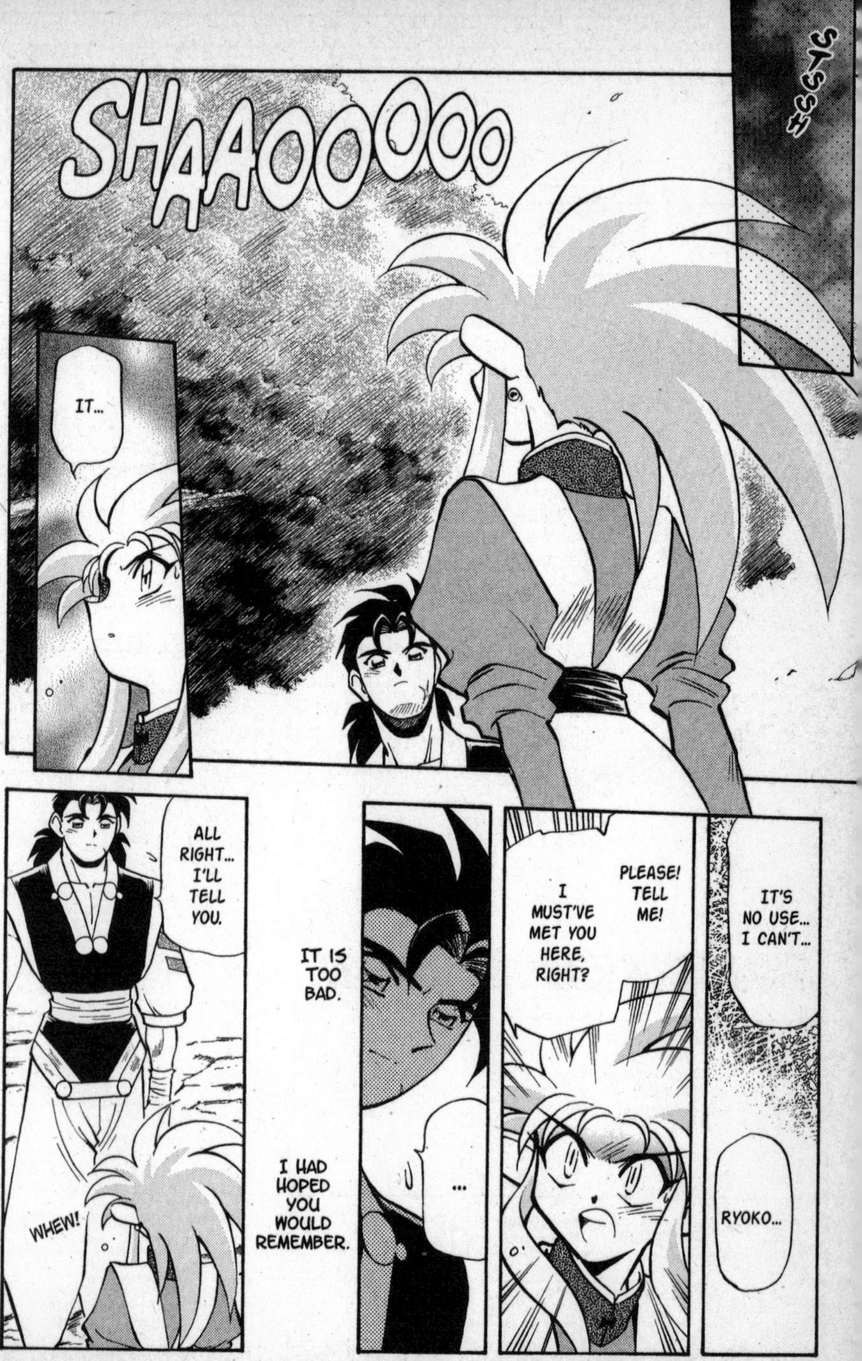
SISSH
SHAAOOOOO
IT...
IT'S NO USE... I CAN'T...
RYOKO...
PLEASE! TELL ME!
I MUST'VE MET YOU HERE, RIGHT?
IT IS TOO BAD.
...
I HAD HOPED YOU WOULD REMEMBER.
ALL RIGHT... I'LL TELL YOU.
WHEW!

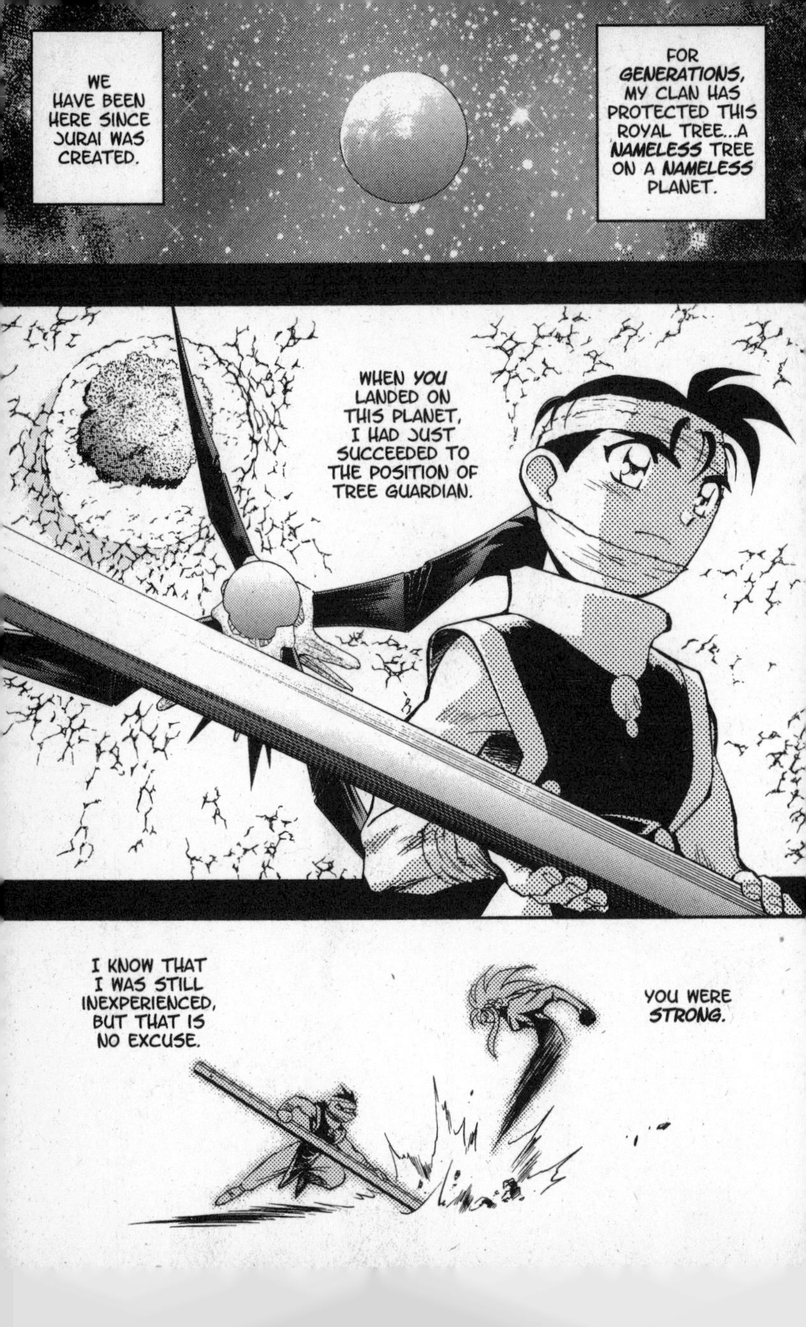
FOR GENERATIONS, MY CLAN HAS PROTECTED THIS ROYAL TREE...A NAMELESS TREE ON A NAMELESS PLANET.
WE HAVE BEEN HERE SINCE JURAI WAS CREATED.
WHEN YOU LANDED ON THIS PLANET, I HAD JUST SUCCEEDED TO THE POSITION OF TREE GUARDIAN.
YOU WERE STRONG.
I KNOW THAT I WAS STILL INEXPERIENCED, BUT THAT IS NO EXCUSE.

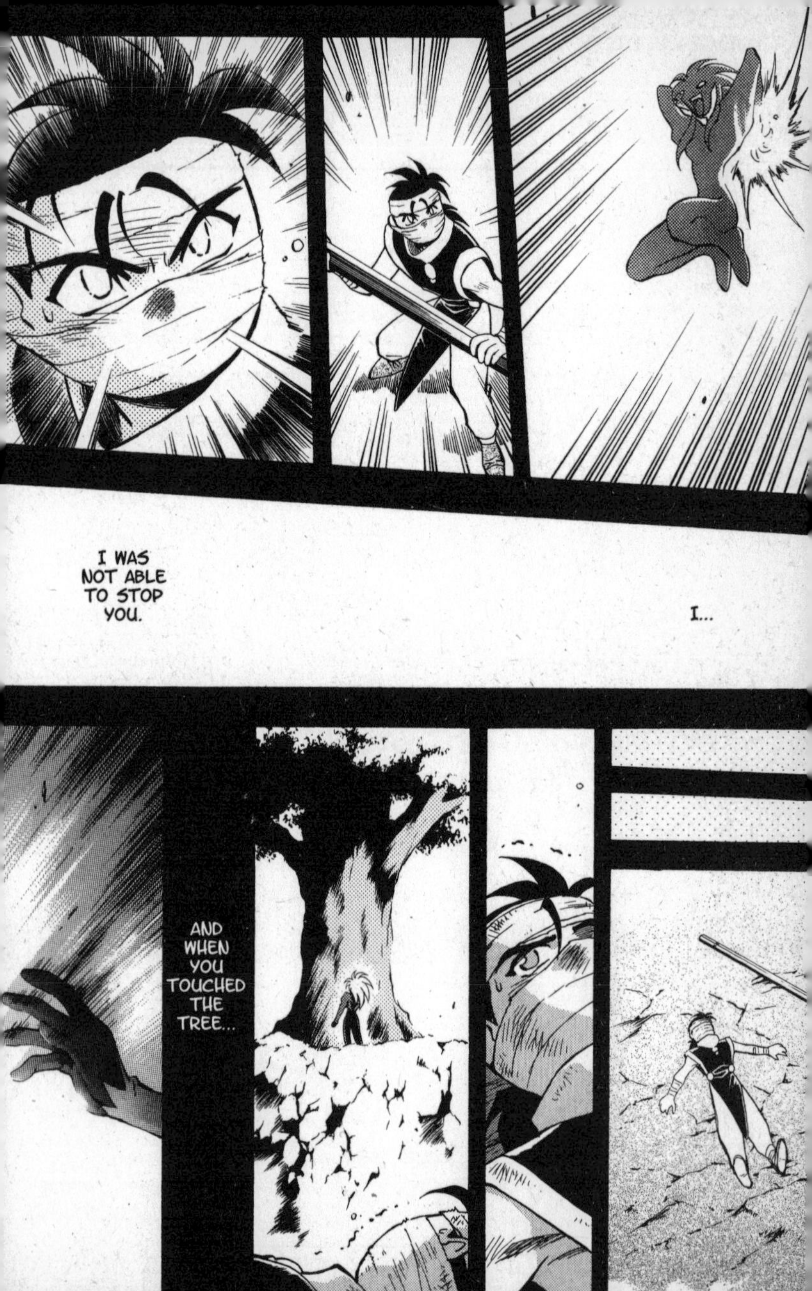
I...
I WAS NOT ABLE TO STOP YOU.
AND WHEN YOU TOUCHED THE TREE...

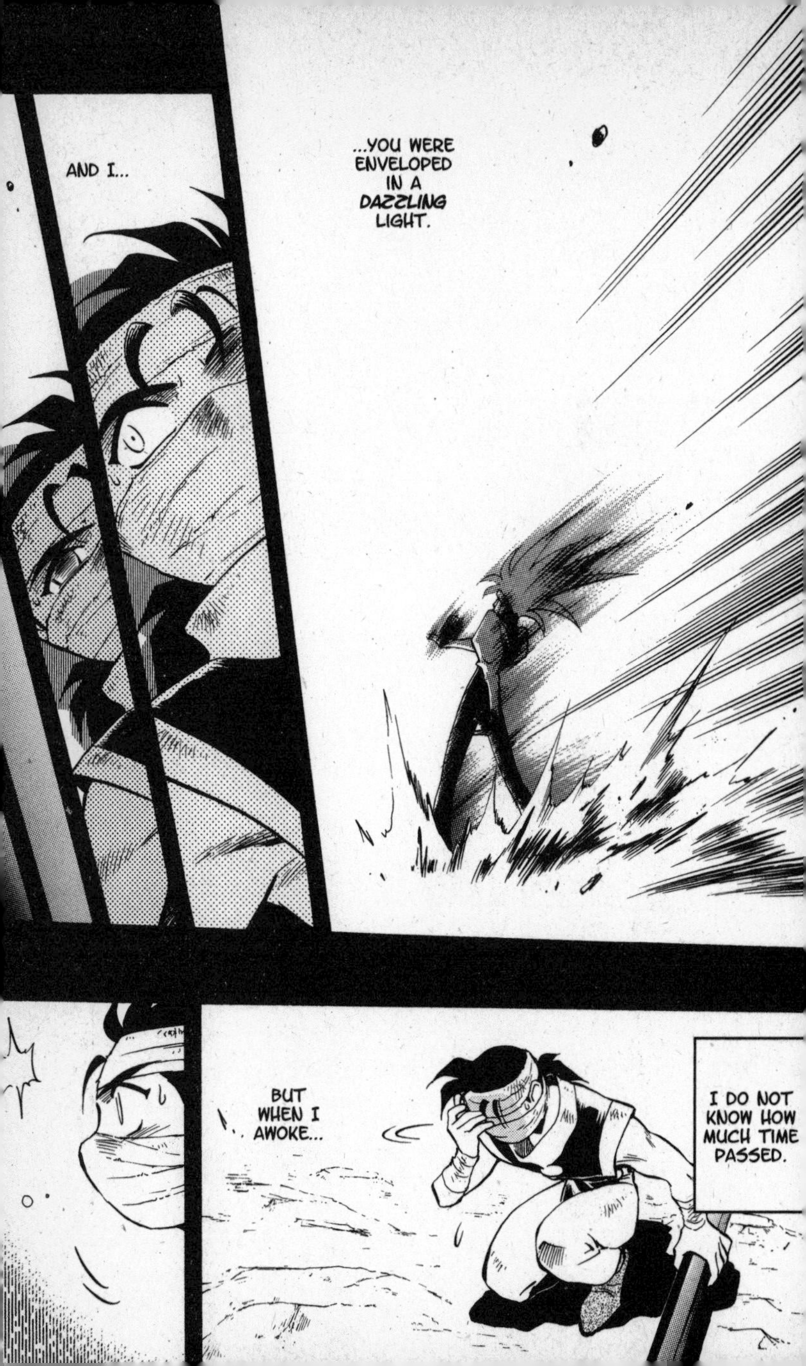
...YOU WERE ENVELOPED IN A DAZZLING LIGHT.
AND I...
I DO NOT KNOW HOW MUCH TIME PASSED.
BUT WHEN I AWOKE...

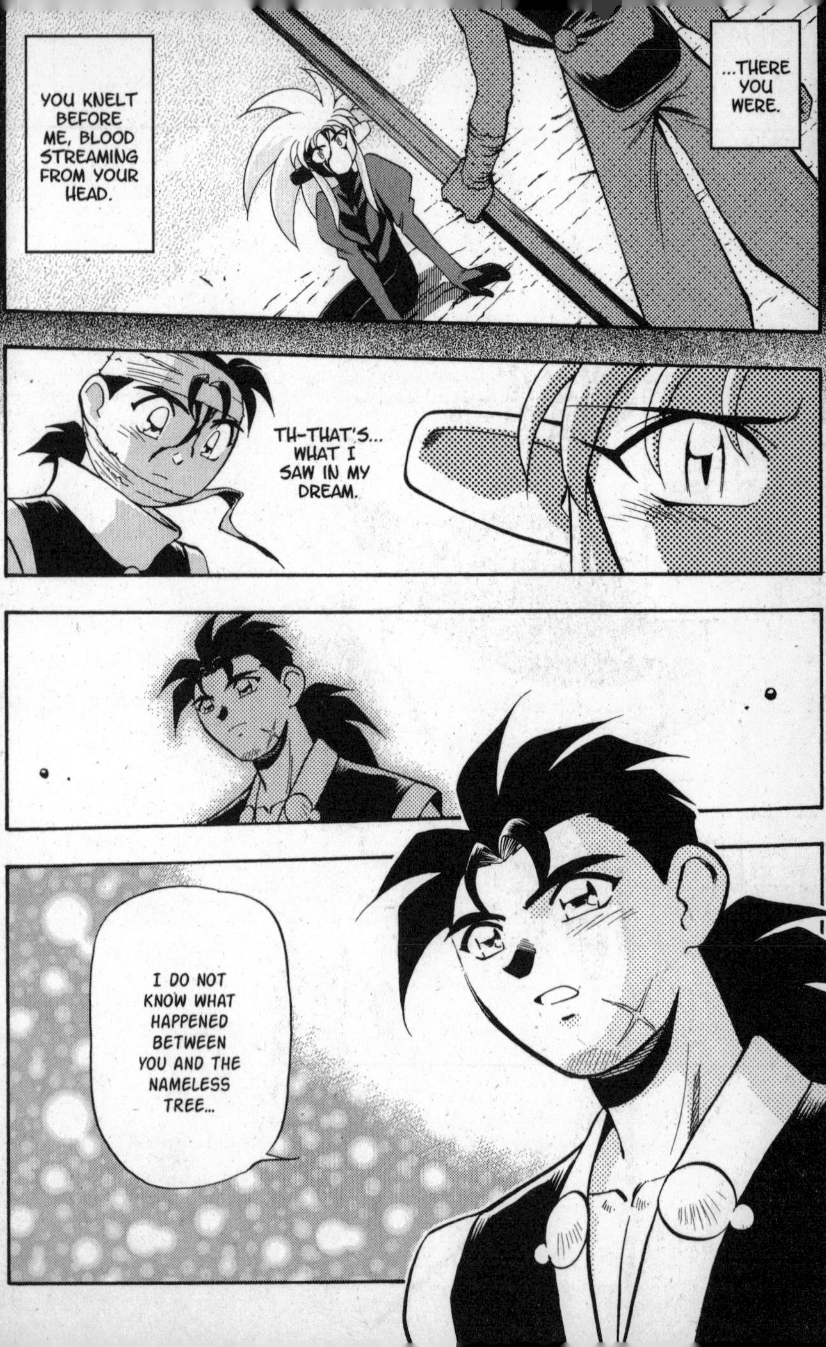
...THERE YOU WERE.
YOU KNELT BEFORE ME, BLOOD STREAMING FROM YOUR HEAD.
TH-THAT'S... WHAT I SAW IN MY DREAM.
I DO NOT KNOW WHAT HAPPENED BETWEEN YOU AND THE NAMELESS TREE...

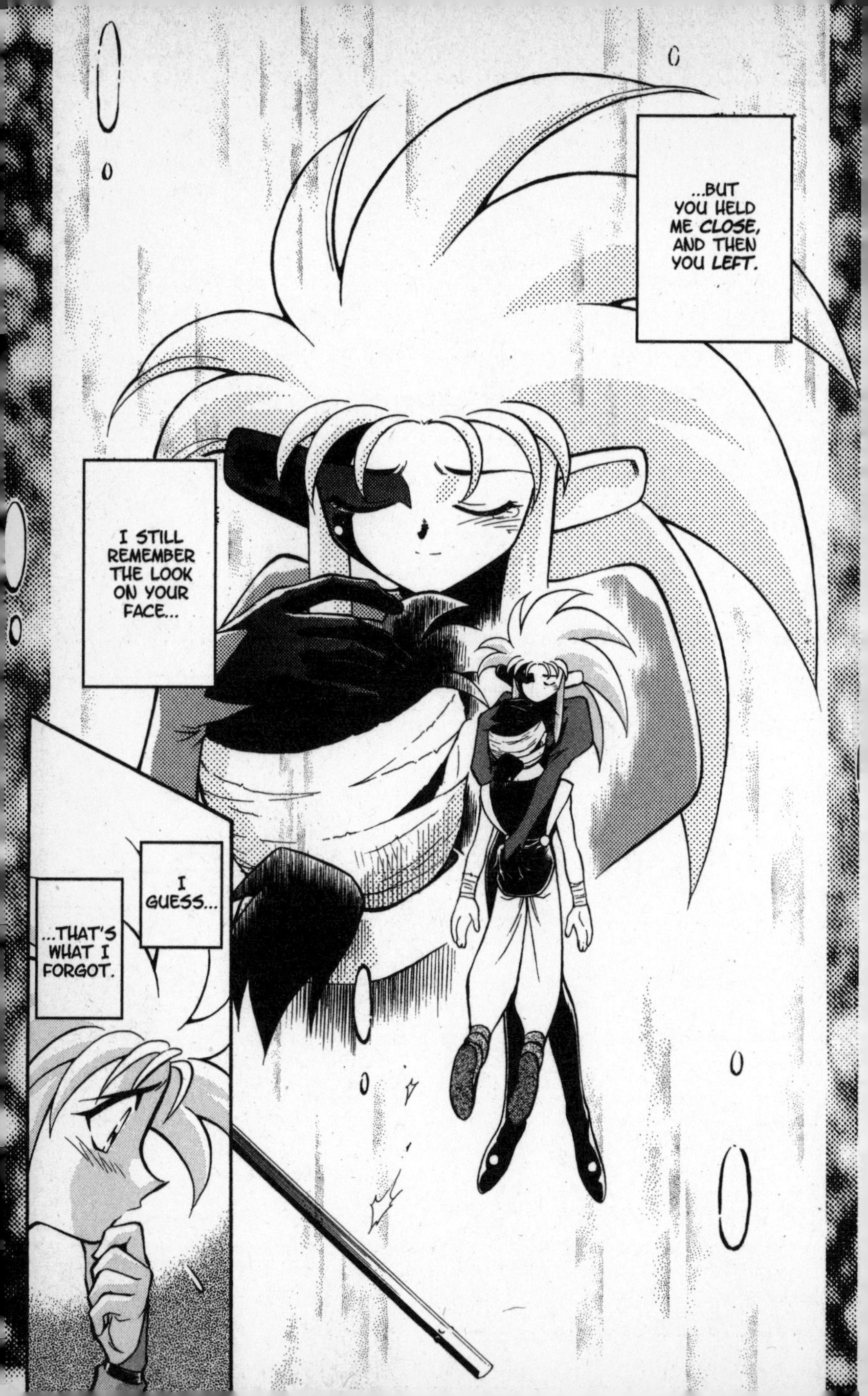
...BUT YOU HELD ME CLOSE, AND THEN YOU LEFT.
I STILL REMEMBER THE LOOK ON YOUR FACE...
I GUESS...
...THAT'S WHAT I FORGOT.

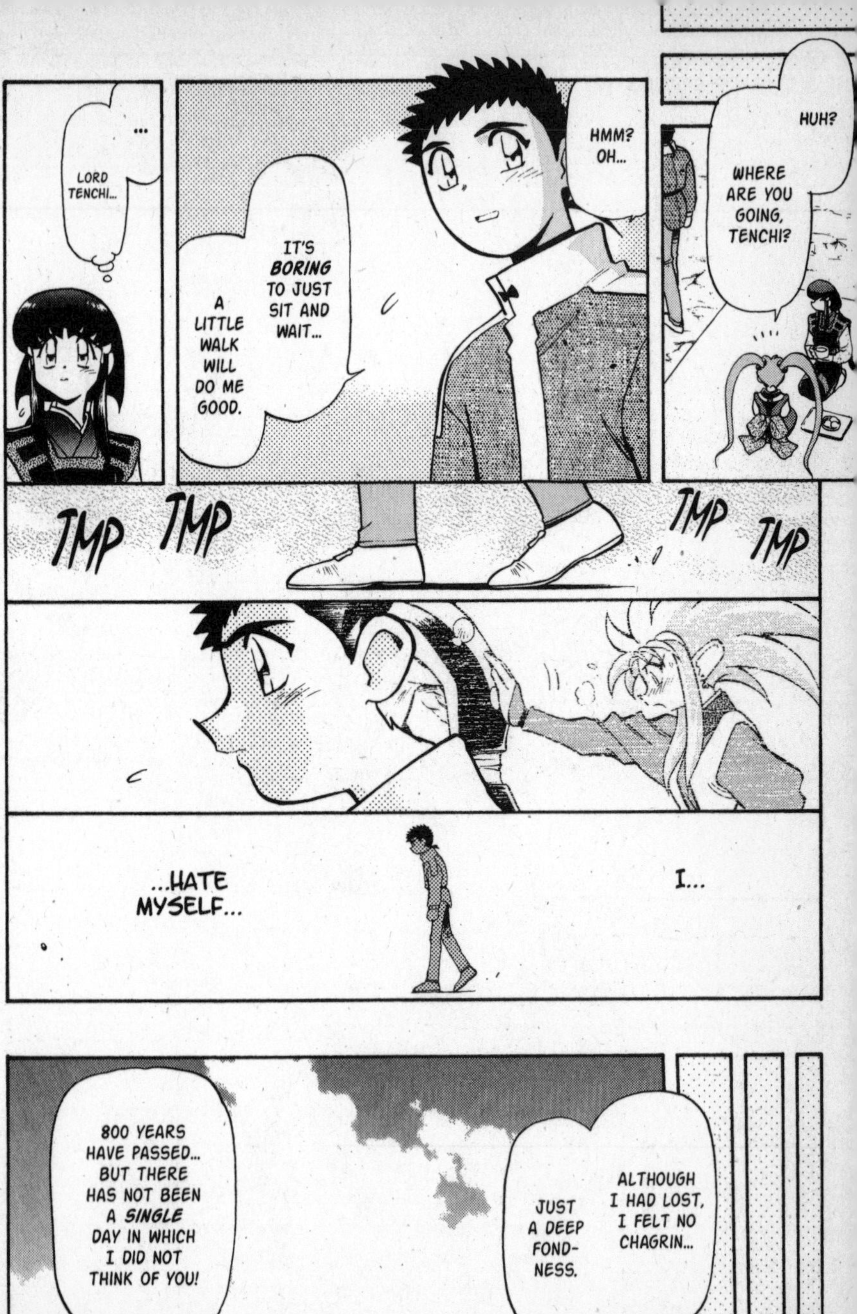
HUH?
WHERE ARE YOU GOING, TENCHI?
HMM? OH...
IT'S *BORING* TO JUST SIT AND WAIT...
A LITTLE WALK WILL DO ME GOOD.
...
LORD TENCHI...
TMP
TMP
TMP
TMP
I...
...HATE MYSELF...
ALTHOUGH I HAD LOST, I FELT NO CHAGRIN...
JUST A DEEP FOND-NESS.
800 YEARS HAVE PASSED... BUT THERE HAS NOT BEEN A *SINGLE* DAY IN WHICH I DID NOT THINK OF YOU!

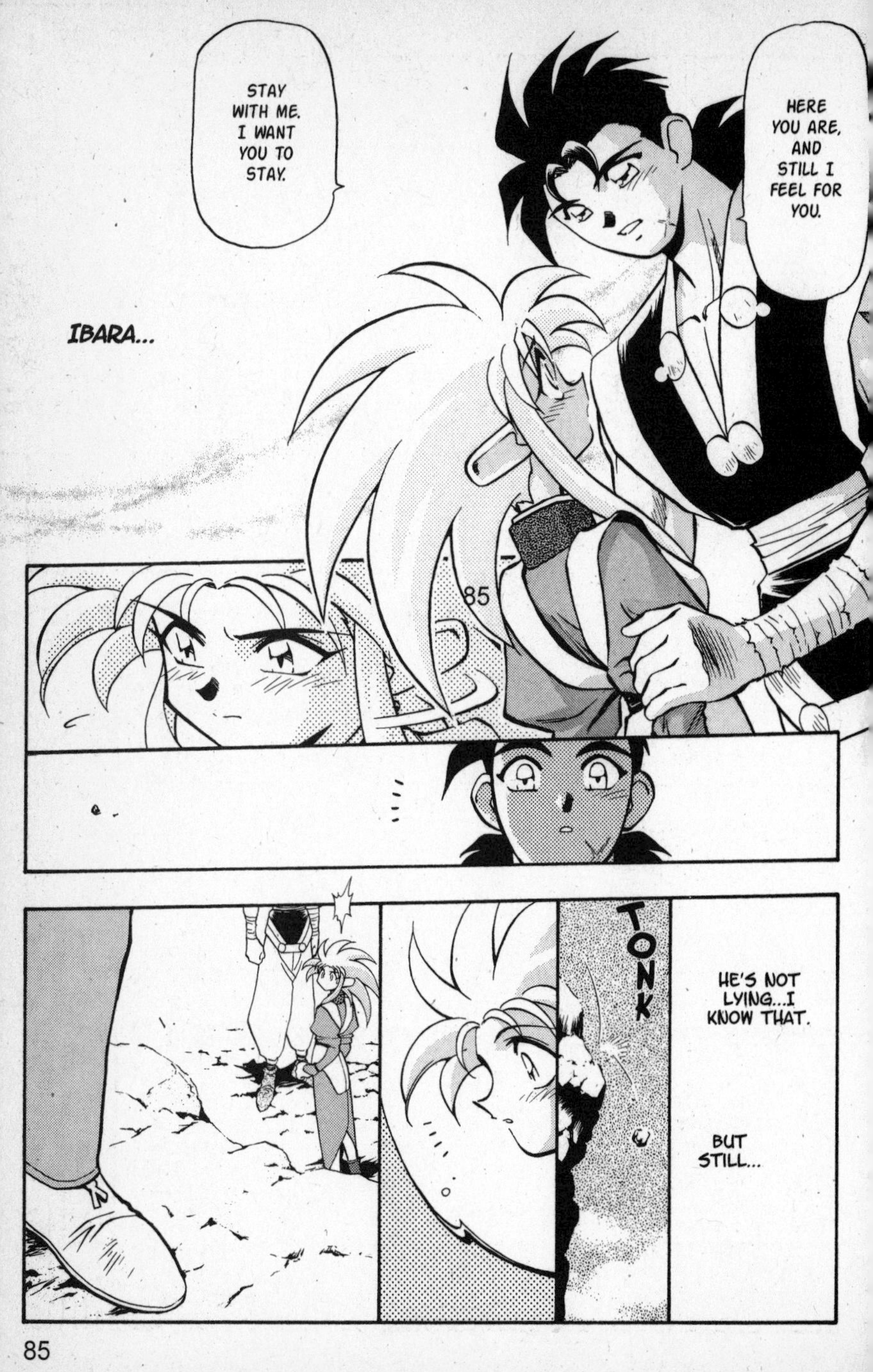
HERE YOU ARE, AND STILL I FEEL FOR YOU.
STAY WITH ME. I WANT YOU TO STAY.
IBARA...
HE'S NOT LYING...I KNOW THAT.
BUT STILL...
TONK

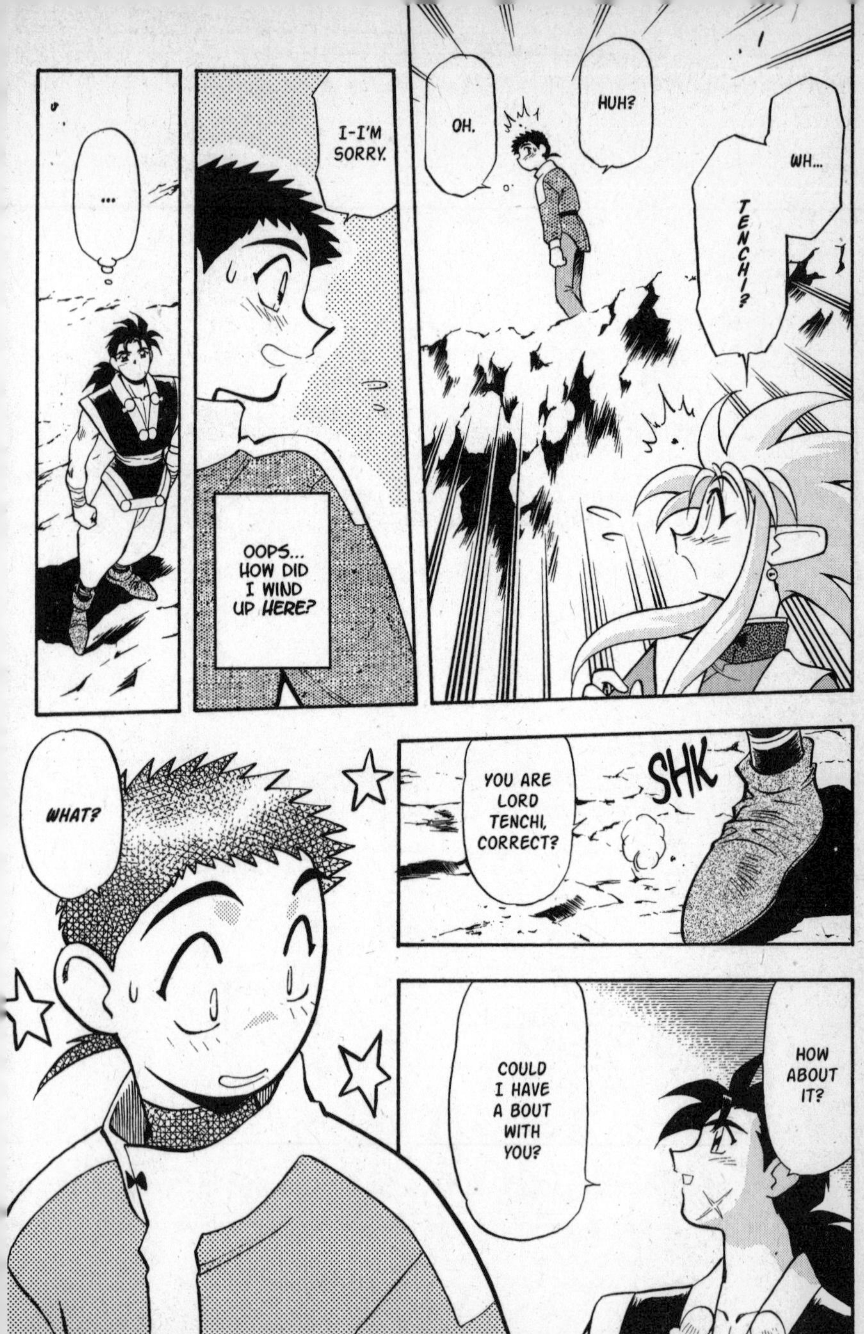
WH... TENCHI?
HUH?
OH.
I-I'M SORRY.
OOPS... HOW DID I WIND UP *HERE?*
...
SHK
YOU ARE LORD TENCHI, CORRECT?
HOW ABOUT IT?
COULD I HAVE A BOUT WITH YOU?
WHAT?

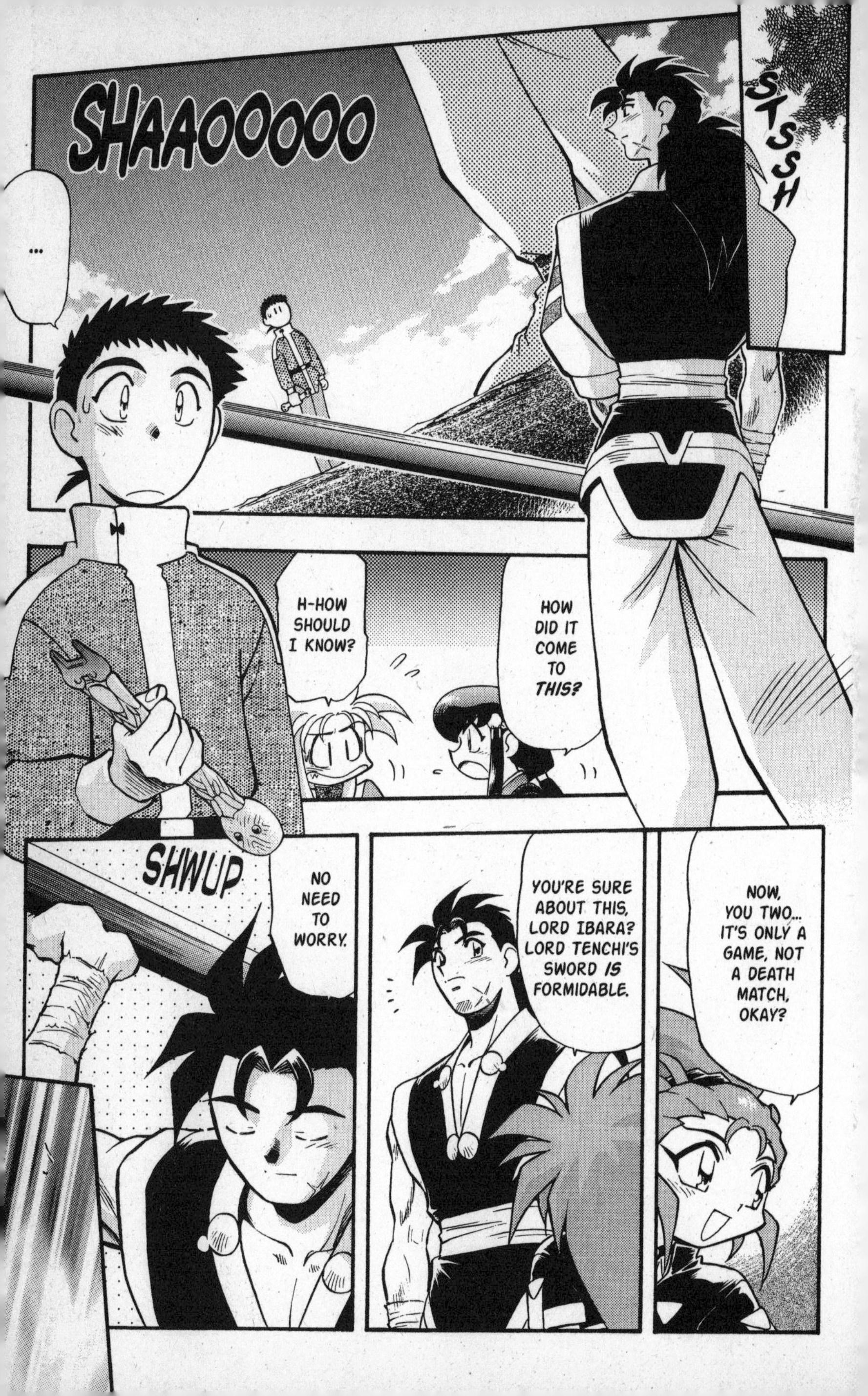
STSSH
SHAAOOOOO
...
HOW DID IT COME TO *THIS?*
H-HOW SHOULD I KNOW?
NOW, YOU TWO... IT'S ONLY A GAME, NOT A DEATH MATCH, OKAY?
YOU'RE SURE ABOUT THIS, LORD IBARA? LORD TENCHI'S SWORD *IS* FORMIDABLE.
SHWUP
NO NEED TO WORRY.

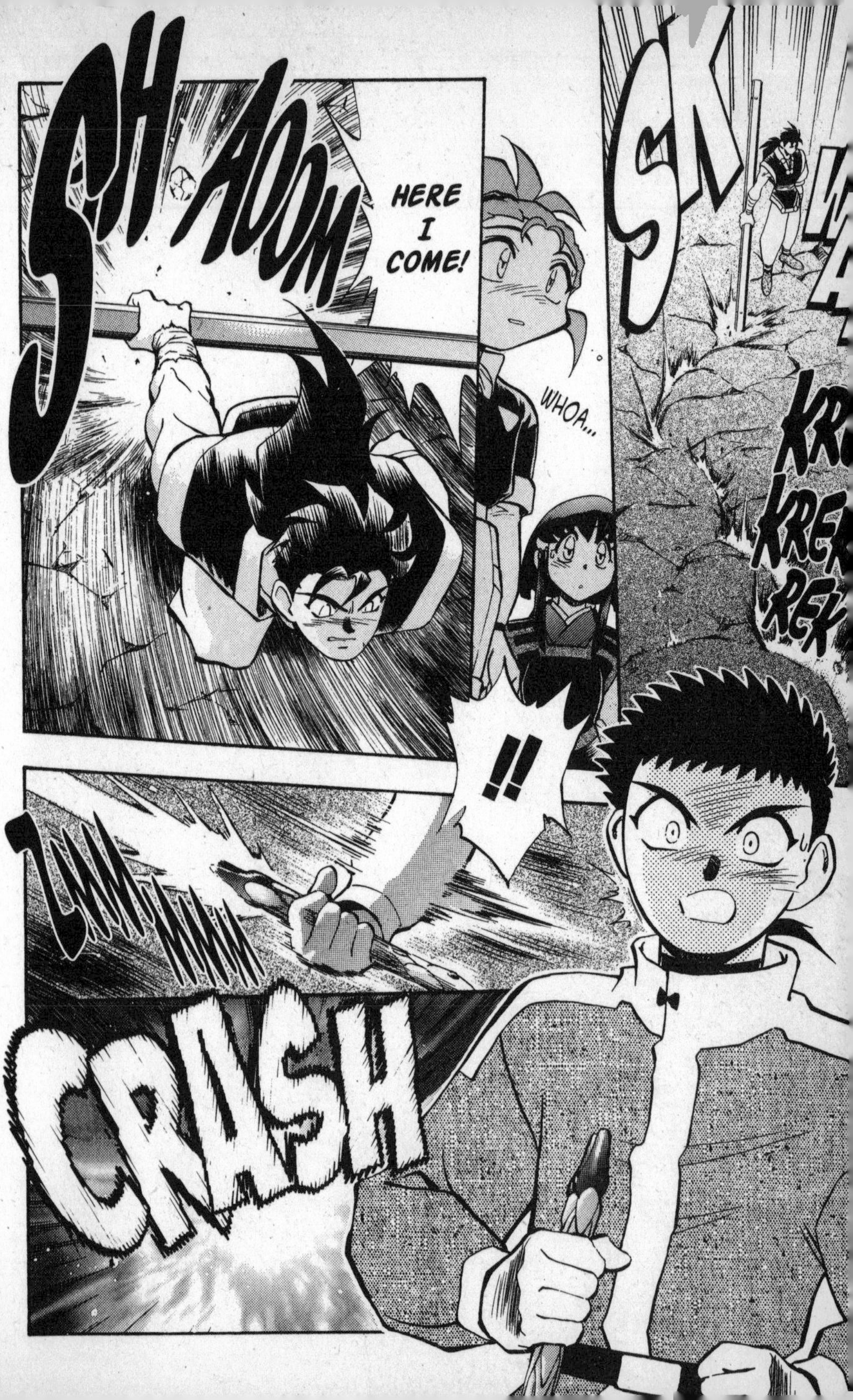
SK
WHOA...
SHAOOM
HERE I COME!
!!
ZWMMMM
CRASH

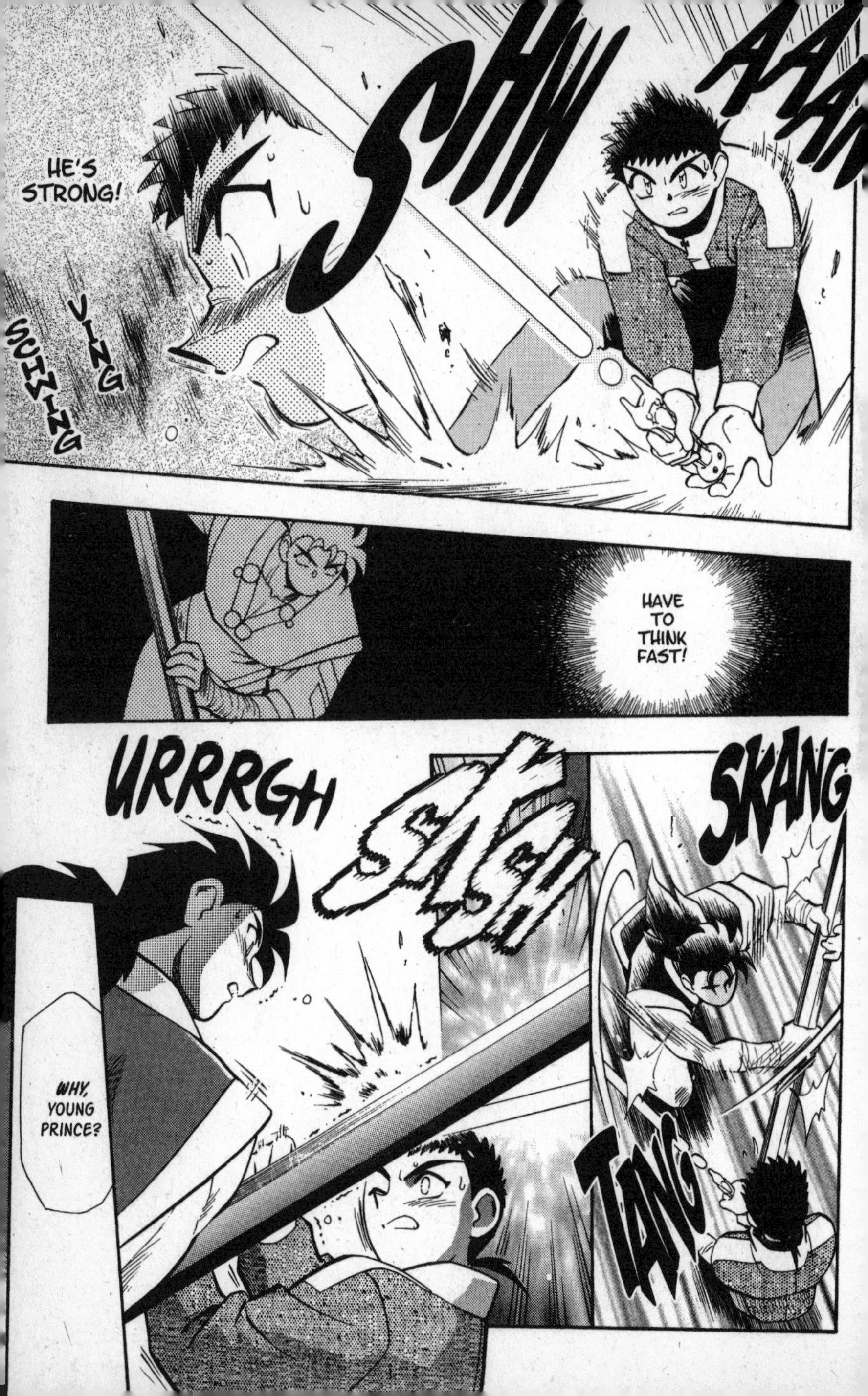
SCHW
AAA
HE'S STRONG!
VING
SCHWING
HAVE TO THINK FAST!
SKANG
TANG
URRRGH
WHY, YOUNG PRINCE?

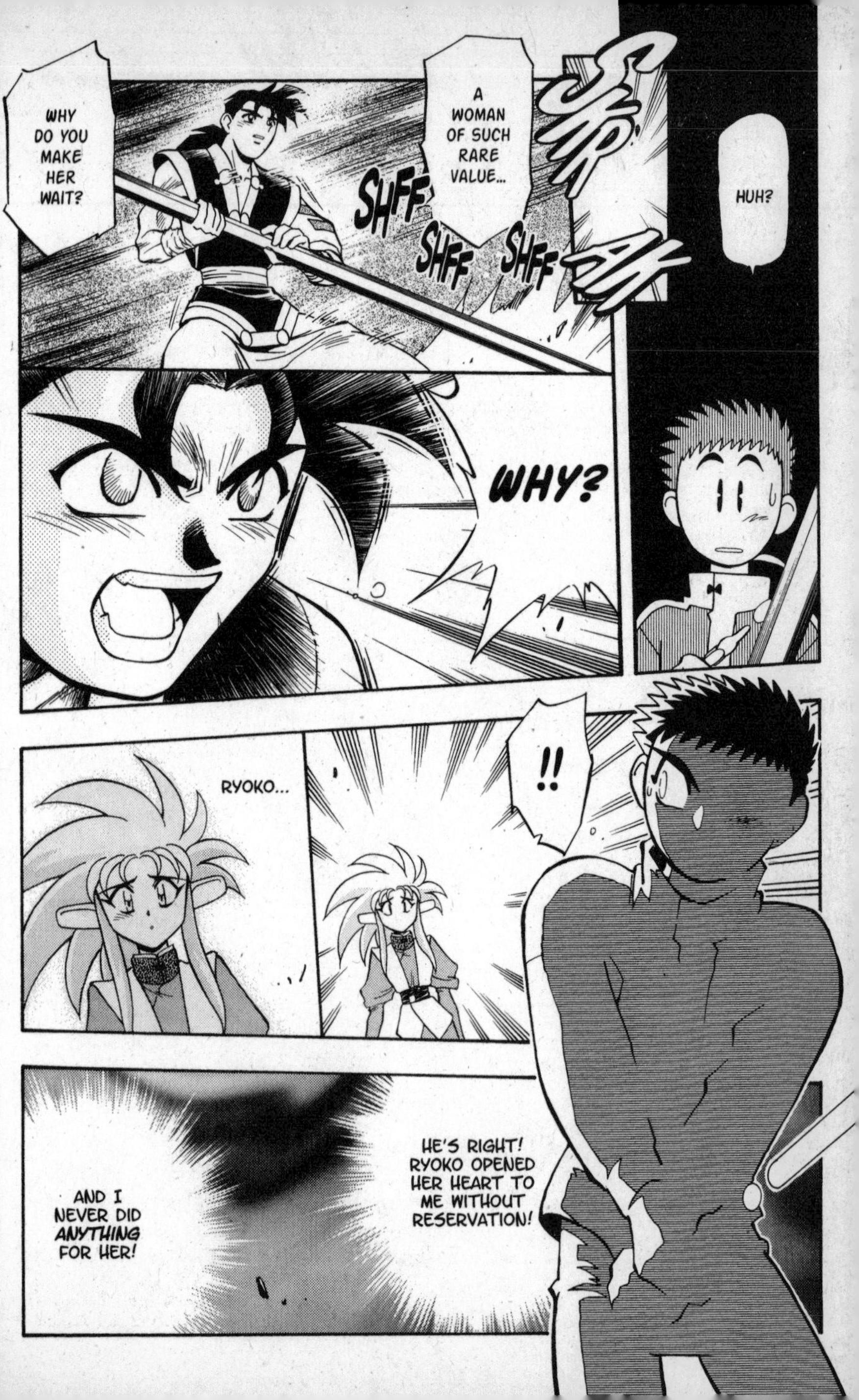
SKRAK
HUH?
A WOMAN OF SUCH RARE VALUE...
WHY DO YOU MAKE HER WAIT?
SHFF
SHFF
SHFF
WHY?
!!
RYOKO...
HE'S RIGHT! RYOKO OPENED HER HEART TO ME WITHOUT RESERVATION!
AND I NEVER DID *ANYTHING* FOR HER!

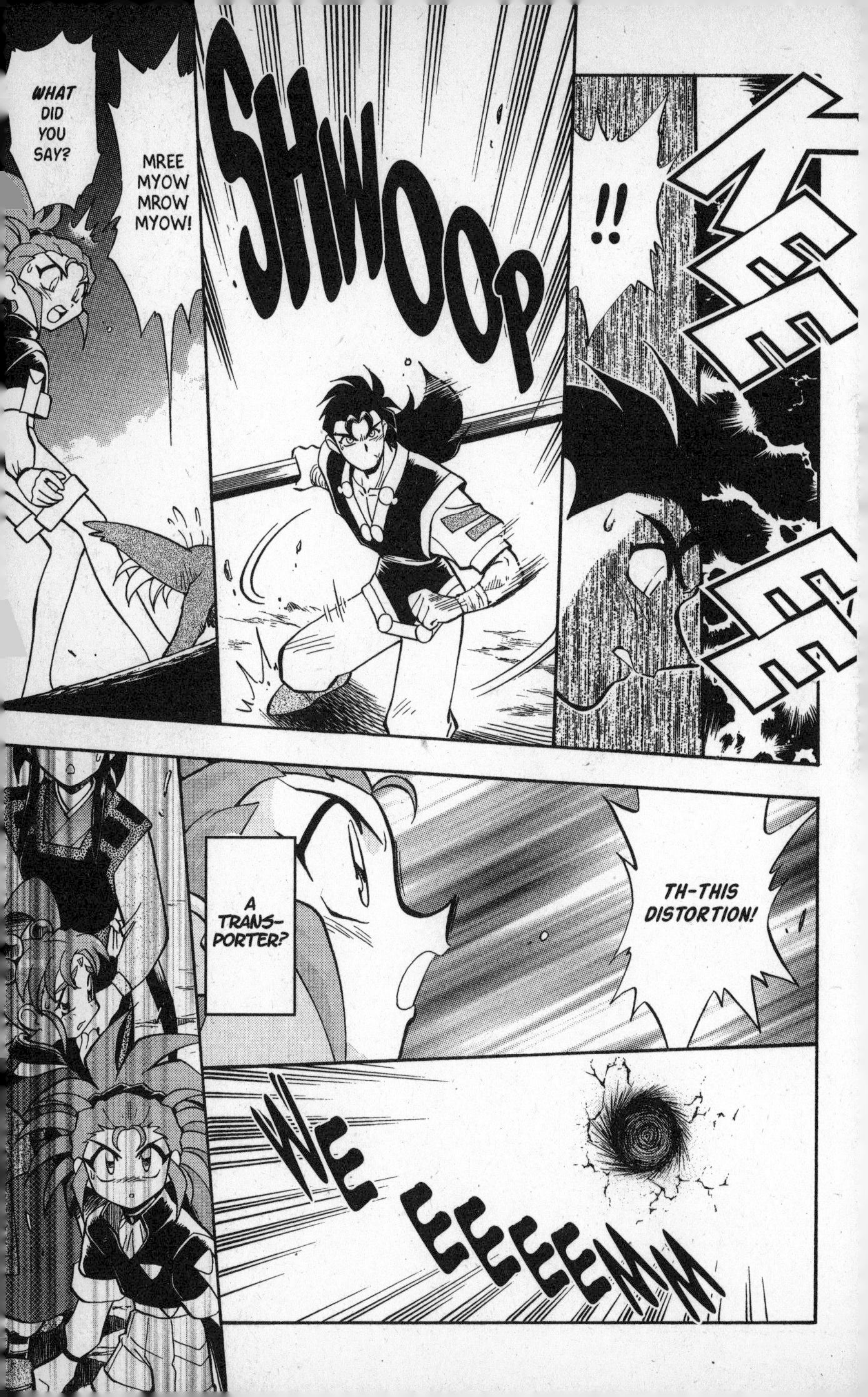
!!
SHWOOP
WHAT DID YOU SAY?
MREE MYOW MROW MYOW!
TH-THIS DISTORTION!
A TRANS-PORTER?
WEEEEEEMM

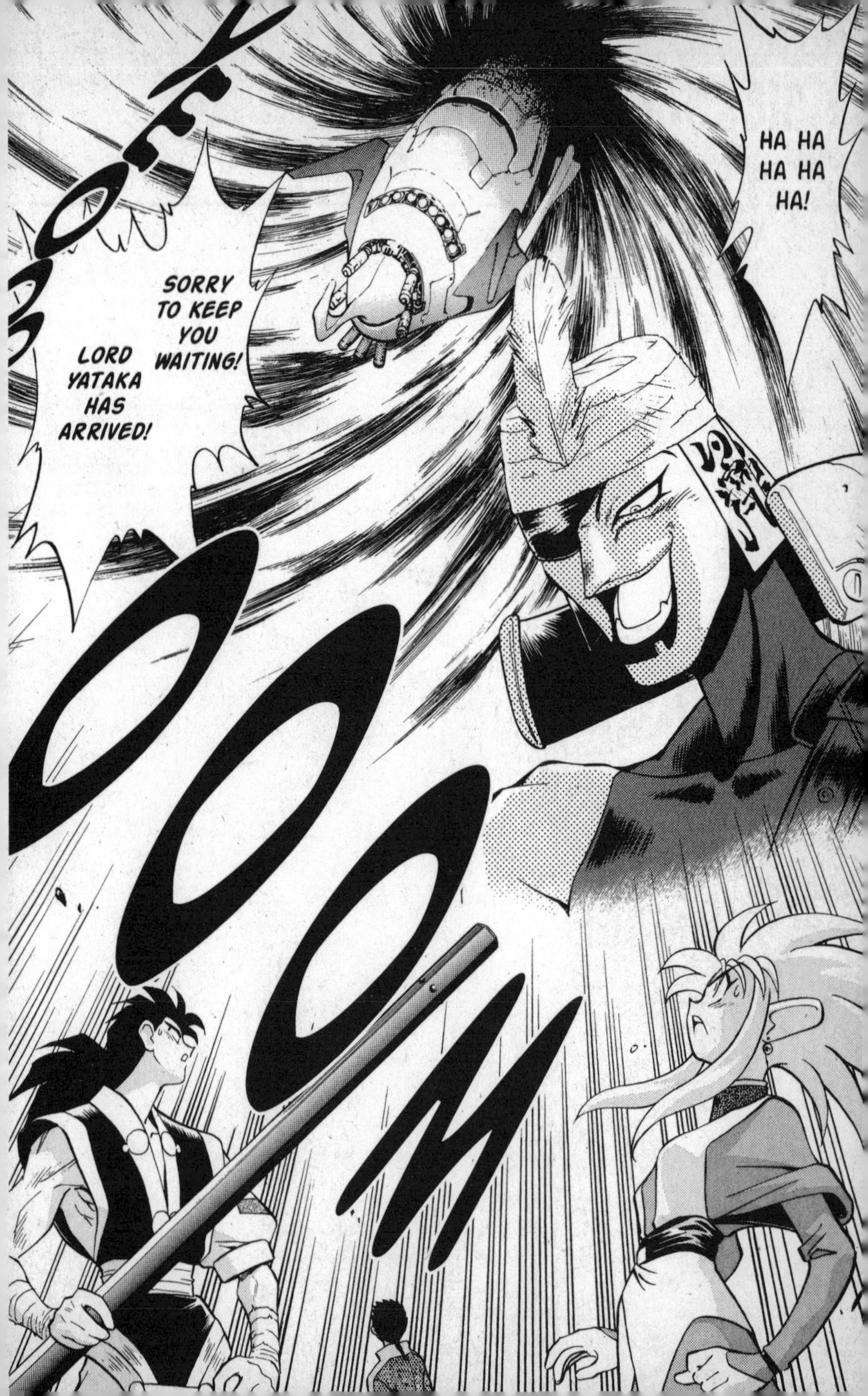
HA HA HA HA HA!
SORRY TO KEEP YOU WAITING!
LORD YATAKA HAS ARRIVED!
YEOOOOOOOM

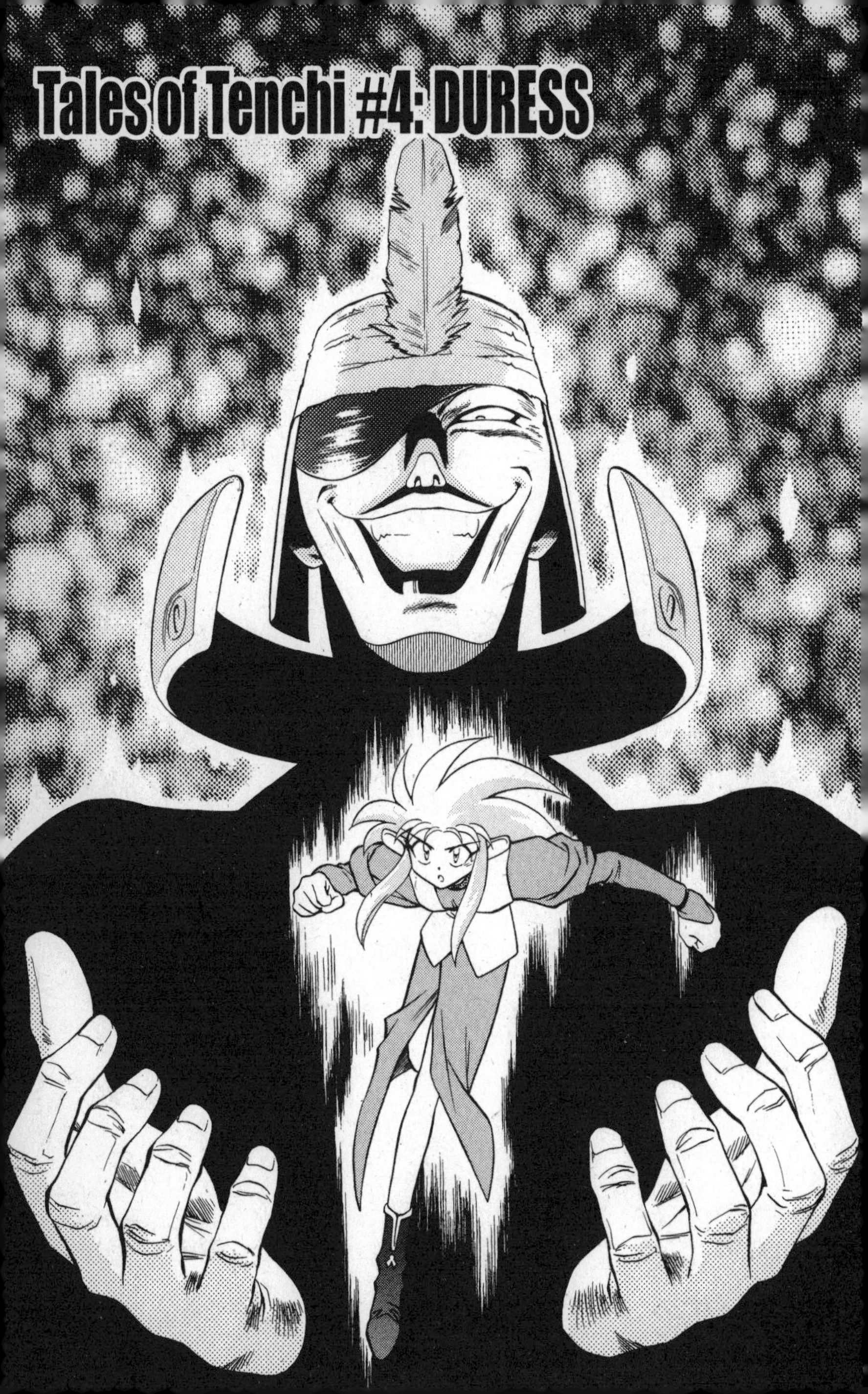
Tales of Tenchi #4: DURESS

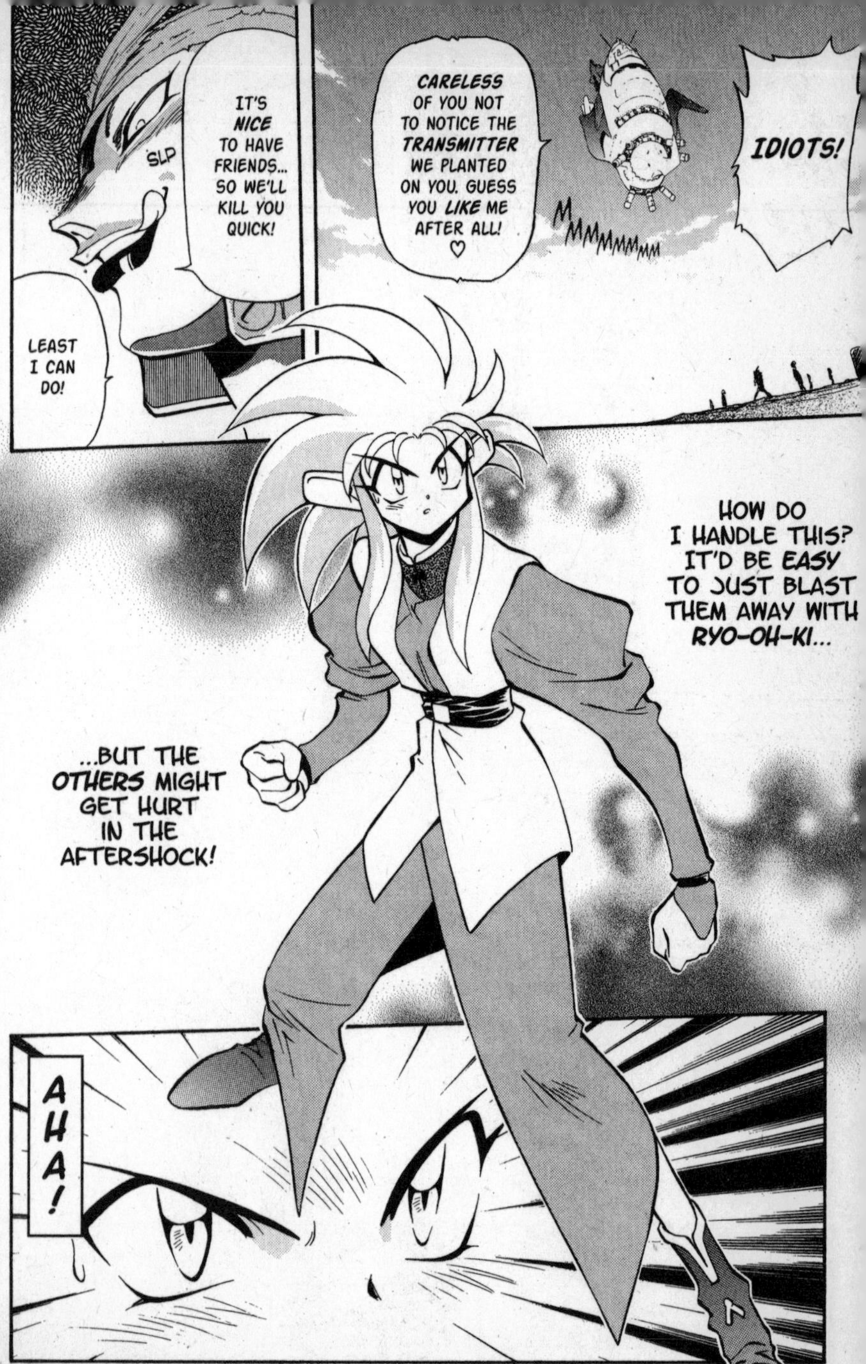
IDIOTS!
CARELESS OF YOU NOT TO NOTICE THE TRANSMITTER WE PLANTED ON YOU. GUESS YOU LIKE ME AFTER ALL! ♡
MMMMMMMMM
IT'S NICE TO HAVE FRIENDS... SO WE'LL KILL YOU QUICK!
SLP
LEAST I CAN DO!
HOW DO I HANDLE THIS? IT'D BE EASY TO JUST BLAST THEM AWAY WITH RYO-OH-KI...
...BUT THE OTHERS MIGHT GET HURT IN THE AFTERSHOCK!
AHA!

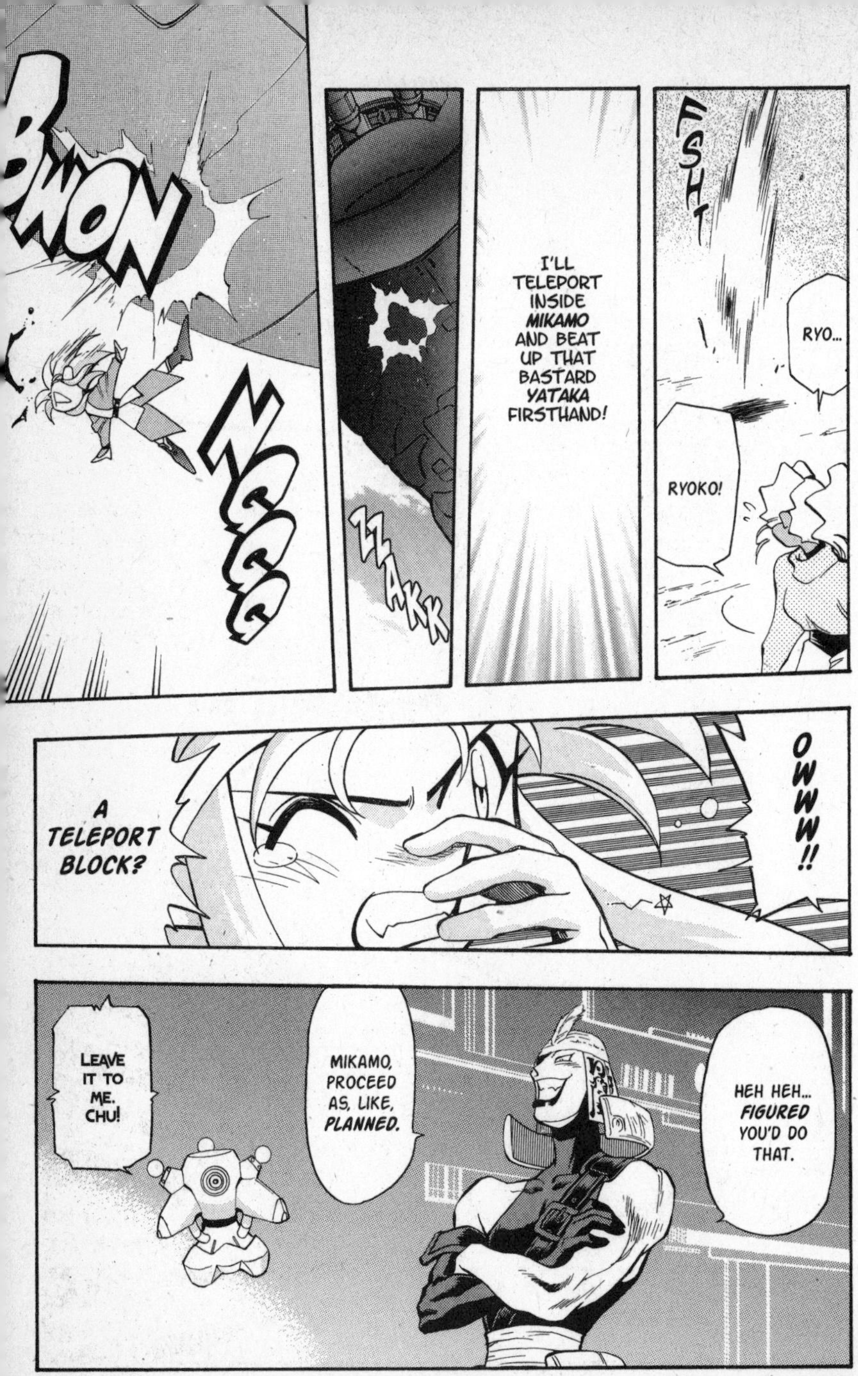
FSHT
RYO...
RYOKO!
I'LL TELEPORT INSIDE MIKAMO AND BEAT UP THAT BASTARD YATAKA FIRSTHAND!
ZZAKK
BWON
NGGG
OWWW!!
A TELEPORT BLOCK?
HEH HEH... FIGURED YOU'D DO THAT.
MIKAMO, PROCEED AS, LIKE, PLANNED.
LEAVE IT TO ME. CHU!

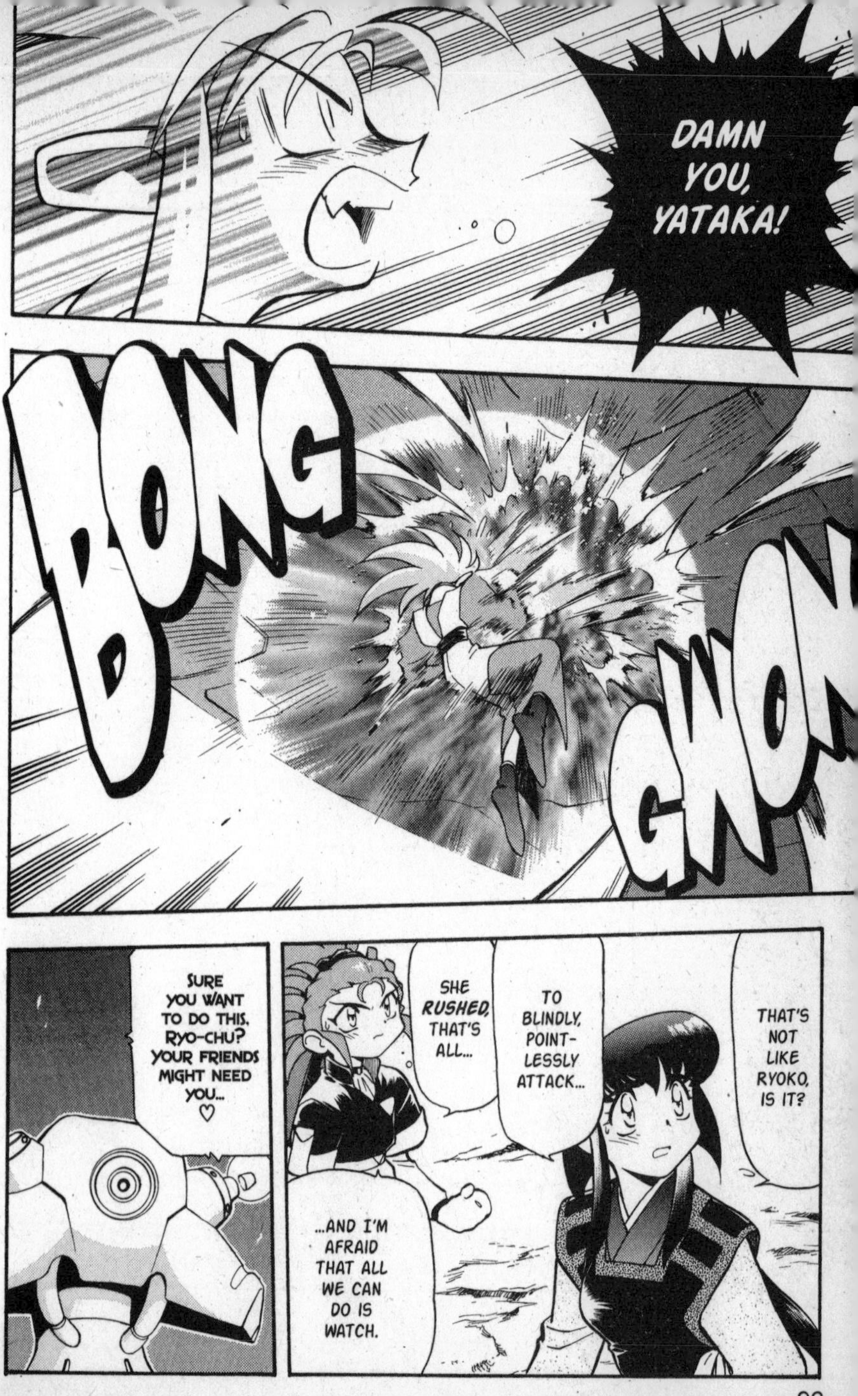
DAMN YOU, YATAKA!
BONG
GWON
THAT'S NOT LIKE RYOKO, IS IT?
TO BLINDLY, POINT-LESSLY ATTACK...
SHE *RUSHED*, THAT'S ALL...
...AND I'M AFRAID THAT ALL WE CAN DO IS WATCH.
SURE YOU WANT TO DO THIS, RYO-CHU? YOUR FRIENDS MIGHT NEED YOU... ♡

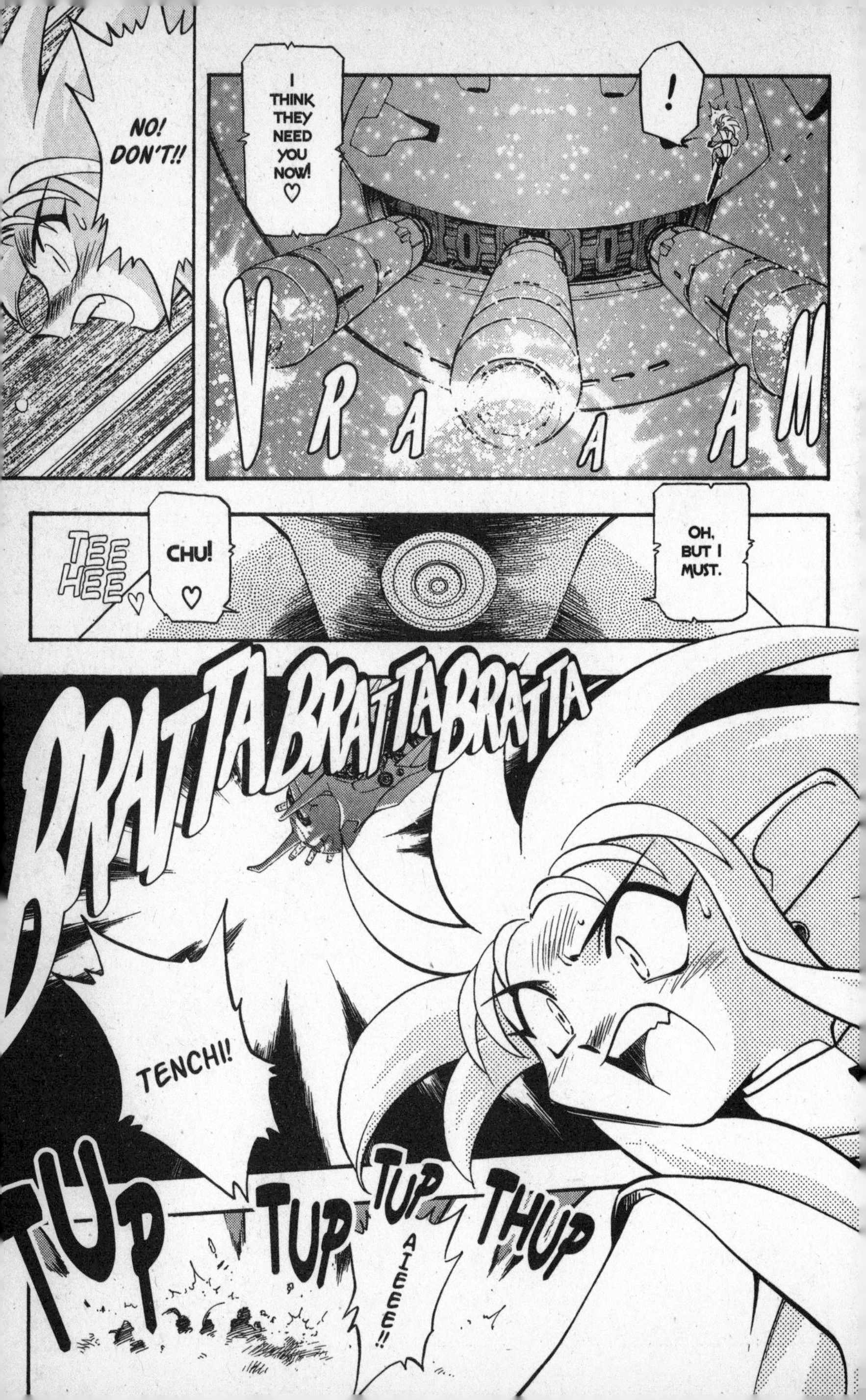
!
I THINK THEY NEED YOU NOW! ♡
VRAAAM
NO! DON'T!!
OH, BUT I MUST.
CHU! ♡
TEE HEE ♡
BRATTA BRATTA BRATTA
TENCHI!
TUP TUP TUP THUP
AIEEEE!!

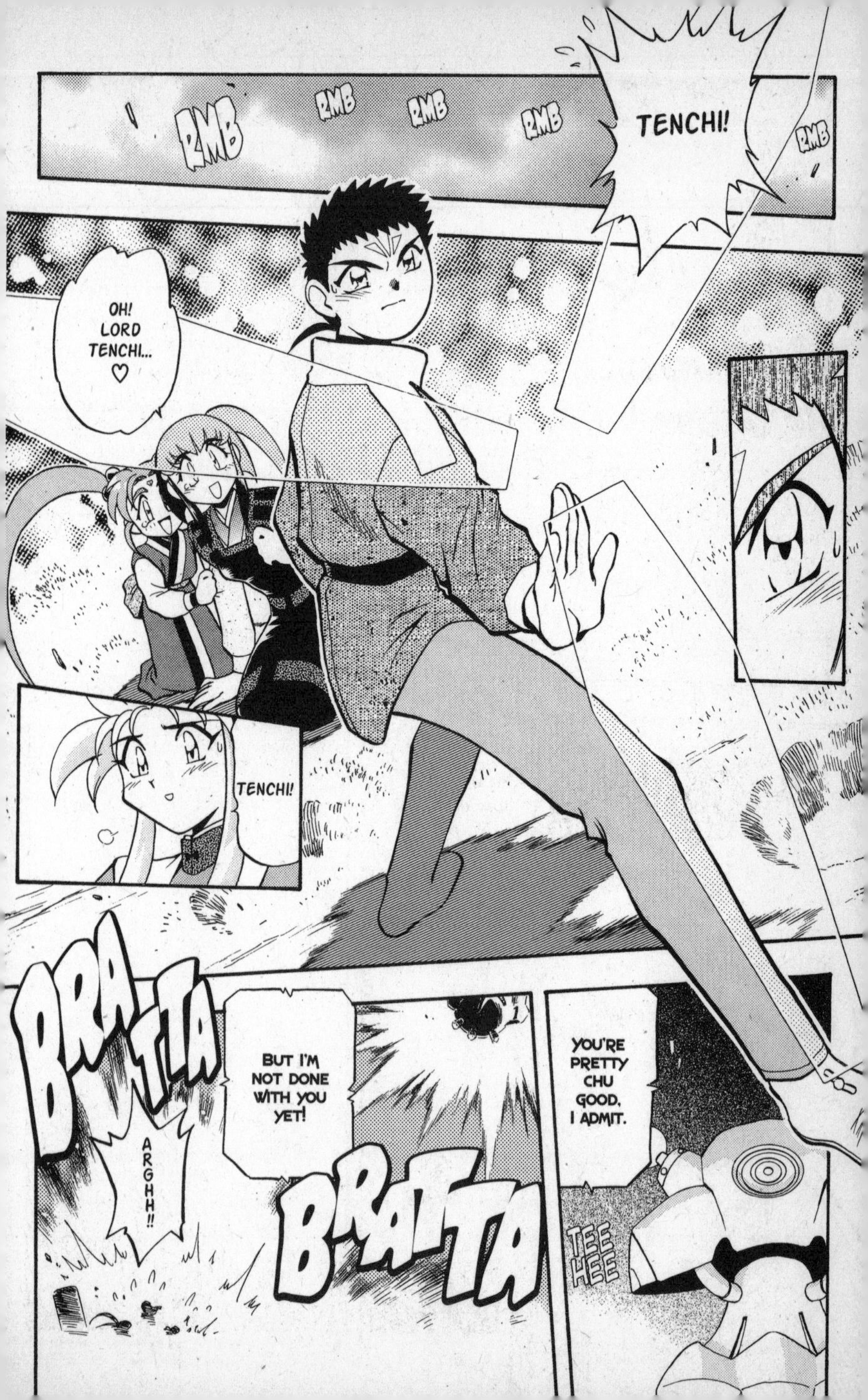
TENCHI!
RMB
RMB
RMB
RMB
RMB
OH! LORD TENCHI... ♡
TENCHI!
YOU'RE PRETTY CHU GOOD, I ADMIT.
TEE HEE
BRATTA
BUT I'M NOT DONE WITH YOU YET!
BRATTA
ARGHH!!

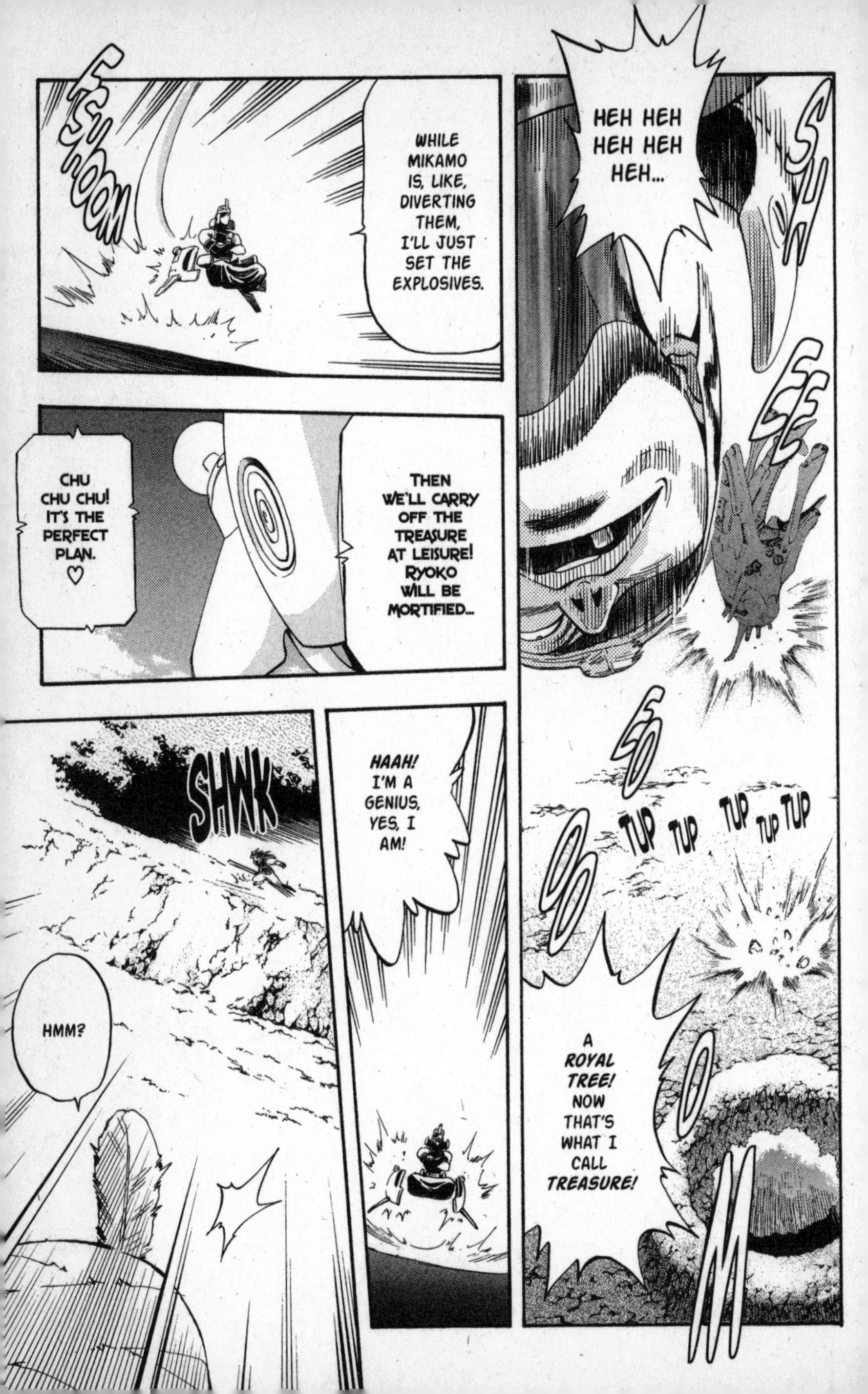
HEH HEH HEH HEH HEH...
TUP TUP TUP TUP TUP
A *ROYAL TREE!* NOW THAT'S WHAT I CALL *TREASURE!*
FSHOOM
WHILE MIKAMO IS, LIKE, DIVERTING THEM, I'LL JUST SET THE EXPLOSIVES.
THEN WE'LL CARRY OFF THE TREASURE AT LEISURE! RYOKO WILL BE MORTIFIED...
CHU CHU CHU! IT'S THE PERFECT PLAN. ♡
HAAH! I'M A GENIUS, YES, I AM!
SHWK
HMM?

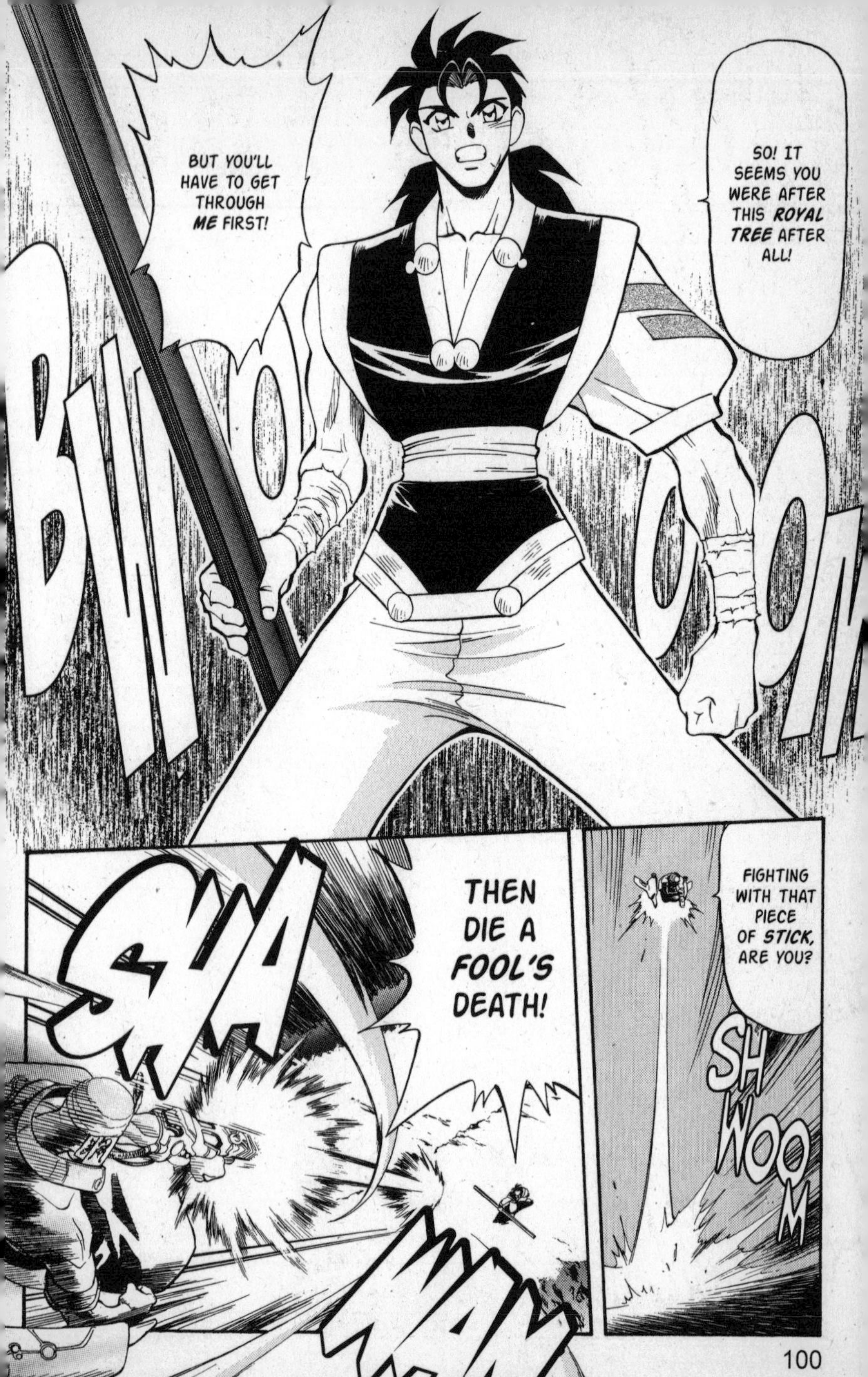

SO! IT SEEMS YOU WERE AFTER THIS *ROYAL TREE* AFTER ALL!
BUT YOU'LL HAVE TO GET THROUGH *ME* FIRST!
BWOOOM
FIGHTING WITH THAT PIECE OF *STICK,* ARE YOU?
SHWOOM
THEN DIE A *FOOL'S* DEATH!
GWA
WAM

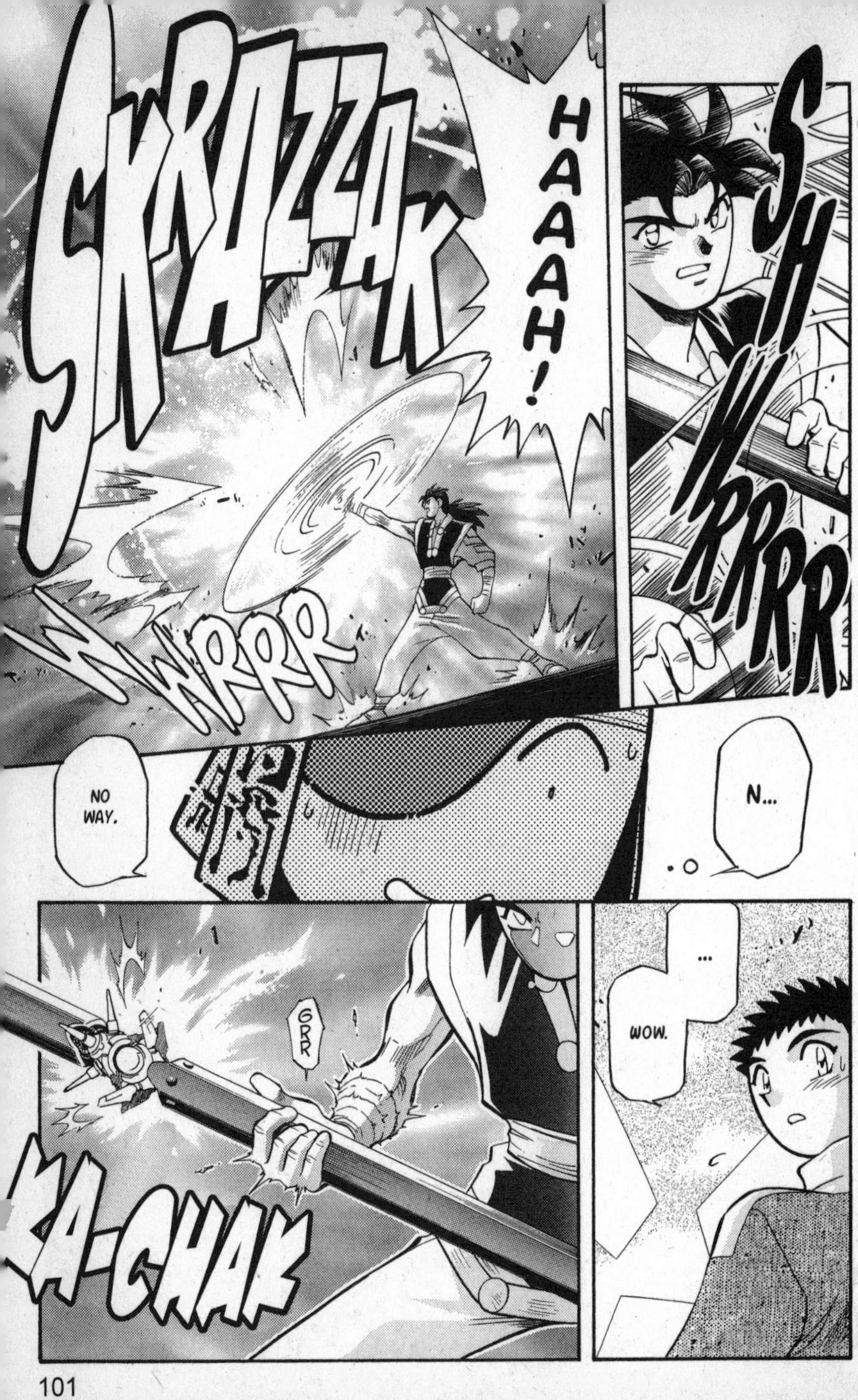
SHWRRRR
HAAAAH!
SKRAZZAK
WRRR
N...
NO WAY.
... WOW.
GRR
KA-CHAK

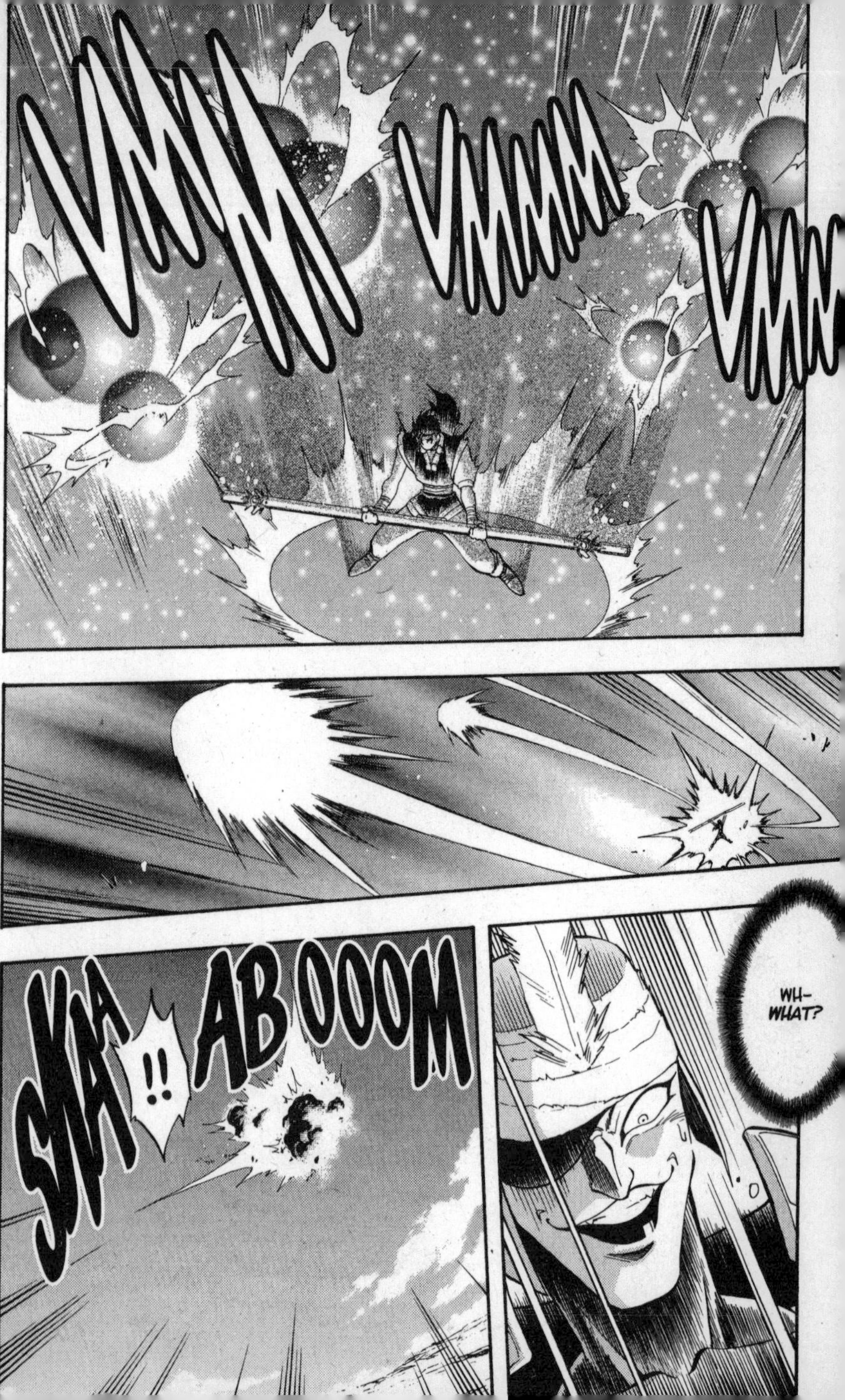
VMMM VMMMM VMM
WH- WHAT?
SKA!! ABOOOM

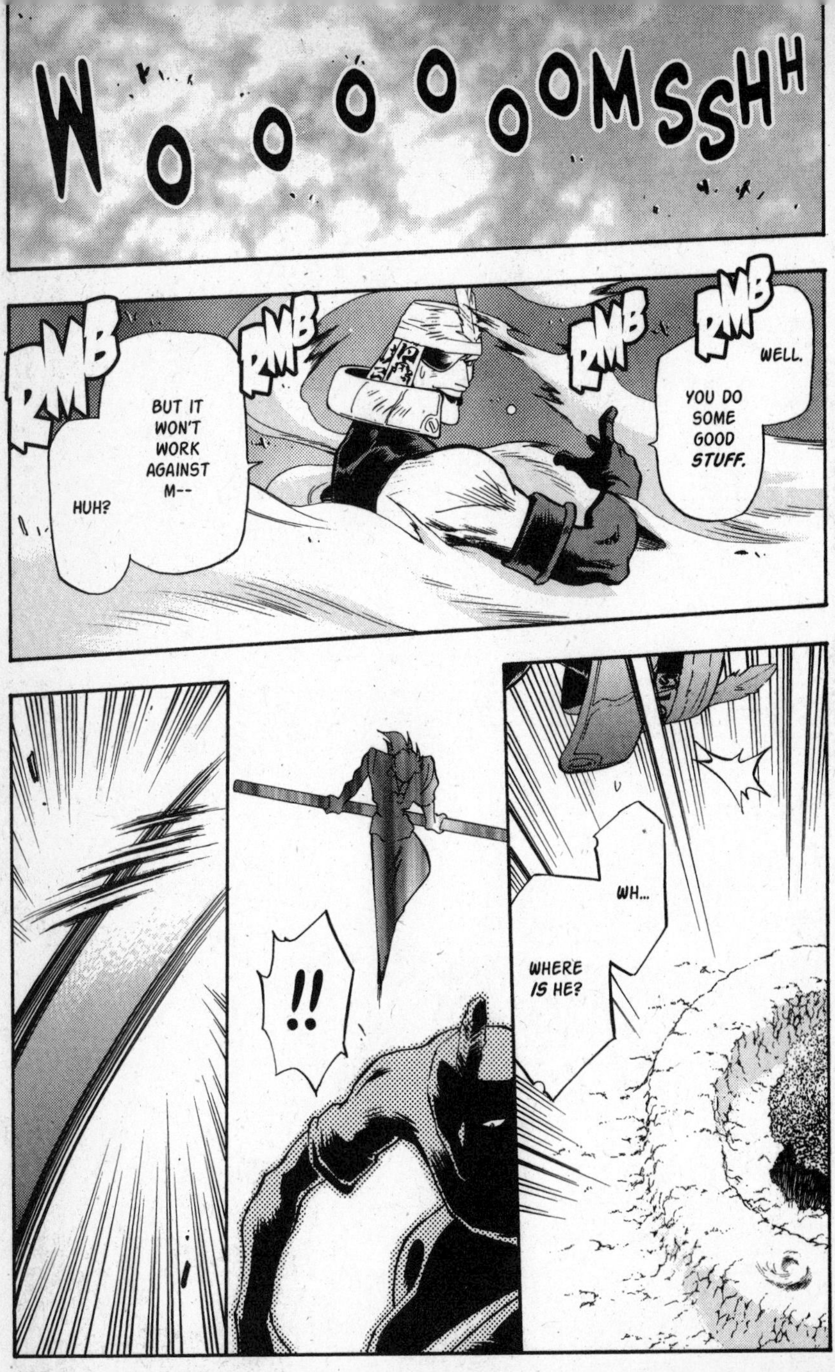
WOOOOOOMSSHH
RMB RMB
WELL.
YOU DO SOME GOOD STUFF.
RMB
RMB
BUT IT WON'T WORK AGAINST M--
HUH?
WH...
WHERE IS HE?
!!

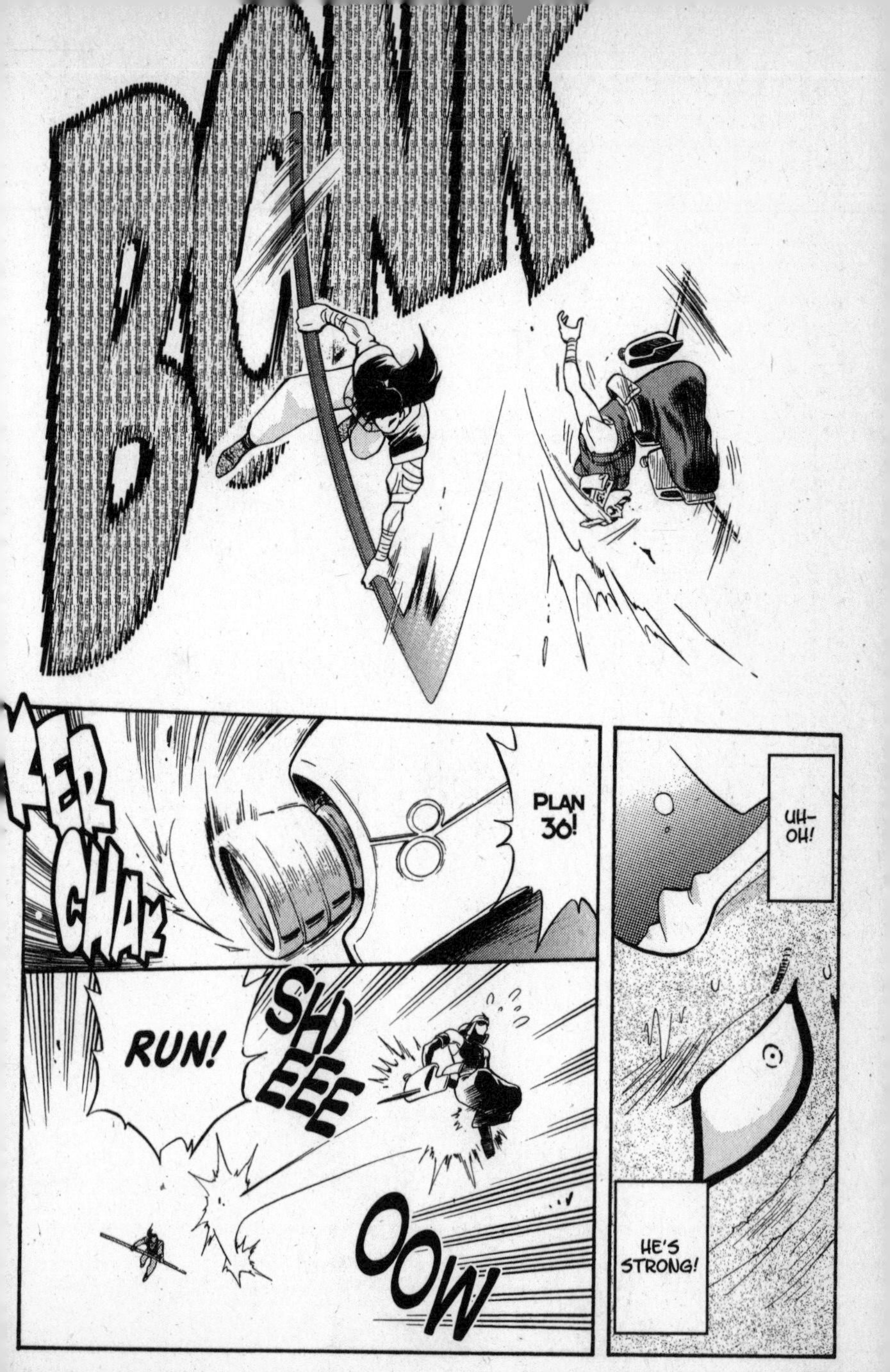
BONK
UH-OH!
HE'S STRONG!
PLAN 36!
KER CHAK
SHIEEE
RUN!
OOW

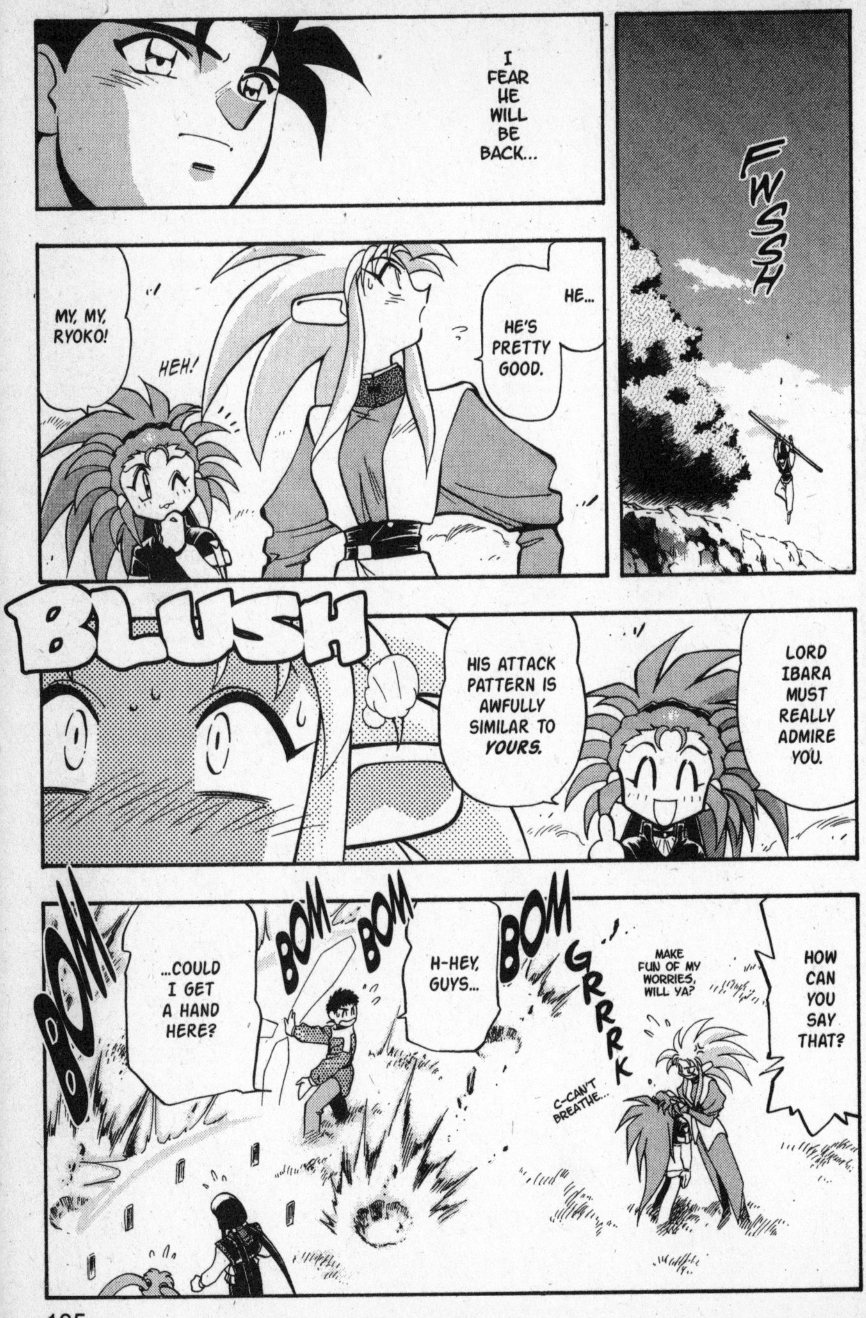
FWSSH
I FEAR HE WILL BE BACK...
HE...
HE'S PRETTY GOOD.
HEH!
MY, MY, RYOKO!
LORD IBARA MUST REALLY ADMIRE YOU.
HIS ATTACK PATTERN IS AWFULLY SIMILAR TO *YOURS.*
BLUSH
HOW CAN YOU SAY THAT?
MAKE FUN OF MY WORRIES, WILL YA?
GRRRK
C-CAN'T BREATHE...
BOM
H-HEY, GUYS...
BOM
BOM
...COULD I GET A HAND HERE?
BOOM

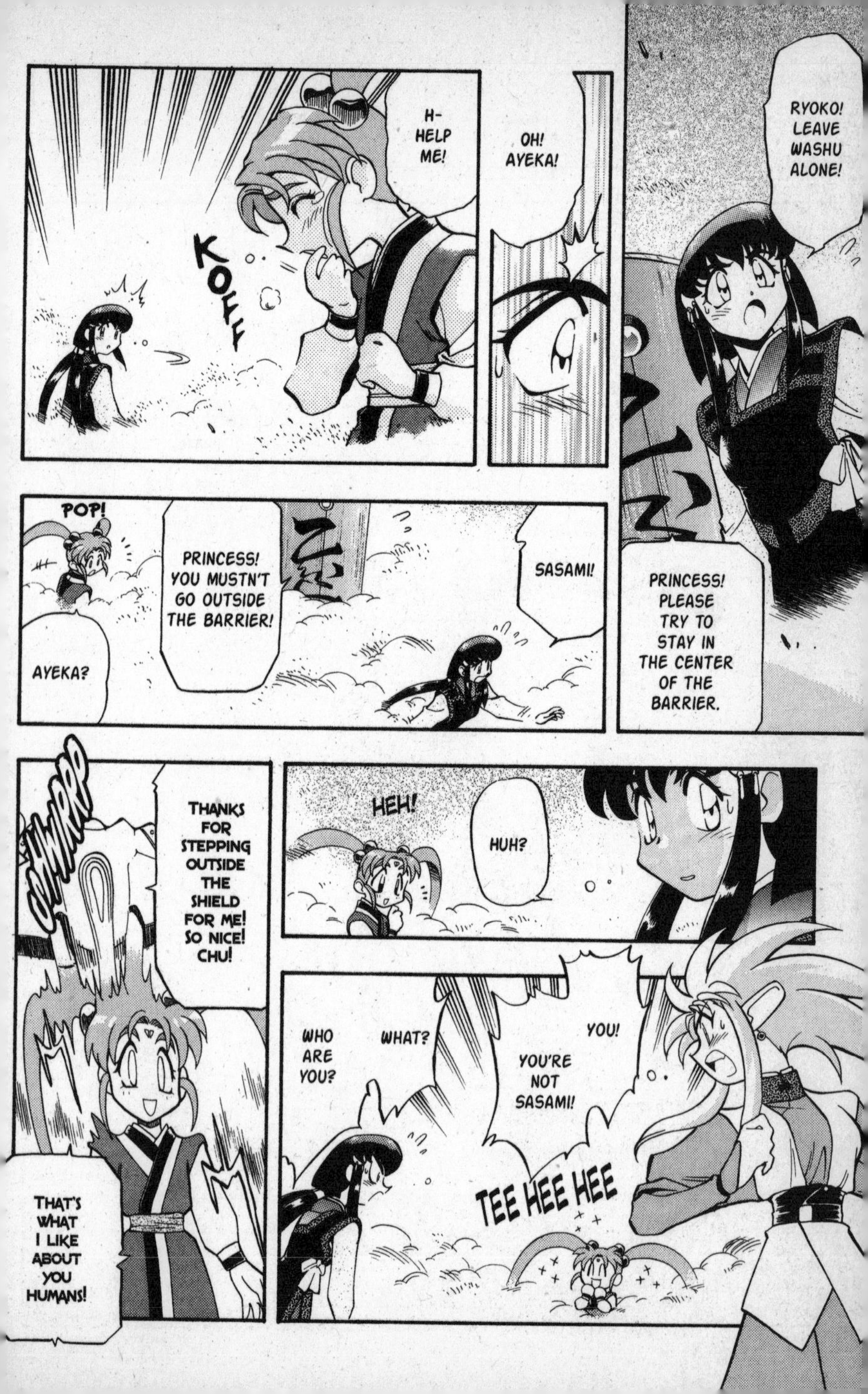
RYOKO! LEAVE WASHU ALONE!
PRINCESS! PLEASE TRY TO STAY IN THE CENTER OF THE BARRIER.
OH! AYEKA!
H- HELP ME!
KOFF
SASAMI!
PRINCESS! YOU MUSTN'T GO OUTSIDE THE BARRIER!
POP!
AYEKA?
HUH?
HEH!
YOU!
YOU'RE NOT SASAMI!
WHAT?
WHO ARE YOU?
TEE HEE HEE
THANKS FOR STEPPING OUTSIDE THE SHIELD FOR ME! SO NICE! CHU!
THAT'S WHAT I LIKE ABOUT YOU HUMANS!

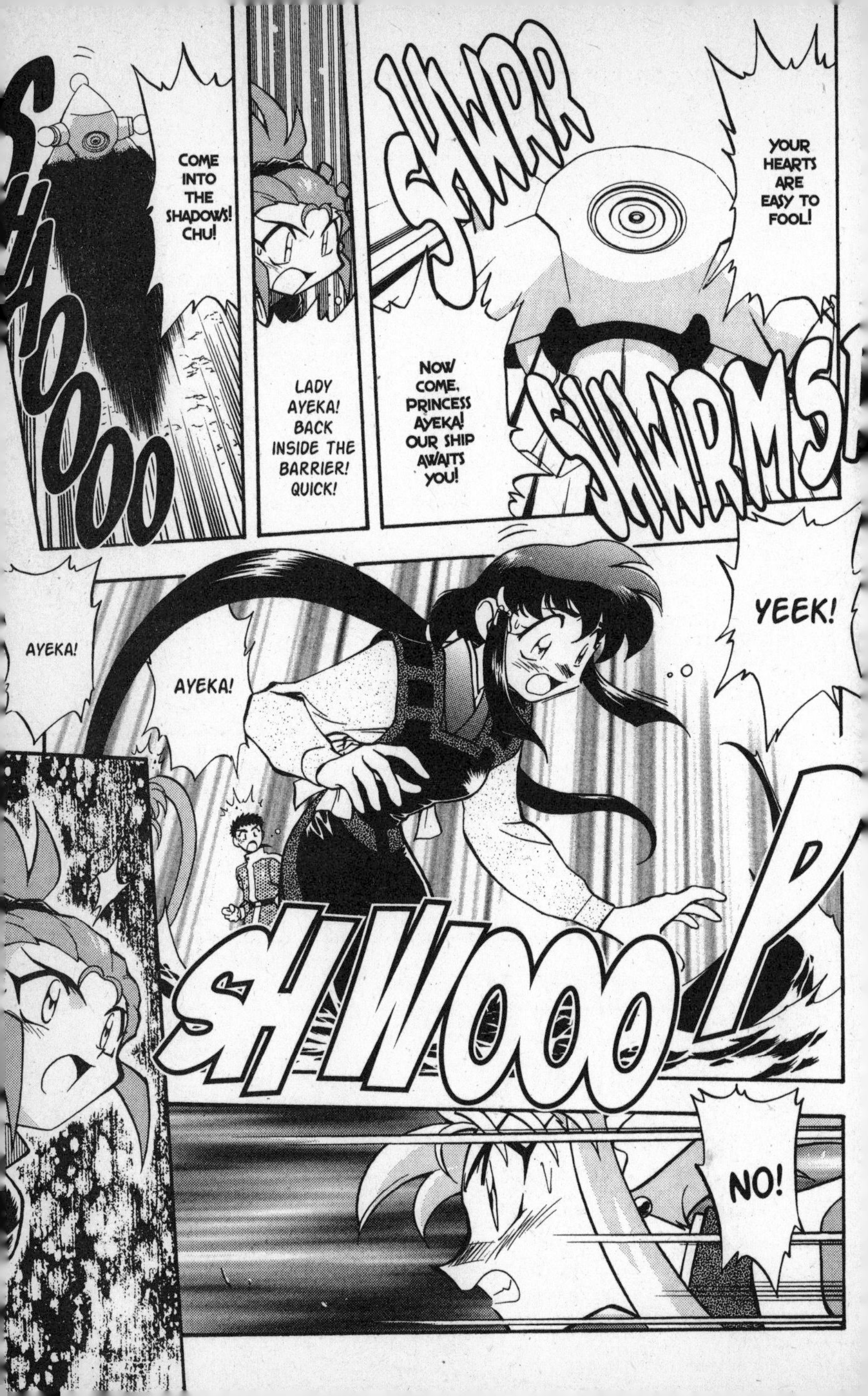
YOUR HEARTS ARE EASY TO FOOL!
SHWRR
SHWRMS!
NOW COME, PRINCESS AYEKA! OUR SHIP AWAITS YOU!
LADY AYEKA! BACK INSIDE THE BARRIER! QUICK!
COME INTO THE SHADOWS! CHU!
SHAOOOO
YEEK!
AYEKA!
AYEKA!
SHWOOOP
NO!

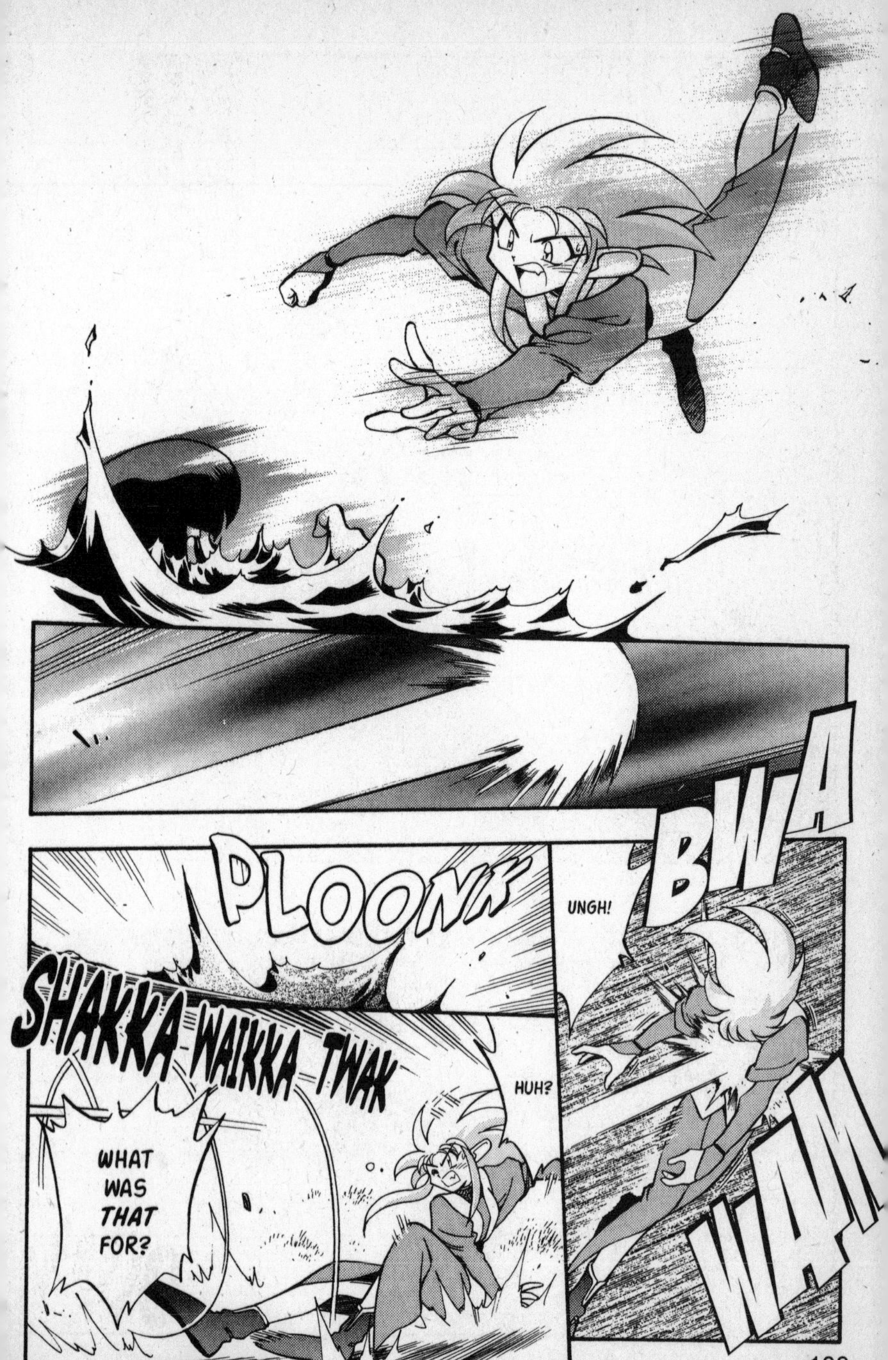
BWA
UNGH!
WAM
PLOONK
SHAKKA WAIKKA TWAK
HUH?
WHAT WAS THAT FOR?

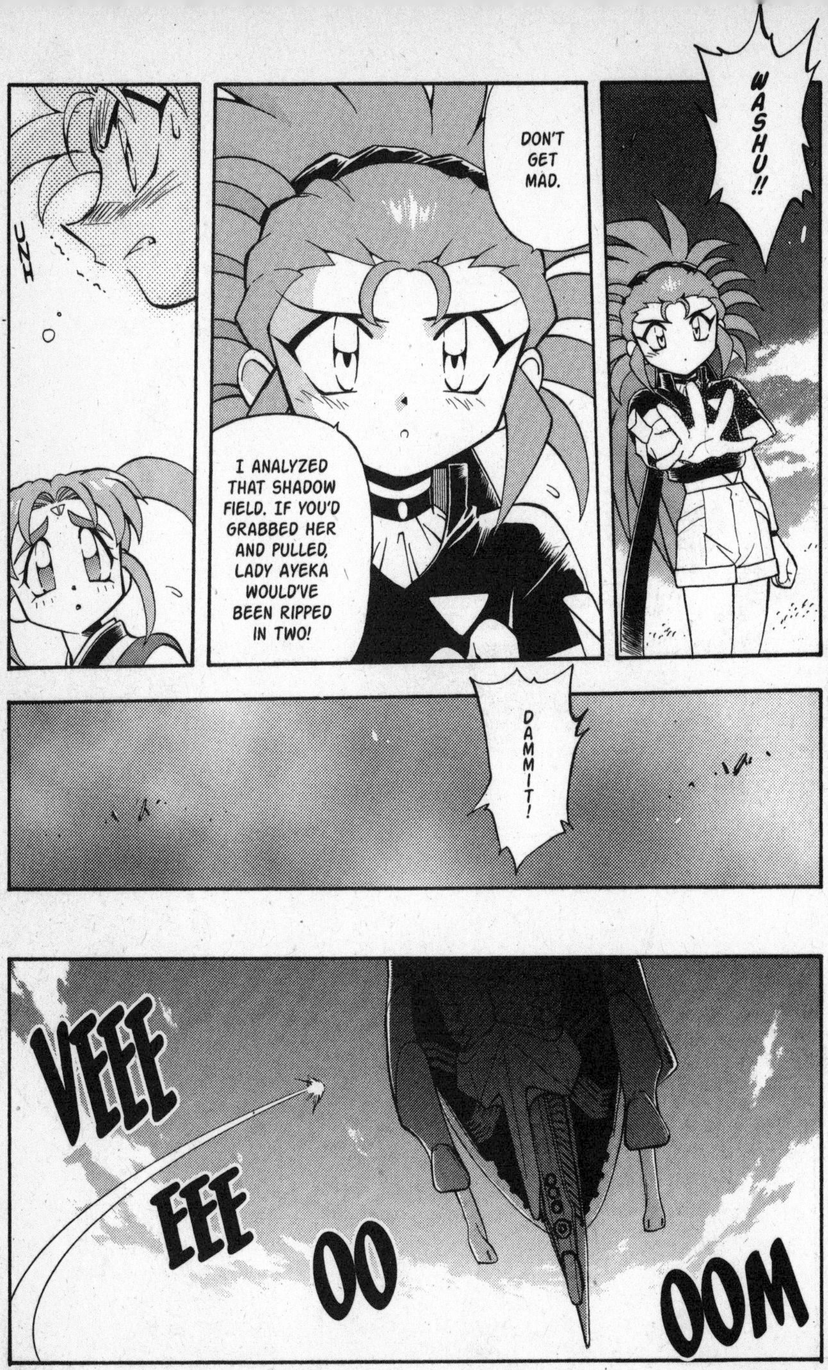
WASHU!!
DON'T GET MAD.
I ANALYZED THAT SHADOW FIELD. IF YOU'D GRABBED HER AND PULLED, LADY AYEKA WOULD'VE BEEN RIPPED IN TWO!
UNH
DAMMIT!
VEEEEEE
OOOOM

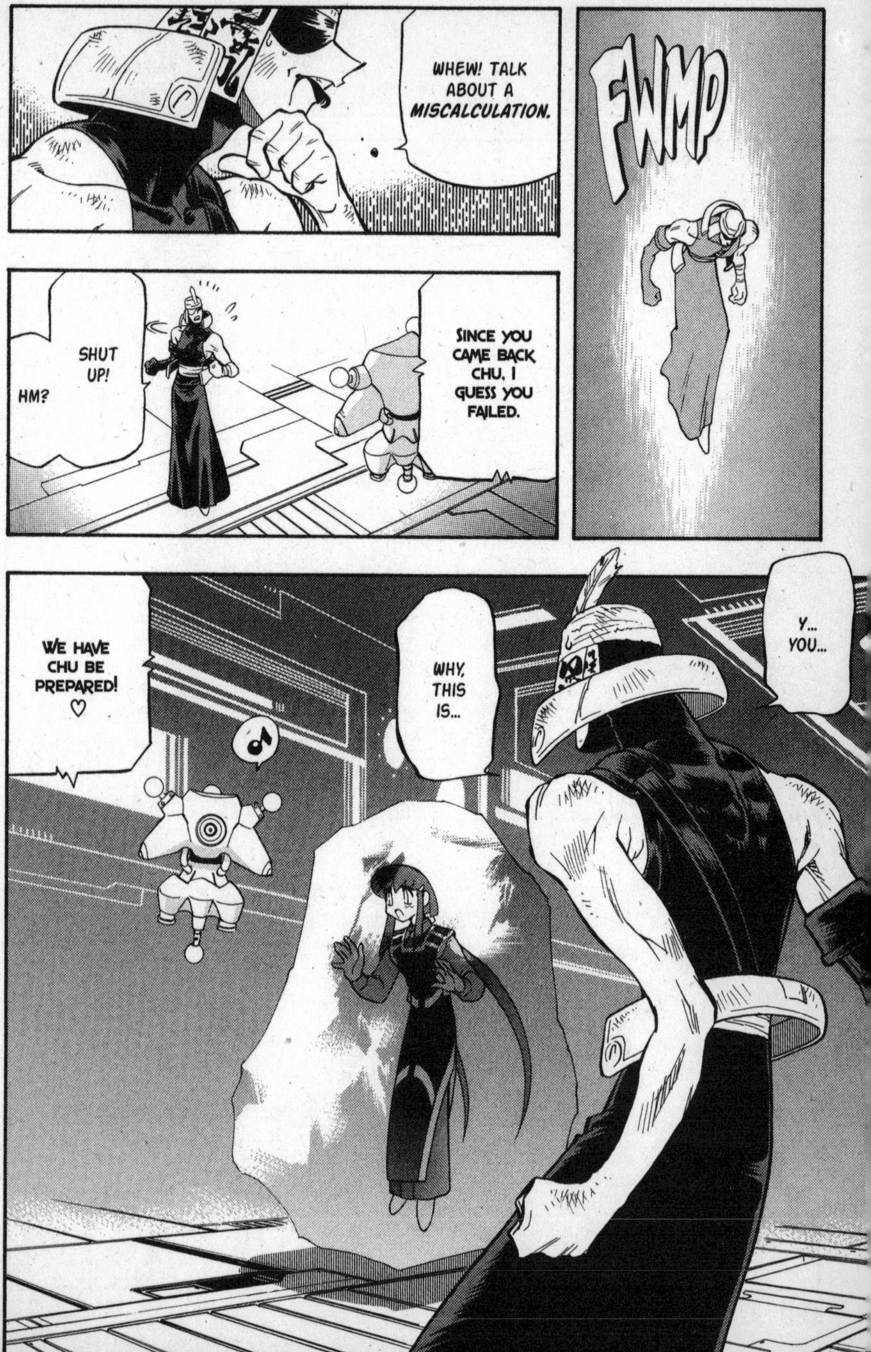
FWMP
WHEW! TALK ABOUT A *MISCALCULATION.*
SINCE YOU CAME BACK CHU, I GUESS YOU FAILED.
SHUT UP!
HM?
Y... YOU...
WHY, THIS IS...
WE HAVE CHU BE PREPARED! ♡

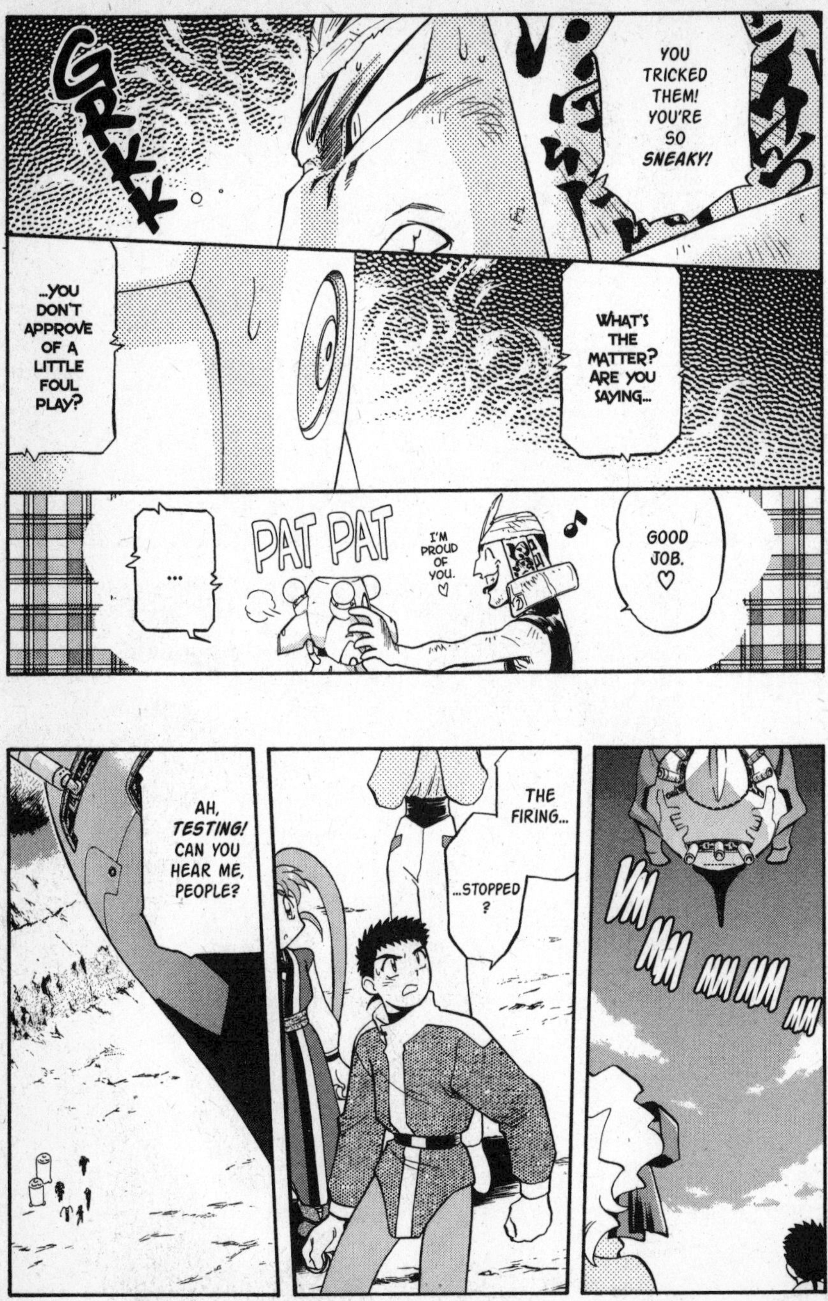
YOU TRICKED THEM! YOU'RE SO *SNEAKY!*
GRKK
WHAT'S THE MATTER? ARE YOU SAYING...
...YOU DON'T APPROVE OF A LITTLE FOUL PLAY?
GOOD JOB. ♡
I'M PROUD OF YOU. ♡
PAT PAT
...
VMMMMMMMMMMMMMM
THE FIRING...
...STOPPED?
AH, *TESTING!* CAN YOU HEAR ME, PEOPLE?

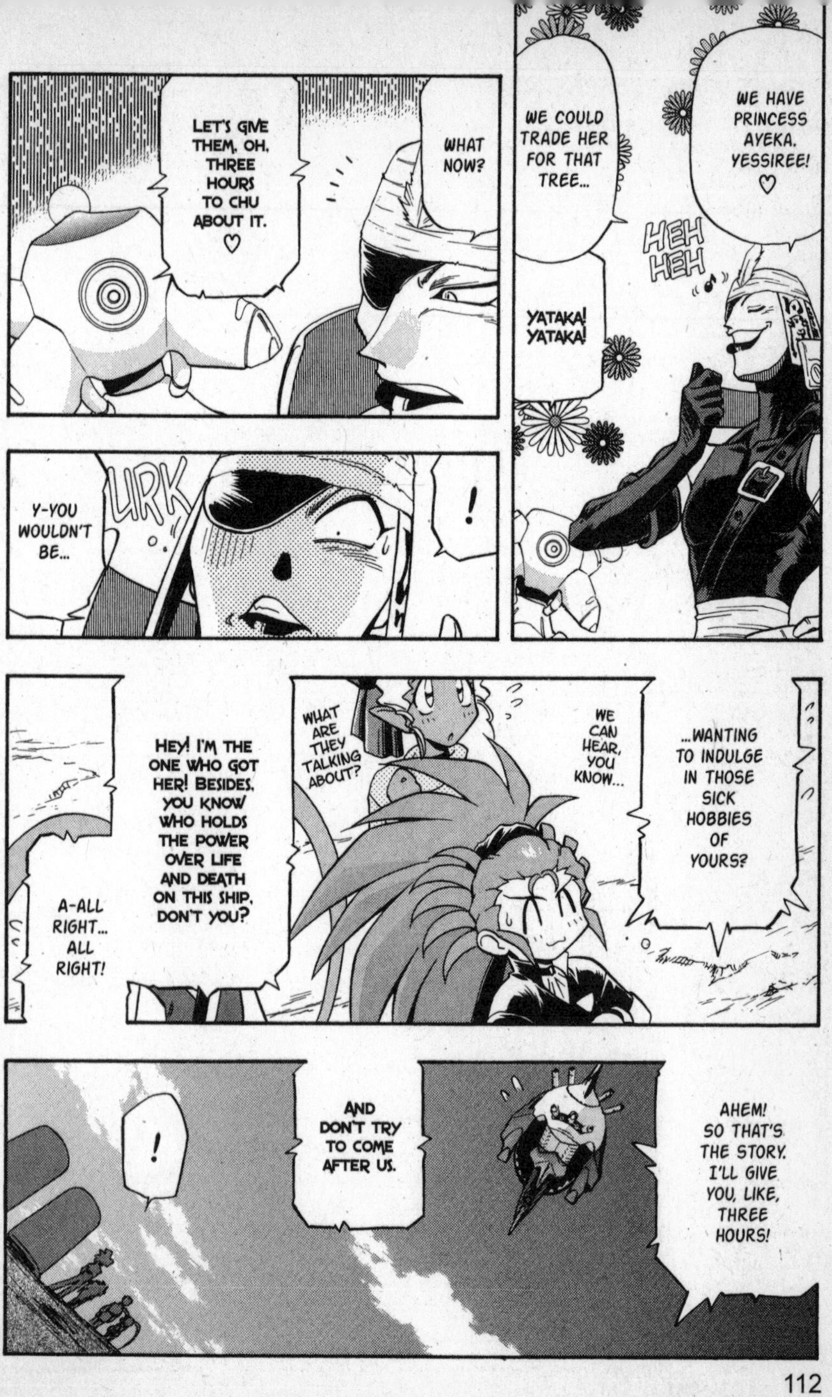
WE HAVE PRINCESS AYEKA. YESSIREE! ♡
WE COULD TRADE HER FOR THAT TREE...
HEH HEH
YATAKA! YATAKA!
WHAT NOW?
LET'S GIVE THEM, OH, THREE HOURS TO CHU ABOUT IT. ♡
!
URK
Y-YOU WOULDN'T BE...
...WANTING TO INDULGE IN THOSE SICK HOBBIES OF YOURS?
WE CAN HEAR, YOU KNOW...
WHAT ARE THEY TALKING ABOUT?
HEY! I'M THE ONE WHO GOT HER! BESIDES, YOU KNOW WHO HOLDS THE POWER OVER LIFE AND DEATH ON THIS SHIP, DON'T YOU?
A-ALL RIGHT... ALL RIGHT!
AHEM! SO THAT'S THE STORY. I'LL GIVE YOU, LIKE, THREE HOURS!
AND DON'T TRY TO COME AFTER US.
!

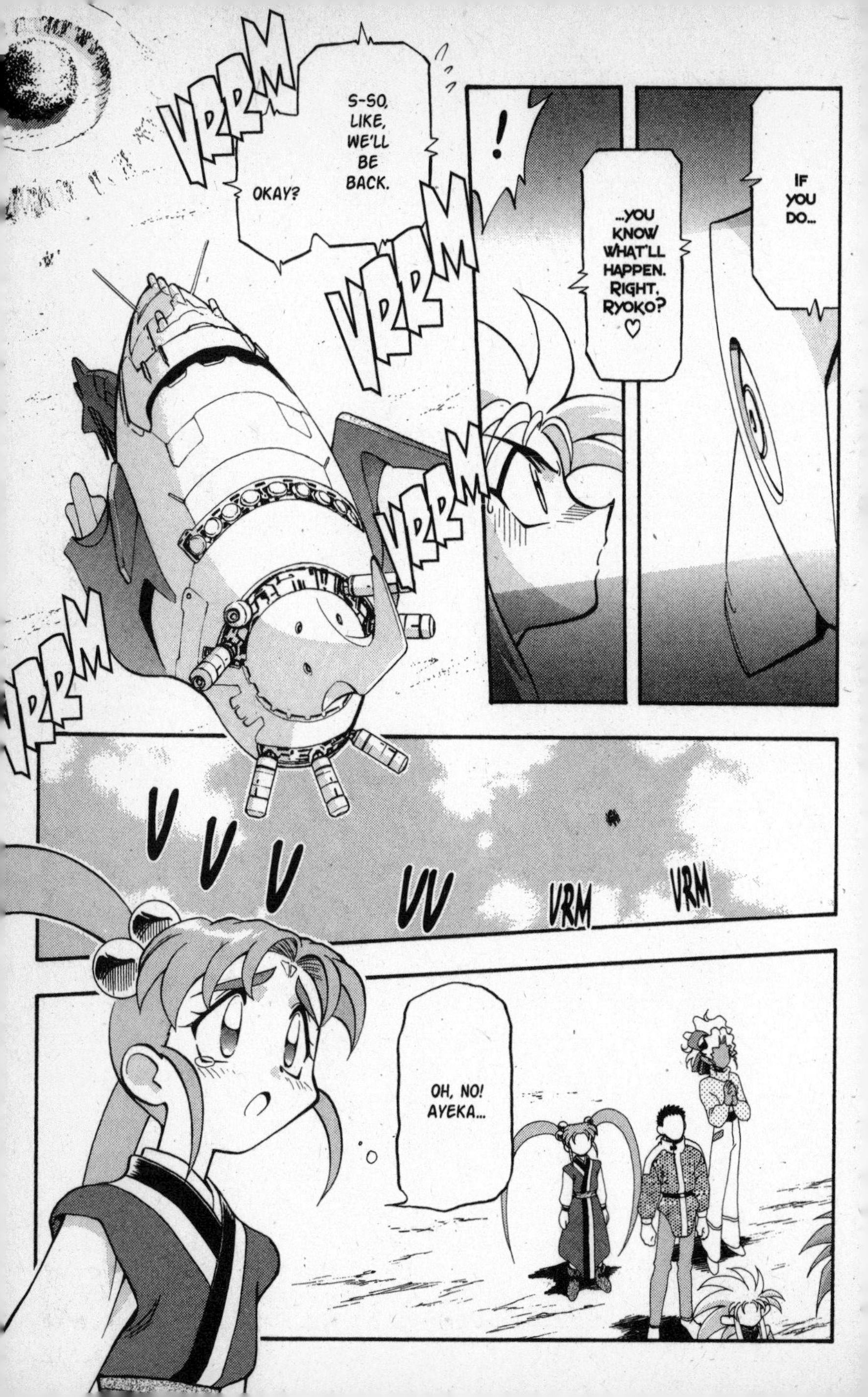
IF YOU DO...
...YOU KNOW WHAT'LL HAPPEN. RIGHT, RYOKO? ♡
!
VRRM
S-SO, LIKE, WE'LL BE BACK.
OKAY?
VRRM
VRRM
VRRM
VRM
VRM
VV
V
V
V
OH, NO! AYEKA...

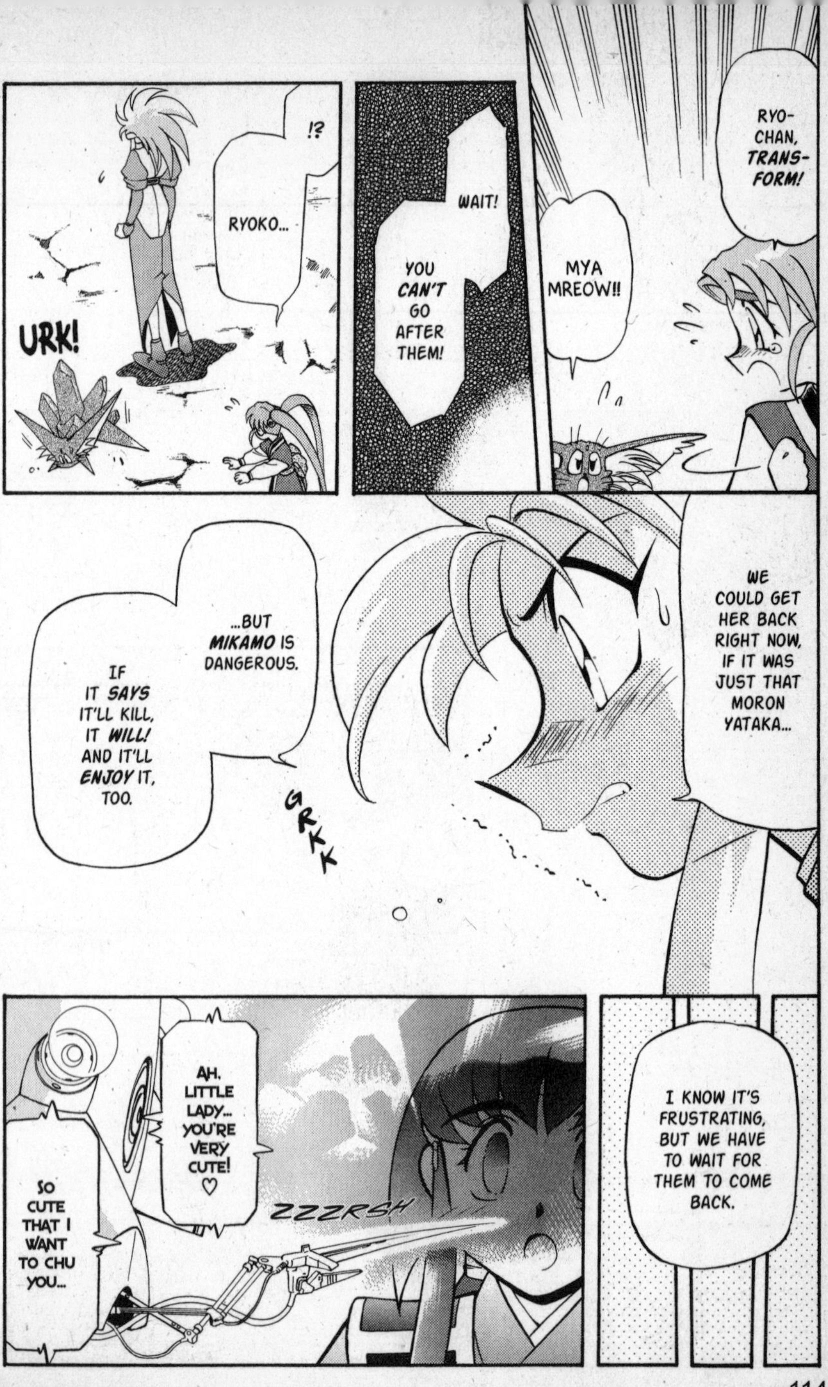
RYO-CHAN, *TRANSFORM!*
MYA MREOW!!
WAIT!
YOU *CAN'T* GO AFTER THEM!
!?
RYOKO...
URK!
WE COULD GET HER BACK RIGHT NOW, IF IT WAS JUST THAT MORON YATAKA...
...BUT *MIKAMO* IS DANGEROUS.
IF IT *SAYS* IT'LL KILL, IT *WILL!* AND IT'LL *ENJOY* IT, TOO.
GRKK
I KNOW IT'S FRUSTRATING, BUT WE HAVE TO WAIT FOR THEM TO COME BACK.
AH, LITTLE LADY... YOU'RE VERY CUTE! ♡
SO CUTE THAT I WANT TO CHU YOU...
ZZZRSH

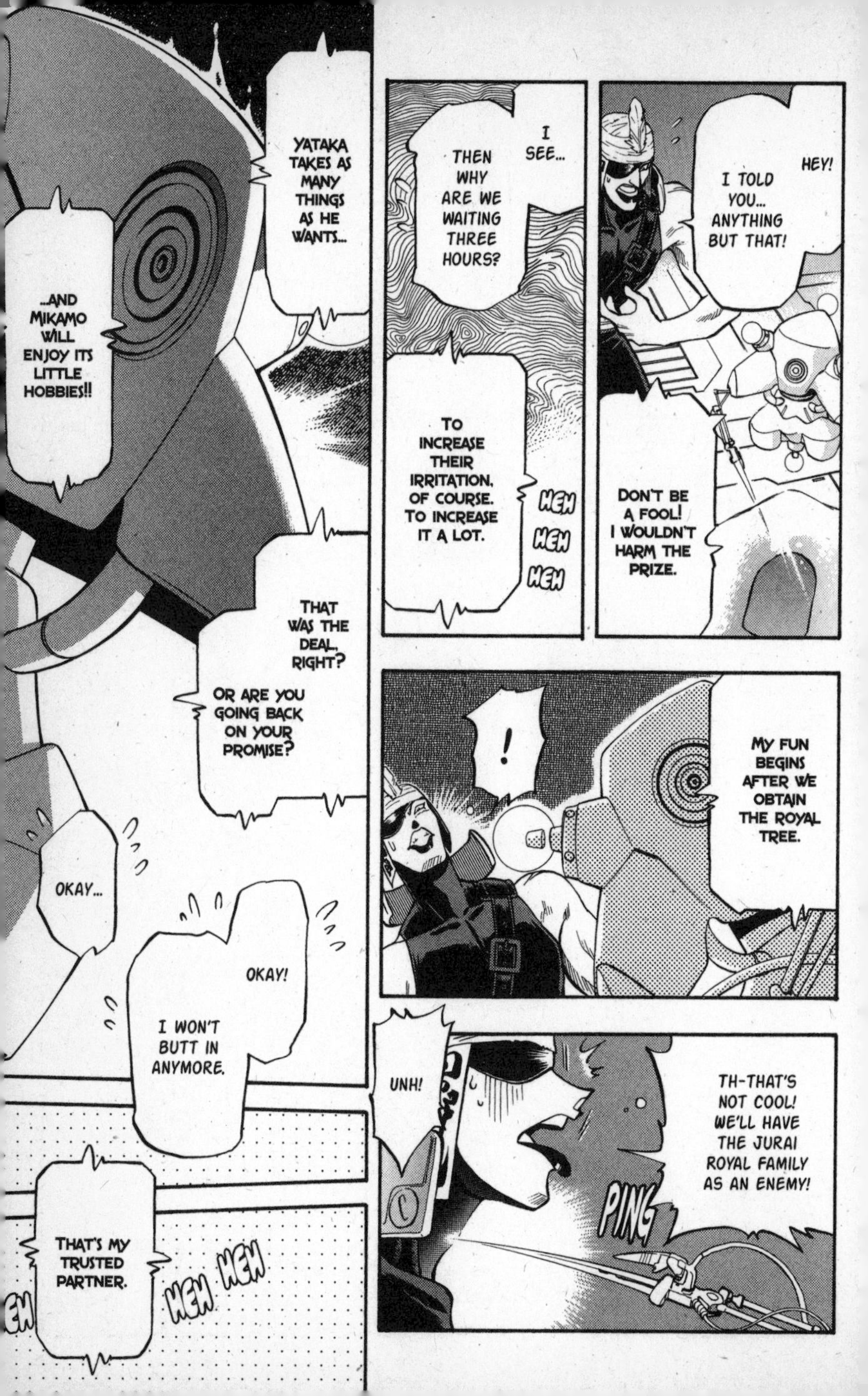
HEY! I TOLD YOU... ANYTHING BUT THAT!
DON'T BE A FOOL! I WOULDN'T HARM THE PRIZE.
I SEE...
THEN WHY ARE WE WAITING THREE HOURS?
TO INCREASE THEIR IRRITATION, OF COURSE. TO INCREASE IT A LOT.
HEH HEH HEH
!
MY FUN BEGINS AFTER WE OBTAIN THE ROYAL TREE.
UNH!
TH-THAT'S NOT COOL! WE'LL HAVE THE JURAI ROYAL FAMILY AS AN ENEMY!
PING
YATAKA TAKES AS MANY THINGS AS HE WANTS...
...AND MIKAMO WILL ENJOY ITS LITTLE HOBBIES!!
THAT WAS THE DEAL, RIGHT?
OR ARE YOU GOING BACK ON YOUR PROMISE?
OKAY...
OKAY!
I WON'T BUTT IN ANYMORE.
THAT'S MY TRUSTED PARTNER.
HEH HEH HEH

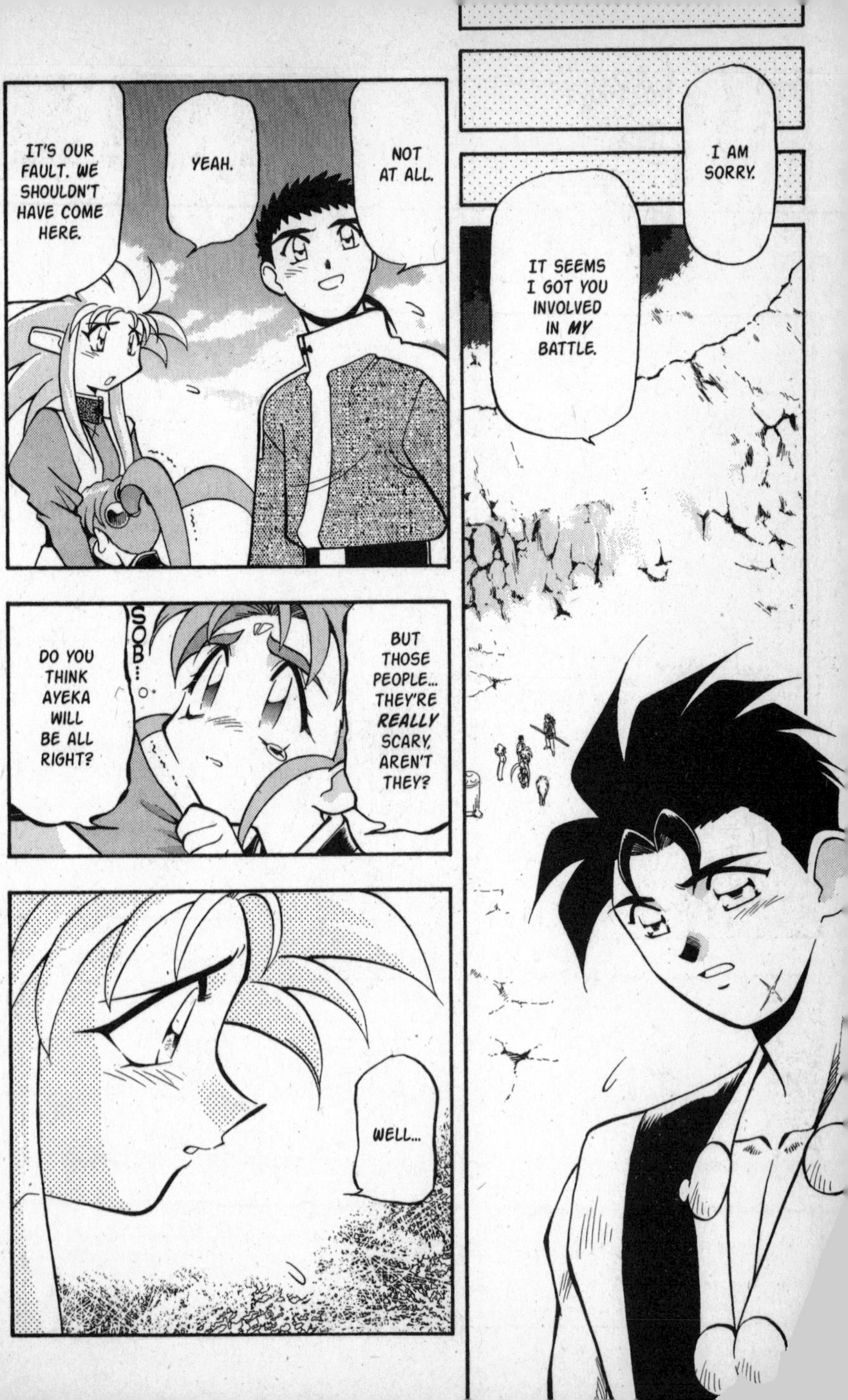
I AM SORRY.
IT SEEMS I GOT YOU INVOLVED IN *MY* BATTLE.
NOT AT ALL.
YEAH.
IT'S OUR FAULT. WE SHOULDN'T HAVE COME HERE.
BUT THOSE PEOPLE... THEY'RE *REALLY* SCARY, AREN'T THEY?
SOB...
DO YOU THINK AYEKA WILL BE ALL RIGHT?
WELL...

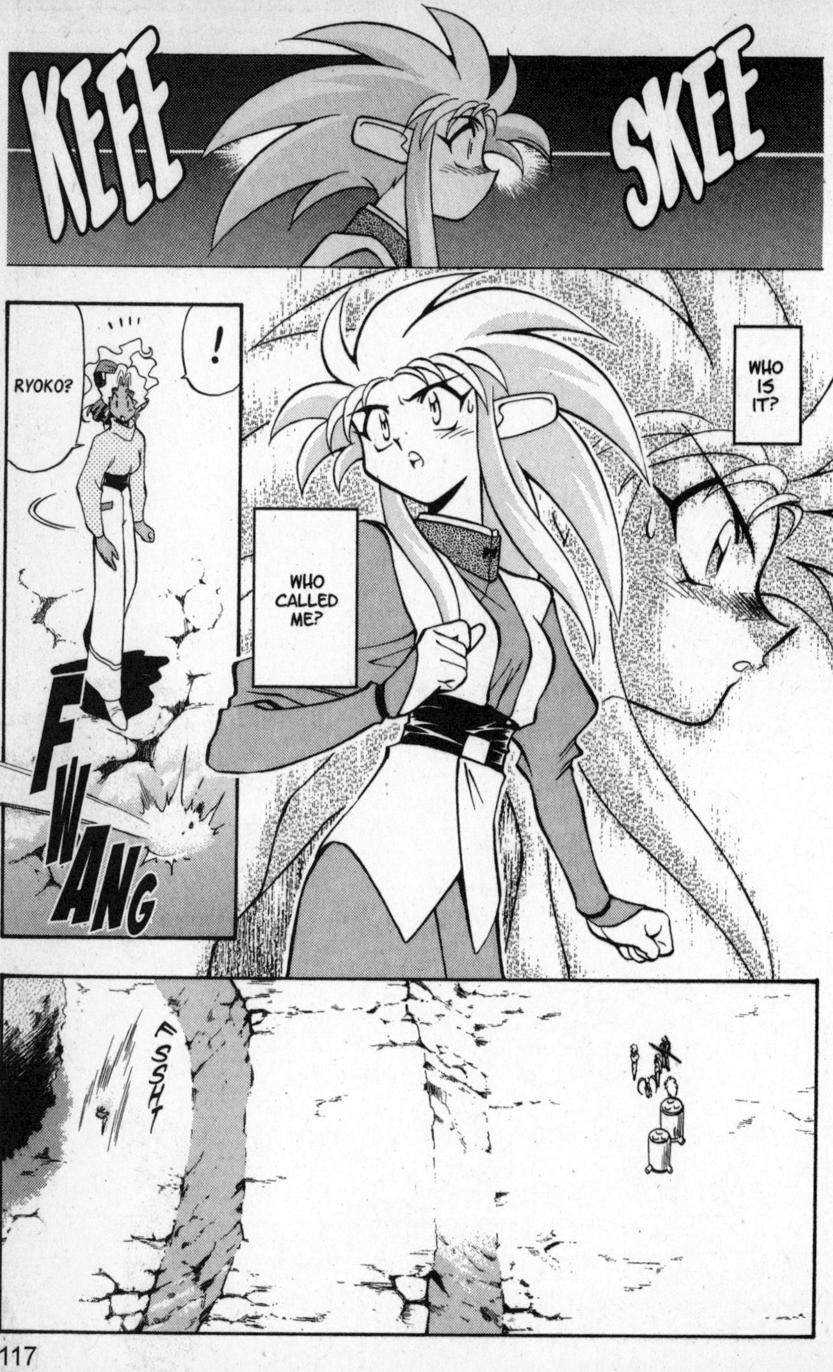
SKEE
KEEE
WHO IS IT?
WHO CALLED ME?
!
RYOKO?
FWANG
FSSHT

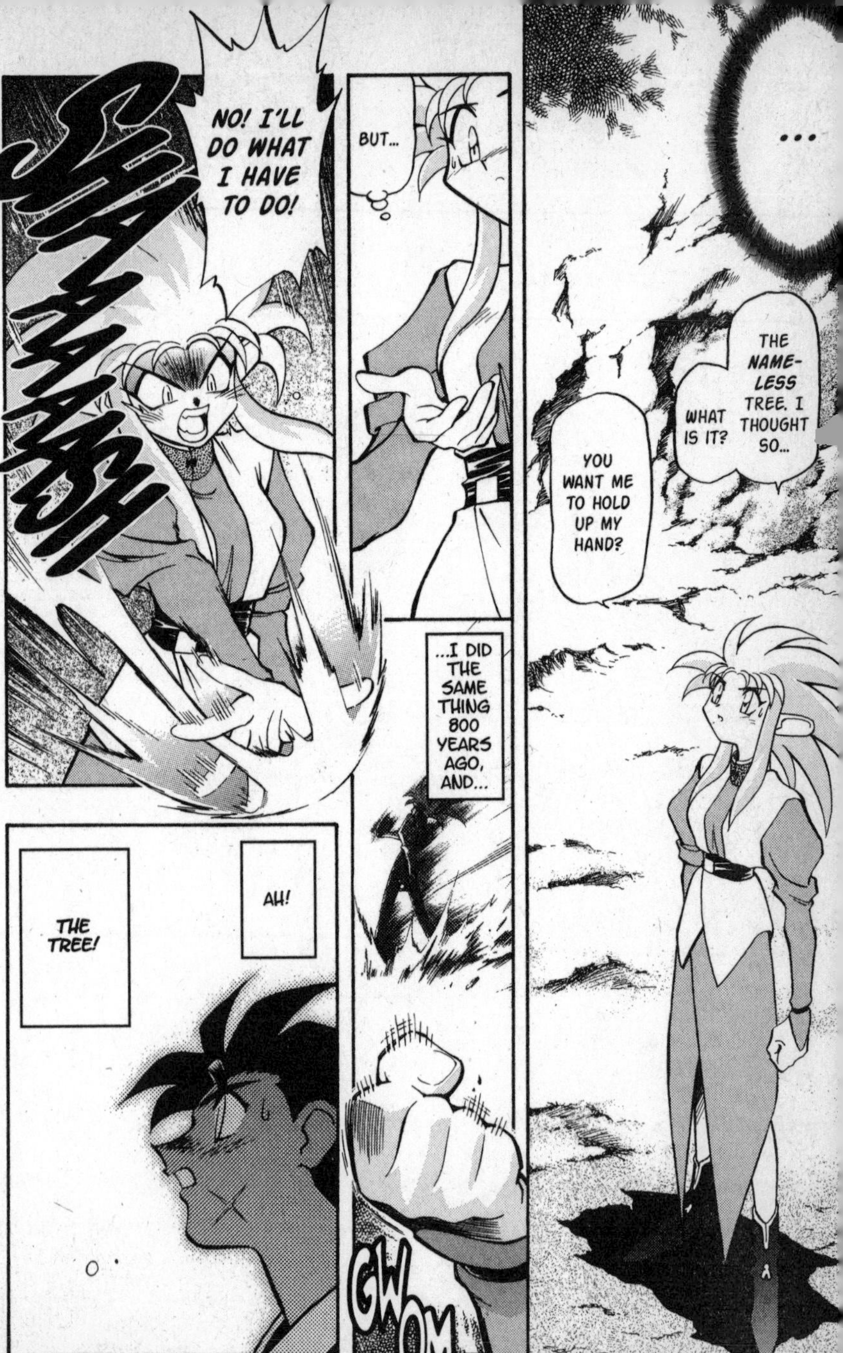
...
THE NAME-LESS TREE. I THOUGHT SO...
WHAT IS IT?
YOU WANT ME TO HOLD UP MY HAND?
BUT...
...I DID THE SAME THING 800 YEARS AGO, AND...
NO! I'LL DO WHAT I HAVE TO DO!
SHAAAASH
GWOM
AH!
THE TREE!

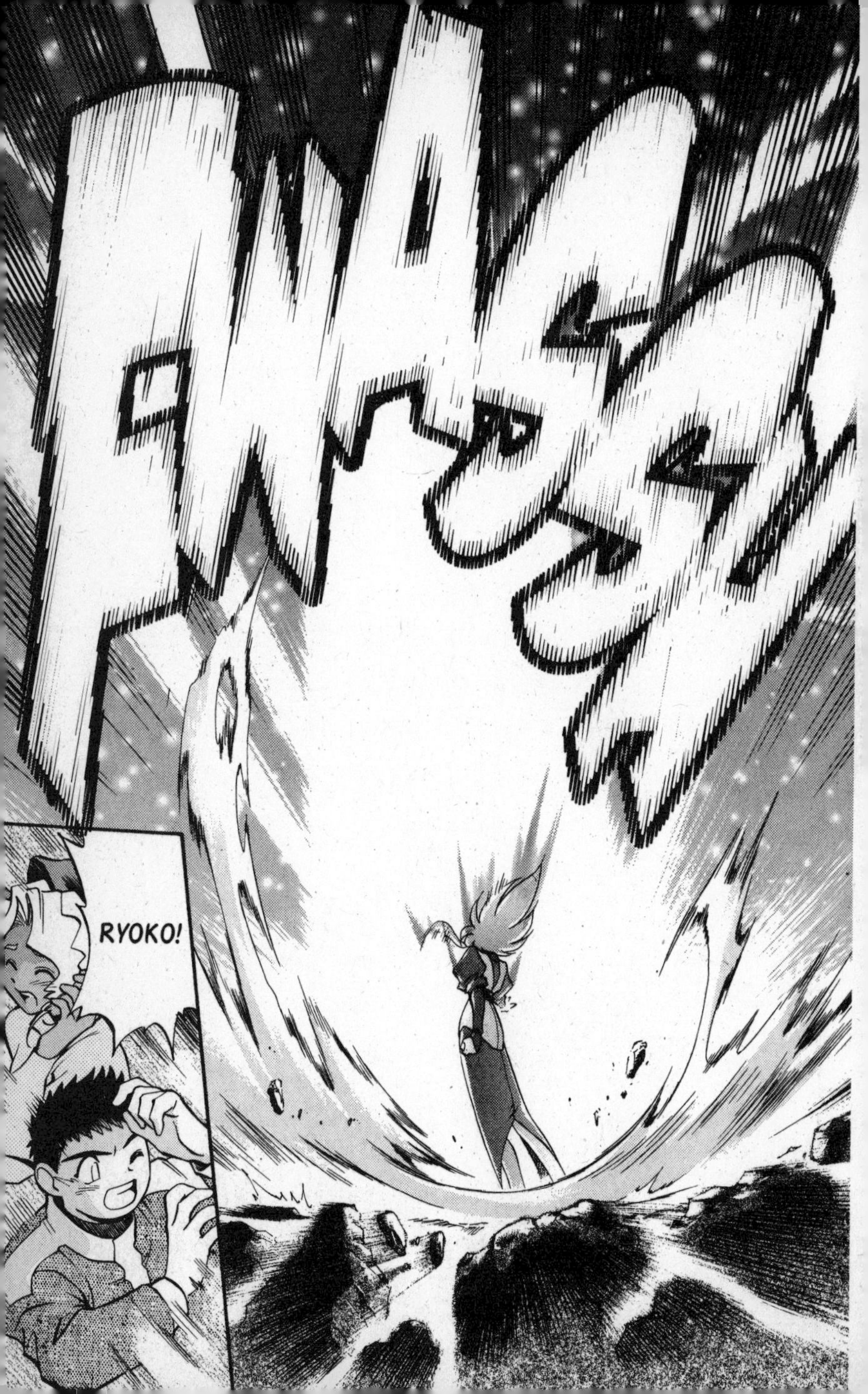
RYOKO!

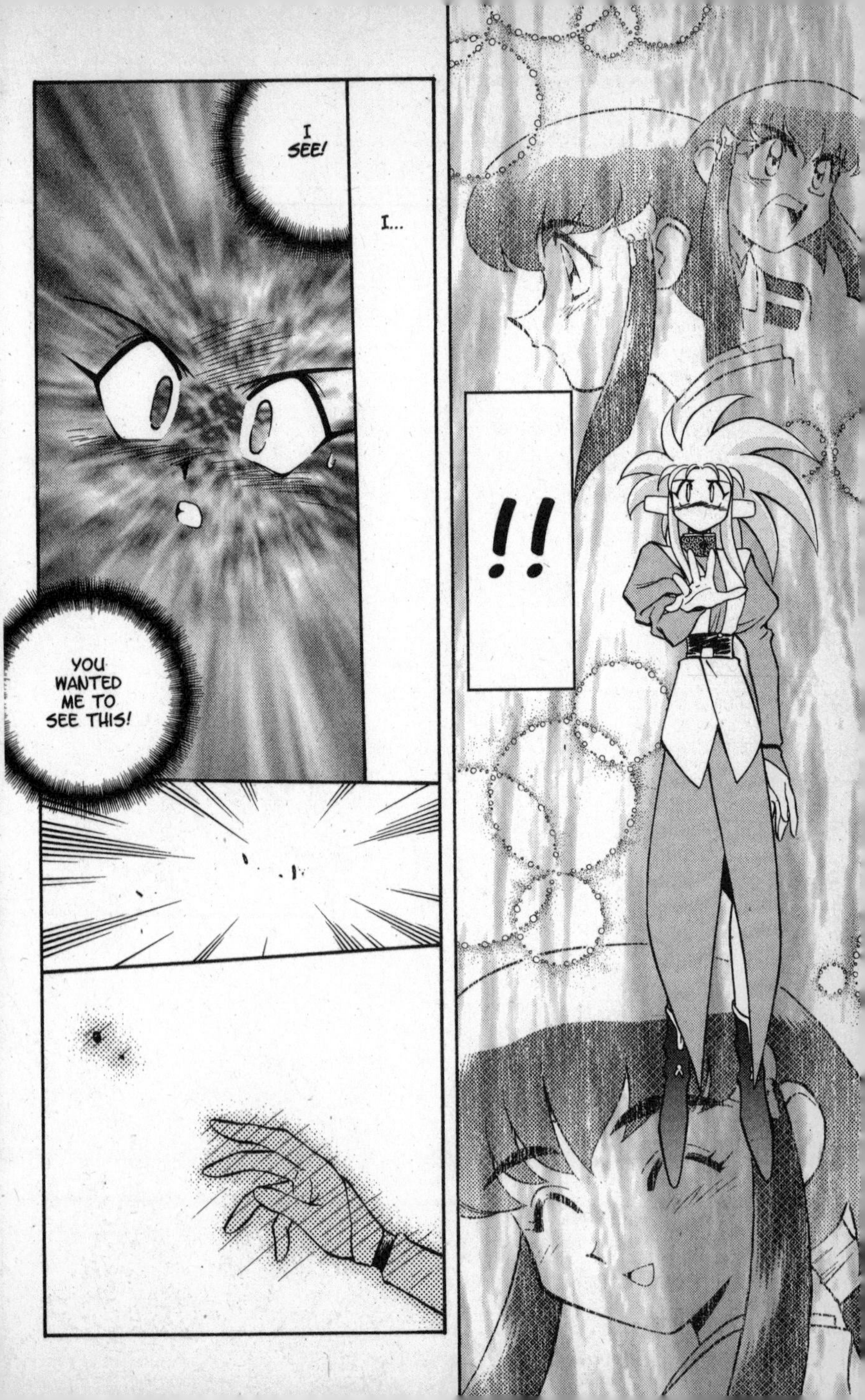
!!
I...
I SEE!
YOU WANTED ME TO SEE THIS!

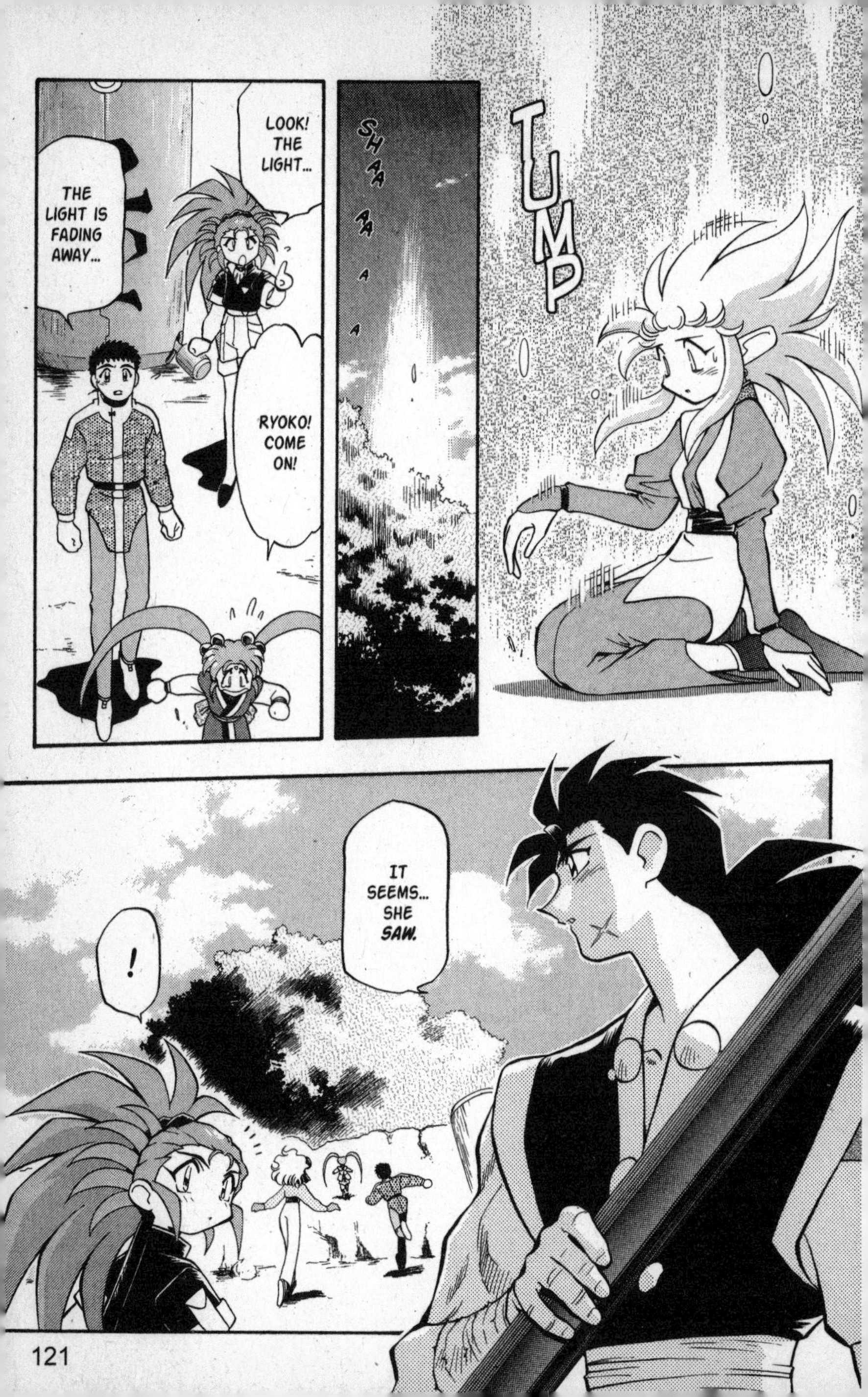
TUMP
SHAAAAAA
LOOK! THE LIGHT...
THE LIGHT IS FADING AWAY...
RYOKO! COME ON!
IT SEEMS... SHE SAW.
!

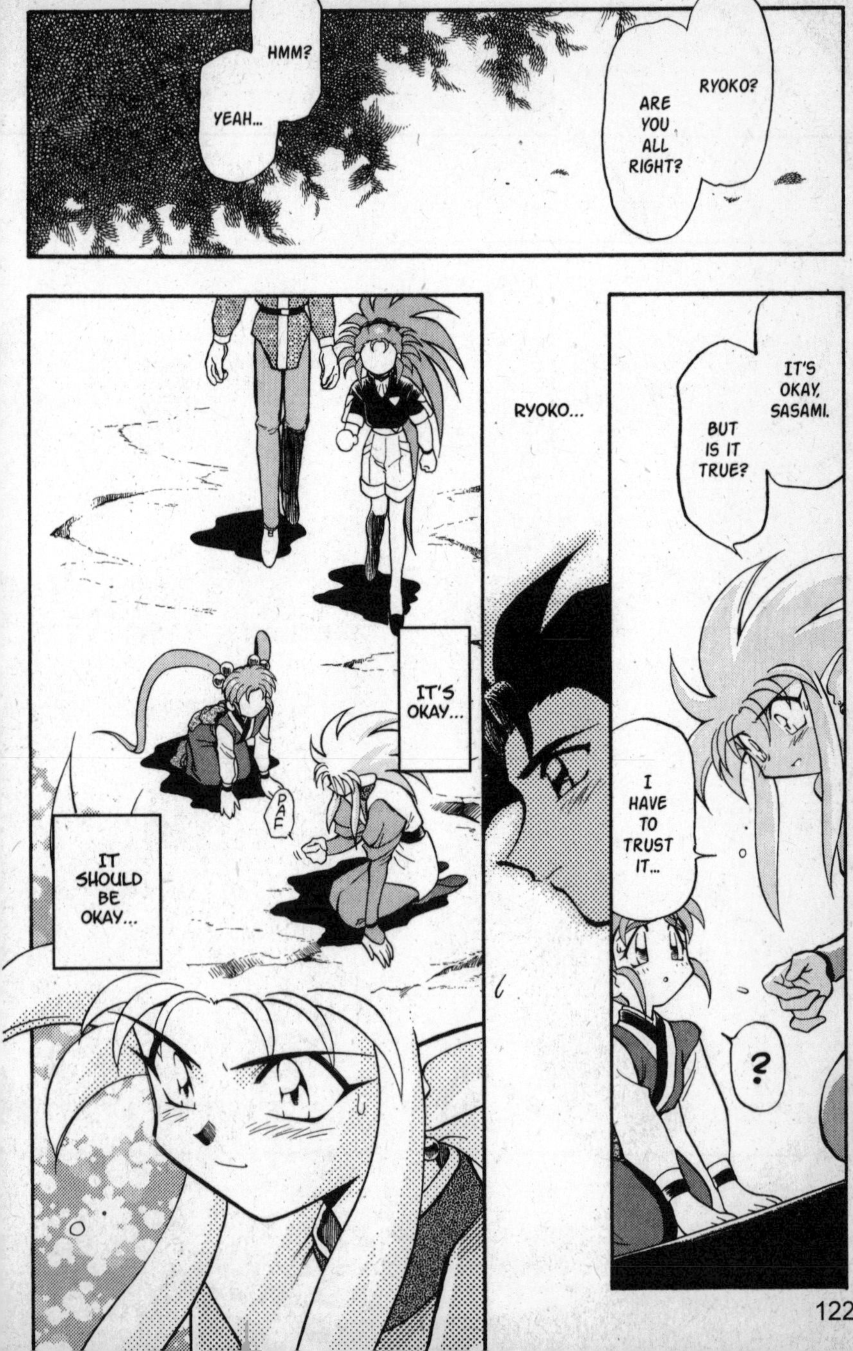
RYOKO? ARE YOU ALL RIGHT?
HMM? YEAH...
IT'S OKAY, SASAMI.
BUT IS IT TRUE?
I HAVE TO TRUST IT...
?
RYOKO...
IT'S OKAY...
PAF
IT SHOULD BE OKAY...

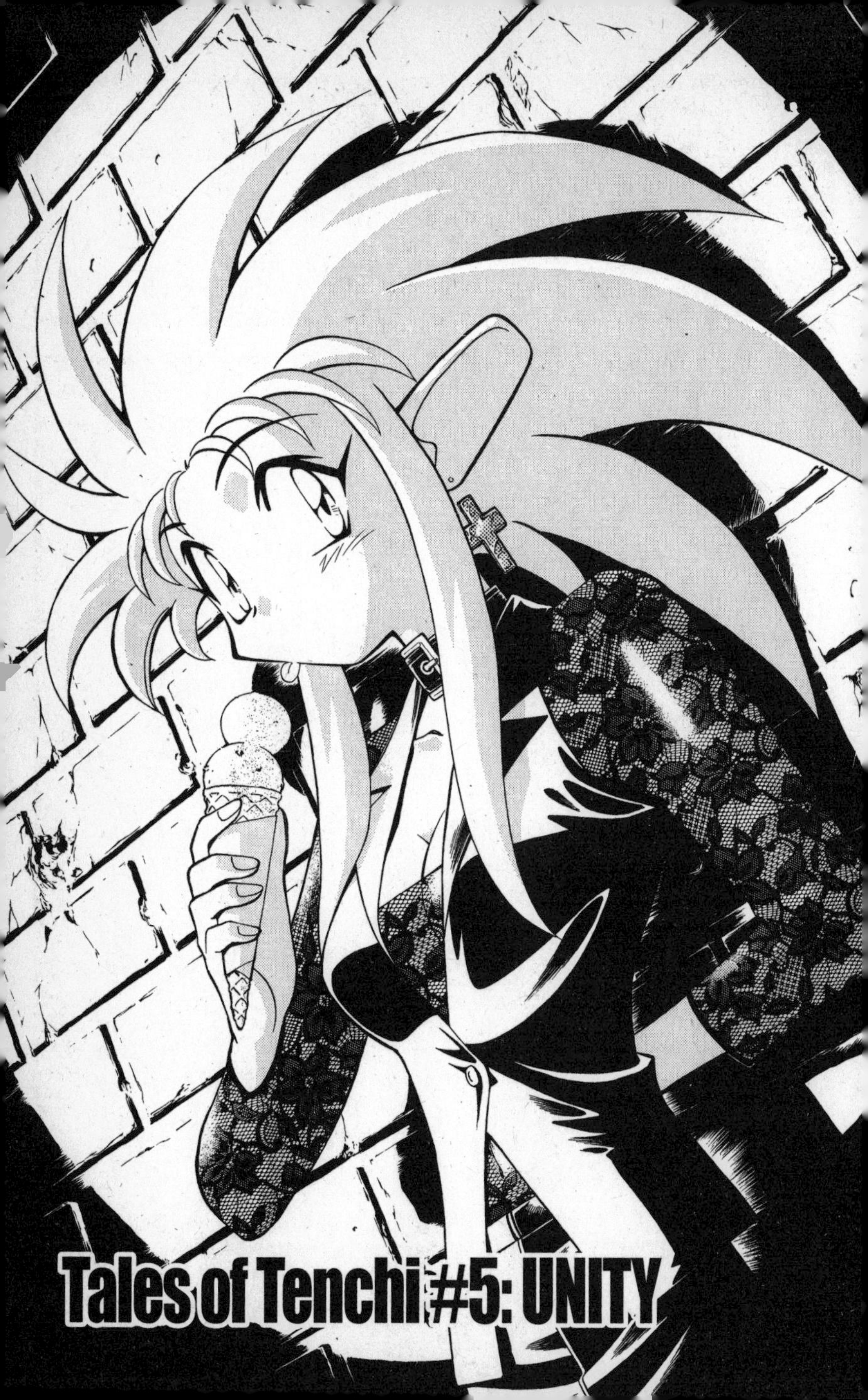
Tales of Tenchi #5: UNITY

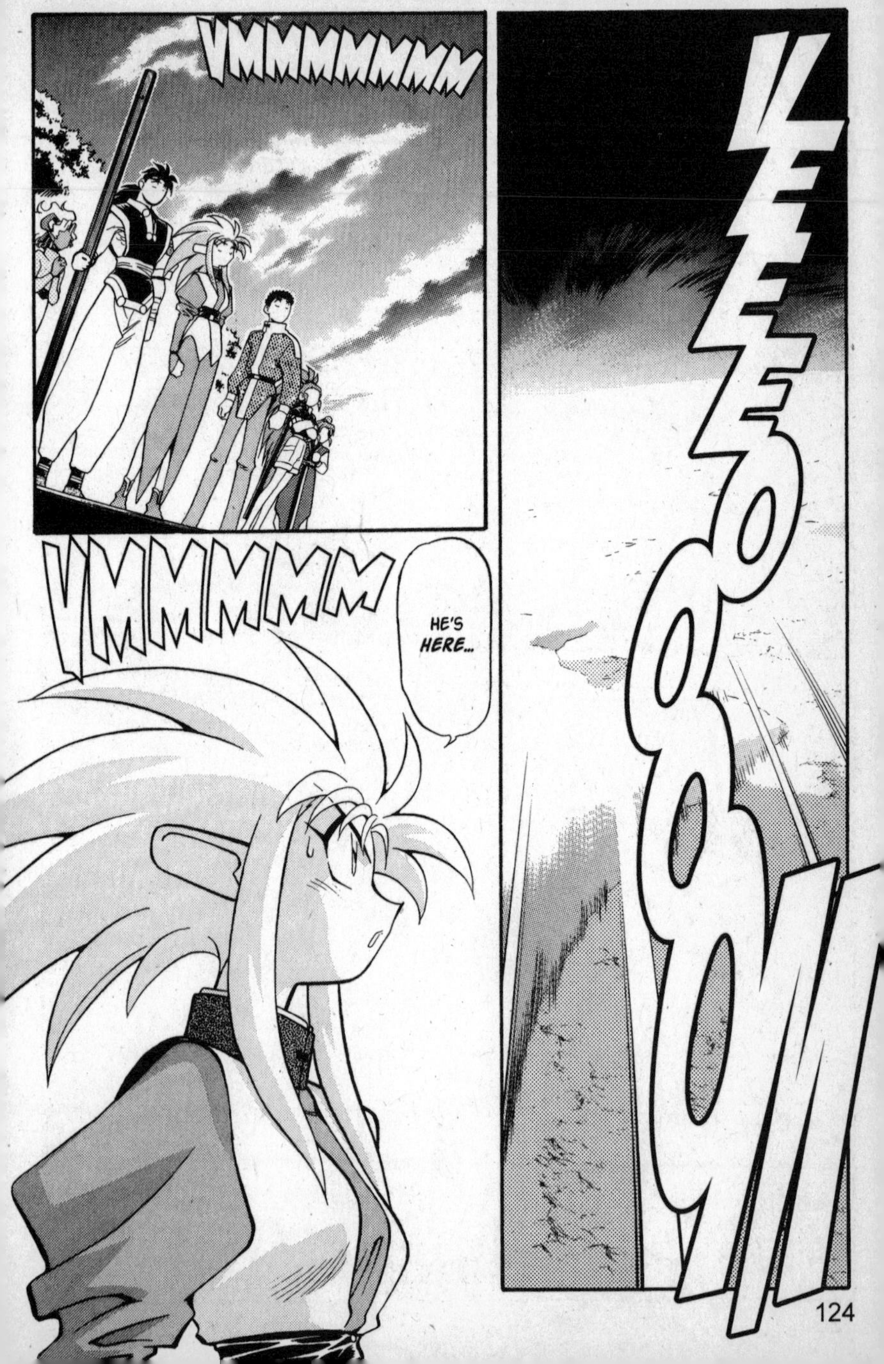
VEEEEOOOOOM
VMMMMMMMM
VMMMMMMM
HE'S HERE...

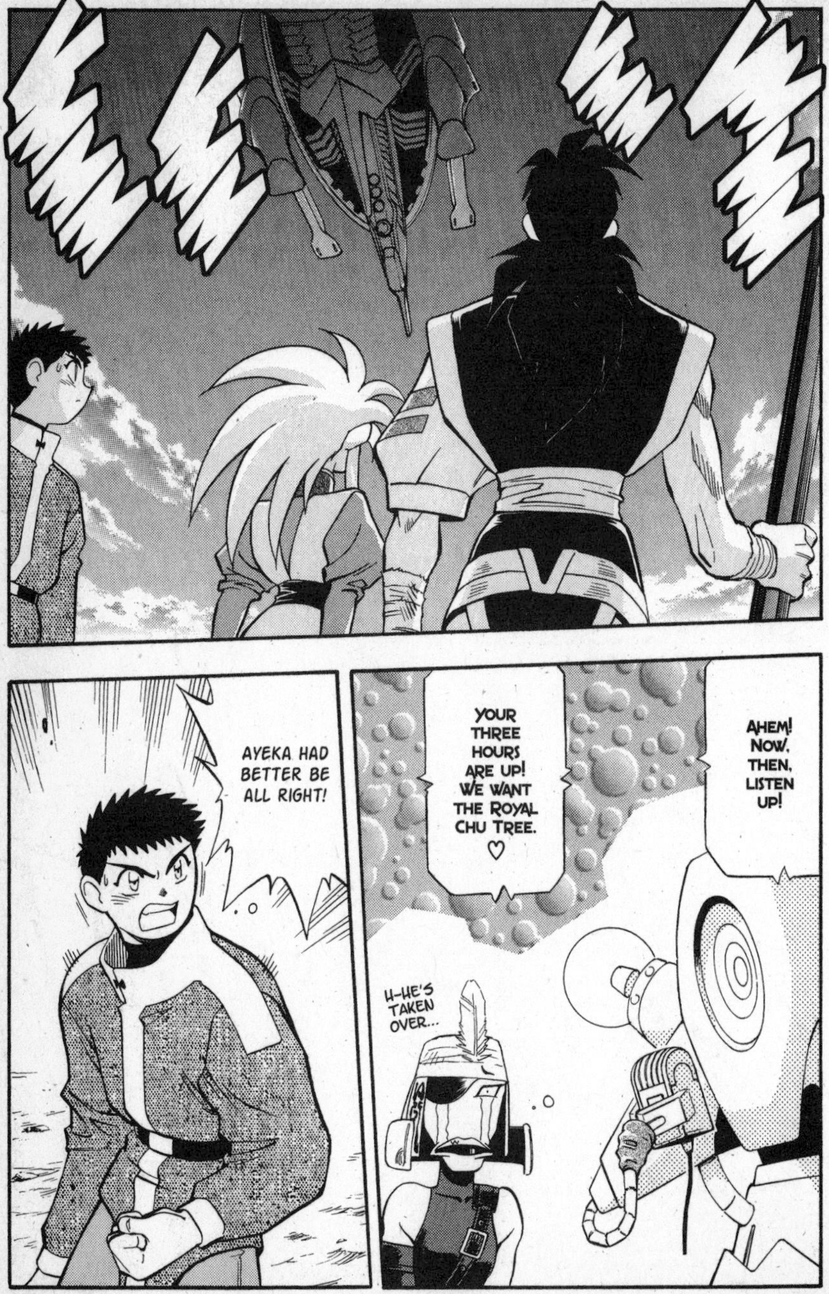
AHEM! NOW, THEN, LISTEN UP!
YOUR THREE HOURS ARE UP! WE WANT THE ROYAL CHU TREE. ♡
H-HE'S TAKEN OVER...
AYEKA HAD BETTER BE ALL RIGHT!

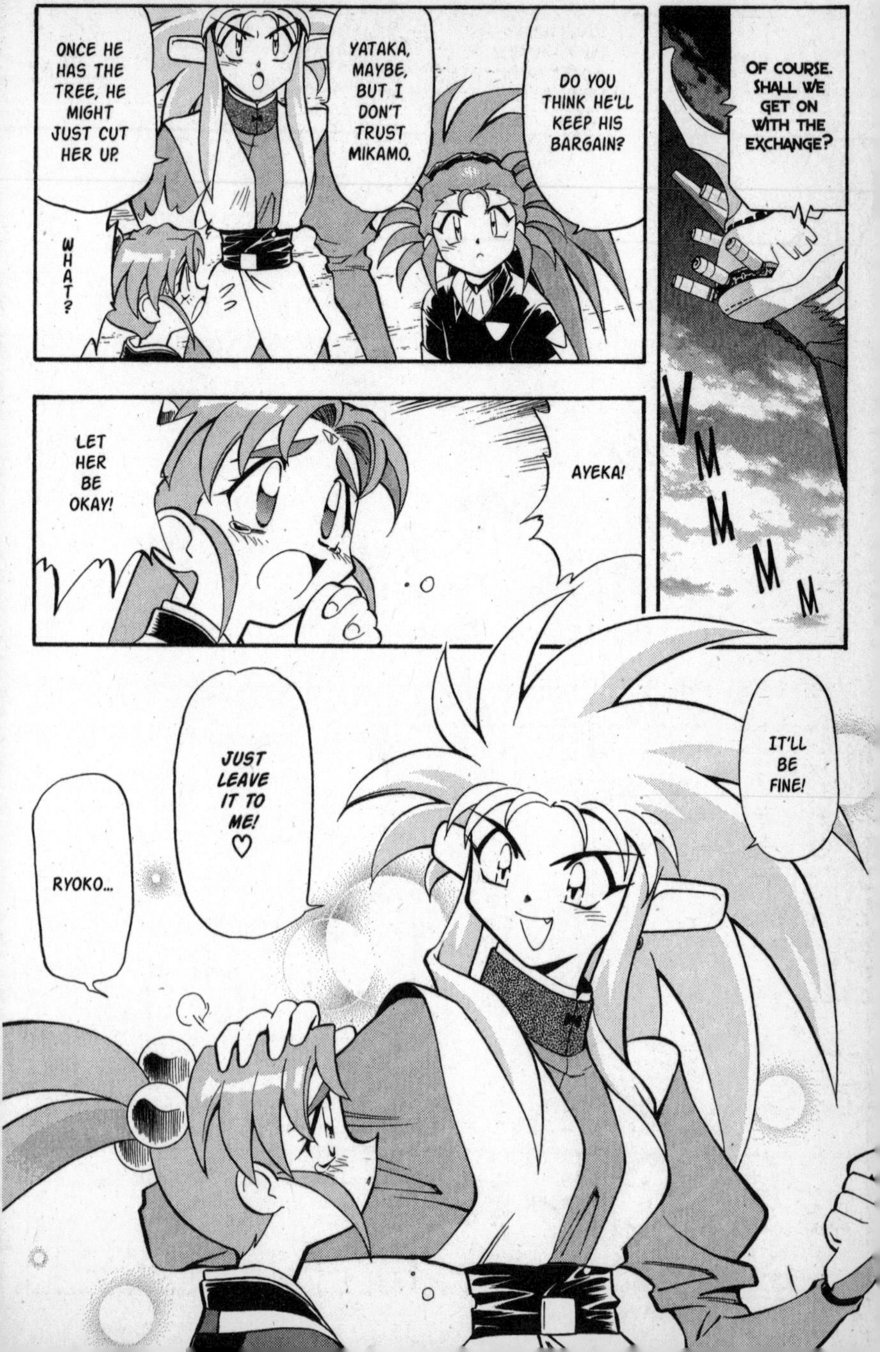
OF COURSE. SHALL WE GET ON WITH THE EXCHANGE?
VMMMMM
DO YOU THINK HE'LL KEEP HIS BARGAIN?
YATAKA, MAYBE, BUT I DON'T TRUST MIKAMO.
ONCE HE HAS THE TREE, HE MIGHT JUST CUT HER UP.
WHAT?
AYEKA!
LET HER BE OKAY!
IT'LL BE FINE!
JUST LEAVE IT TO ME! ♡
RYOKO...

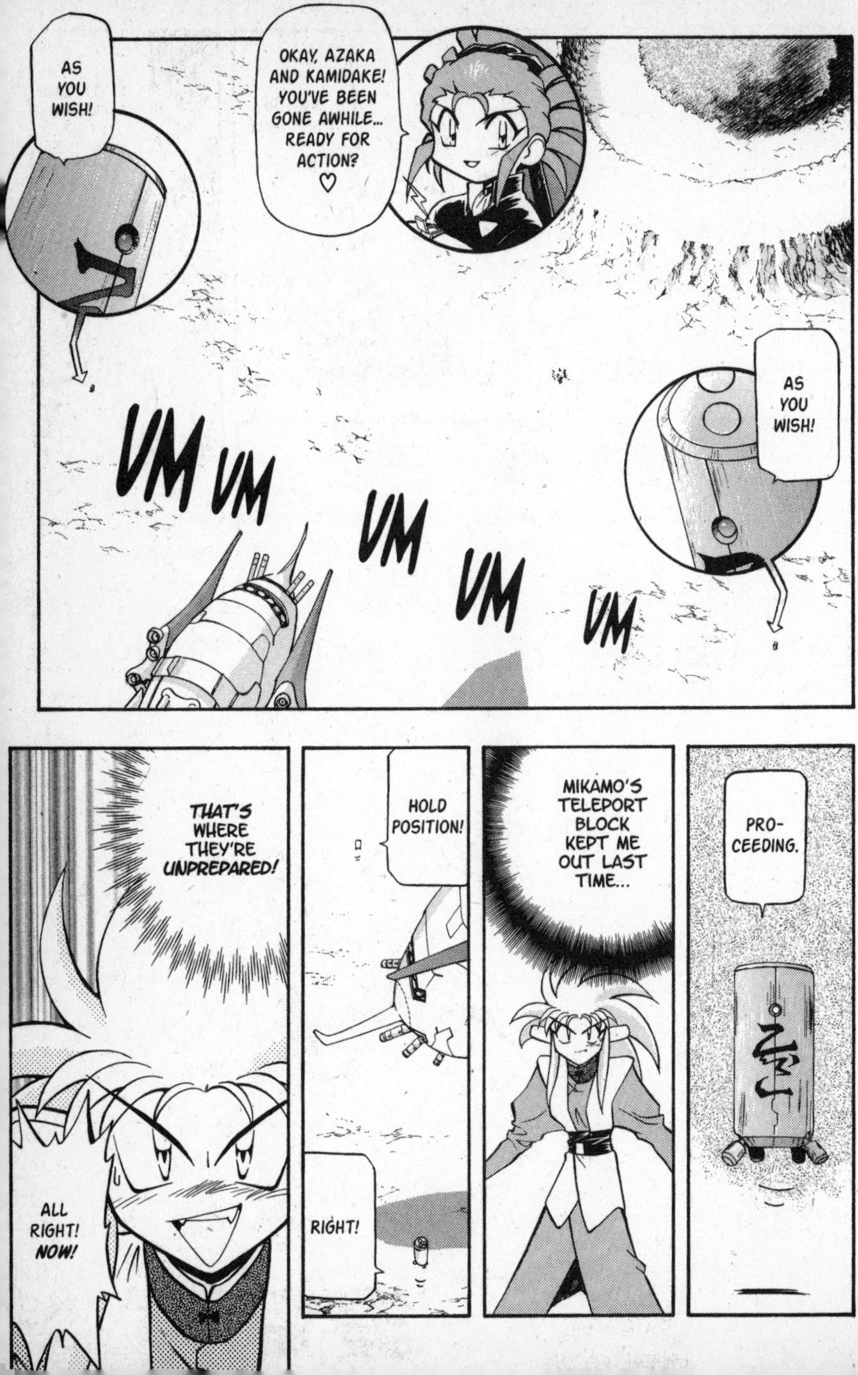
OKAY, AZAKA AND KAMIDAKE! YOU'VE BEEN GONE AWHILE... READY FOR ACTION? ♡
AS YOU WISH!
AS YOU WISH!
UM UM UM UM UM
PRO-CEEDING.
MIKAMO'S TELEPORT BLOCK KEPT ME OUT LAST TIME...
HOLD POSITION!
RIGHT!
THAT'S WHERE THEY'RE UNPREPARED!
ALL RIGHT! NOW!

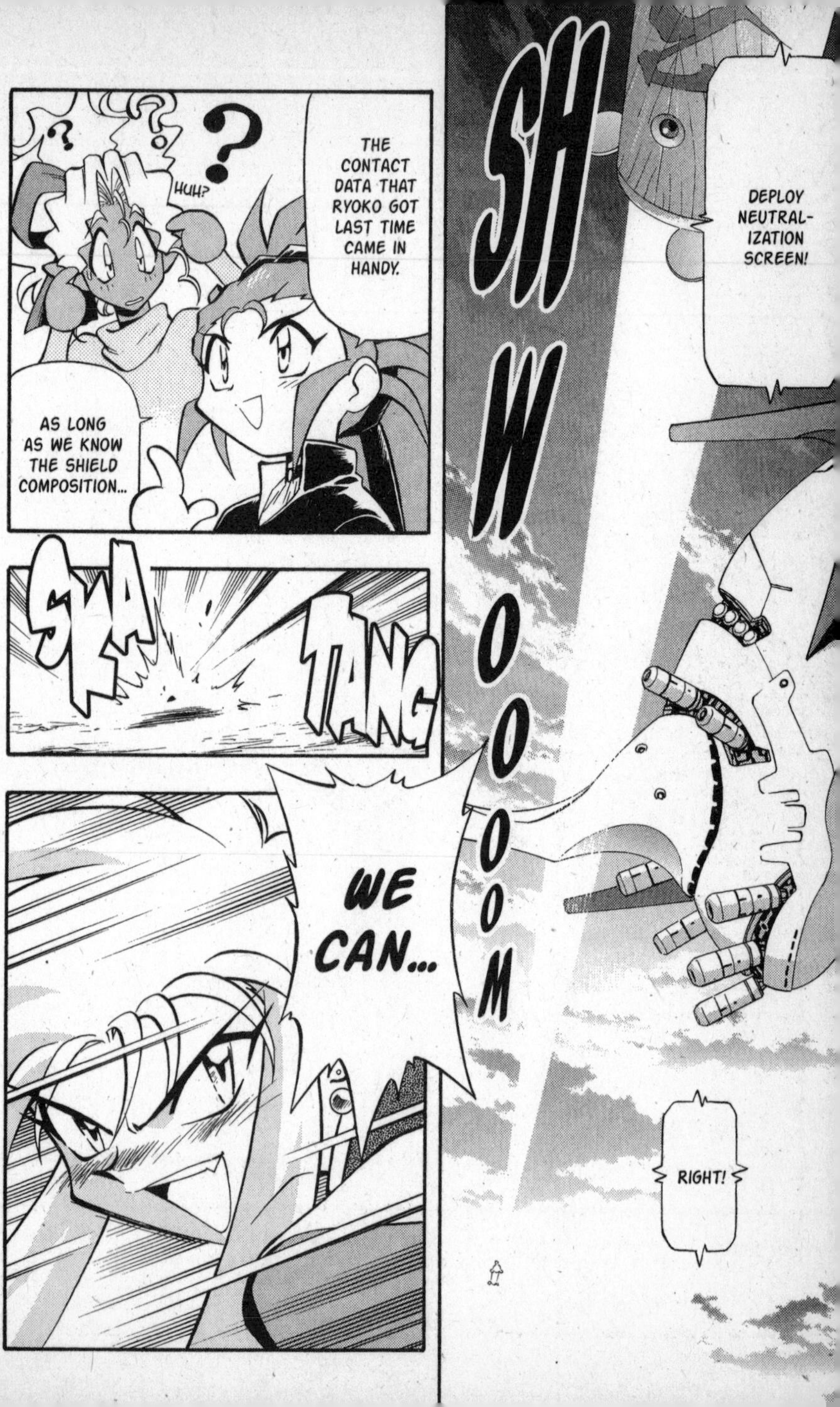
DEPLOY NEUTRAL-IZATION SCREEN!
SHWOOOOM
RIGHT!
THE CONTACT DATA THAT RYOKO GOT LAST TIME CAME IN HANDY.
?
HUH?
AS LONG AS WE KNOW THE SHIELD COMPOSITION...
TANG
SKA
WE CAN...

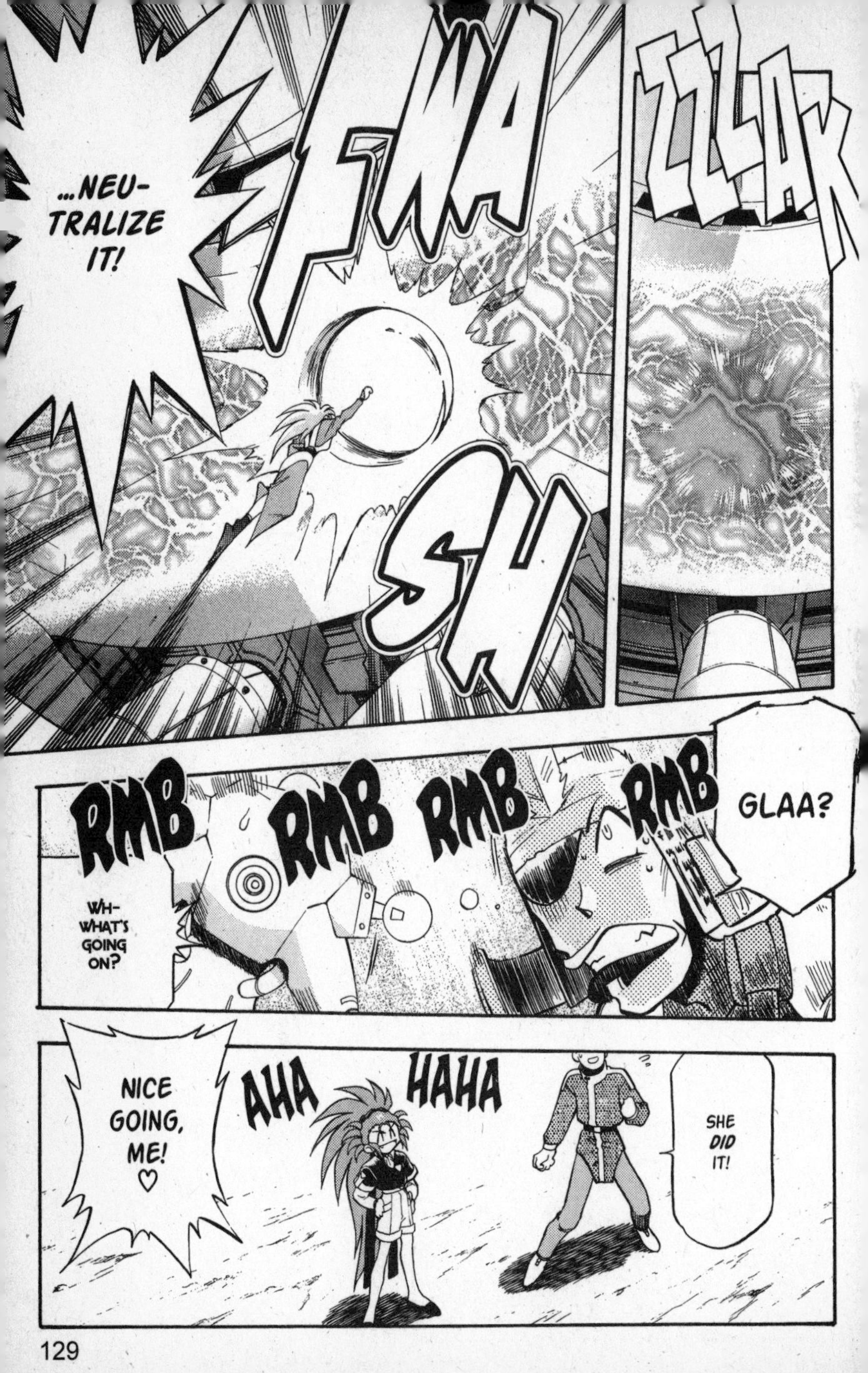
ZZLAK
SHWA
...NEU-TRALIZE IT!
SH
GLAA?
RMB RMB RMB RMB
WH-WHAT'S GOING ON?
SHE DID IT!
AHA HAHA
NICE GOING, ME! ♡

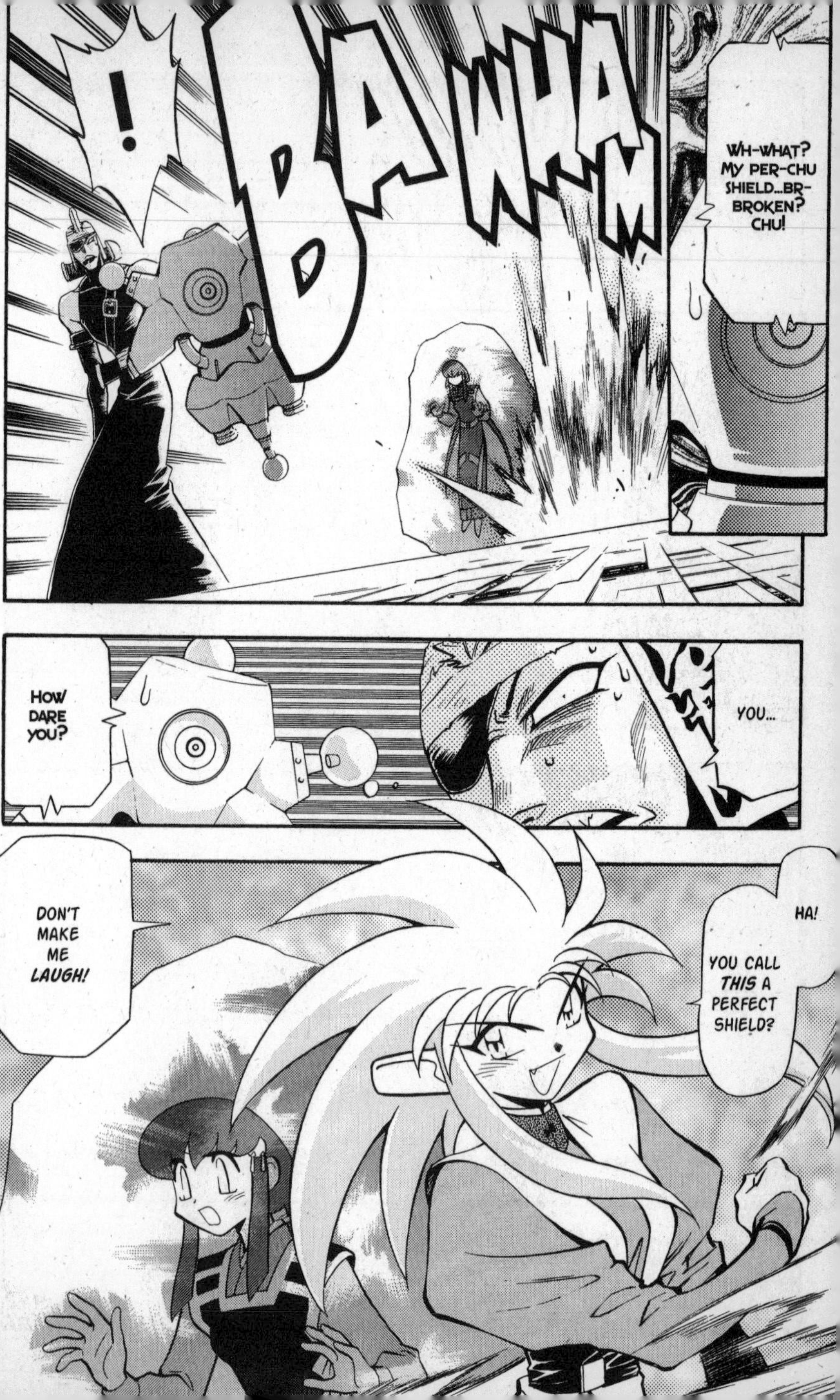
WH-WHAT? MY PER-CHU SHIELD...BR-BROKEN? CHU!
BAWHAM!
!
YOU...
HOW DARE YOU?
HA!
YOU CALL *THIS* A PERFECT SHIELD?
DON'T MAKE ME *LAUGH!*

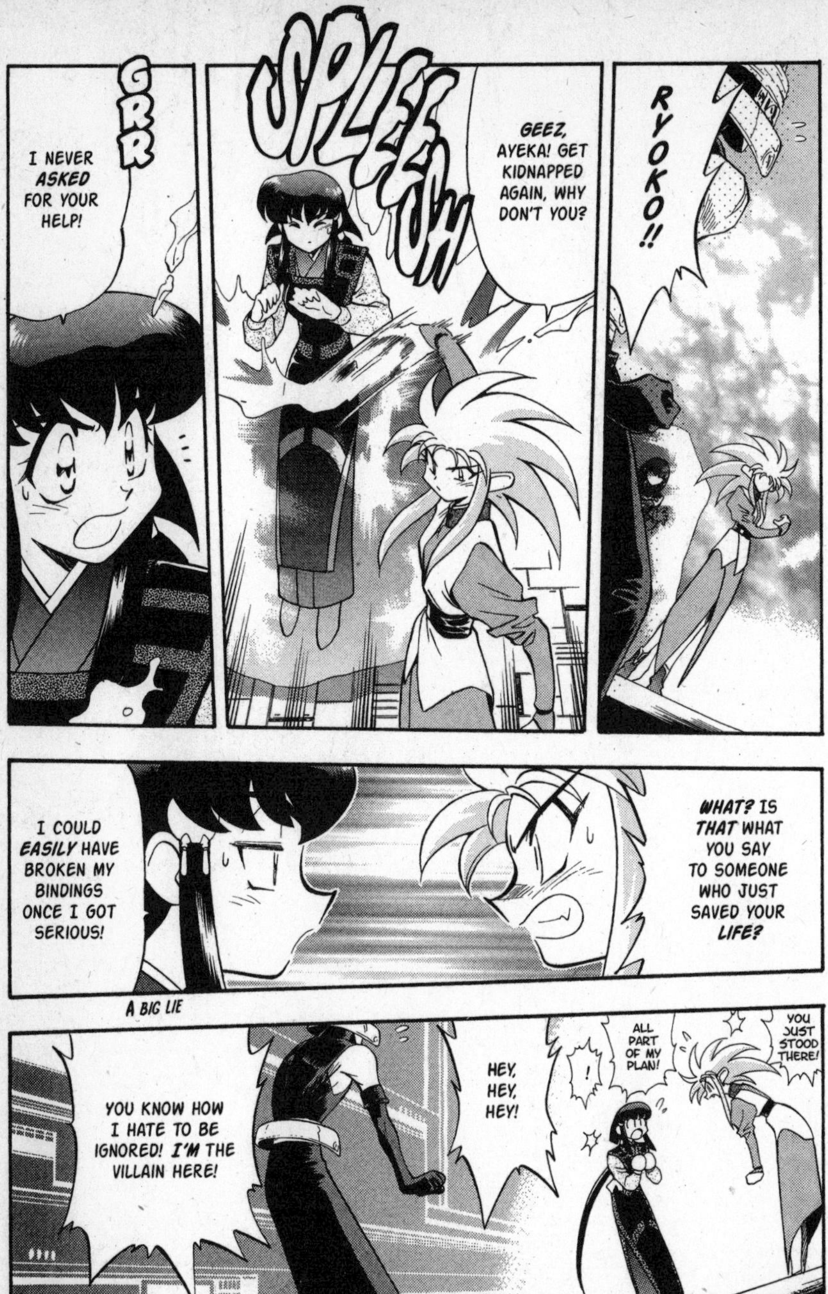

RYOKO!!
SPLEESH
GEEZ, AYEKA! GET KIDNAPPED AGAIN, WHY DON'T YOU?
GRR
I NEVER ASKED FOR YOUR HELP!
WHAT? IS THAT WHAT YOU SAY TO SOMEONE WHO JUST SAVED YOUR LIFE?
I COULD EASILY HAVE BROKEN MY BINDINGS ONCE I GOT SERIOUS!
A BIG LIE
YOU JUST STOOD THERE!
ALL PART OF MY PLAN!
!
HEY, HEY, HEY!
YOU KNOW HOW I HATE TO BE IGNORED! I'M THE VILLAIN HERE!

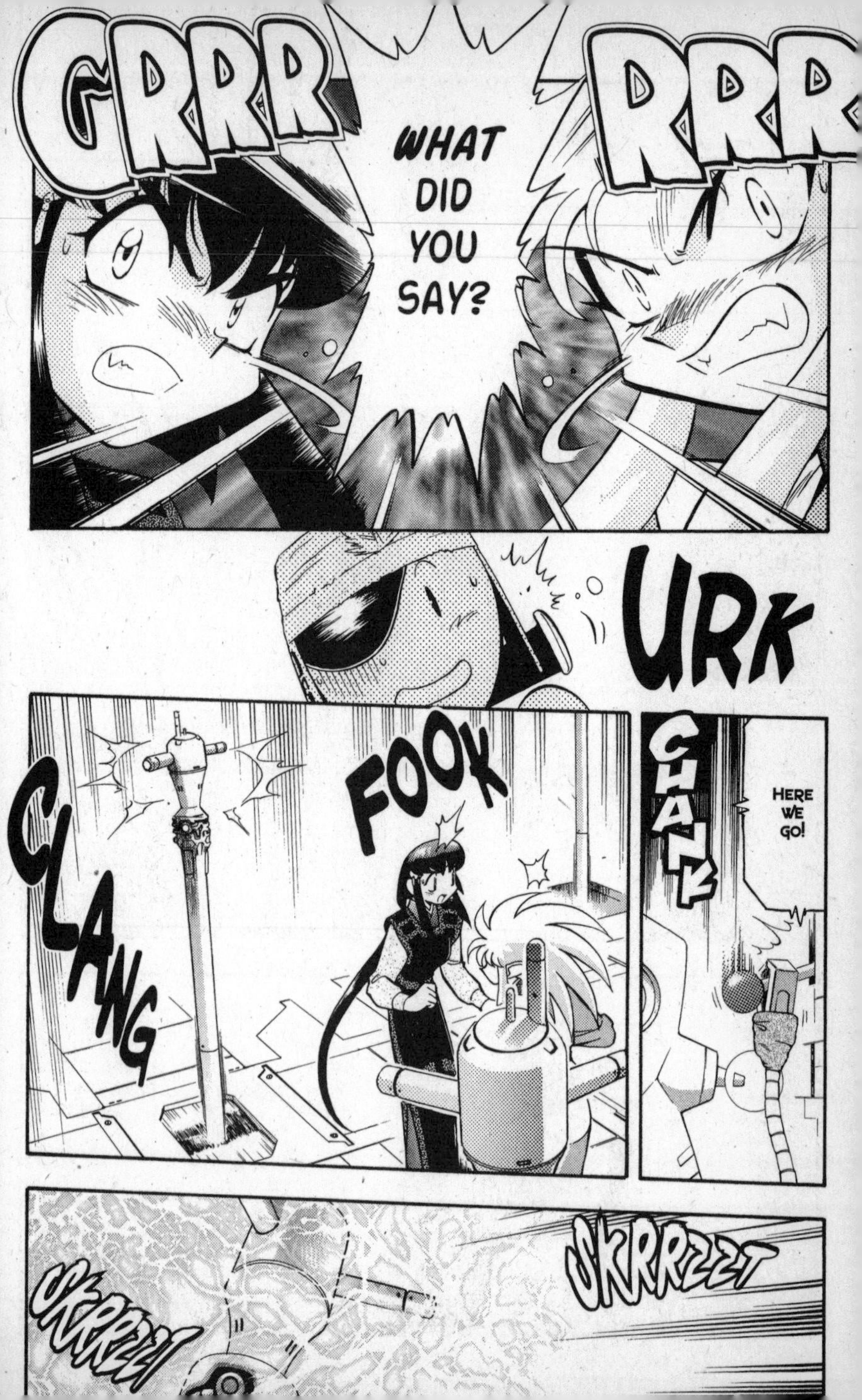
RRRR
WHAT DID YOU SAY?
GRRR
URK
CHANK
HERE WE GO!
FOOK
CLANG
SKRRZEET
SKRRZEET

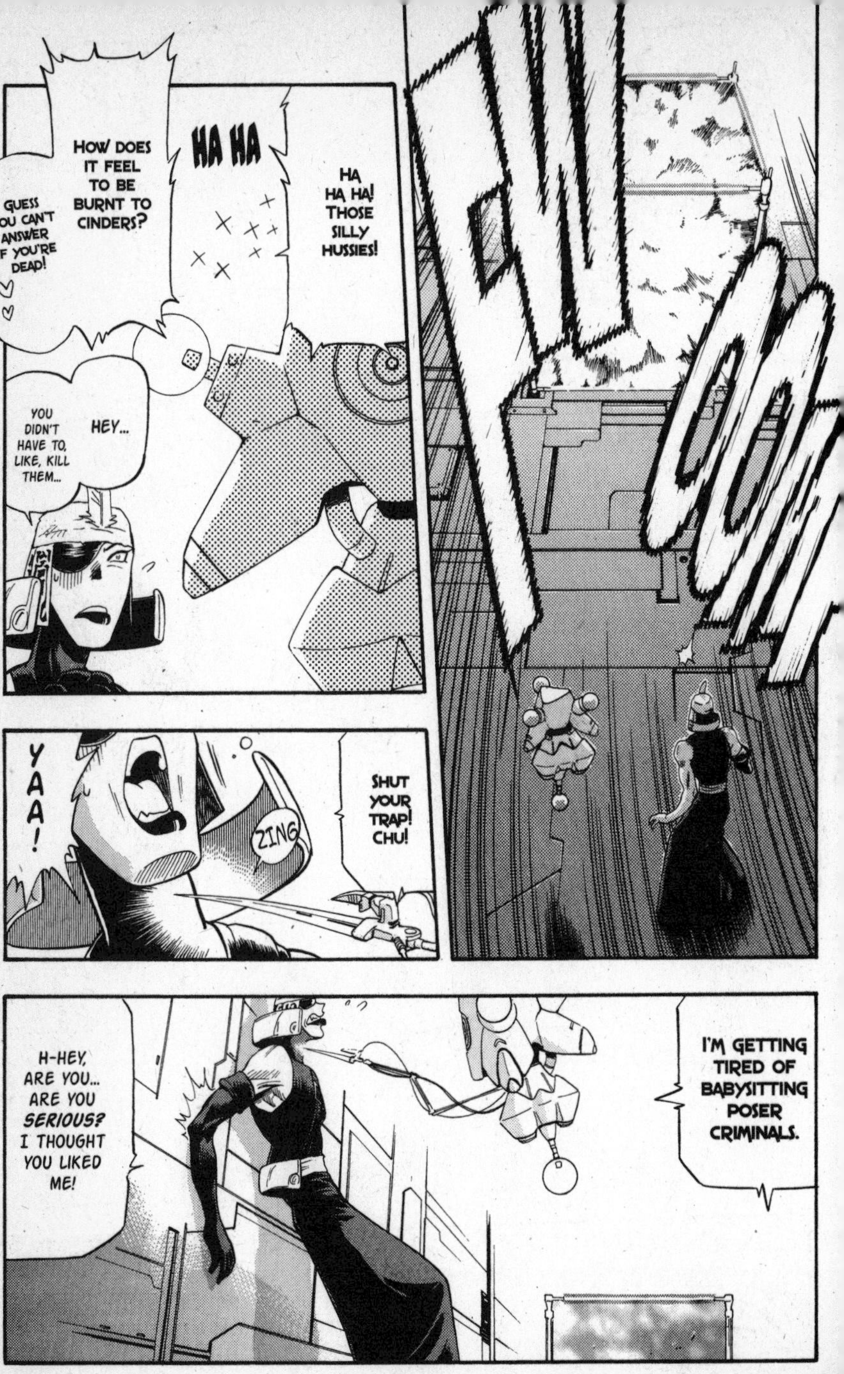
HA HA HA! THOSE SILLY HUSSIES!
HA HA
HOW DOES IT FEEL TO BE BURNT TO CINDERS?
GUESS YOU CAN'T ANSWER IF YOU'RE DEAD! ♡ ♡
HEY...
YOU DIDN'T HAVE TO, LIKE, KILL THEM...
SHUT YOUR TRAP! CHU!
ZING
YAAA!
I'M GETTING TIRED OF BABYSITTING POSER CRIMINALS.
H-HEY, ARE YOU... ARE YOU *SERIOUS?* I THOUGHT YOU LIKED ME!

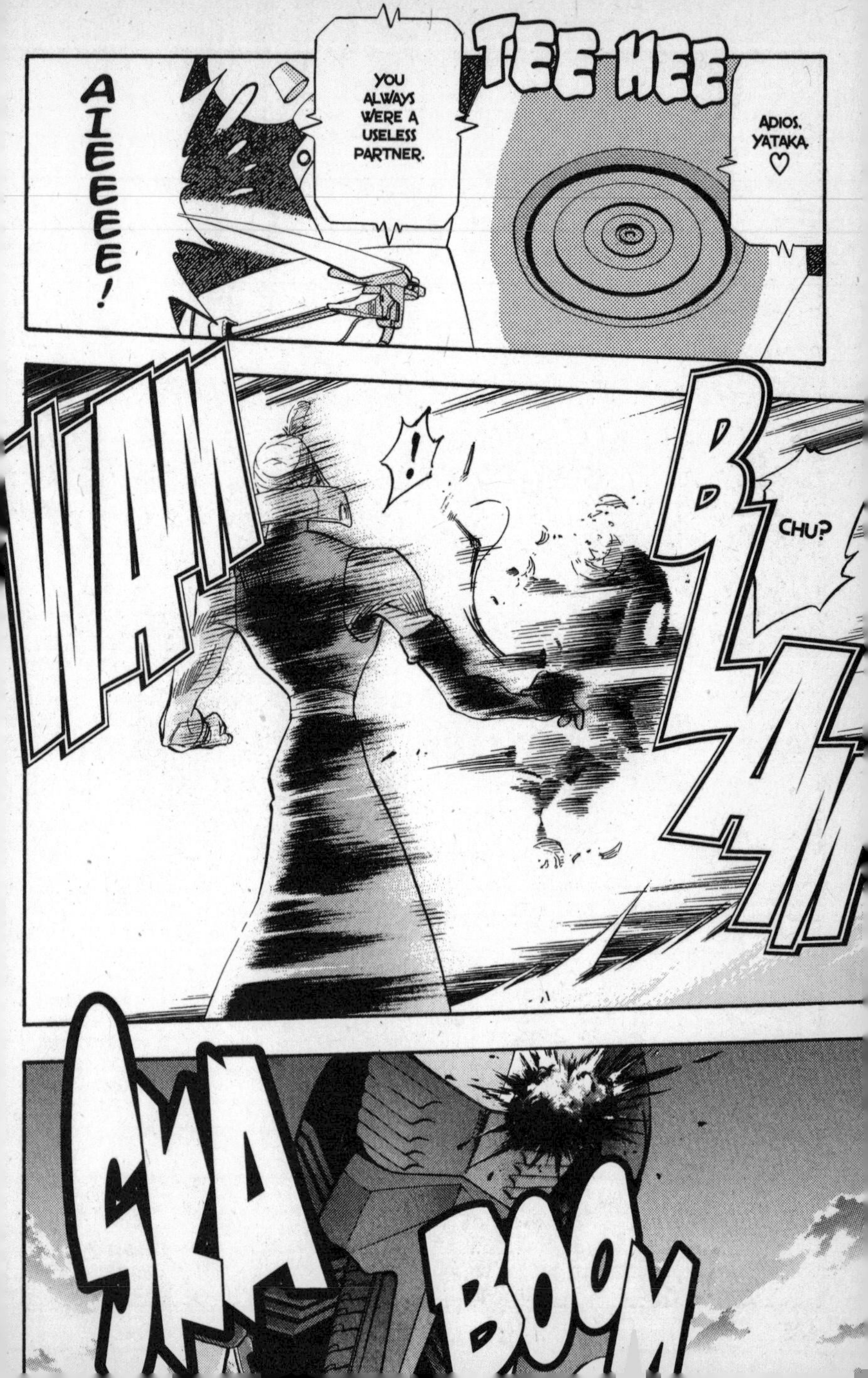
TEE HEE
ADIOS, YATAKA. ♡
YOU ALWAYS WERE A USELESS PARTNER.
AIEEEEE!
BLAM
CHU?
!
WAM
SKA
BOOM

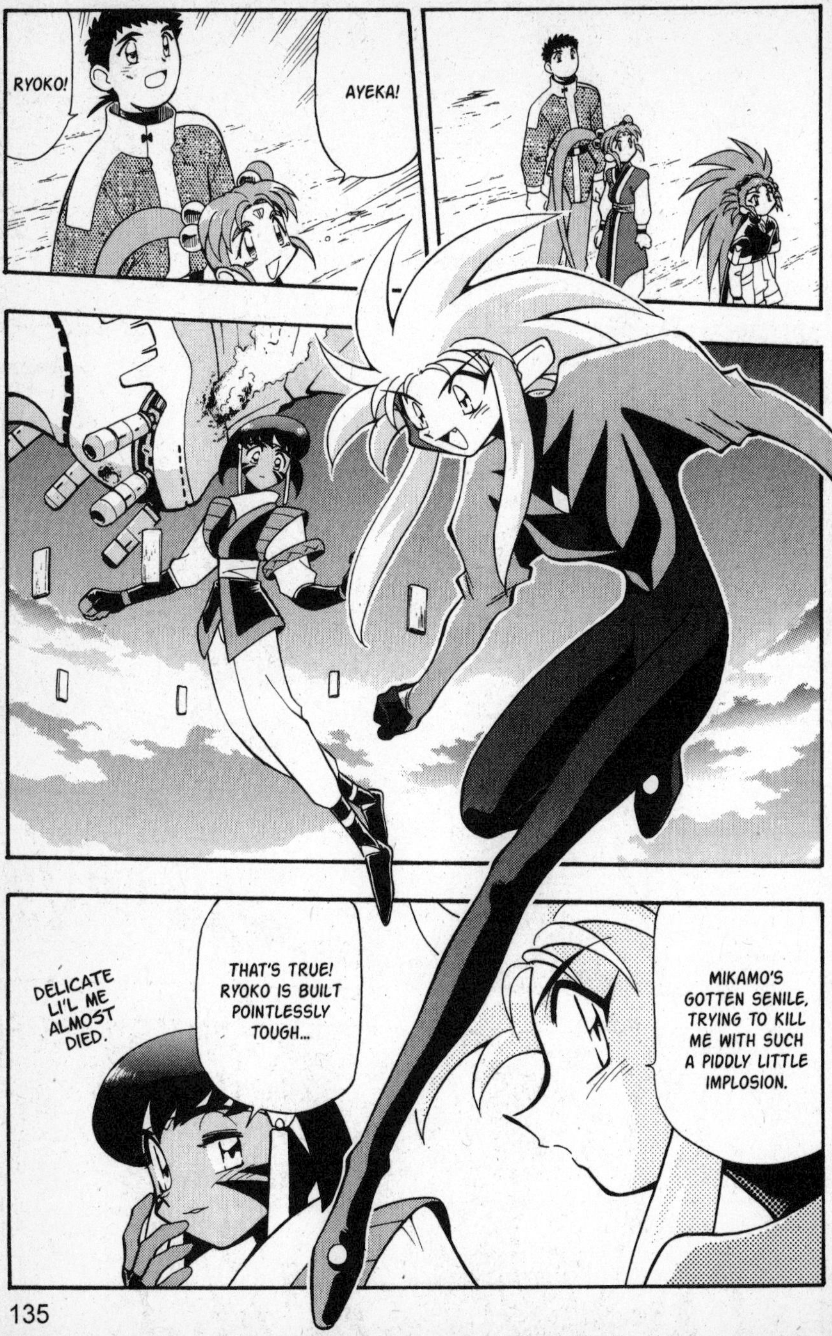
AYEKA!
RYOKO!
MIKAMO'S GOTTEN SENILE, TRYING TO KILL ME WITH SUCH A PIDDLY LITTLE IMPLOSION.
THAT'S TRUE! RYOKO IS BUILT POINTLESSLY TOUGH...
DELICATE LI'L ME ALMOST DIED.

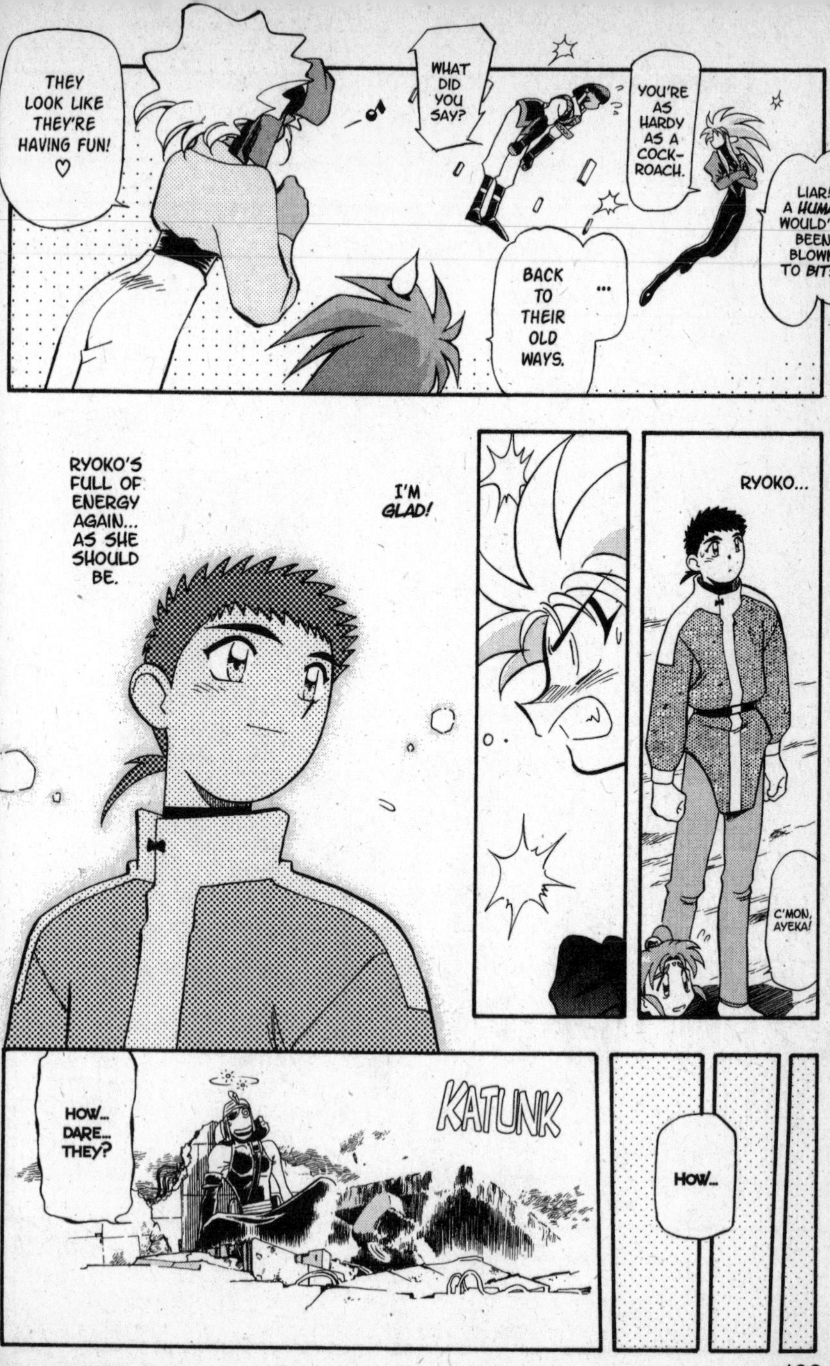

LIAR! A HUMAN WOULD'VE BEEN BLOWN TO BITS.
YOU'RE AS HARDY AS A COCKROACH.
WHAT DID YOU SAY?
...
BACK TO THEIR OLD WAYS.
THEY LOOK LIKE THEY'RE HAVING FUN! ♡
RYOKO...
C'MON, AYEKA!
I'M GLAD!
RYOKO'S FULL OF ENERGY AGAIN... AS SHE SHOULD BE.
HOW...
KATUNK
HOW... DARE... THEY?

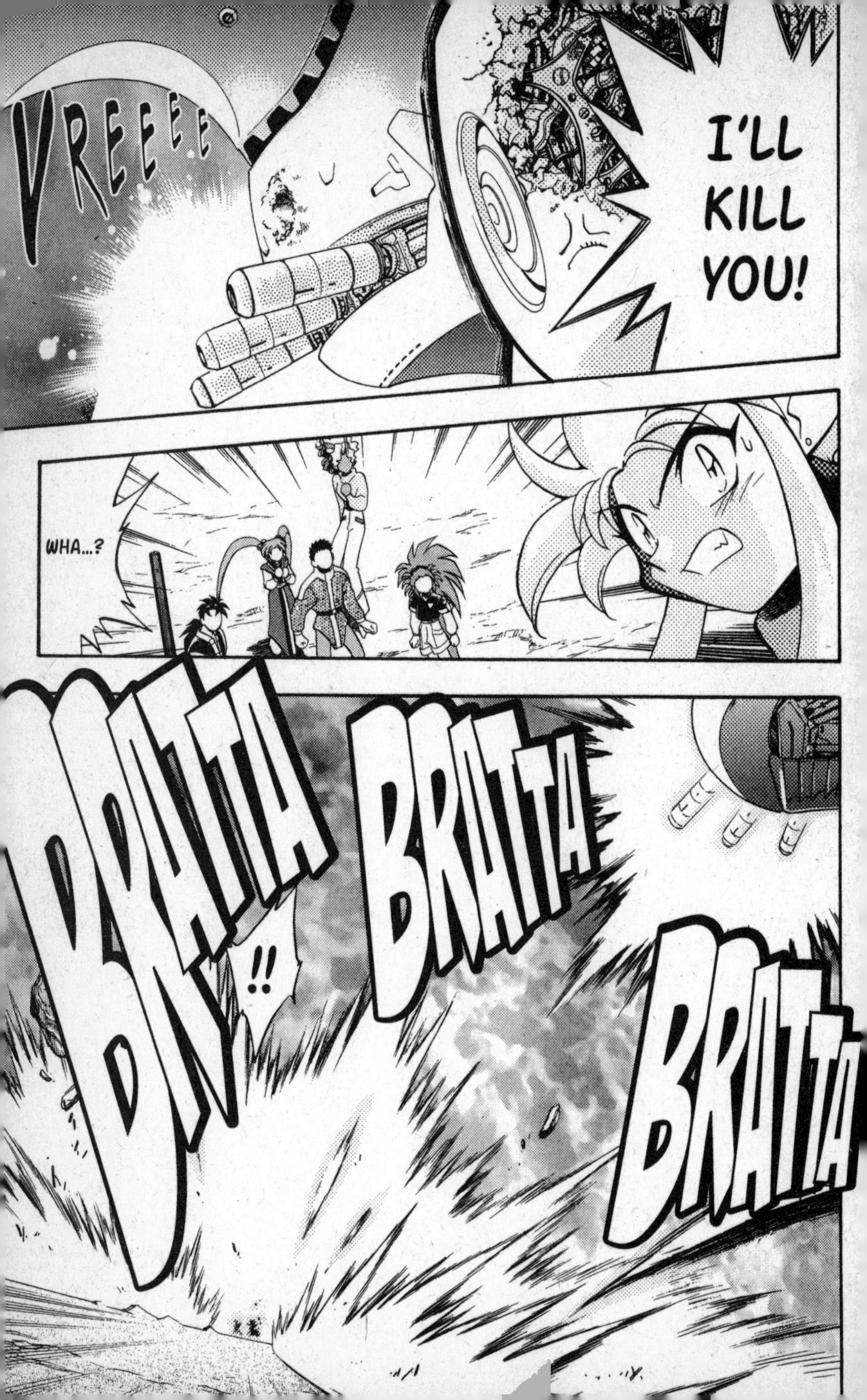
I'LL KILL YOU!
VREEEE
WHA...?
BRATTA
BRATTA
BRATTA
!!

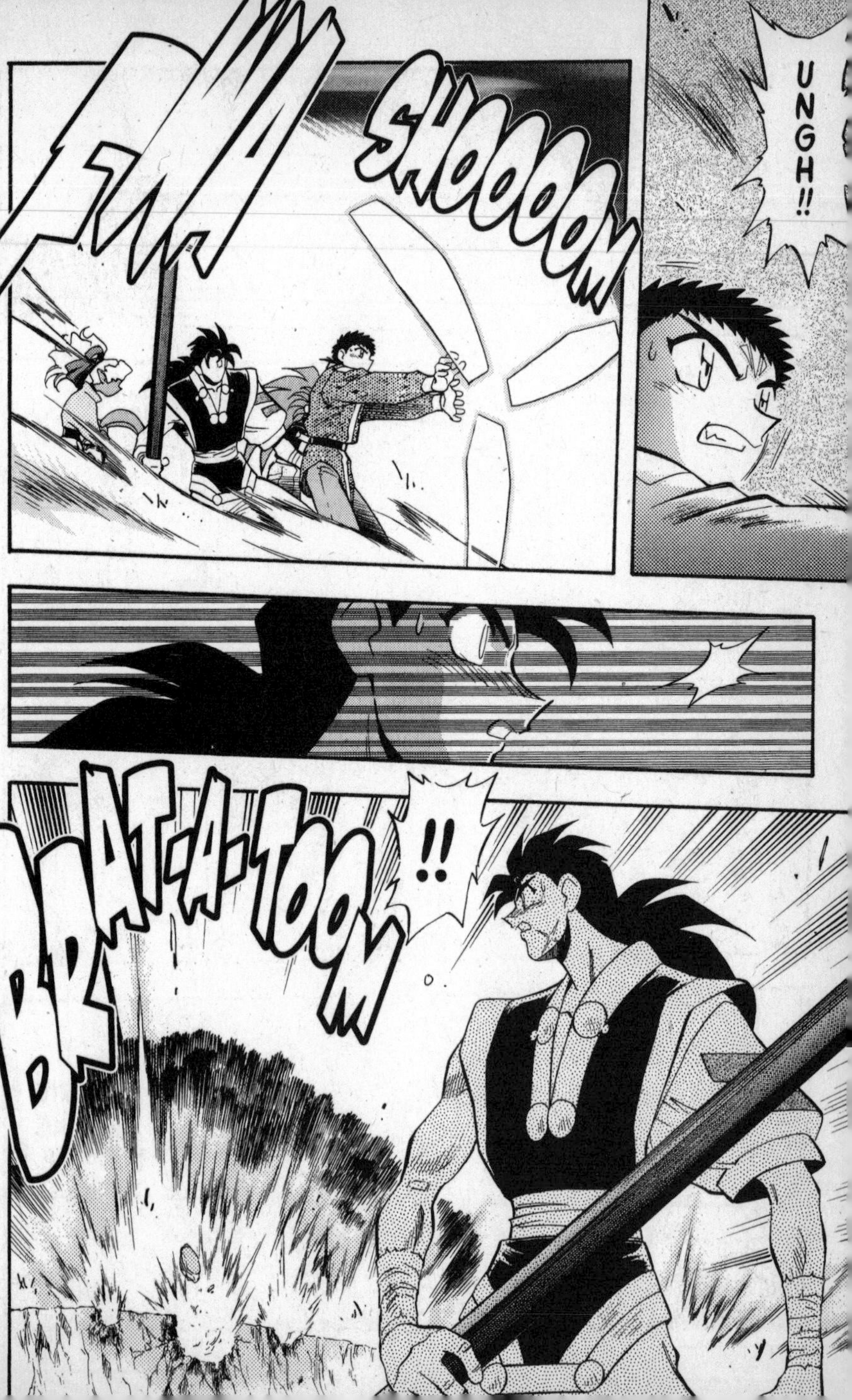
UNGH!!
SHOOOOM
FWAM
!!
BRAT-A-TOOM

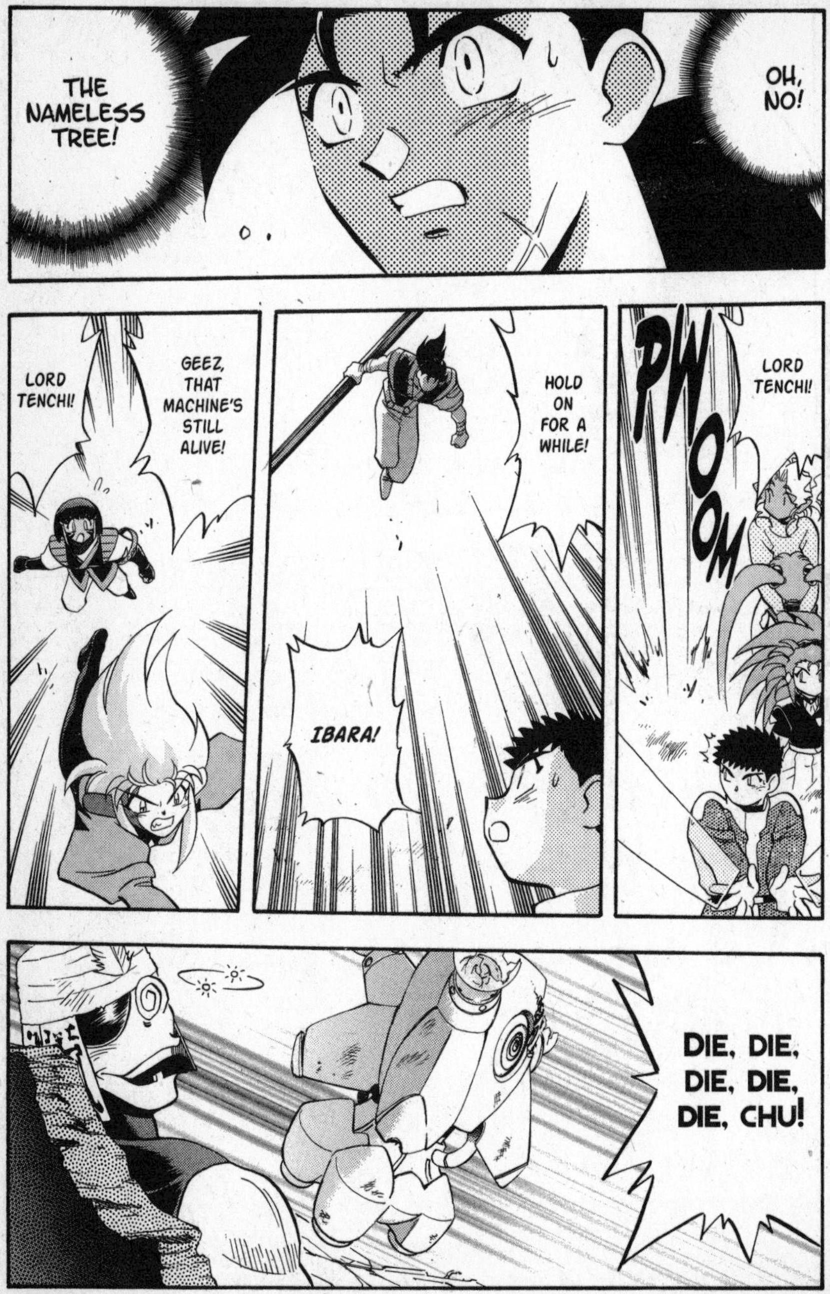
OH, NO!
THE NAMELESS TREE!
PWOOM
LORD TENCHI!
HOLD ON FOR A WHILE!
IBARA!
GEEZ, THAT MACHINE'S STILL ALIVE!
LORD TENCHI!
DIE, DIE, DIE, DIE, DIE, CHU!

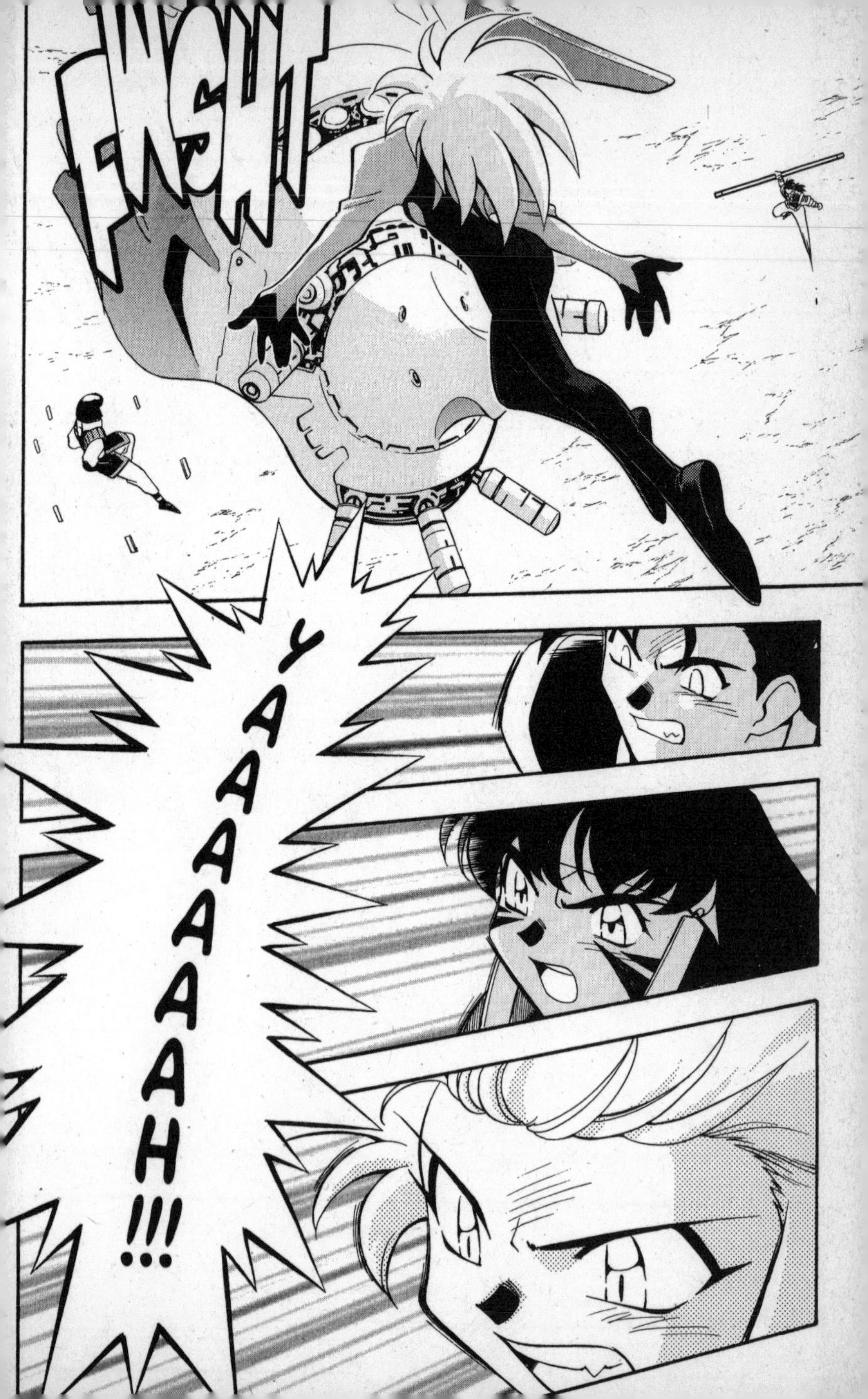
FWSHT
YAAAAAAAAH!!!

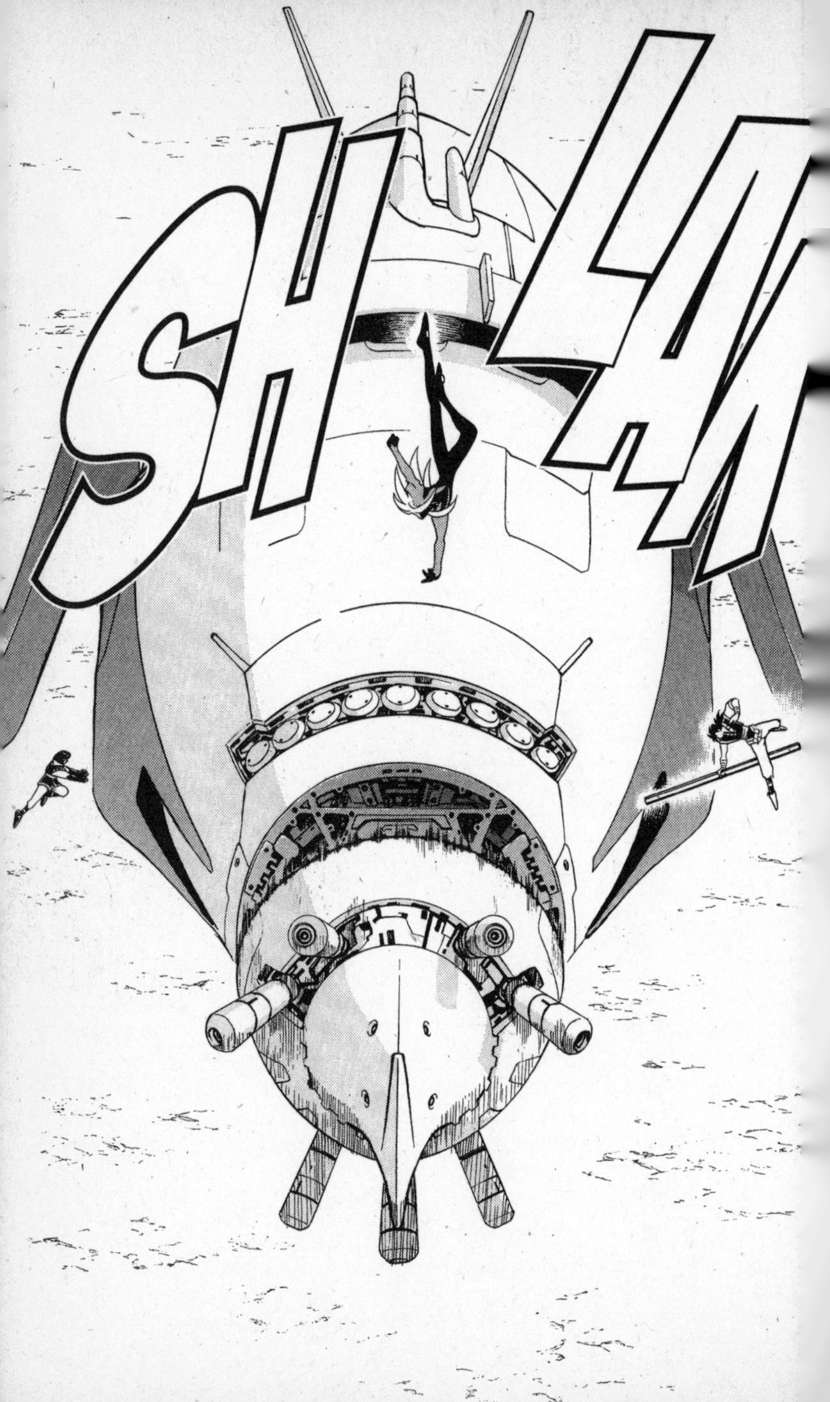
SH-LA

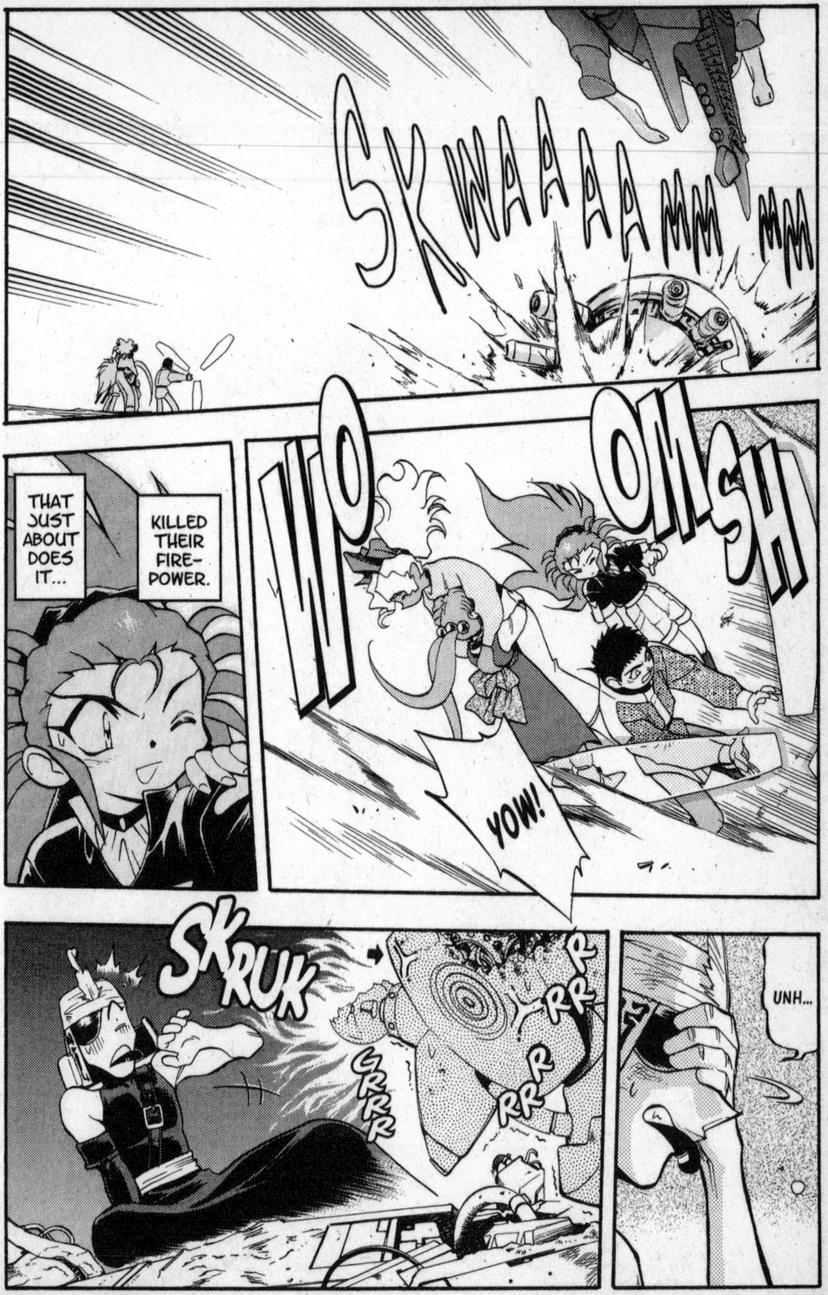
SKWAAAAMMMM
WHOOMSH
YOW!
KILLED THEIR FIRE-POWER.
THAT JUST ABOUT DOES IT...
UNH...
SKRUK
RRRRRRRR
GRRR

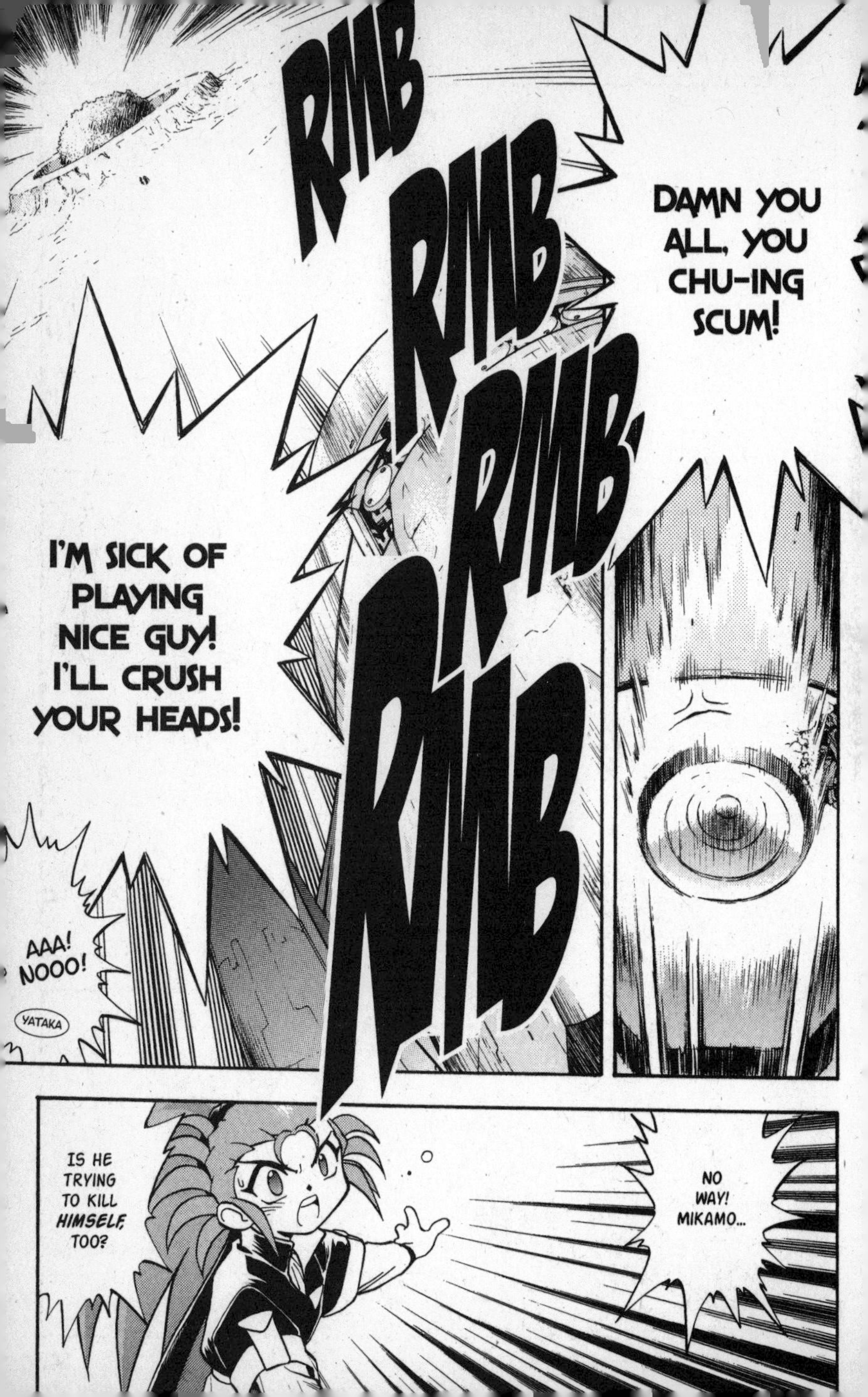
DAMN YOU ALL, YOU CHU-ING SCUM!
RMB RMB RMB RMB
I'M SICK OF PLAYING NICE GUY! I'LL CRUSH YOUR HEADS!
AAA! NOOO!
YATAKA
NO WAY! MIKAMO...
IS HE TRYING TO KILL *HIMSELF*, TOO?

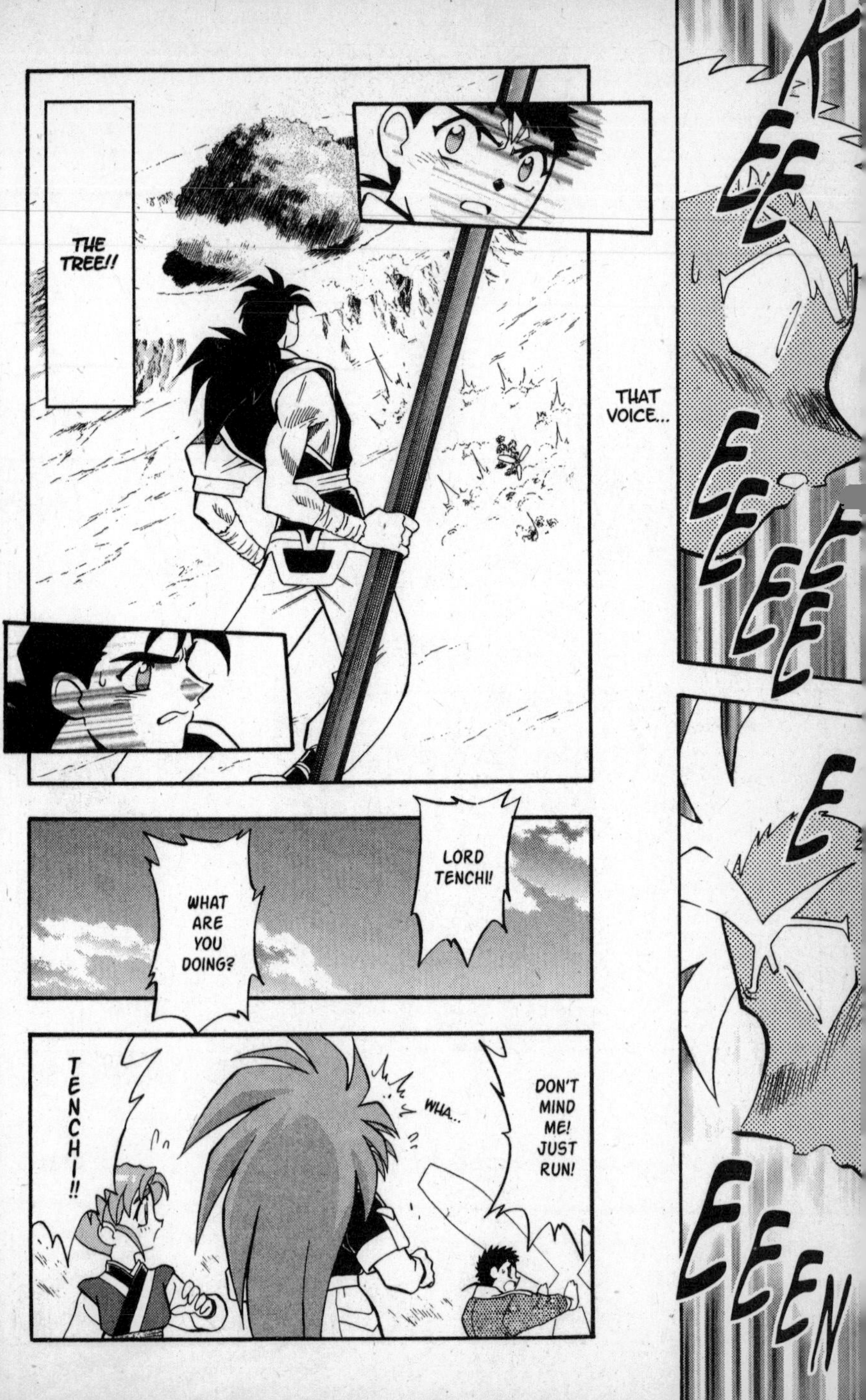
KEEEEEEEEEEEN
THAT VOICE...
THE TREE!!
LORD TENCHI!
WHAT ARE YOU DOING?
DON'T MIND ME! JUST RUN!
WHA...
TENCHI!!

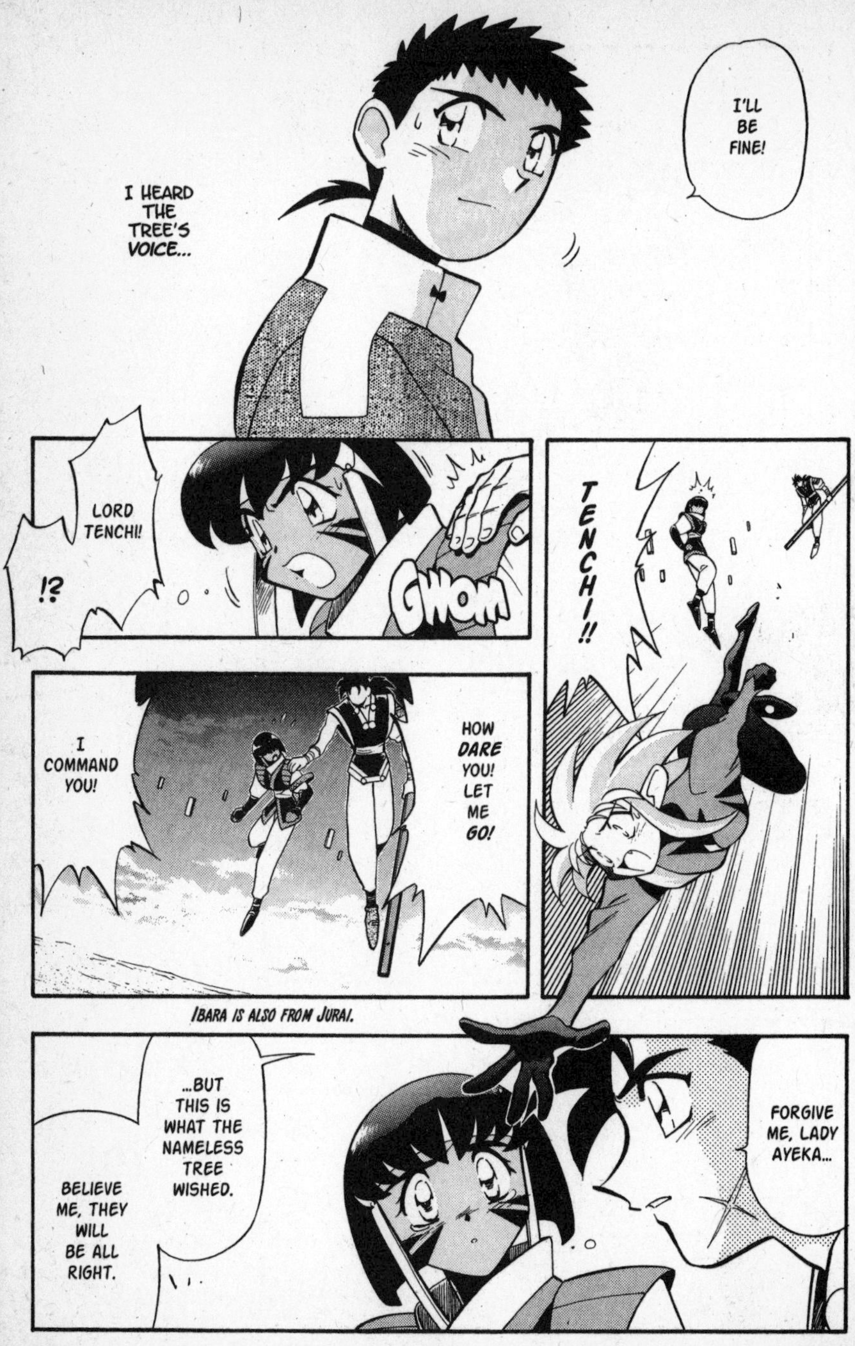
I'LL BE FINE!
I HEARD THE TREE'S VOICE...
TENCHI!!
LORD TENCHI!
!?
GWOM
HOW DARE YOU! LET ME GO!
I COMMAND YOU!
IBARA IS ALSO FROM JURAI.
FORGIVE ME, LADY AYEKA...
...BUT THIS IS WHAT THE NAMELESS TREE WISHED.
BELIEVE ME, THEY WILL BE ALL RIGHT.

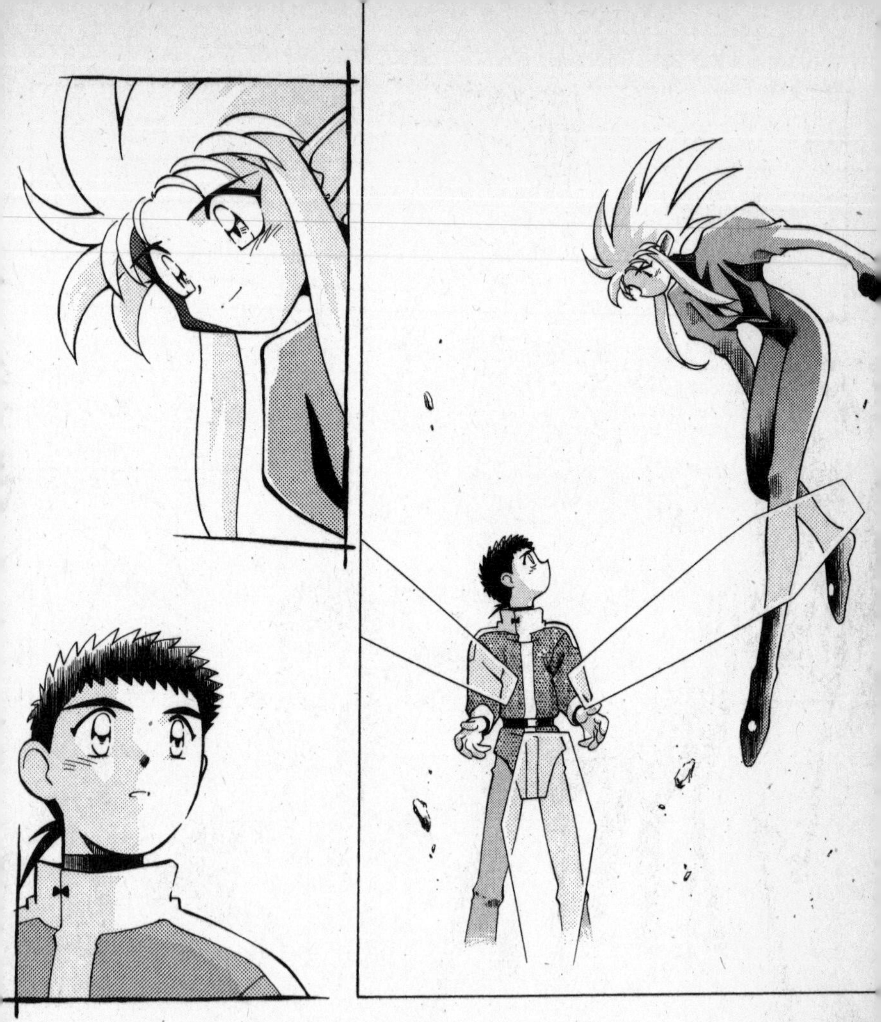
YOU HEARD THE VOICE, RYOKO?
YEAH...
IT'S OKAY. WE CAN DO IT.
RIGHT, TENCHI?

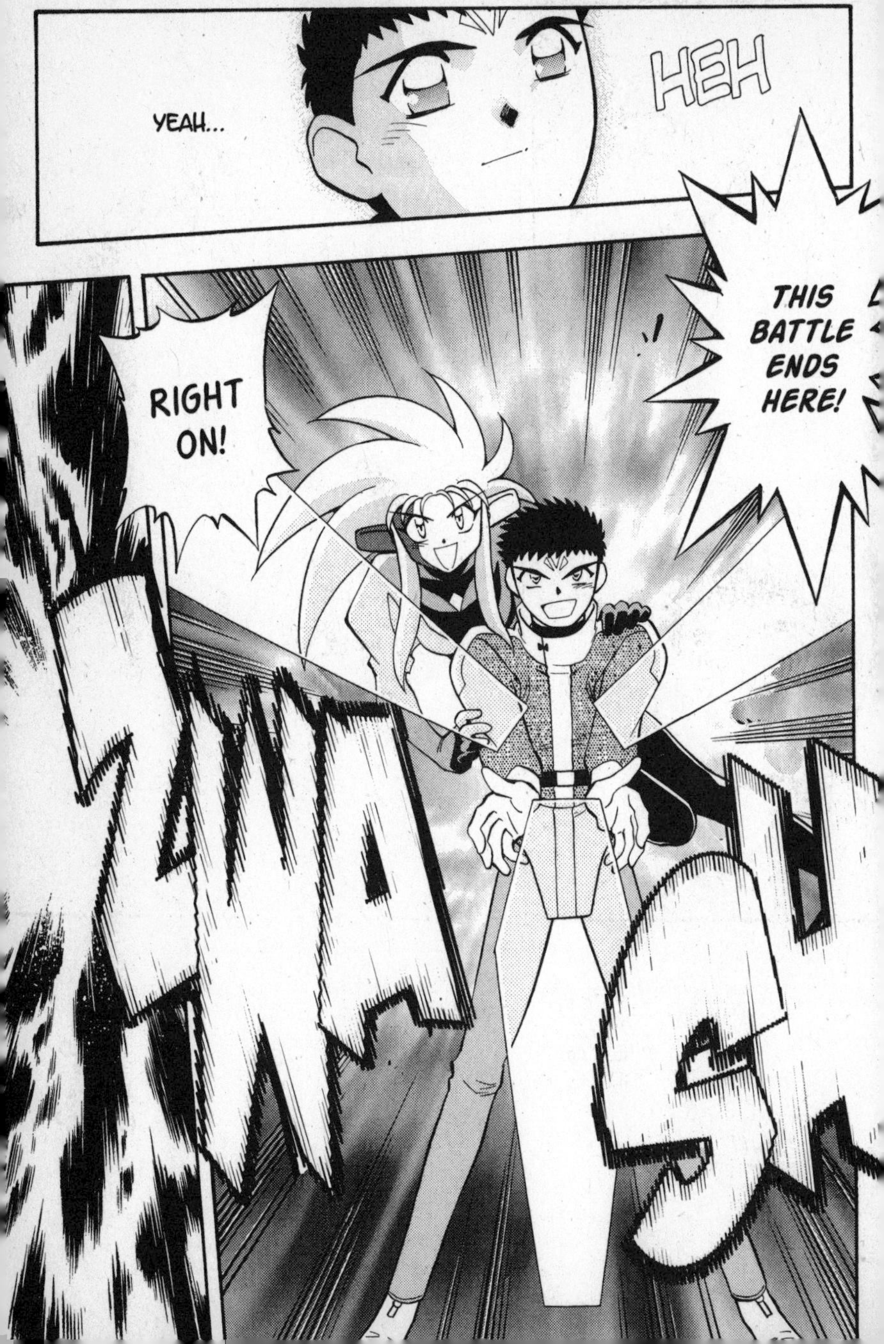
HEH
YEAH...
THIS BATTLE ENDS HERE!
RIGHT ON!
ZWASH

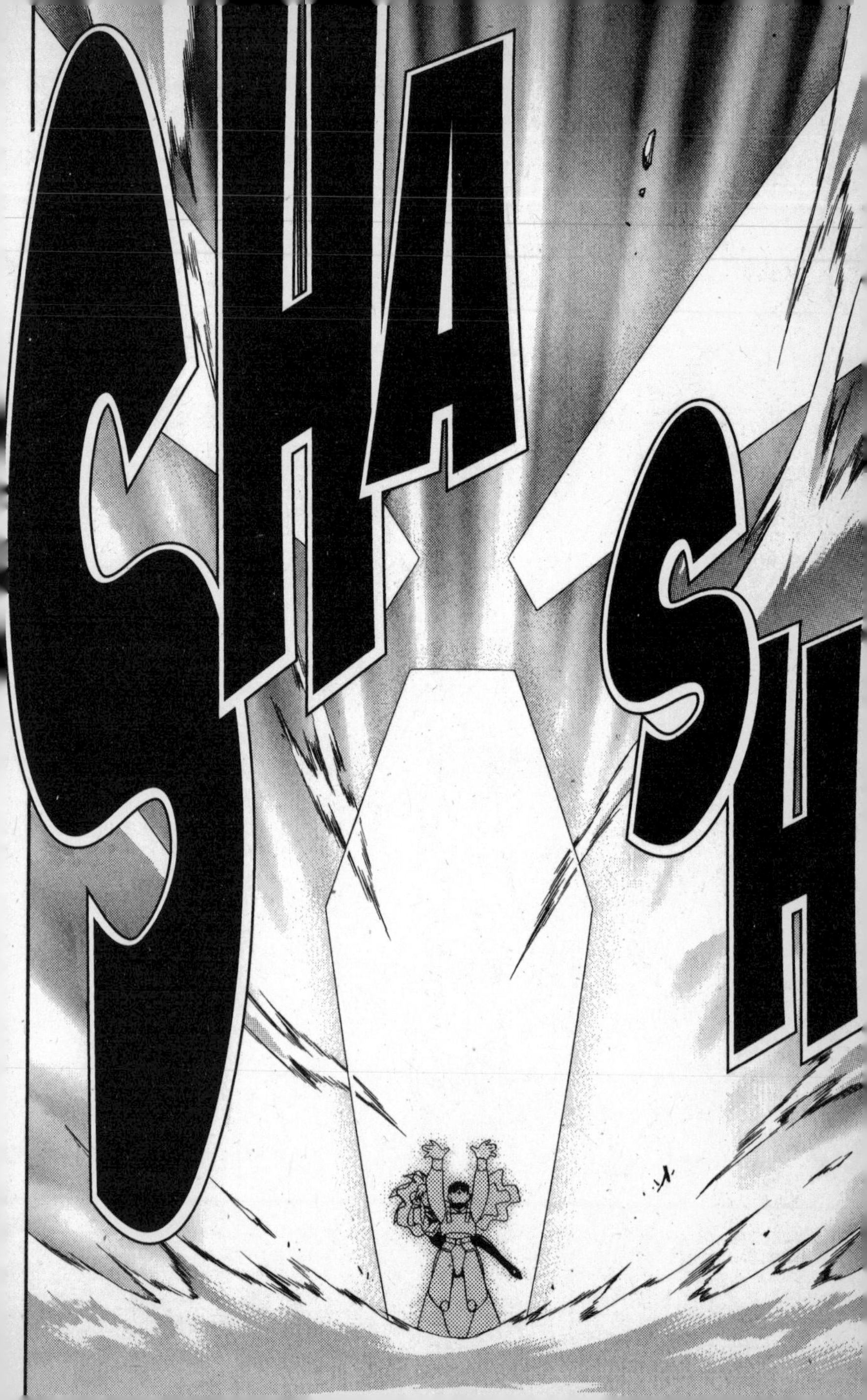
SHA
SH

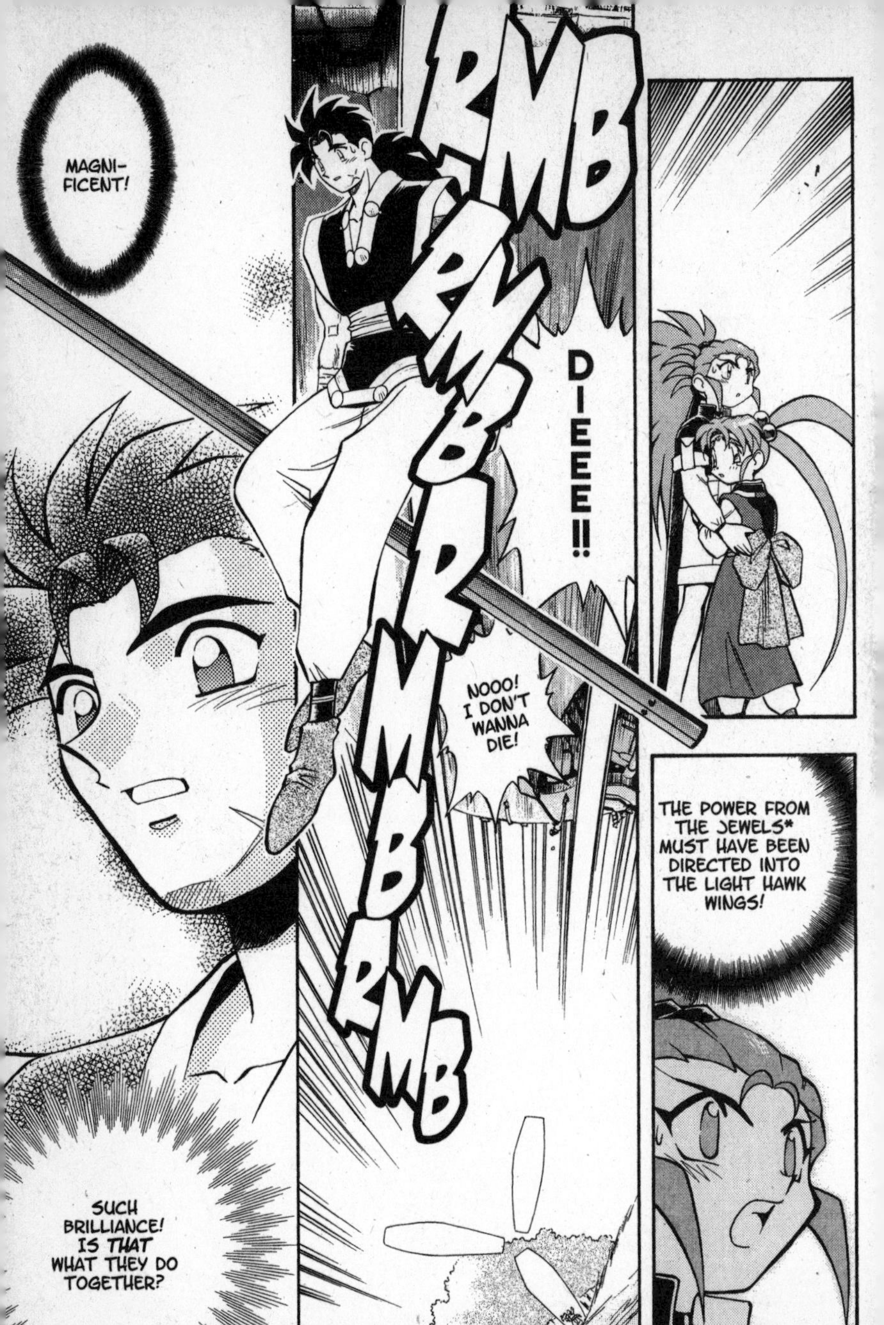
THE POWER FROM THE JEWELS* MUST HAVE BEEN DIRECTED INTO THE LIGHT HAWK WINGS!
RMB
RMBRMBRMBRMB
DIEEE!!
NOOO! I DON'T WANNA DIE!
MAGNI-FICENT!
SUCH BRILLIANCE! IS THAT WHAT THEY DO TOGETHER?
*THE THREE JEWELS THAT POWER RYOKO! REMEMBER THE OAV SERIES?

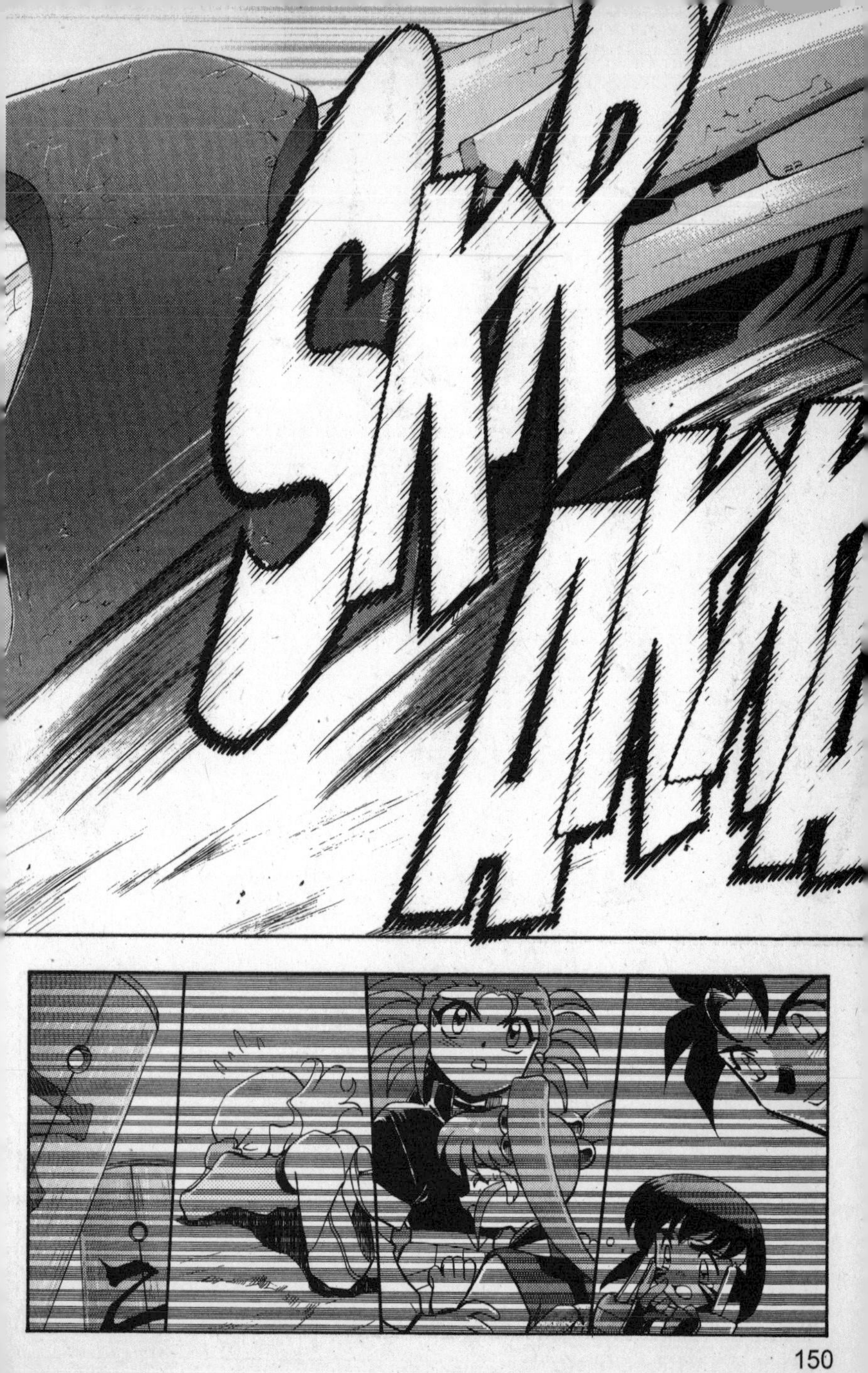

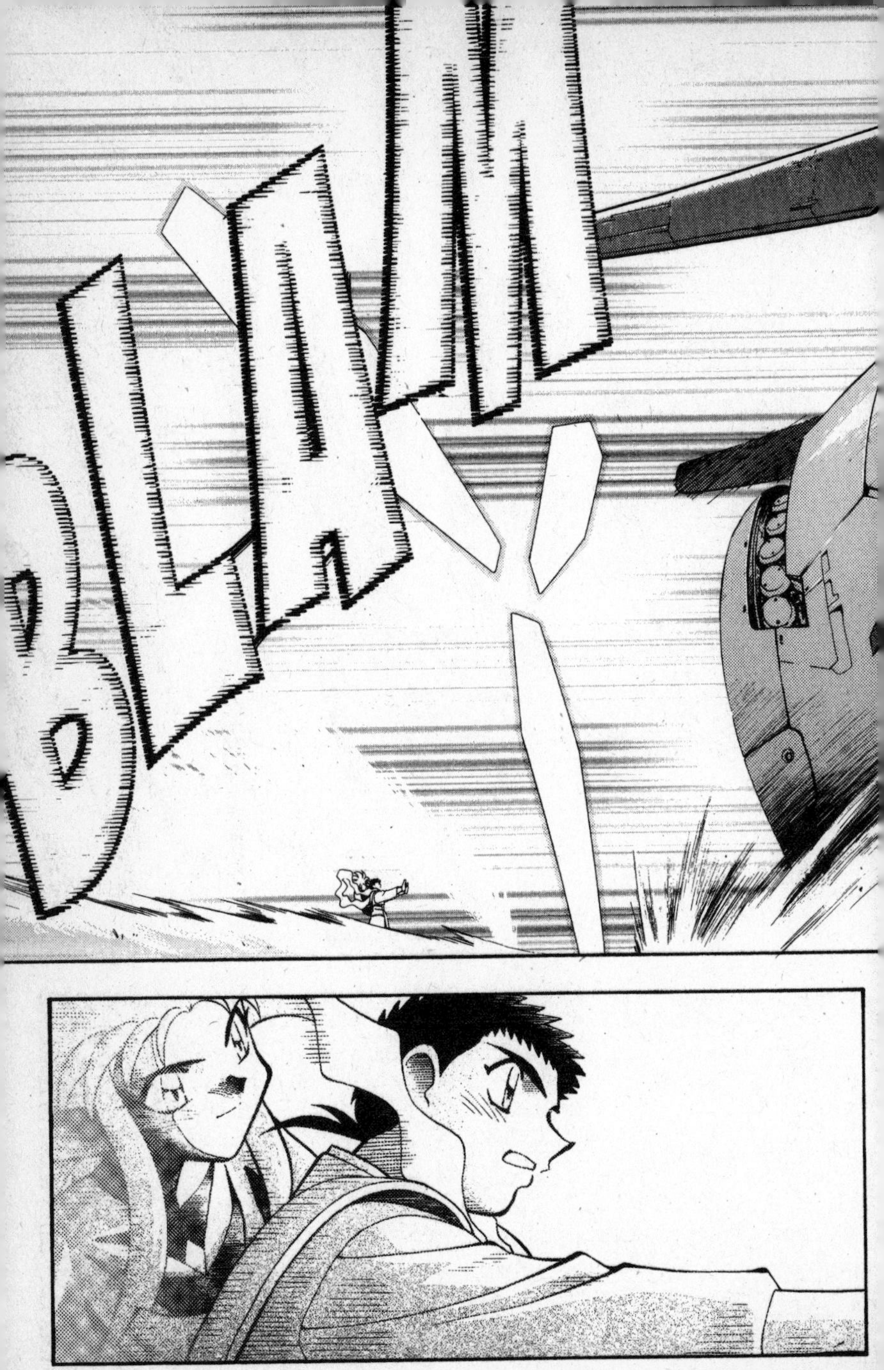
BLAM

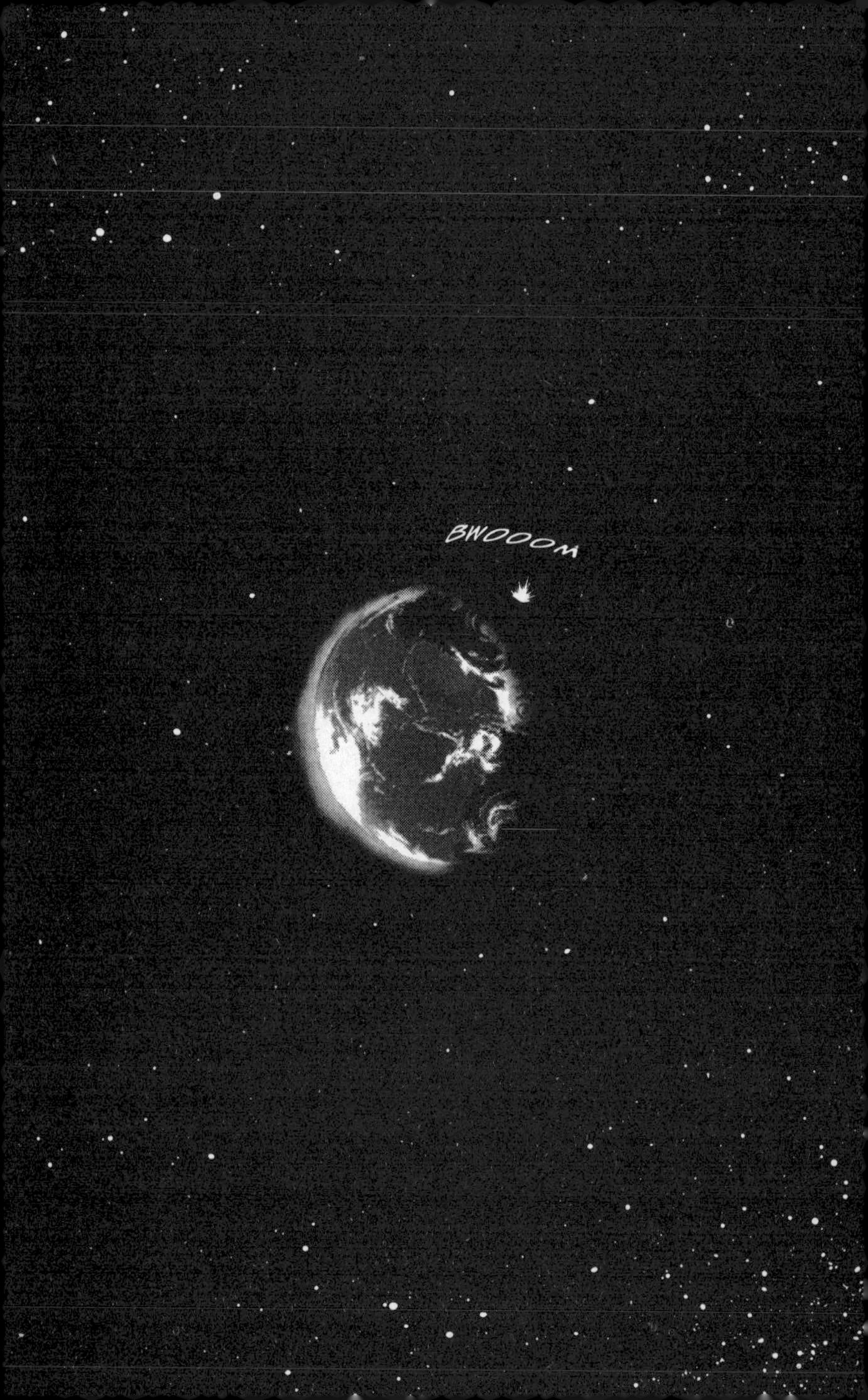
BWOOOM

Tales of Tenchi #6: IN THE SPOTLIGHT

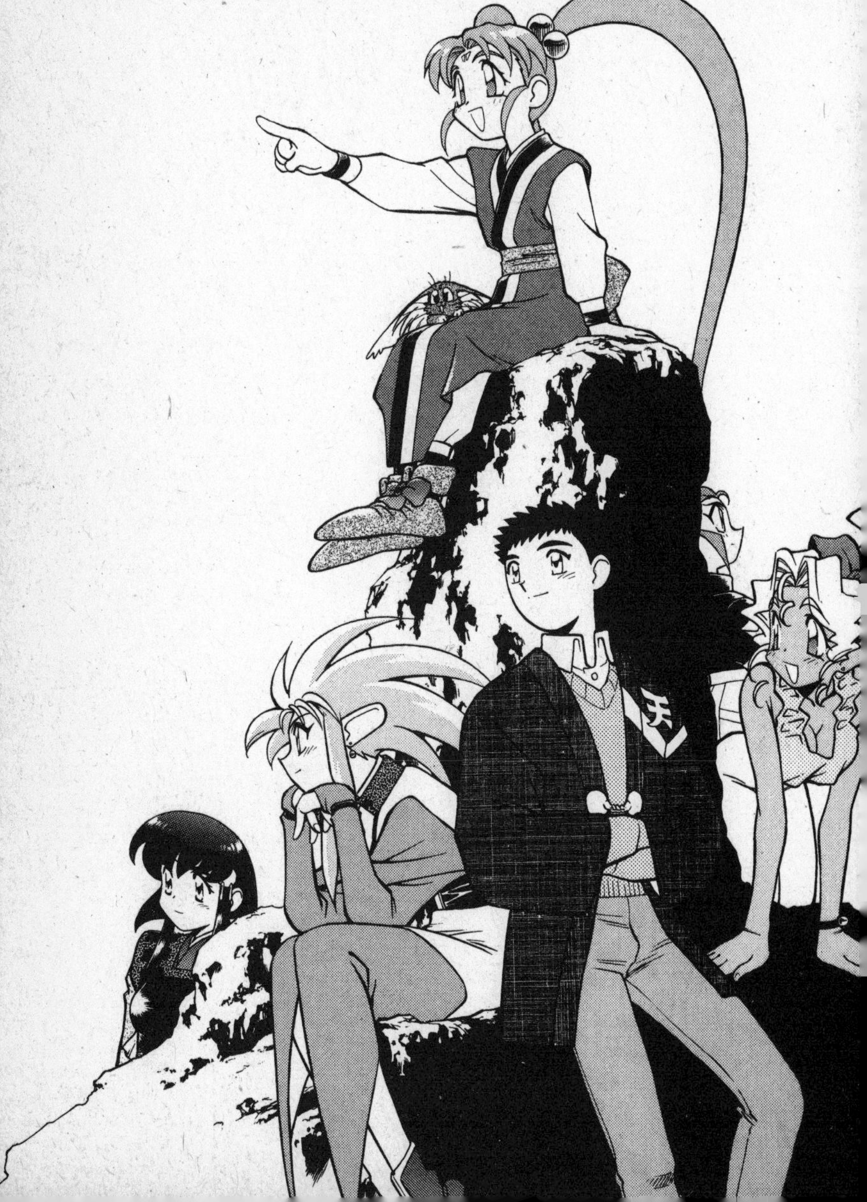

天

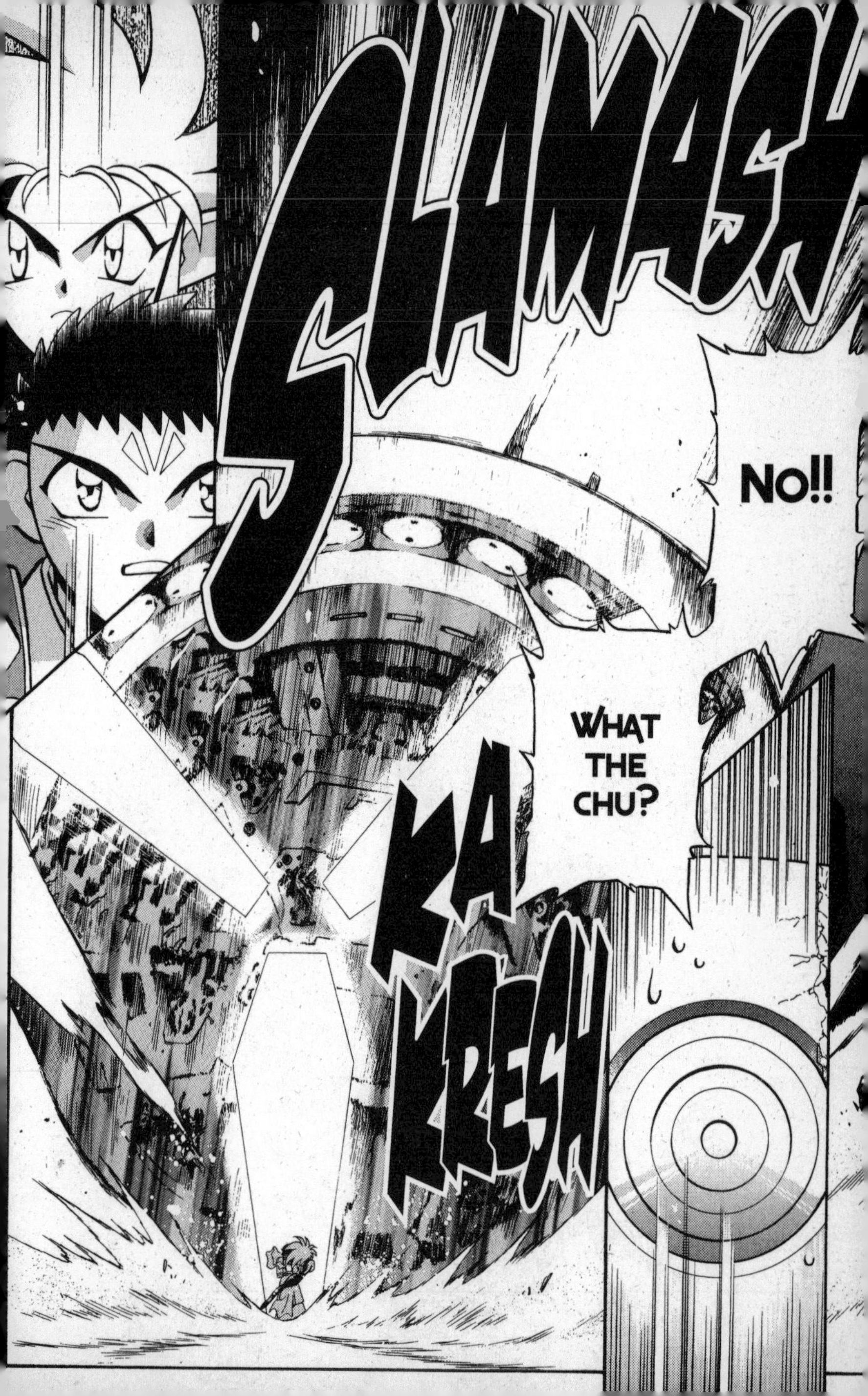
SLAMASH
NO!!
WHAT THE CHU?
KA KRESH

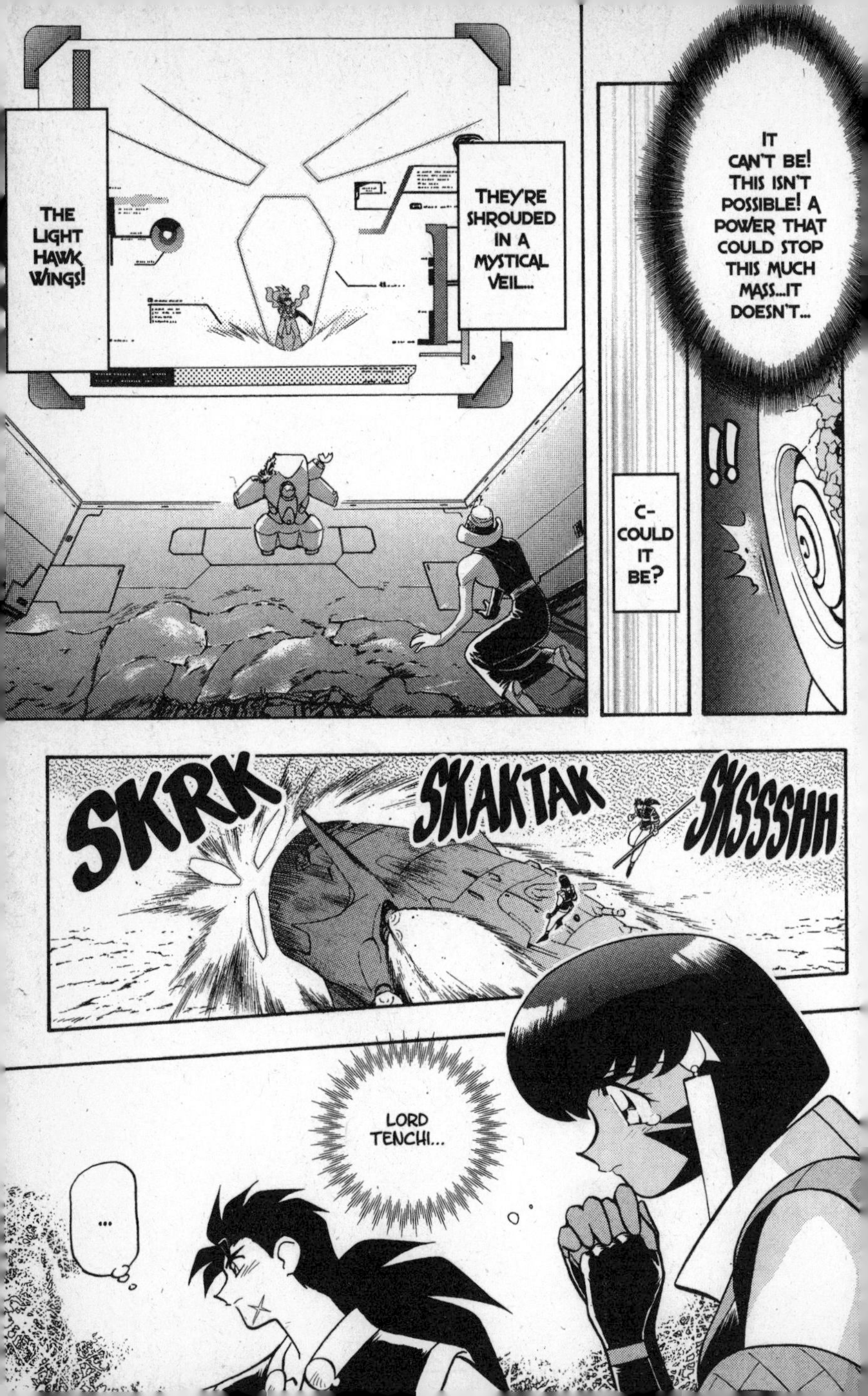
IT CAN'T BE! THIS ISN'T POSSIBLE! A POWER THAT COULD STOP THIS MUCH MASS...IT DOESN'T...
!!
C-COULD IT BE?
THE LIGHT HAWK WINGS!
THEY'RE SHROUDED IN A MYSTICAL VEIL...
SKSSSHH
SKAKTAK
SKRK
LORD TENCHI...
...

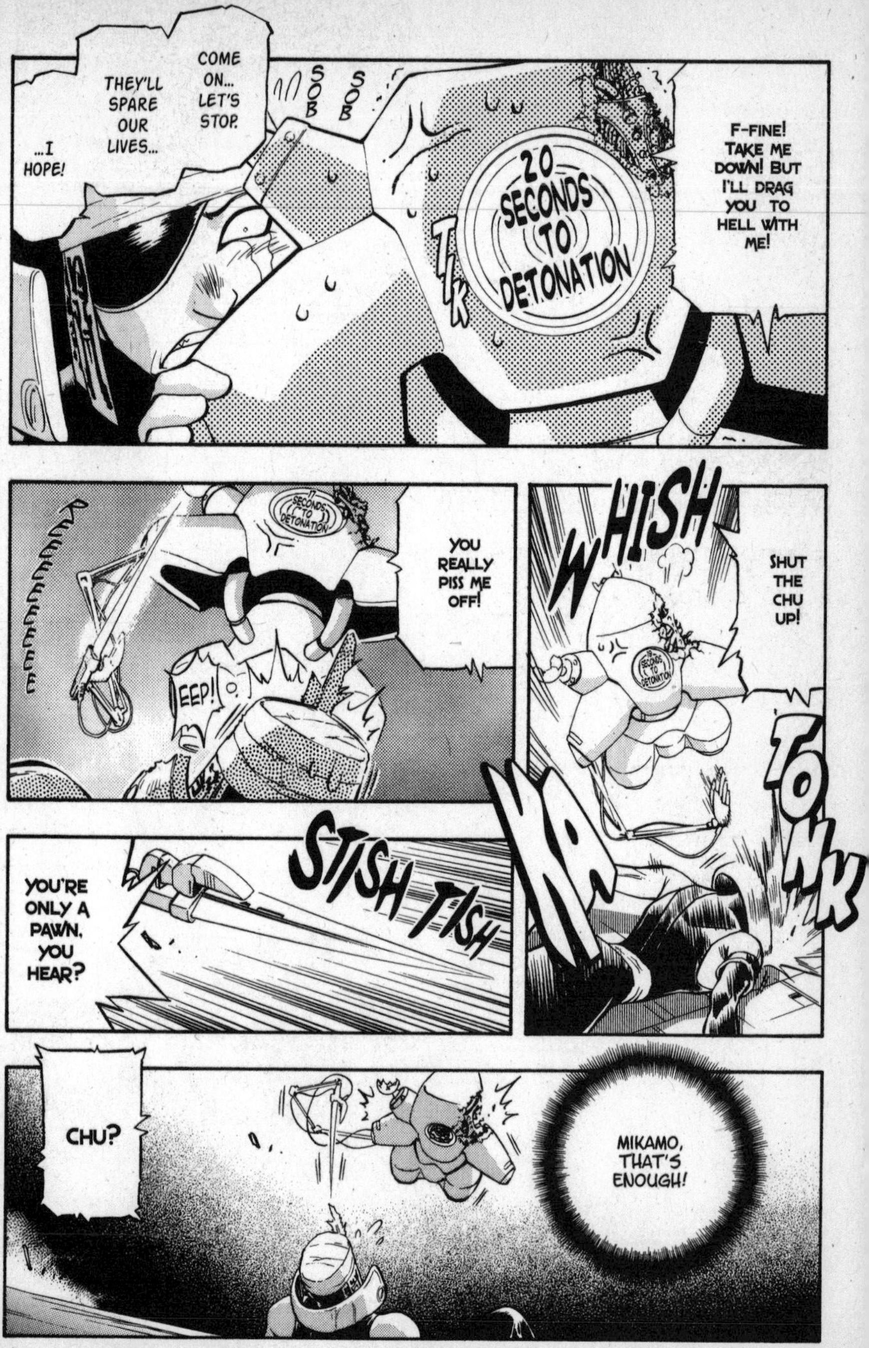
F-FINE! TAKE ME DOWN! BUT I'LL DRAG YOU TO HELL WITH ME!
20 SECONDS TO DETONATION
TIK
SOB SOB
COME ON... LET'S STOP.
THEY'LL SPARE OUR LIVES...
...I HOPE!
WHISH
SHUT THE CHU UP!
TONK
17 SECONDS TO DETONATION
YOU REALLY PISS ME OFF!
EEP!
STISH TISH
YOU'RE ONLY A PAWN, YOU HEAR?
MIKAMO, THAT'S ENOUGH!
CHU?

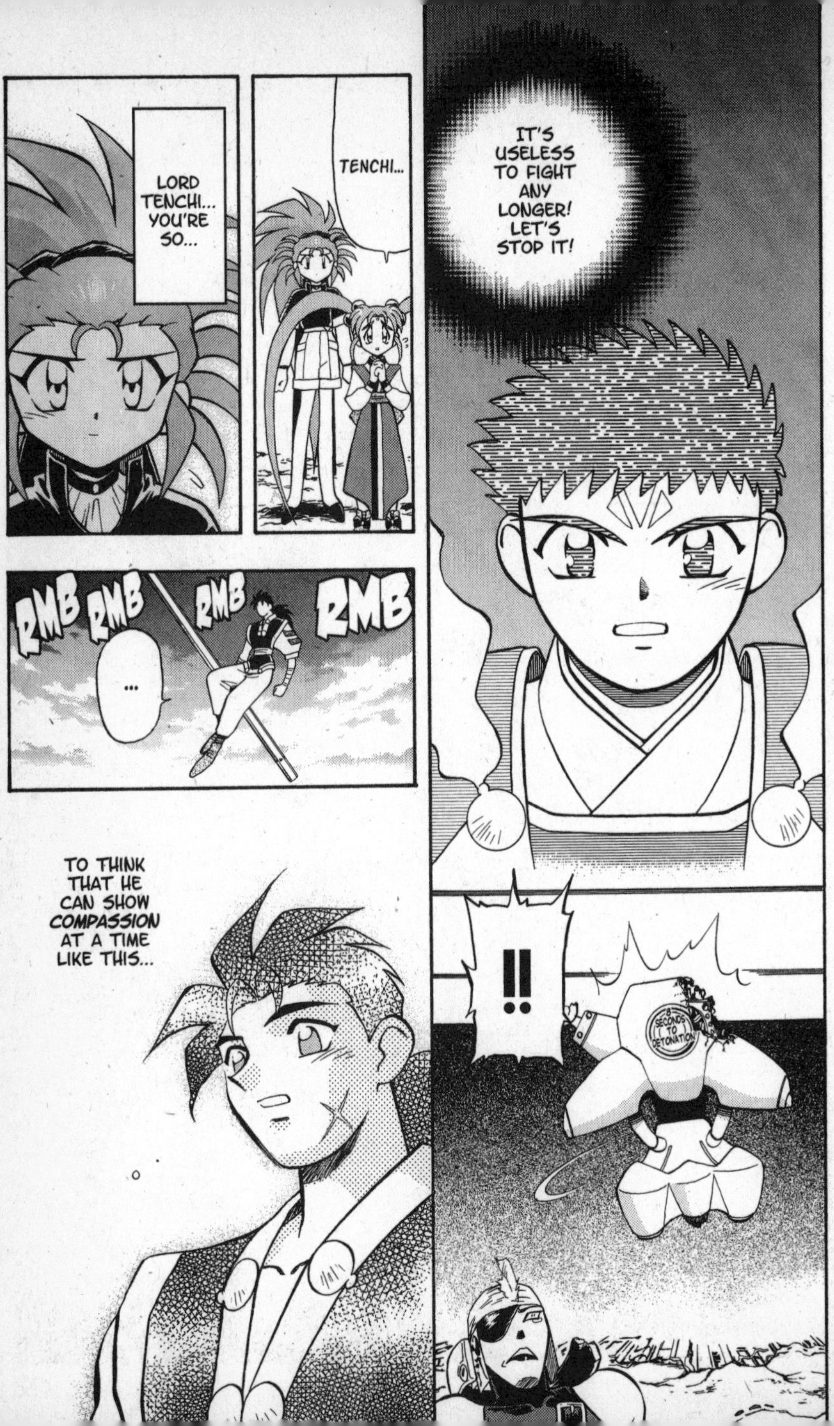
IT'S USELESS TO FIGHT ANY LONGER! LET'S STOP IT!
!!
8 SECONDS TO DETONATION
TENCHI...
LORD TENCHI... YOU'RE SO...
RMB
RMB
RMB
RMB
...
TO THINK THAT HE CAN SHOW COMPASSION AT A TIME LIKE THIS...

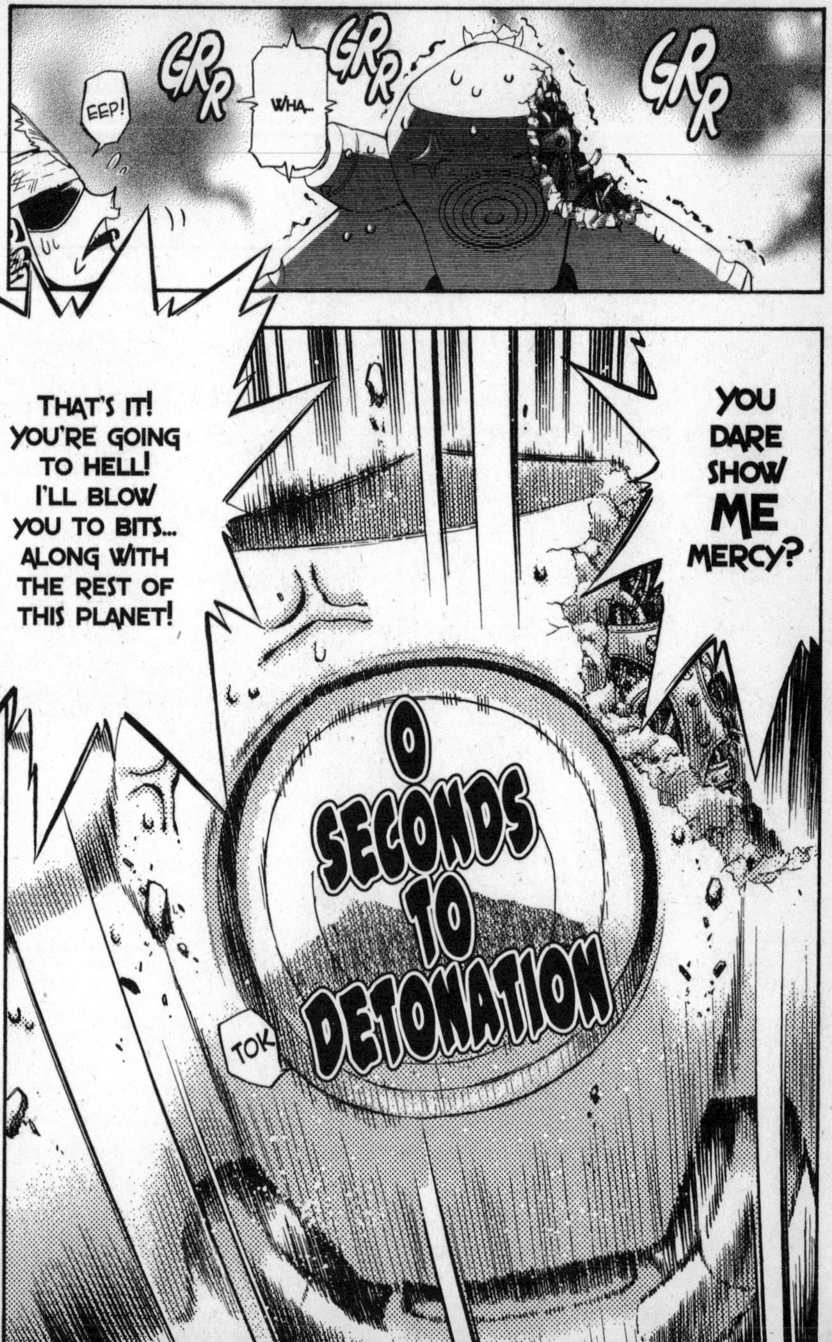
GRR
GRR
WHA...
GRR
EEP!
YOU DARE SHOW ME MERCY?
THAT'S IT! YOU'RE GOING TO HELL! I'LL BLOW YOU TO BITS... ALONG WITH THE REST OF THIS PLANET!
0 SECONDS TO DETONATION
TOK

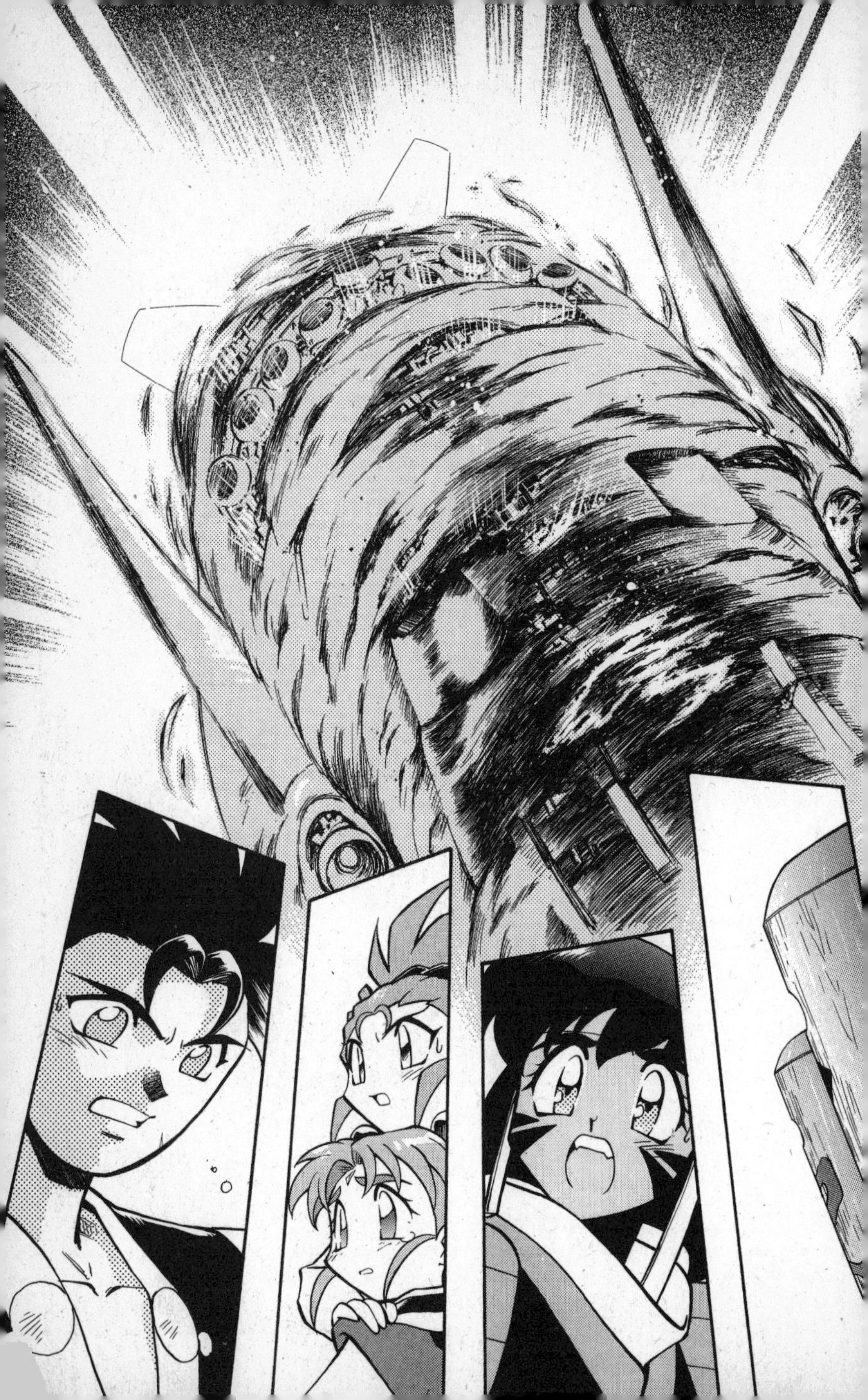

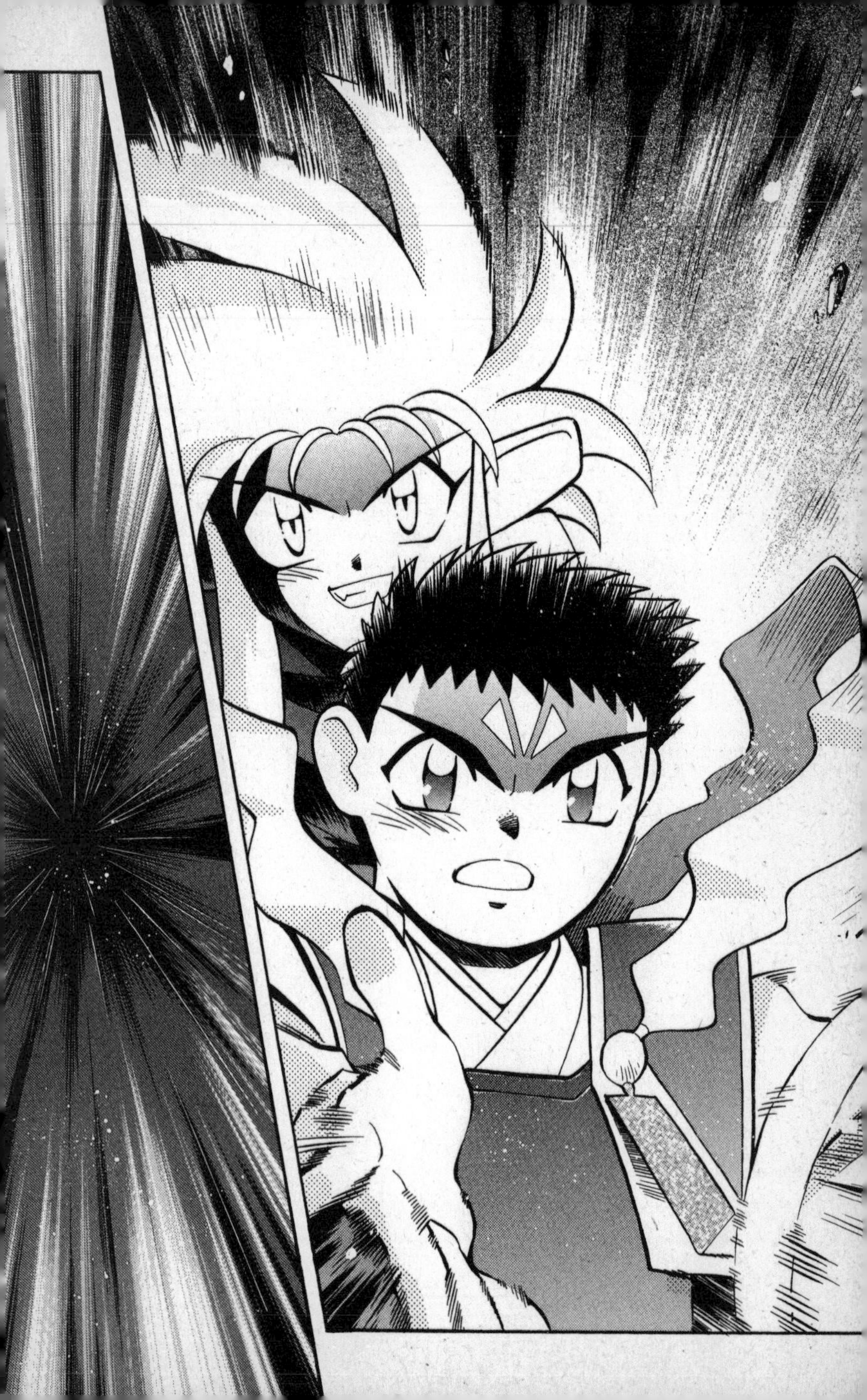

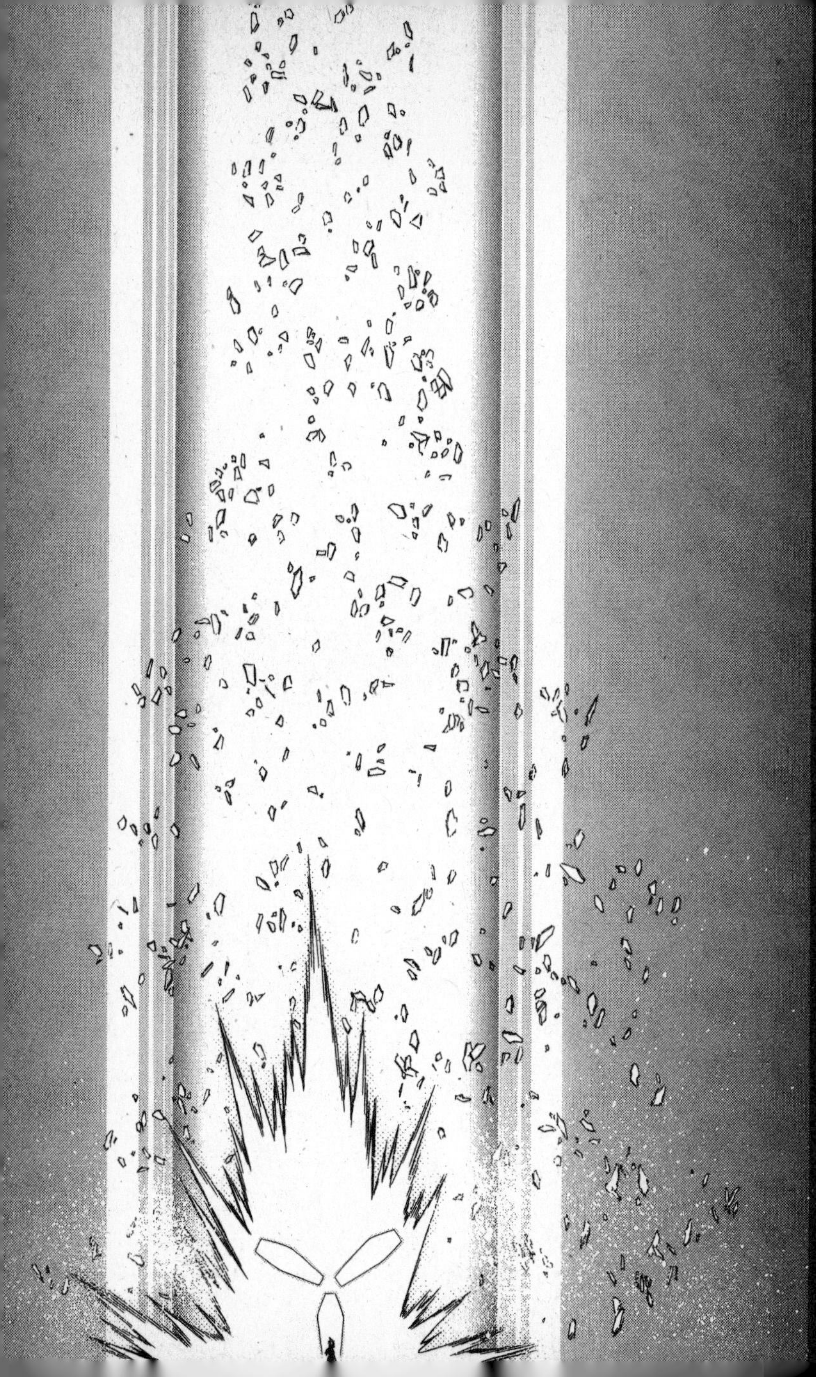

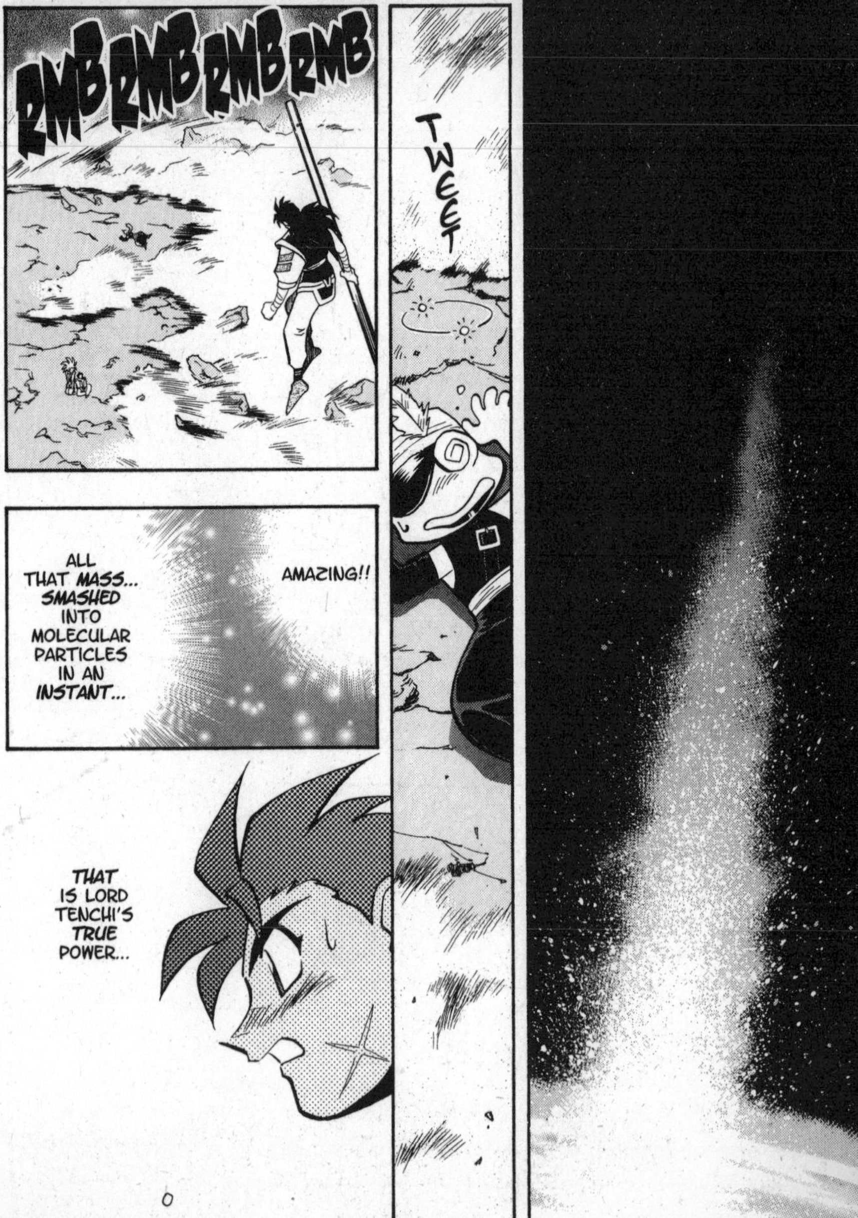
TWEET
RMB RMB RMB RMB
AMAZING!!
ALL THAT MASS... SMASHED INTO MOLECULAR PARTICLES IN AN INSTANT...
THAT IS LORD TENCHI'S TRUE POWER...

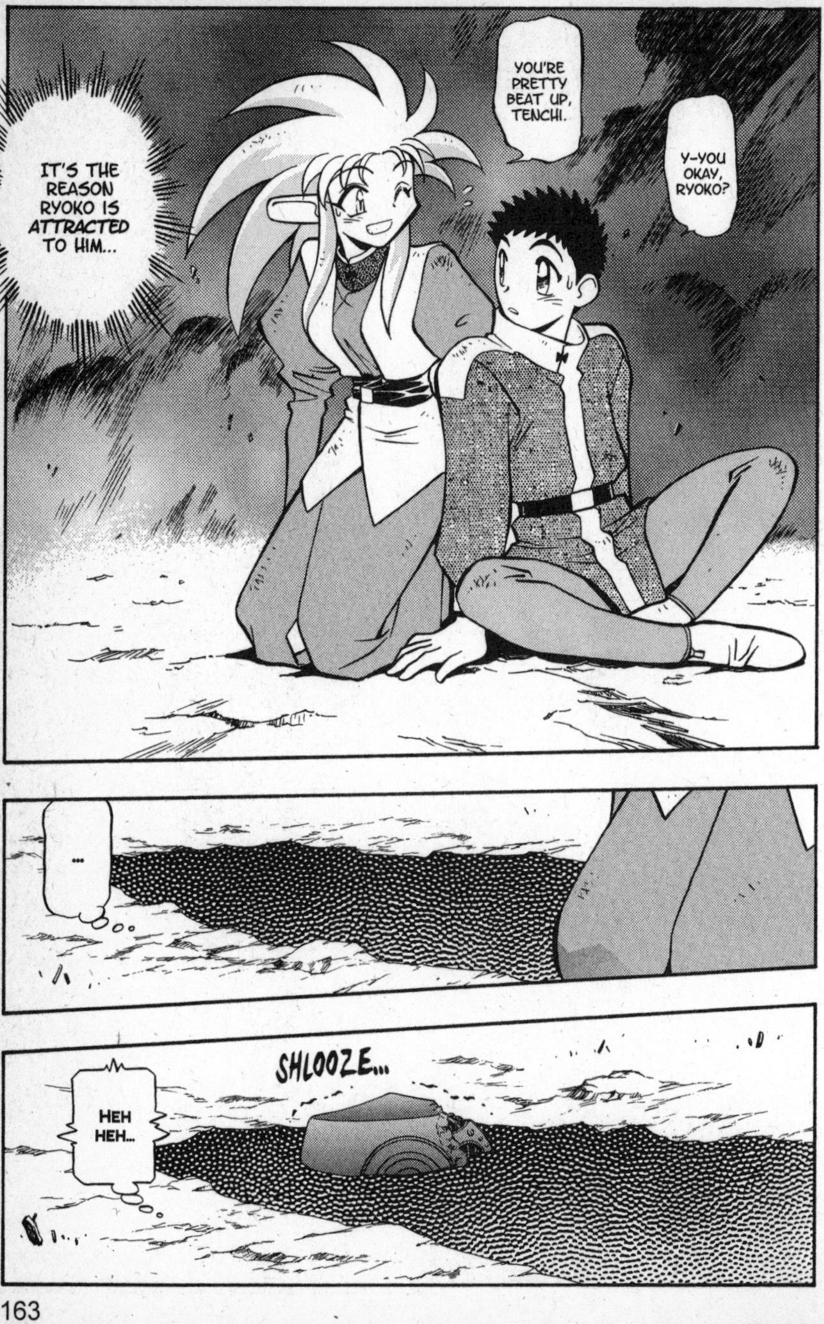
Y-YOU OKAY, RYOKO?
YOU'RE PRETTY BEAT UP, TENCHI.
IT'S THE REASON RYOKO IS ATTRACTED TO HIM...
...
SHLOOZE...
HEH HEH...

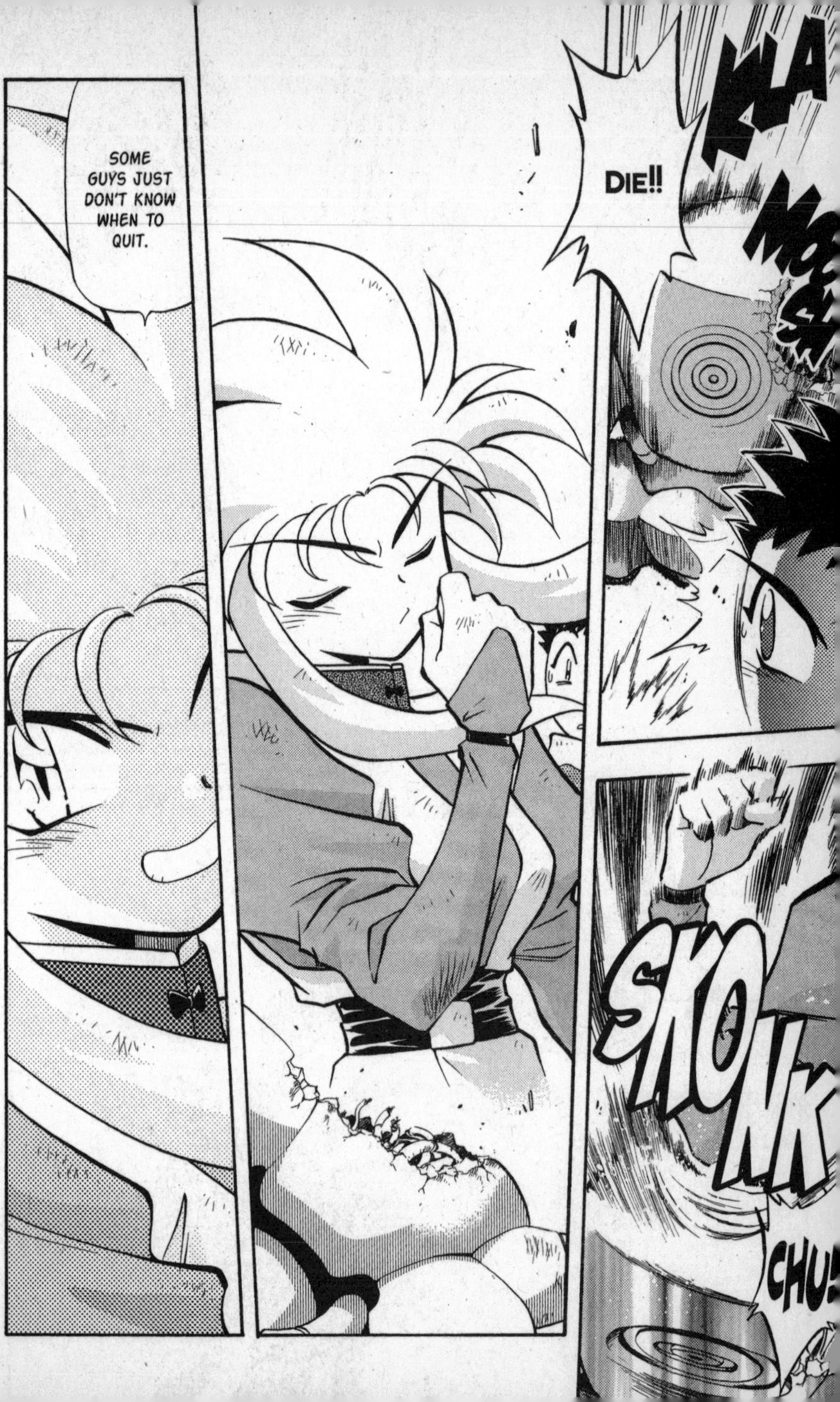
DIE!!
SKONK
SOME GUYS JUST DON'T KNOW WHEN TO QUIT.

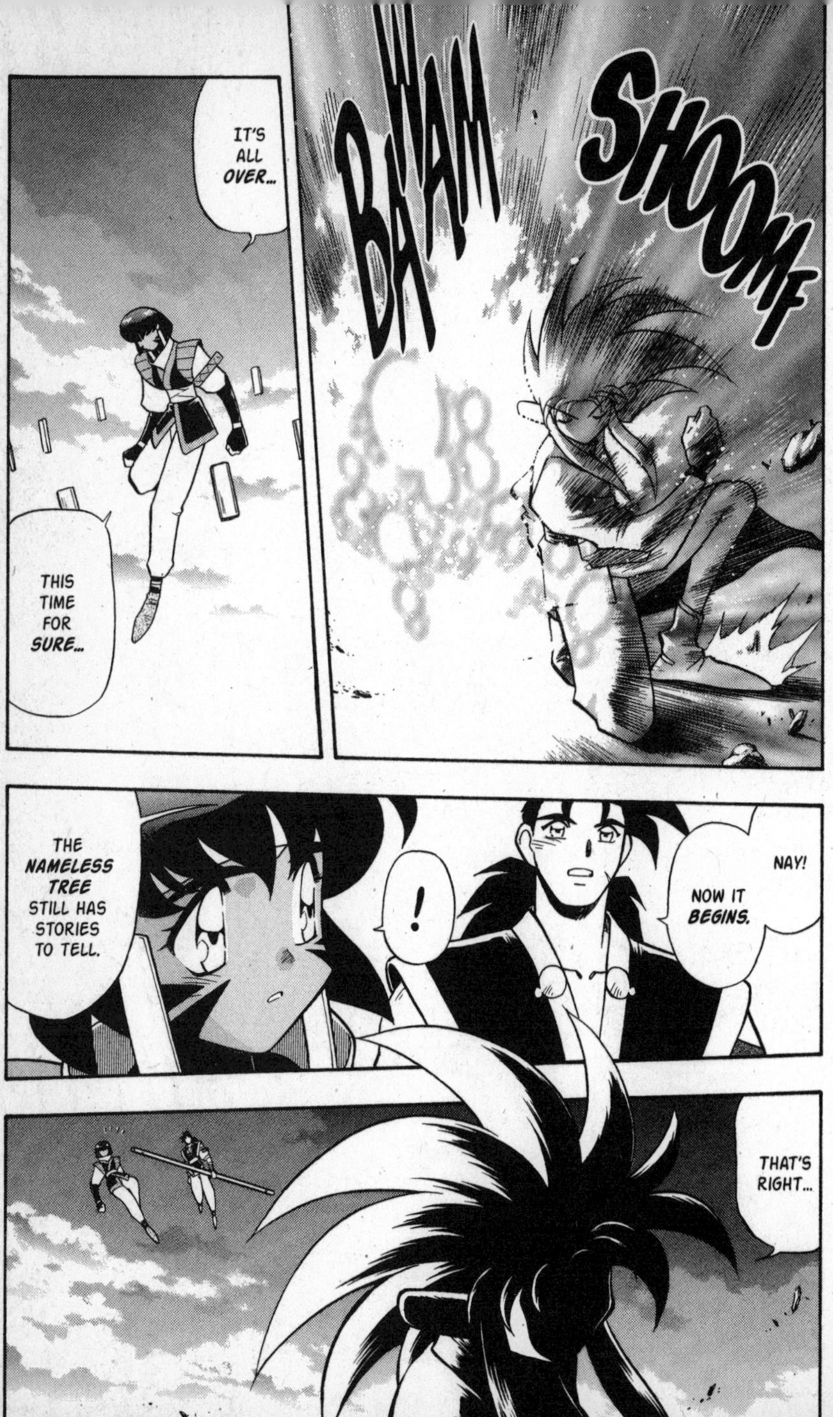
BAAM
SHOOMF
IT'S ALL OVER...
THIS TIME FOR SURE...
NAY! NOW IT BEGINS.
!
THE NAMELESS TREE STILL HAS STORIES TO TELL.
THAT'S RIGHT...

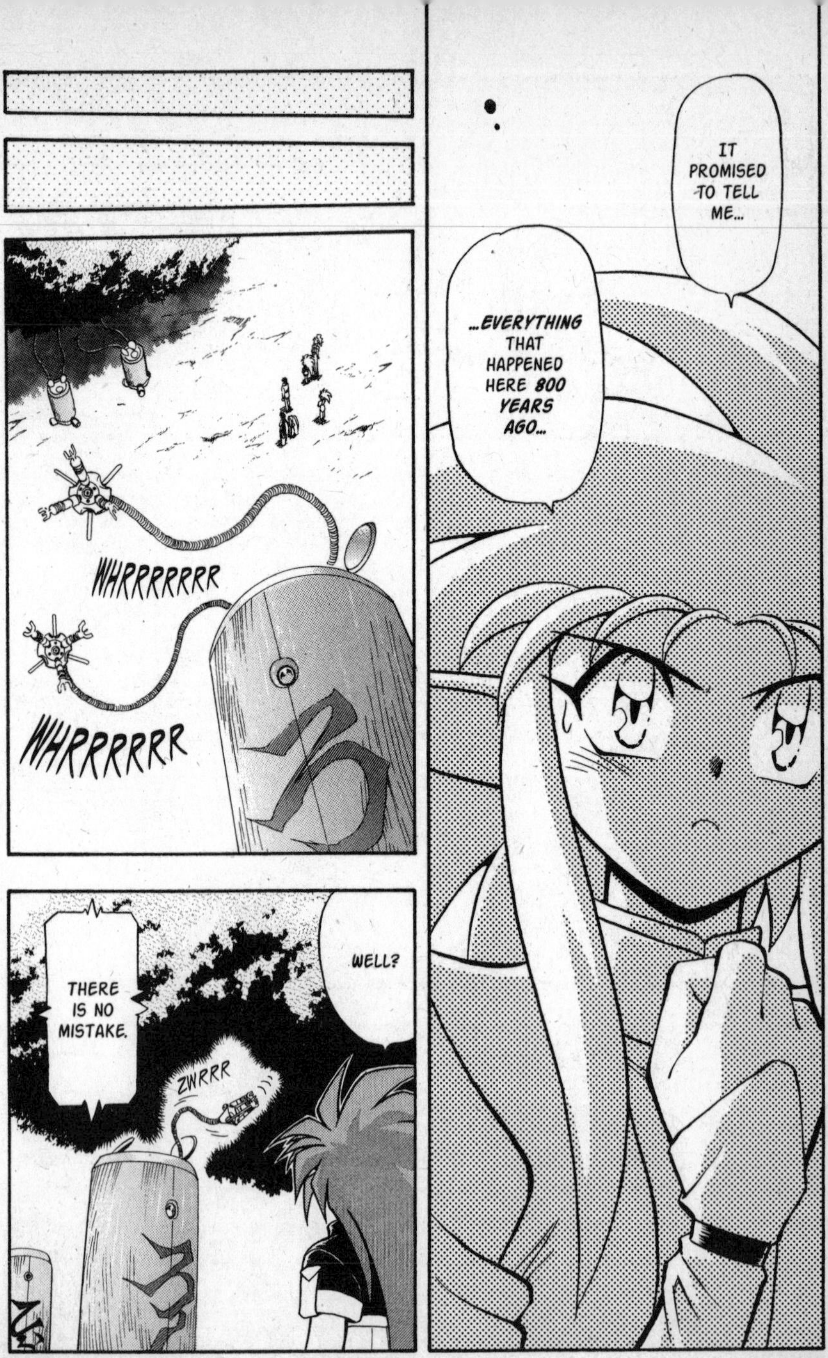
IT PROMISED TO TELL ME...
...EVERYTHING THAT HAPPENED HERE 800 YEARS AGO...
WHRRRRRRR
WHRRRRRR
WELL?
THERE IS NO MISTAKE.
ZWRRR

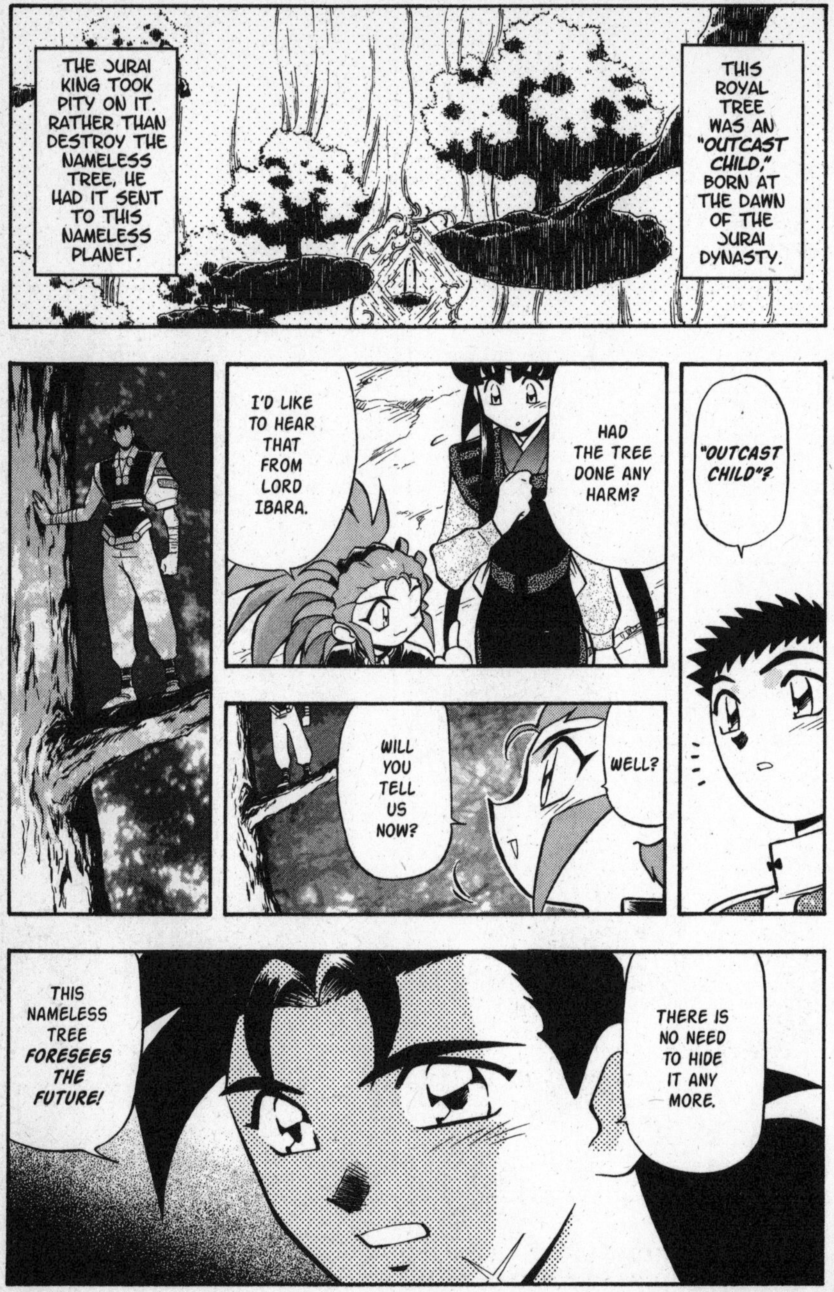
THIS ROYAL TREE WAS AN *"OUTCAST CHILD,"* BORN AT THE DAWN OF THE JURAI DYNASTY.
THE JURAI KING TOOK PITY ON IT. RATHER THAN DESTROY THE NAMELESS TREE, HE HAD IT SENT TO THIS NAMELESS PLANET.
"OUTCAST CHILD"?
HAD THE TREE DONE ANY HARM?
I'D LIKE TO HEAR THAT FROM LORD IBARA.
WELL?
WILL YOU TELL US NOW?
THERE IS NO NEED TO HIDE IT ANY MORE.
THIS NAMELESS TREE *FORESEES THE FUTURE!*

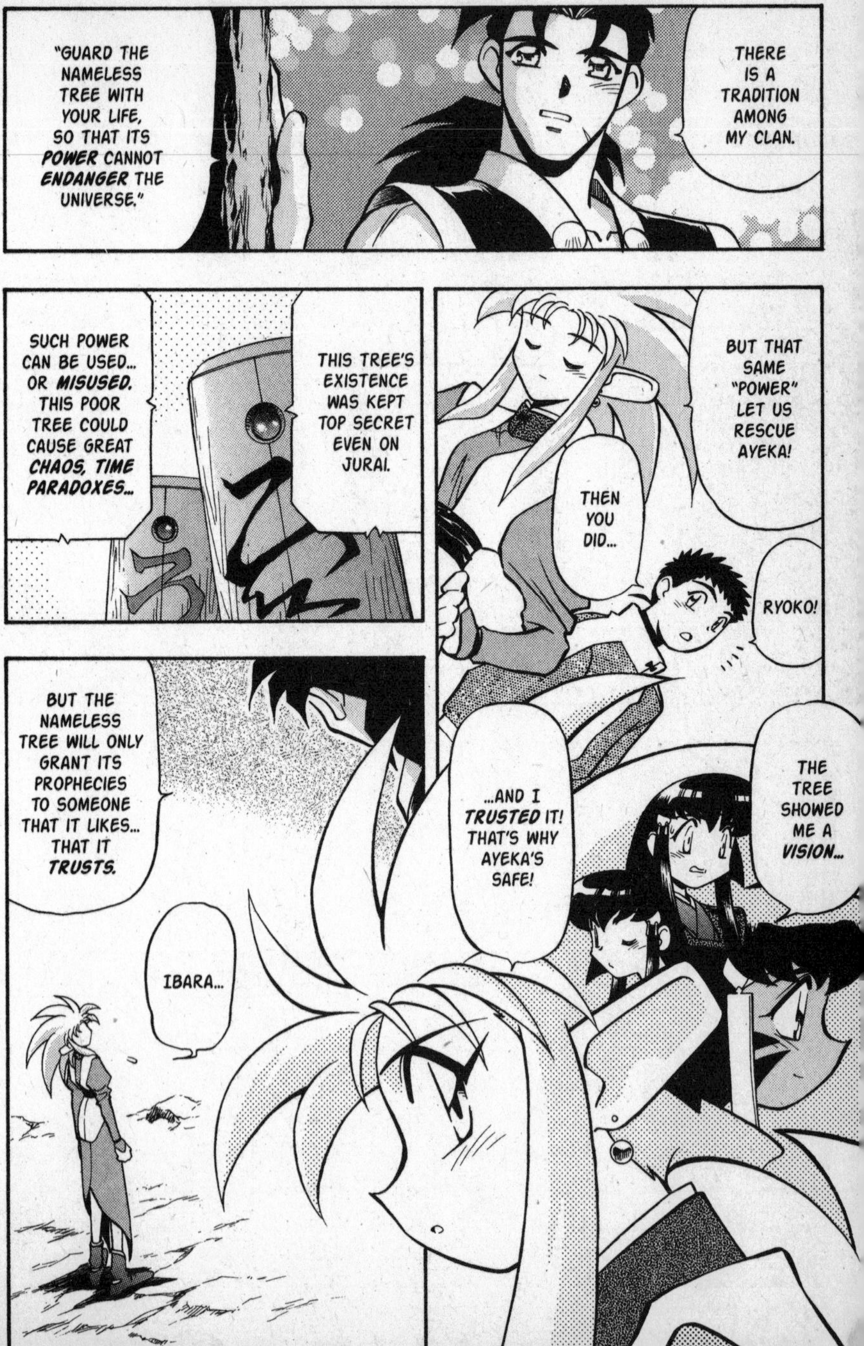
THERE IS A TRADITION AMONG MY CLAN.
"GUARD THE NAMELESS TREE WITH YOUR LIFE, SO THAT ITS *POWER* CANNOT *ENDANGER* THE UNIVERSE."
BUT THAT SAME "POWER" LET US RESCUE AYEKA!
THEN YOU DID...
RYOKO!
THIS TREE'S EXISTENCE WAS KEPT TOP SECRET EVEN ON JURAI.
SUCH POWER CAN BE USED... OR *MISUSED.* THIS POOR TREE COULD CAUSE GREAT *CHAOS, TIME PARADOXES...*
THE TREE SHOWED ME A *VISION...*
...AND I *TRUSTED* IT! THAT'S WHY AYEKA'S SAFE!
BUT THE NAMELESS TREE WILL ONLY GRANT ITS PROPHECIES TO SOMEONE THAT IT LIKES... THAT IT *TRUSTS.*
IBARA...

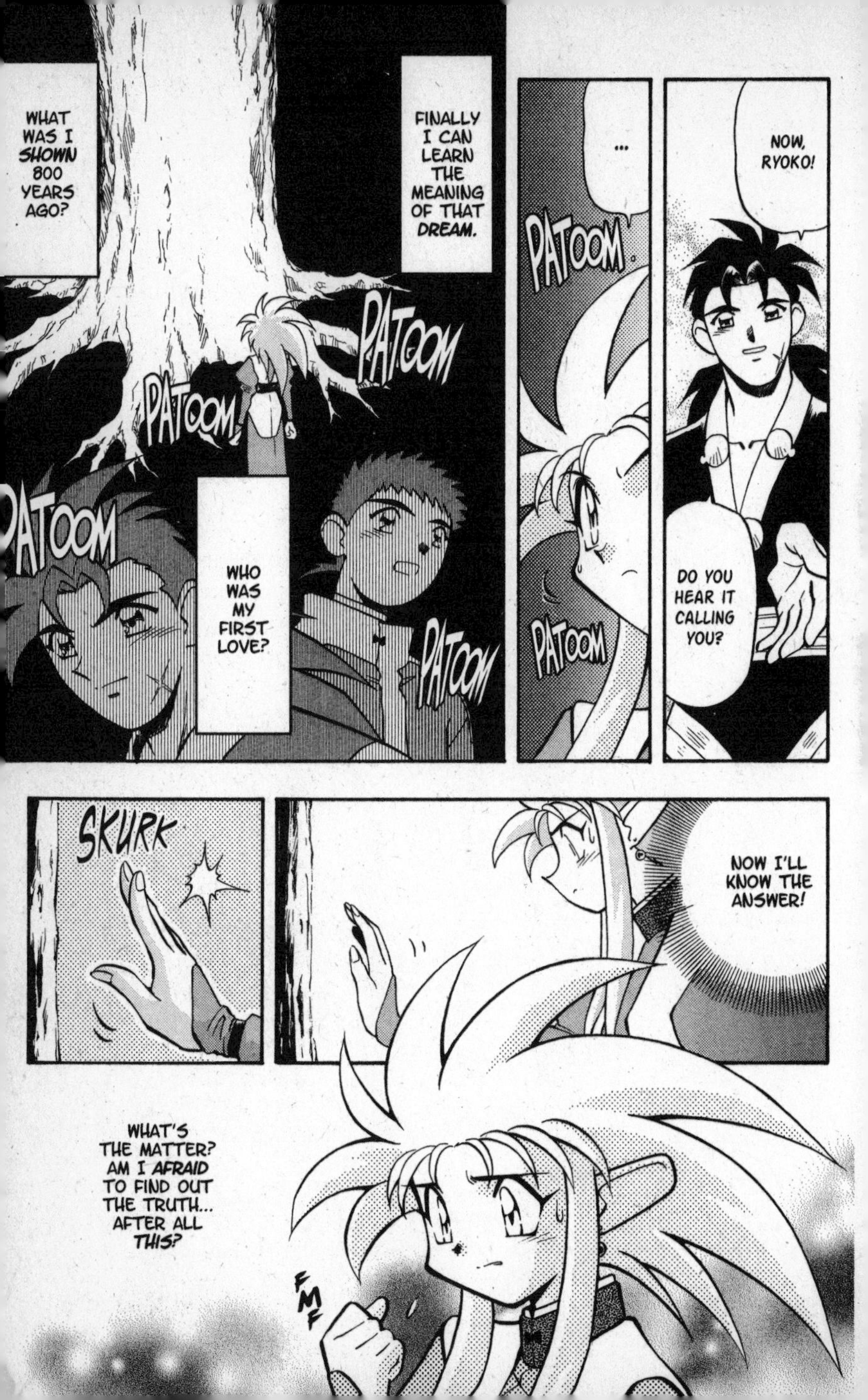
NOW, RYOKO!
DO YOU HEAR IT CALLING YOU?
...
PATOOM
PATOOM
FINALLY I CAN LEARN THE MEANING OF THAT *DREAM.*
PATOOM
WHAT WAS I *SHOWN* 800 YEARS AGO?
PATOOM
PATOOM
WHO WAS MY FIRST LOVE?
PATOOM
NOW I'LL KNOW THE ANSWER!
SKURK
WHAT'S THE MATTER? AM I *AFRAID* TO FIND OUT THE TRUTH... AFTER ALL *THIS?*
FMF

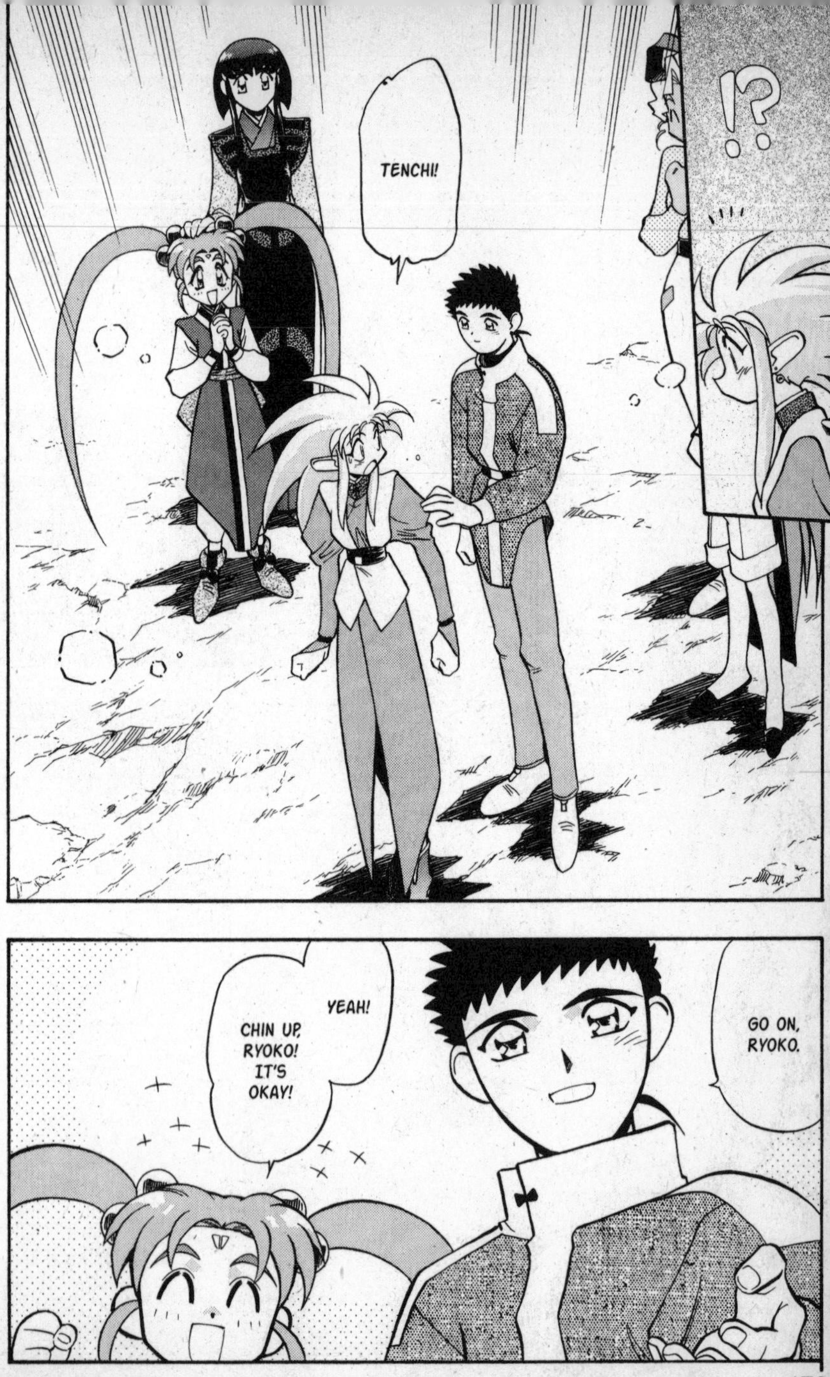
!?
TENCHI!
GO ON, RYOKO.
YEAH! CHIN UP, RYOKO! IT'S OKAY!

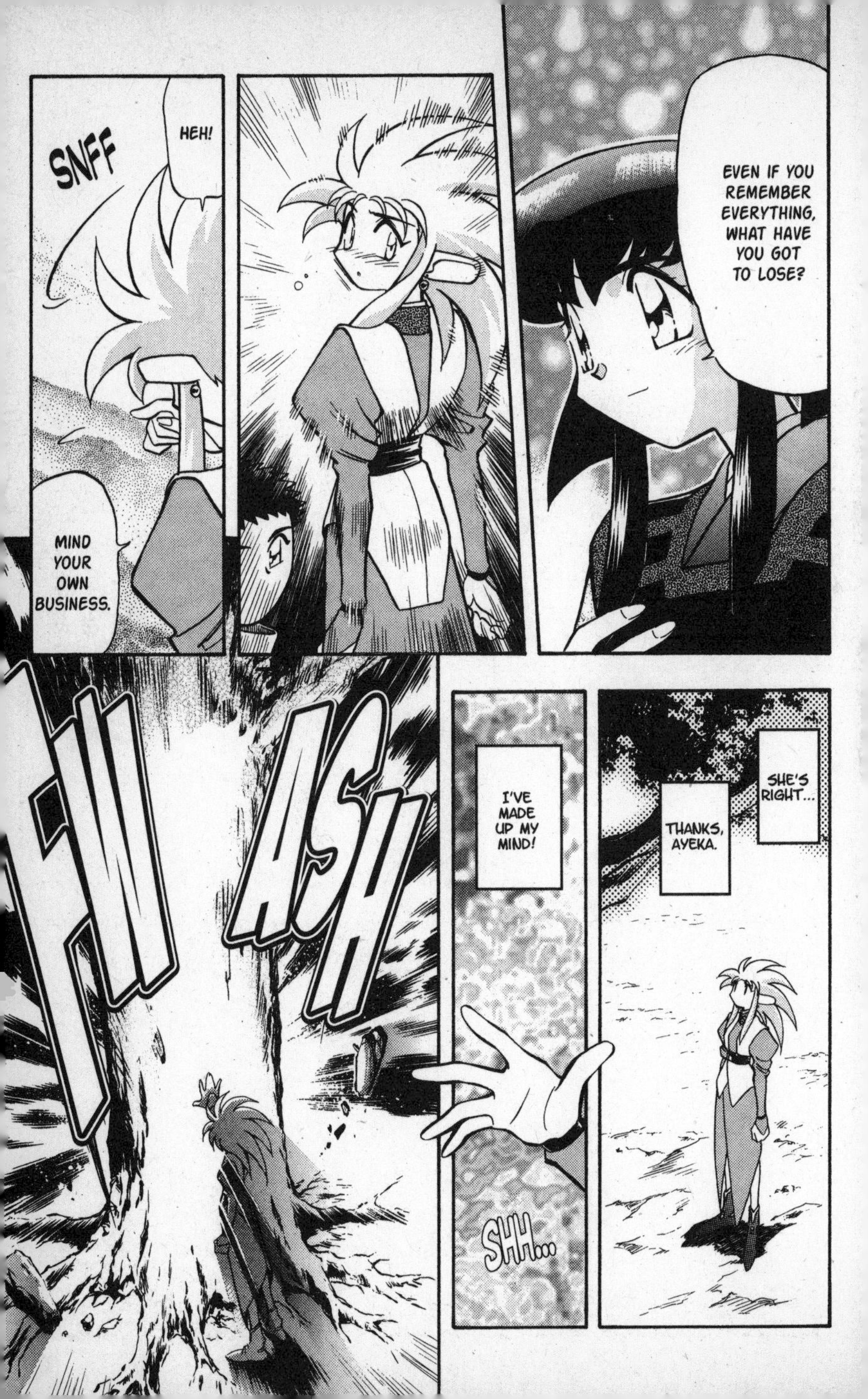
EVEN IF YOU REMEMBER EVERYTHING, WHAT HAVE YOU GOT TO LOSE?
HEH!
SNFF
MIND YOUR OWN BUSINESS.
SHE'S RIGHT...
THANKS, AYEKA.
I'VE MADE UP MY MIND!
SHH...
ASH

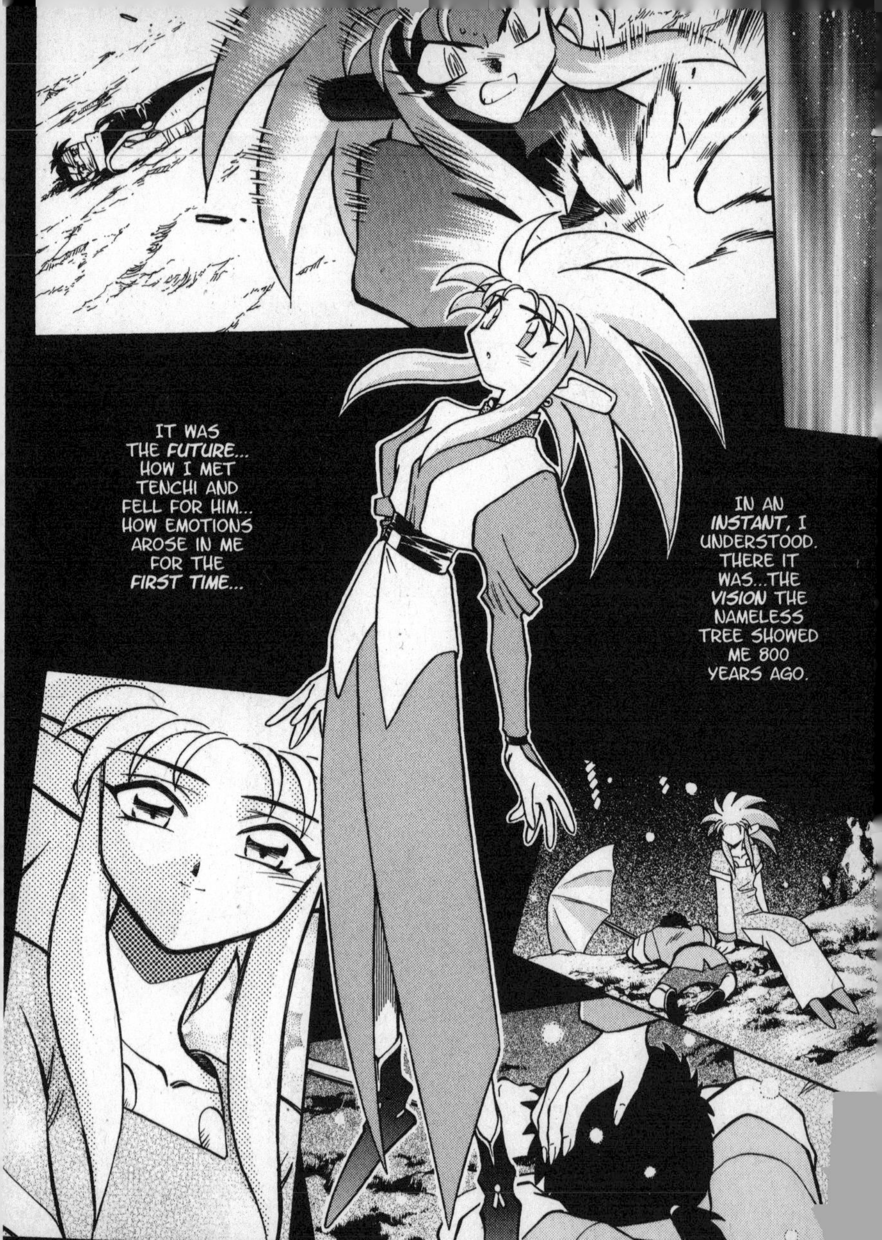
IN AN INSTANT, I UNDERSTOOD. THERE IT WAS...THE VISION THE NAMELESS TREE SHOWED ME 800 YEARS AGO.
IT WAS THE FUTURE... HOW I MET TENCHI AND FELL FOR HIM... HOW EMOTIONS AROSE IN ME FOR THE FIRST TIME...

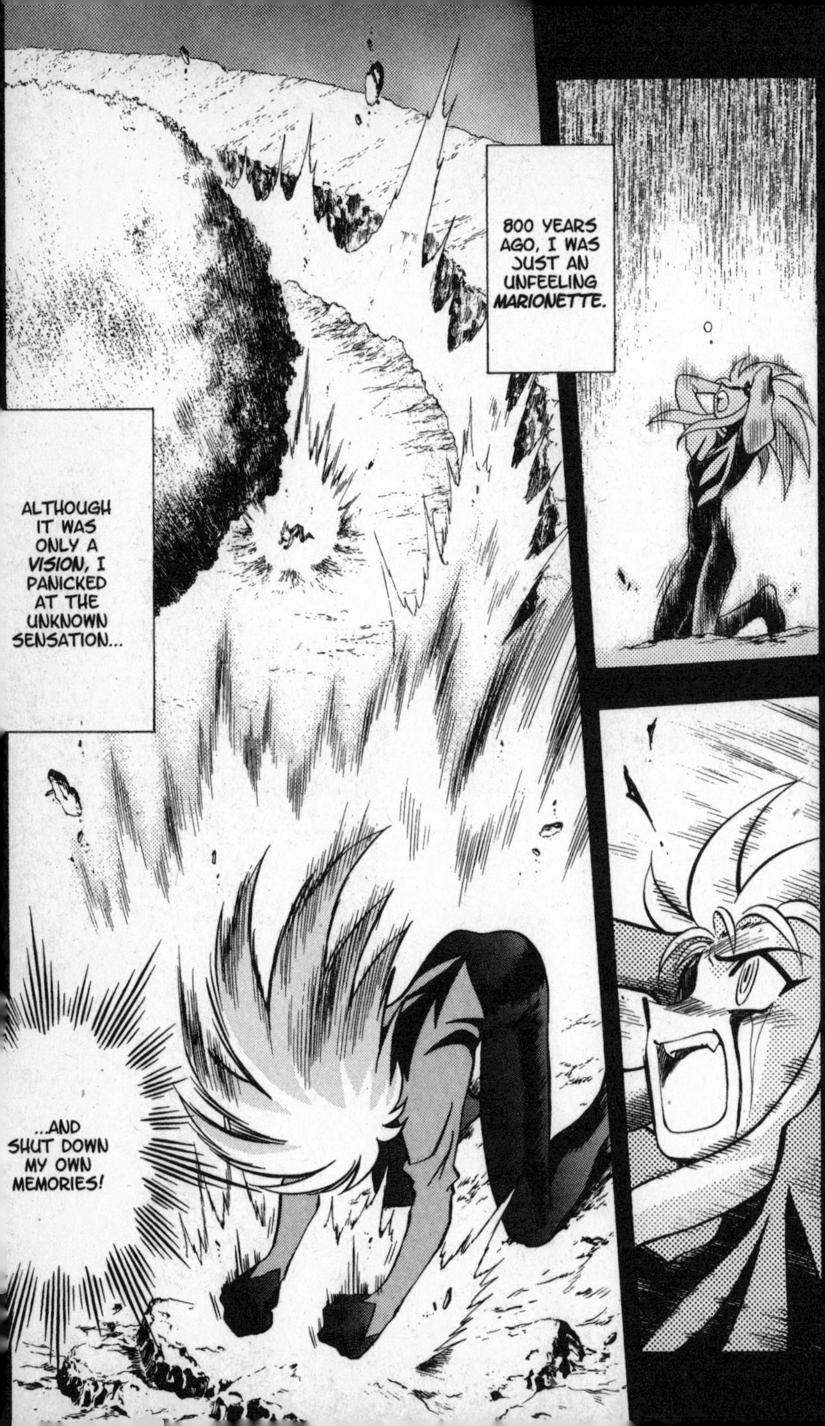
800 YEARS AGO, I WAS JUST AN UNFEELING MARIONETTE.
ALTHOUGH IT WAS ONLY A VISION, I PANICKED AT THE UNKNOWN SENSATION...
...AND SHUT DOWN MY OWN MEMORIES!

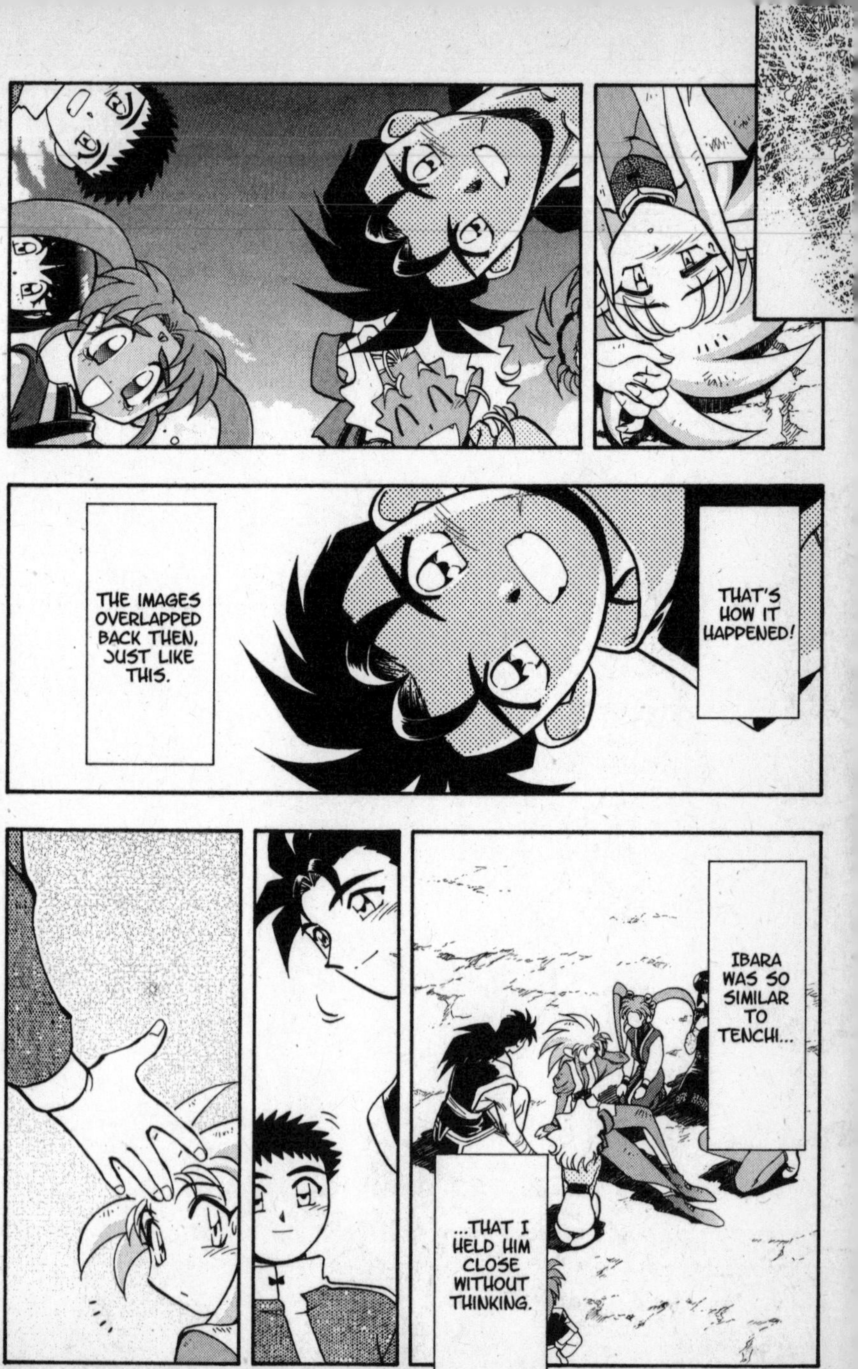
THAT'S HOW IT HAPPENED!
THE IMAGES OVERLAPPED BACK THEN, JUST LIKE THIS.
IBARA WAS SO SIMILAR TO TENCHI...
...THAT I HELD HIM CLOSE WITHOUT THINKING.

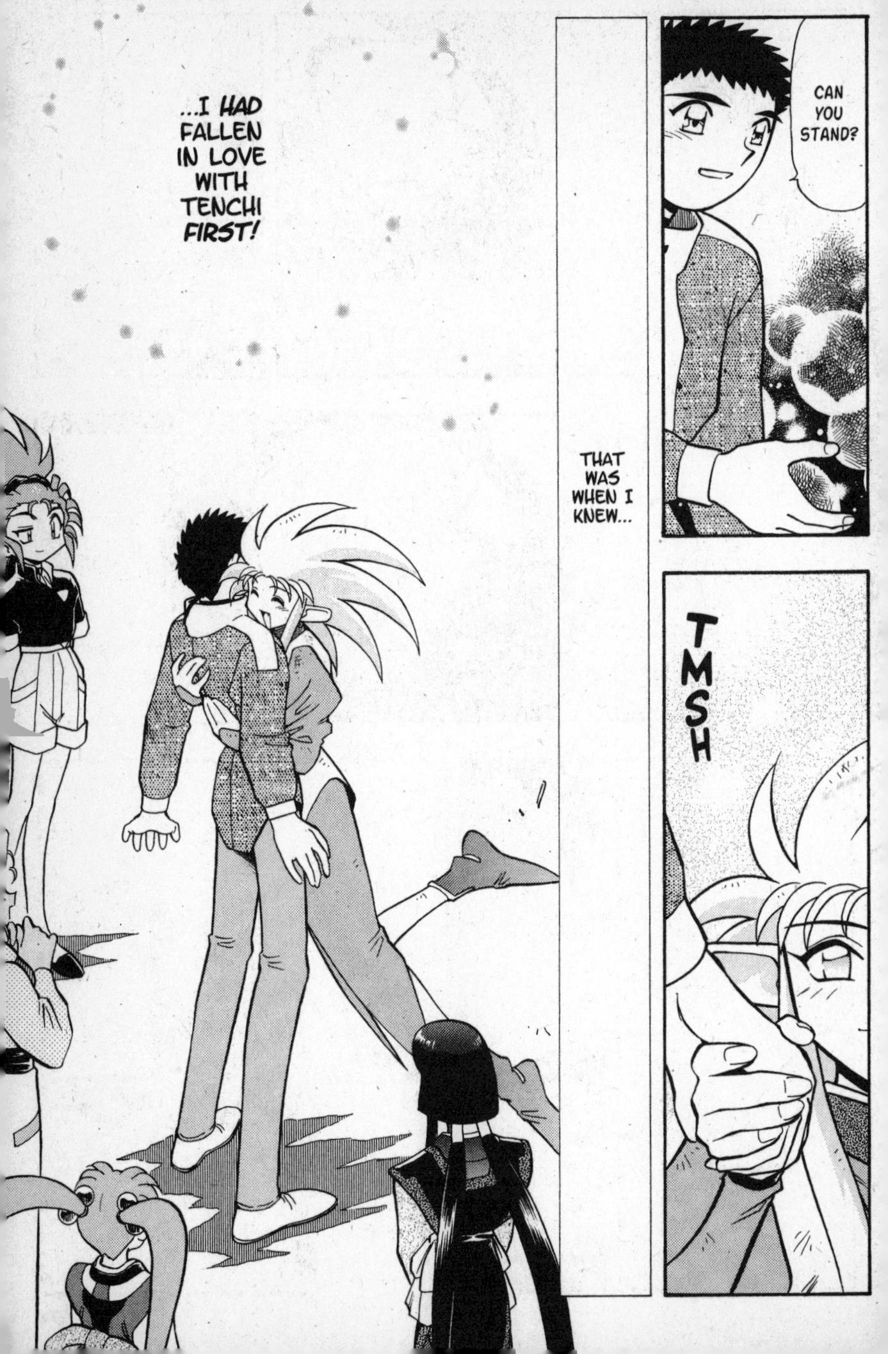
CAN YOU STAND?
TMSH
THAT WAS WHEN I KNEW...
...I HAD FALLEN IN LOVE WITH TENCHI FIRST!

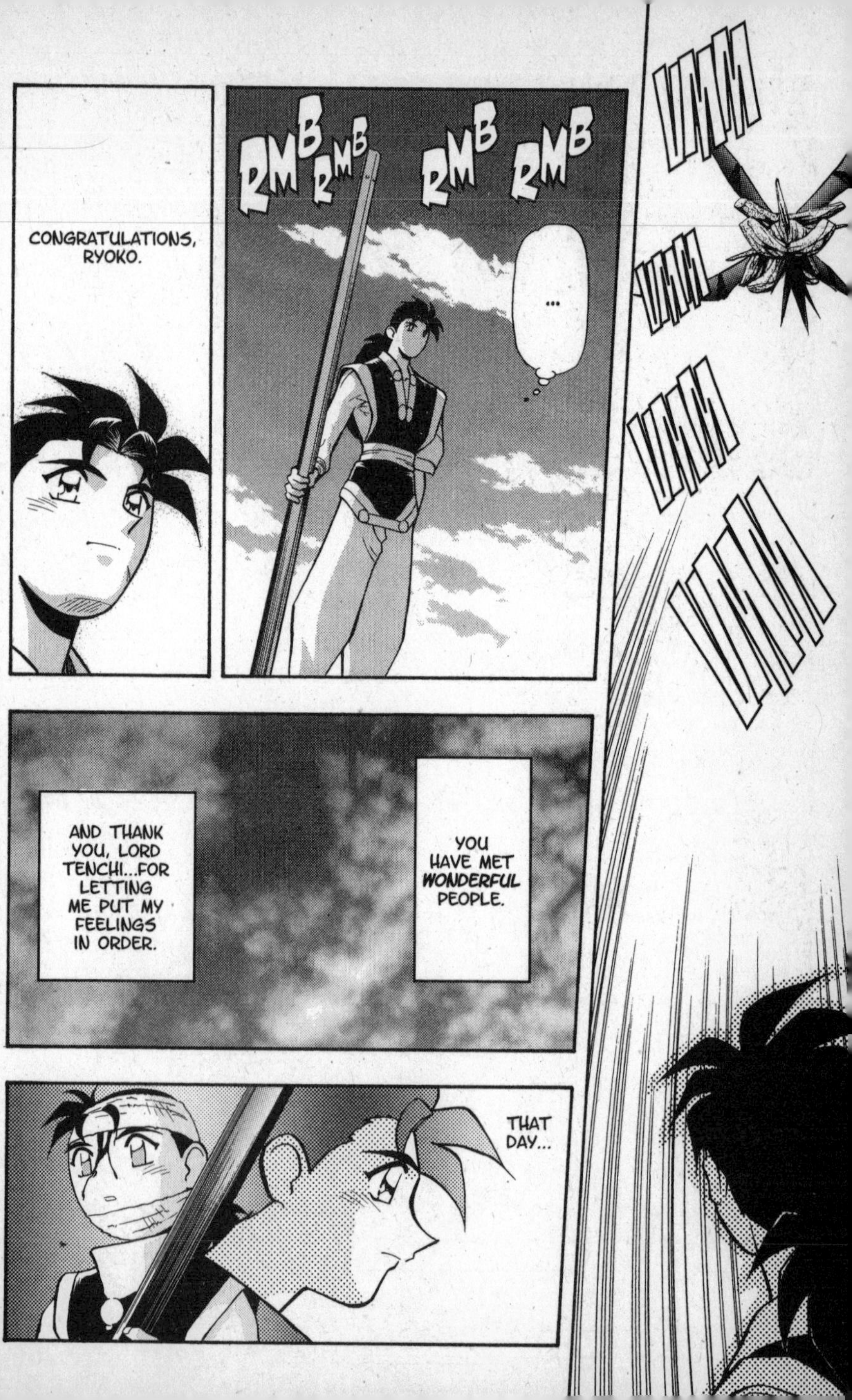
RMB RMB RMB RMB
...
CONGRATULATIONS, RYOKO.
YOU HAVE MET WONDERFUL PEOPLE.
AND THANK YOU, LORD TENCHI...FOR LETTING ME PUT MY FEELINGS IN ORDER.
THAT DAY...

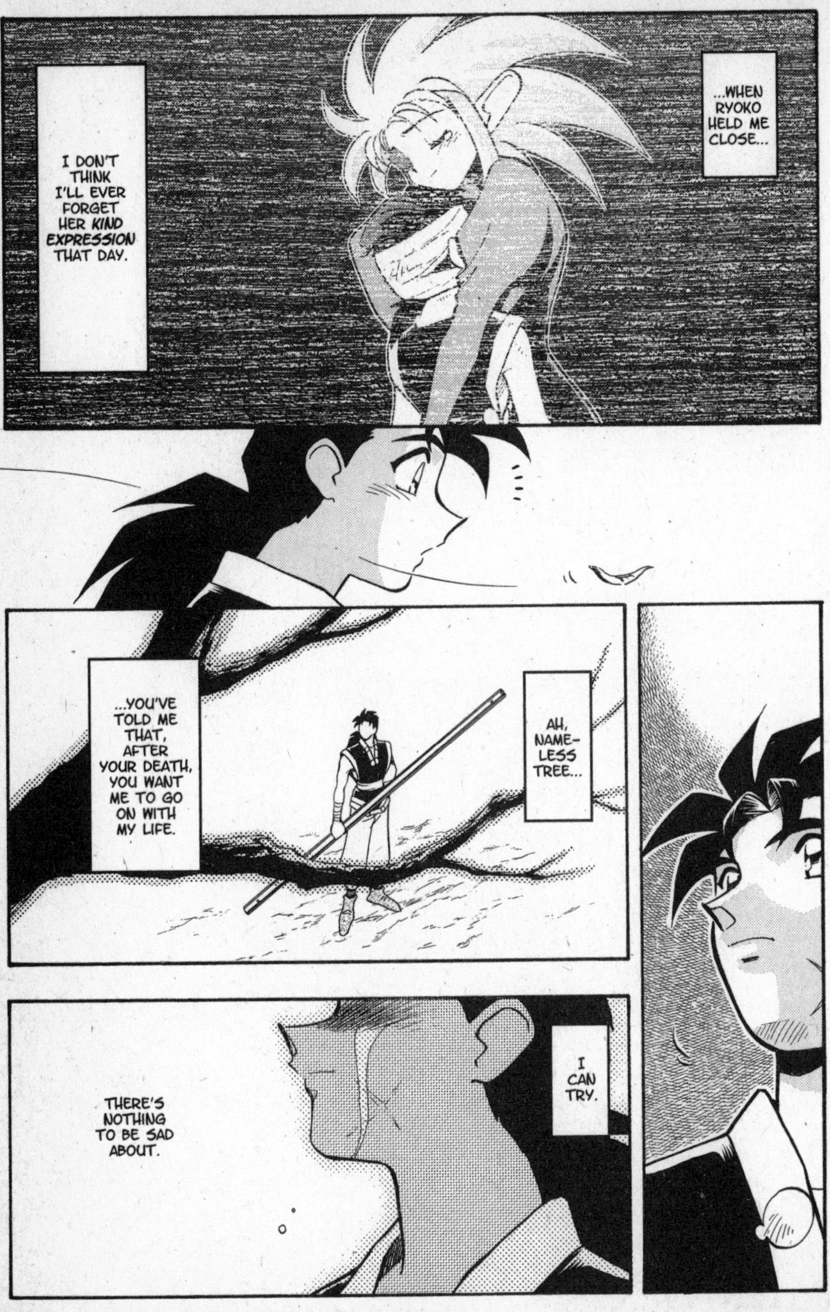
...WHEN RYOKO HELD ME CLOSE...
I DON'T THINK I'LL EVER FORGET HER KIND EXPRESSION THAT DAY.
AH, NAME-LESS TREE...
...YOU'VE TOLD ME THAT, AFTER YOUR DEATH, YOU WANT ME TO GO ON WITH MY LIFE.
I CAN TRY.
THERE'S NOTHING TO BE SAD ABOUT.

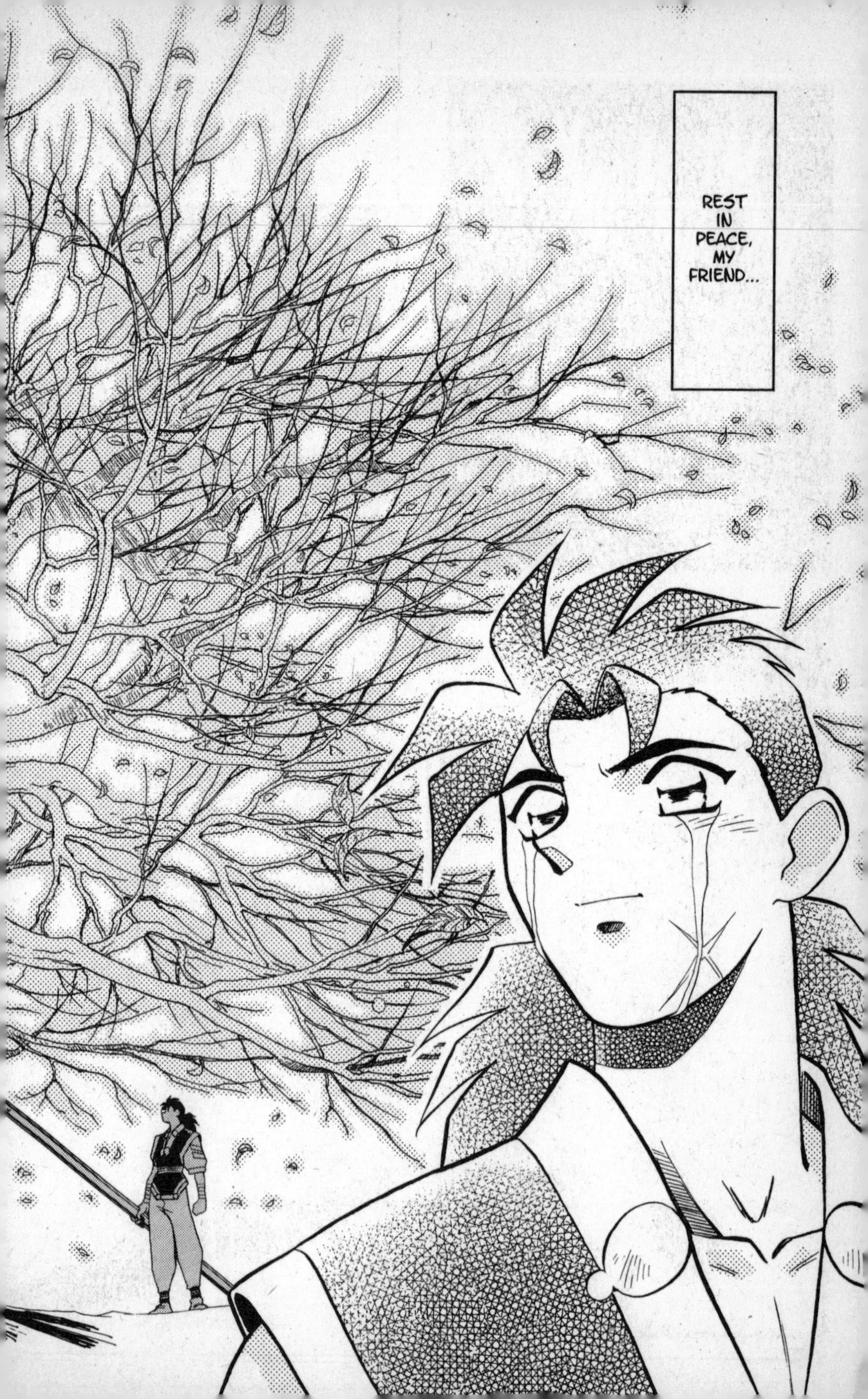
REST IN PEACE, MY FRIEND...

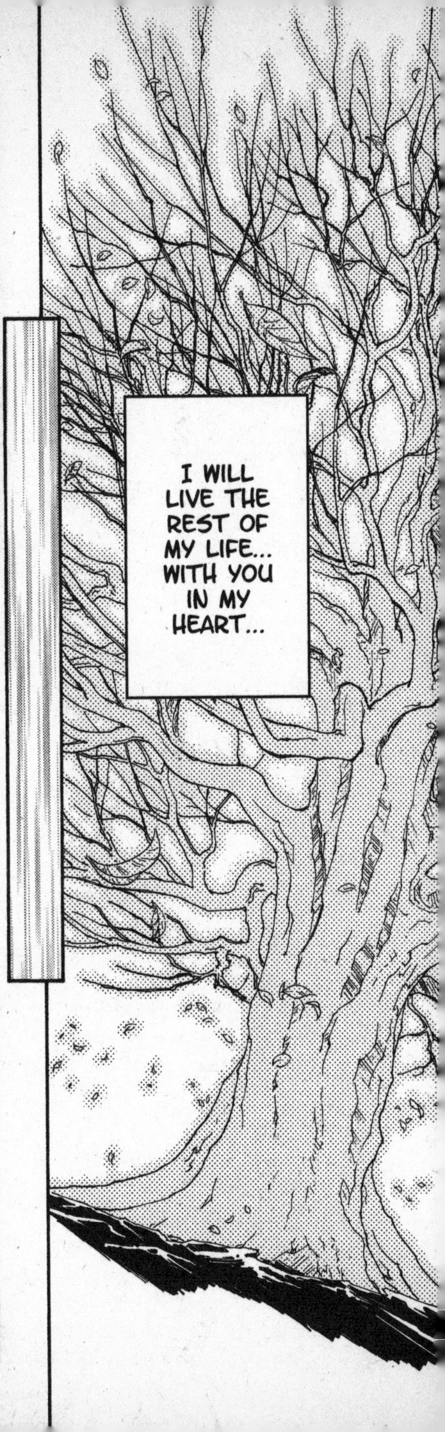
I WILL LIVE THE REST OF MY LIFE... WITH YOU IN MY HEART...

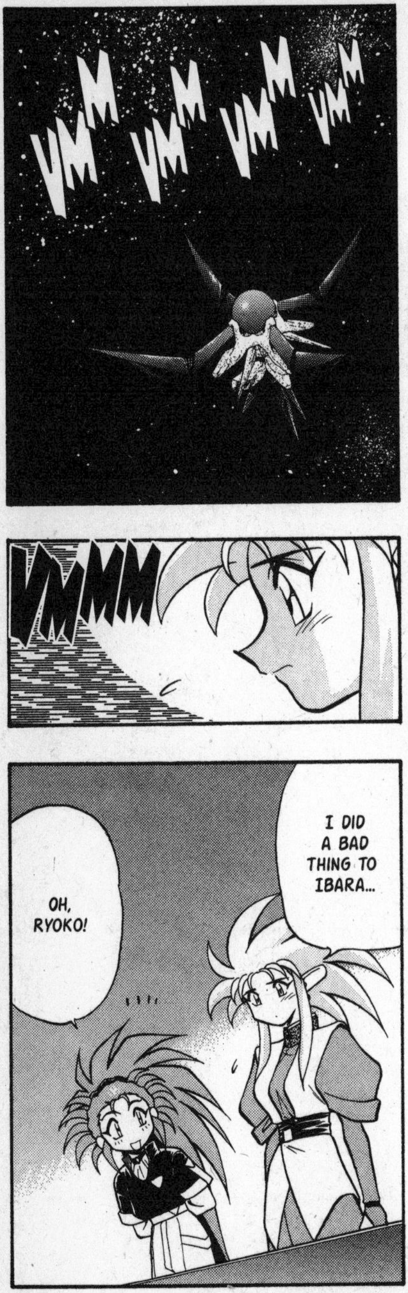
VMM VMM VMM VMM
VMMM
I DID A BAD THING TO IBARA...
OH, RYOKO!

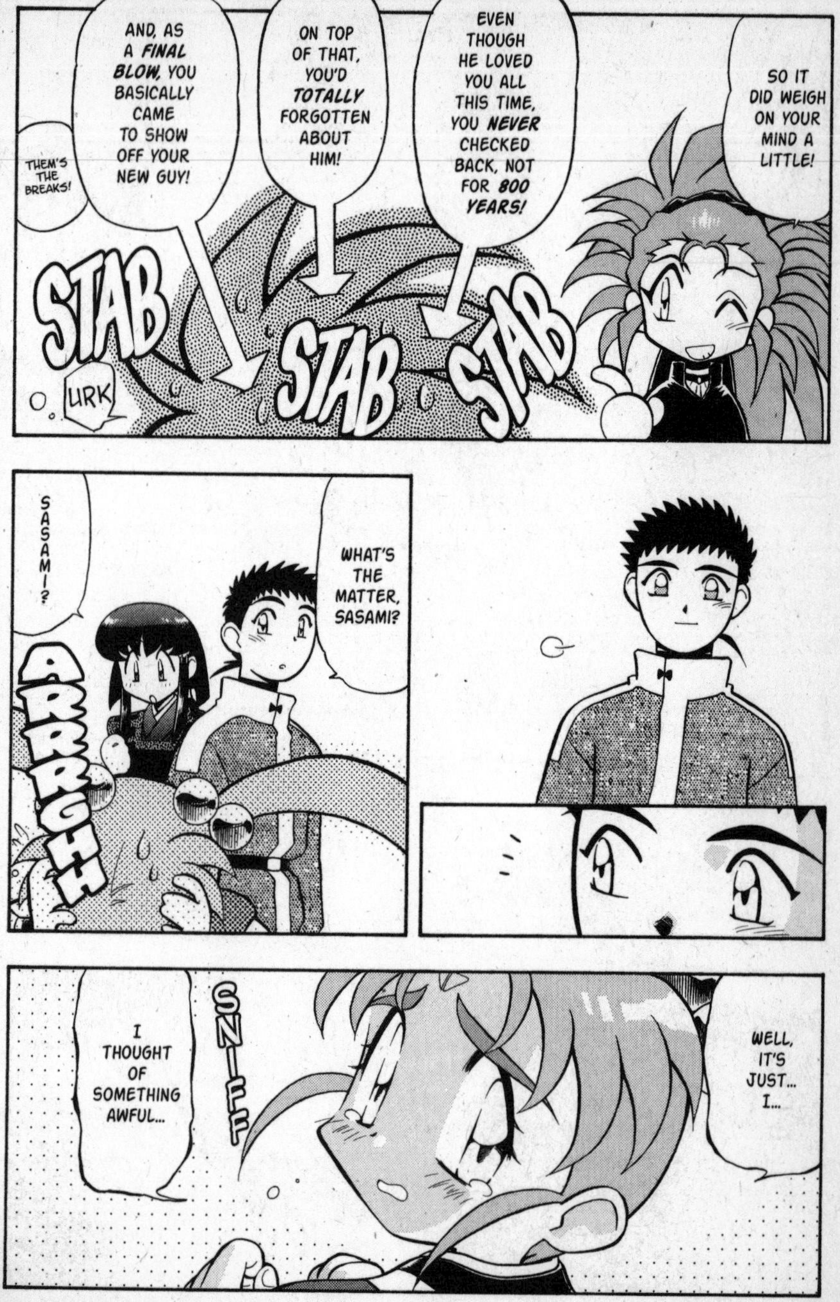
SO IT DID WEIGH ON YOUR MIND A LITTLE!
EVEN THOUGH HE LOVED YOU ALL THIS TIME, YOU NEVER CHECKED BACK, NOT FOR 800 YEARS!
STAB
ON TOP OF THAT, YOU'D TOTALLY FORGOTTEN ABOUT HIM!
STAB
AND, AS A FINAL BLOW, YOU BASICALLY CAME TO SHOW OFF YOUR NEW GUY!
STAB
THEM'S THE BREAKS!
URK
WHAT'S THE MATTER, SASAMI?
SASAMI?
ARRRGHH
WELL, IT'S JUST... I...
SNIFF
I THOUGHT OF SOMETHING AWFUL...

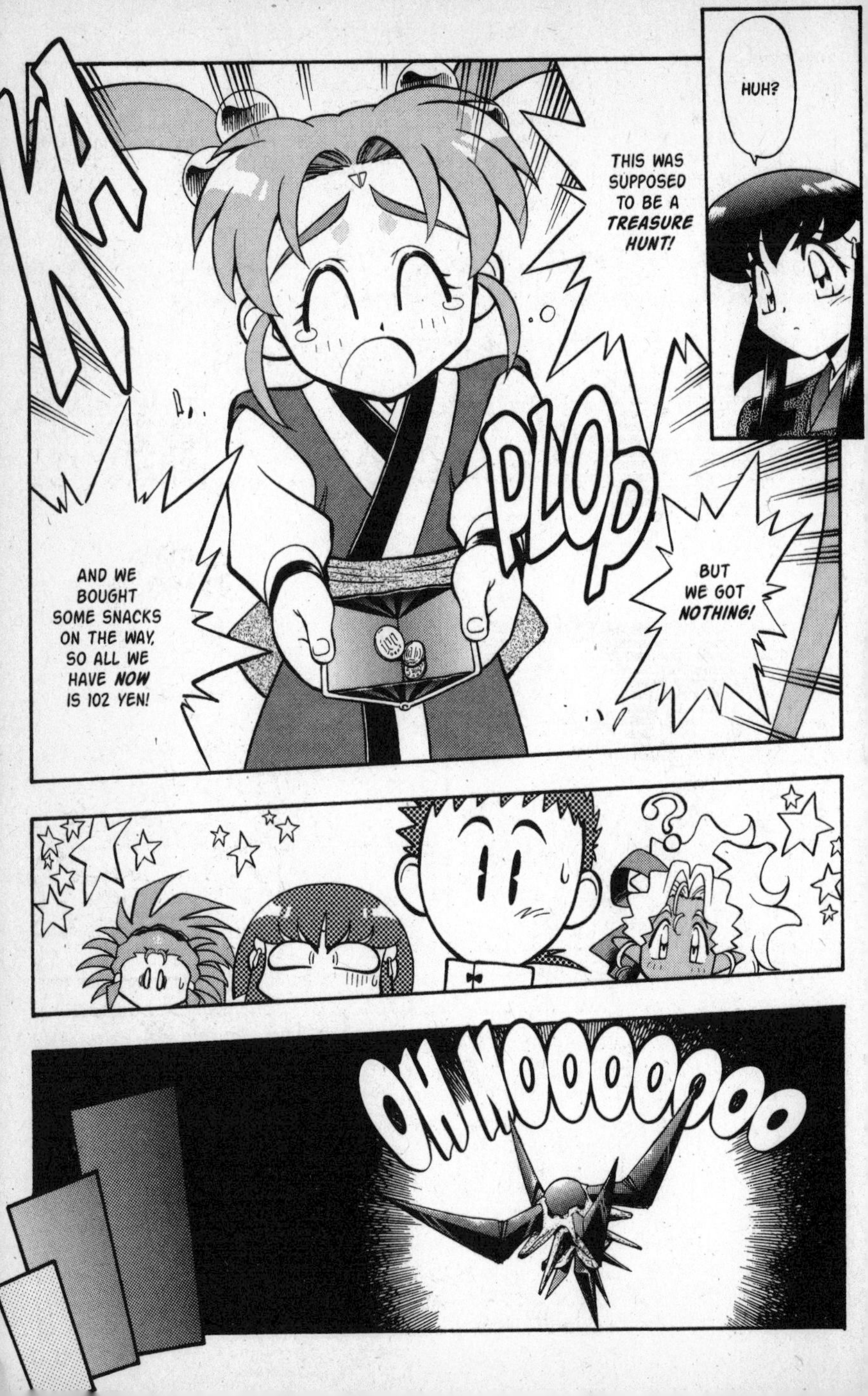
HUH?
THIS WAS SUPPOSED TO BE A *TREASURE HUNT!*
KA
PLOP
BUT WE GOT *NOTHING!*
AND WE BOUGHT SOME SNACKS ON THE WAY, SO ALL WE HAVE *NOW* IS 102 YEN!
OH NOOOOOOOO

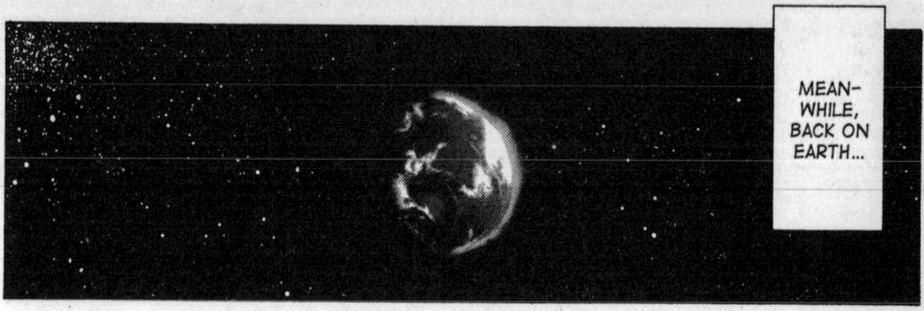
MEAN-WHILE, BACK ON EARTH...

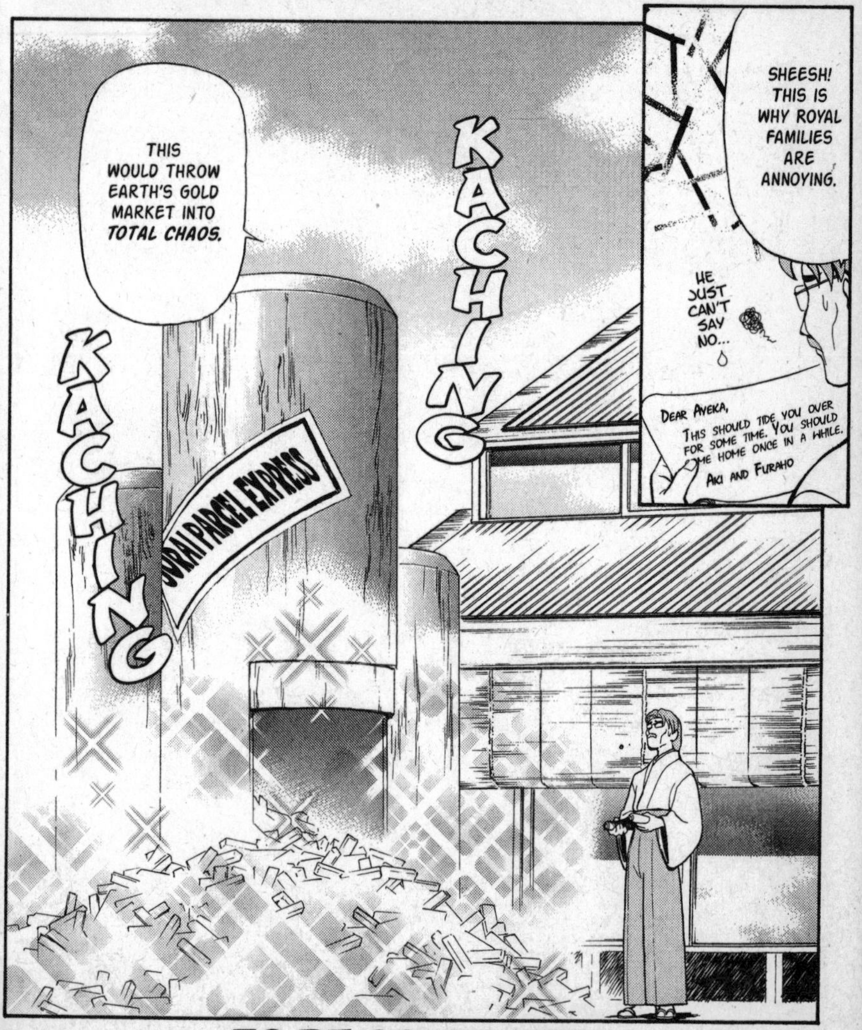
SHEESH! THIS IS WHY ROYAL FAMILIES ARE ANNOYING.
HE JUST CAN'T SAY NO...
DEAR AYEKA,
THIS SHOULD TIDE YOU OVER FOR SOME TIME. YOU SHOULD COME HOME ONCE IN A WHILE.
AKI AND FURAHO
KACHING
THIS WOULD THROW EARTH'S GOLD MARKET INTO TOTAL CHAOS.
KACHING
JURAI PARCEL EXPRESS

TO BE CONTINUED...

At Your Indentured Service

Hayate's parents are bad with money, so they sell his organs to pay their debts. Hayate doesn't like this plan, so he comes up with a new one—kidnap and ransom a girl from a wealthy family. Solid plan... so how did he end up as her butler?

Find out in *Hayate the Combat Butler*— buy the manga at store.viz.com!